GAMMA DRACONIS

WRITER
BENOIST SIMMAT

ARTIST
ELDO YOSHIMIZU

TITAN®
COMICS

TITAN COMICS
SENIOR EDITOR / Jake Devine
DESIGNER / Donna Askem
MANAGING EDITOR / Martin Eden
ASSISTANT EDITOR / Phoebe Hedges
PRODUCTION CONTROLLERS / Caterina Falqui & Kelly Fenlon
PRODUCTION MANAGER / Jackie Flook
SENIOR DESIGNER / Andrew Leung
ART DIRECTOR / Oz Browne
SALES & CIRCULATION MANAGER / Steve Tothill
MARKETING & ADVERTISEMENT ASSISTANT / Lauren Noding
SALES & MARKETING COORDINATOR / George Wickenden
PUBLICIST / Imogen Harris
HEAD OF RIGHTS / Jenny Boyce
ACQUISITIONS EDITOR / Duncan Baizley
PUBLISHING DIRECTOR / Ricky Claydon
PUBLISHING DIRECTOR / John Dziewiatkowski
OPERATIONS DIRECTOR / Leigh Baulch
PUBLISHERS / Vivian Cheung & Nick Landau

HARD CASE CRIME
CONSULTING EDITOR / Charles Ardai

ALSO AVAILABLE:

RYUKO VOL. 1
ISBN: 9781787730946

RYUKO VOL. 2
ISBN: 9781787732551

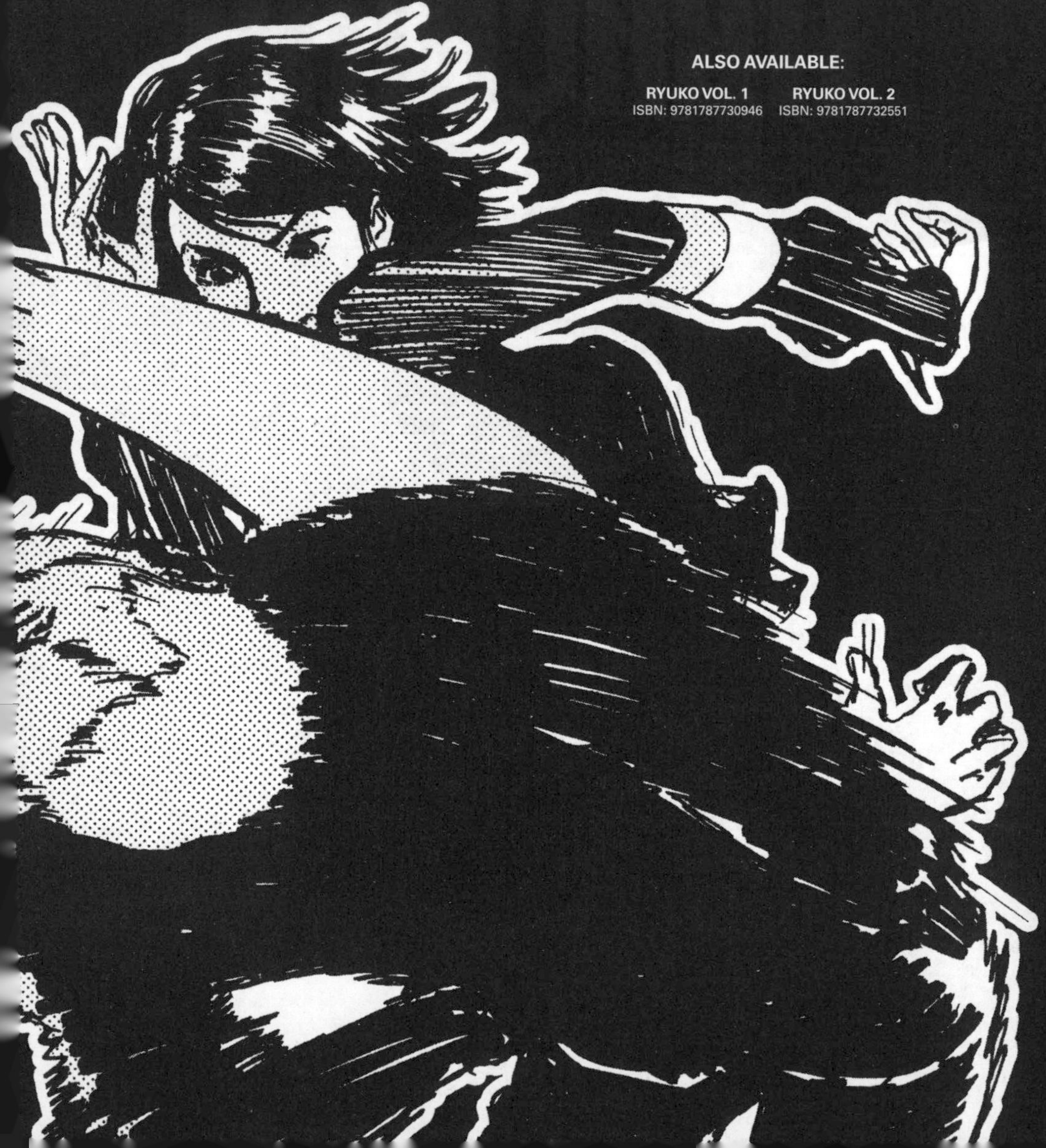

GAMMA DRACONIS

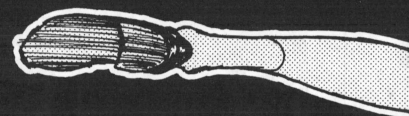

WRITER
BENOIST SIMMAT

ARTIST
ELDO YOSHIMIZU

TRANSLATOR
MARC BOURBON-CROOK

LETTERER
LAUREN BOWES

GAMMA DRACONIS
© 2021 Le Lézard Noir
Eldo Yoshimizu, Benoist Simmat & Stéphane Duval. From an original story by Benoist Simmat & Stéphane Duval. All rights reserved.

This translation first published in 2021 by Titan Comics, a division of Titan Publishing Group, Ltd, 144 Southwark Street, London SE1 0UP, UK.
Titan Comics is a registered trademark of Titan Publishing Group Ltd.

The name Hard Case Crime and the Hard Case Crime logo are trademarks of Winterfall LCC. Hard Case Crime Comics are produced with editorial guidance from Charles Ardai.

10 9 8 7 6 5 4 3 2 1

First edition: August 21
Printed in India
ISBN: 9781787736061

A CIP catalogue record for this title is available from the British Library.

Back cover, diagram (*Sigillum Dei Aemeth*) and original script by John Dee in *De Heptarchia Mystica* (1582). The cover page illustration is taken from Elias Ashmole's *Theatrum Chemicum Britannicum* (London, 1652). The engraving on page 256 is taken from *Tractatus duo egregii, de Lapide Philosophorum, una cum Theatro astronomiae terrestri, cum Figuris, in gratiam filiorum Hermetis nunc primum in lucem editi*, Edward Kelley, Ed. J.L.M.C., (Hamburg, 1676); page 250 from *The Tragical History of the Life and Death of Doctor Faustus*, Christopher Marlowe (London, 1620); Anonymous page 126, in Camille Flammarion, *The atmosphere: popular meteorology* (Paris, 1888). The magic seals on pages 210 and 53 are original creations by Ayis Lertas. Etsuko's House in Tokyo, p.128, p.116 is a realization of Mikan Architects. Mina dress p.9 by Anne Sofie Madsen. The front cover design is by Emilie Bouchon.

CAST OF CHARACTERS

JANNE PAUWELS
Tenacious police officer who
specializes in financial crime.

AIKO MORIYAMA
A brilliant student from Osaka who
traveled to Paris to study religious
art. Or so it would appear.

PIERRE LE PUY
High-ranking initiate with the ideal cover
– professor of history at the Sorbonne.

ETSUKO MORIYAMA
Aiko's mother. Celebrated architect in
Tokyo. She carries a heavy secret which
her daughter will have to confront.

AMIKA MORIYAMA
Aiko's unassuming grandmother
(and mother to Etsuko) is the leader
of an ancient secret society.

KEN'ICHI SHINODA

Bedford's Japanese associate. Shares with Julian a taste for black magic, as well as a complete lack of conscience.

JULIAN BEDFORD

English financier with a thirst for power. He is adept at the occult arts as well as cutting-edge technologies.

KELLEY

Inseparable companion to Nashima, who can pilot anything on the planet with an engine.

NASHIMA

Mysterious adventurer and highly skilled cat burglar.

MINA

A formidable creature and Shinoda's bodyguard, enhanced in her master's secret laboratories.

Act I

PROLOGUE

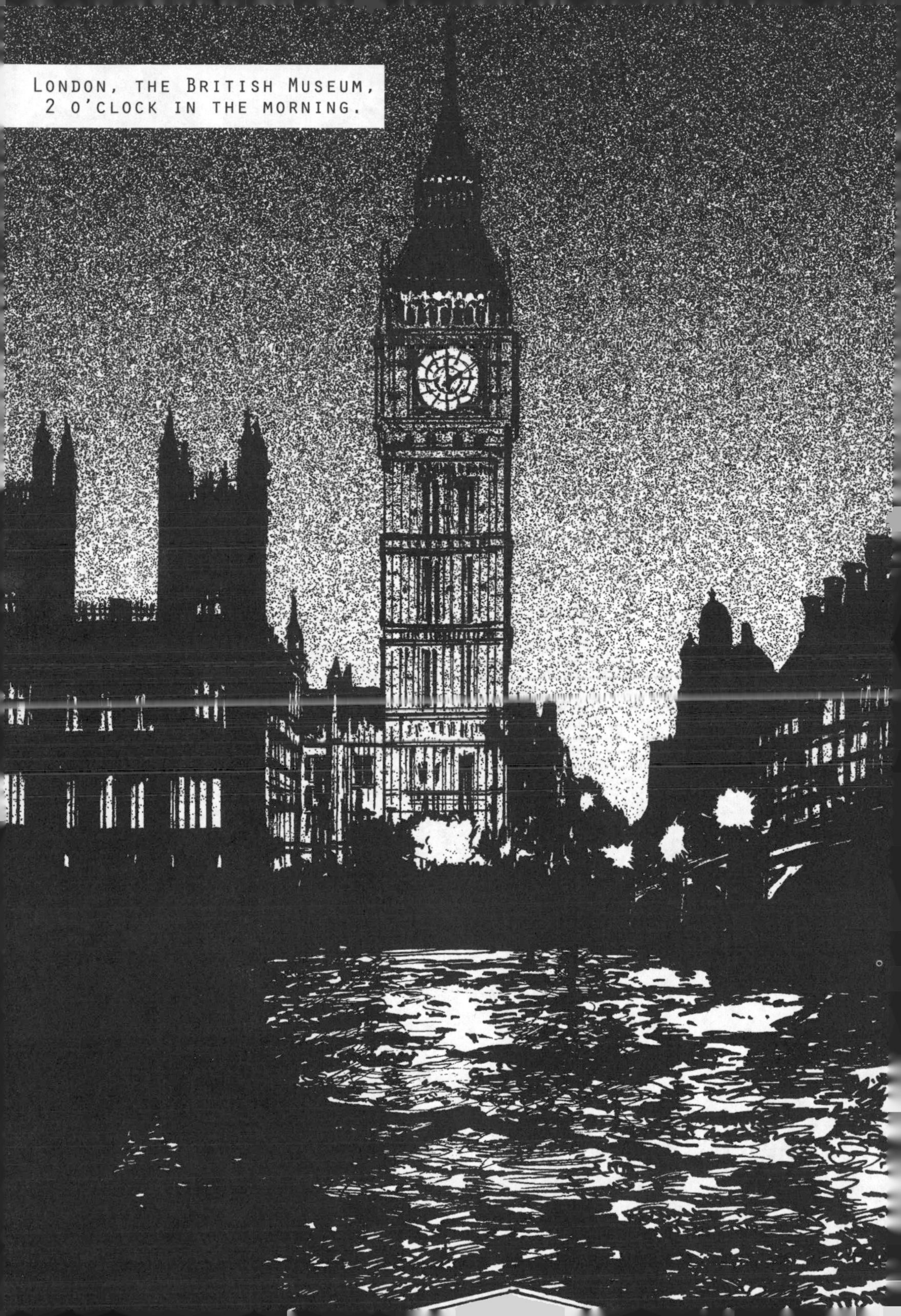
LONDON, THE BRITISH MUSEUM, 2 O'CLOCK IN THE MORNING.

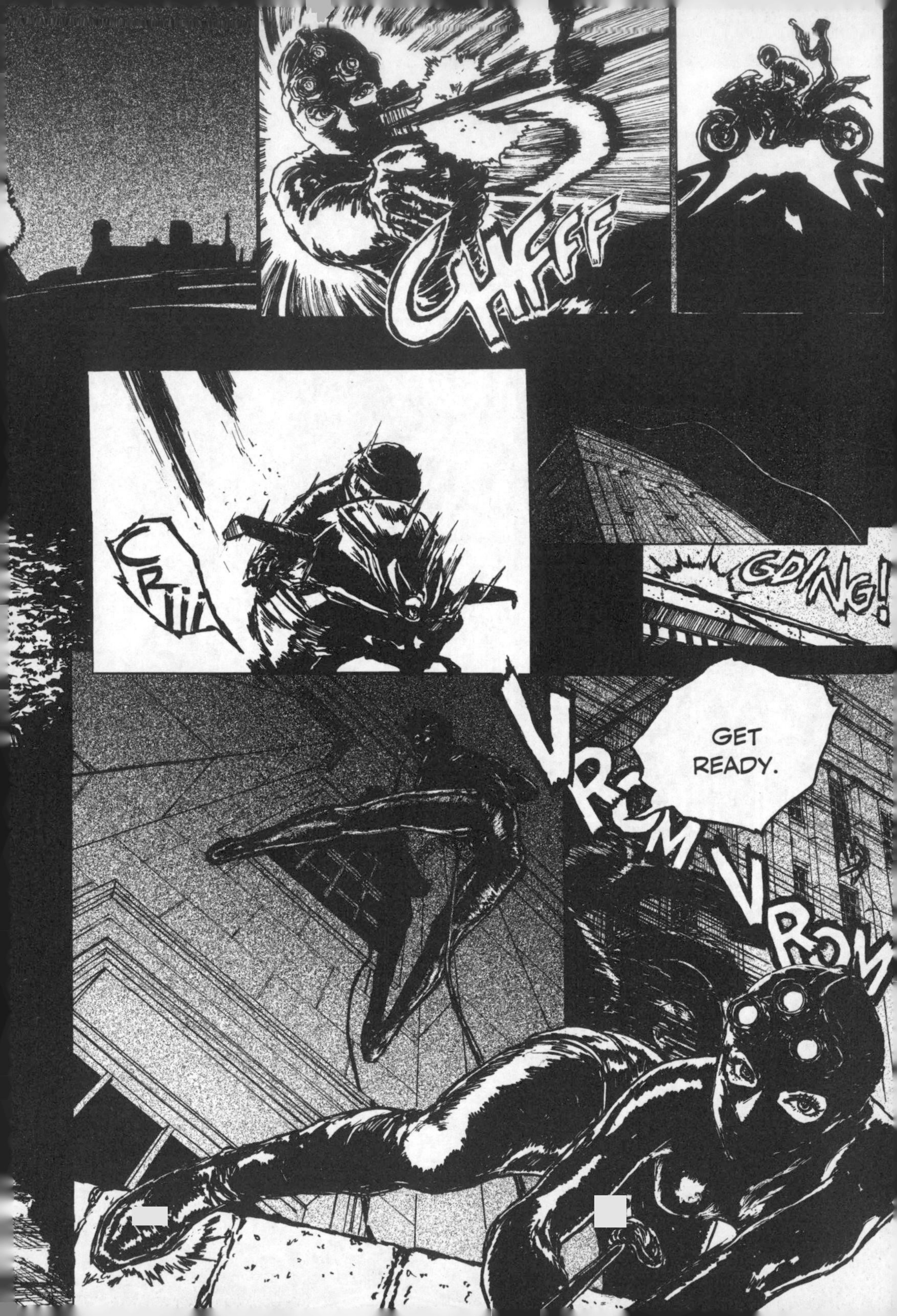
GDING!
CRiii
VROM VROM VROM
GET READY.

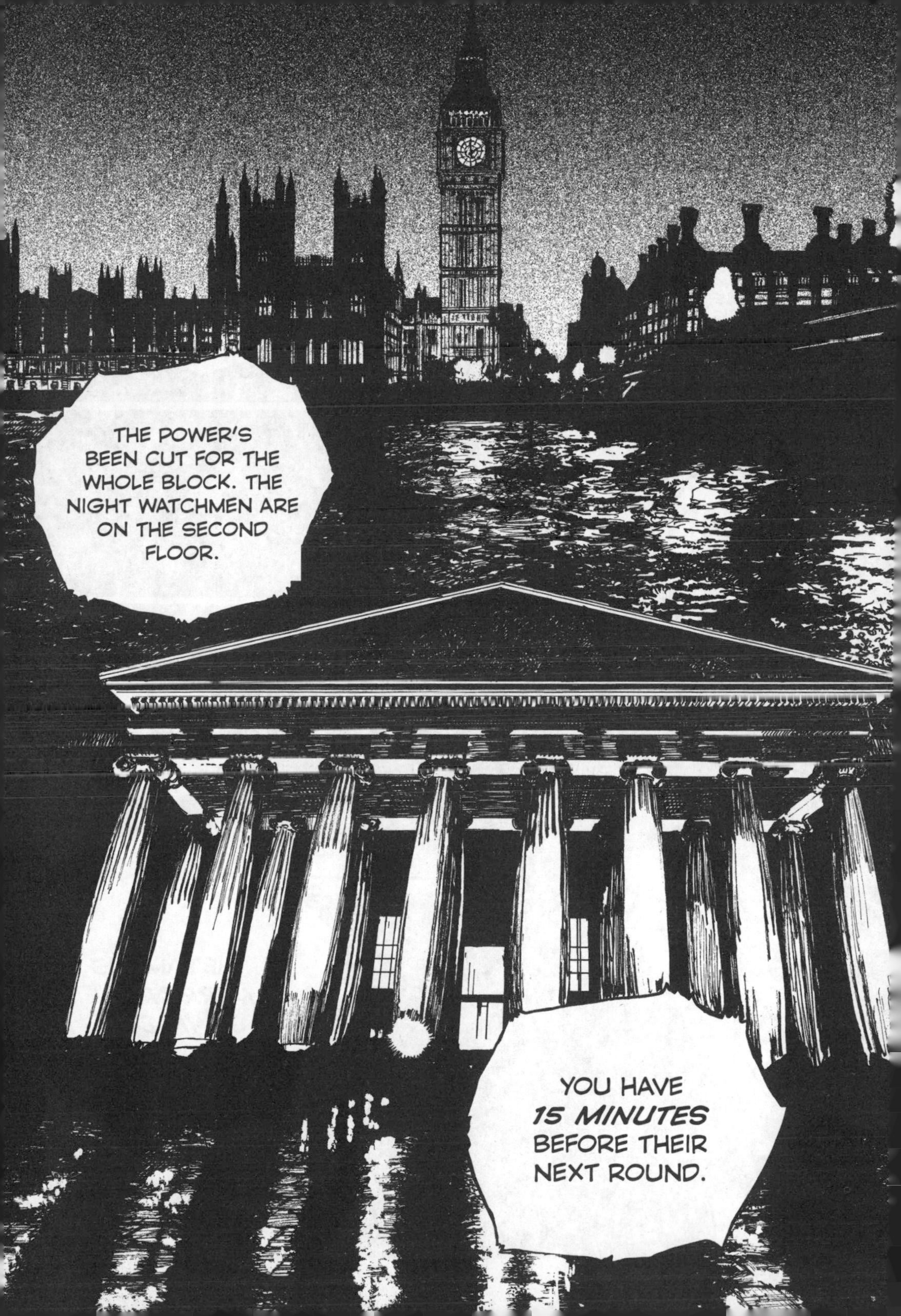
THE POWER'S BEEN CUT FOR THE WHOLE BLOCK. THE NIGHT WATCHMEN ARE ON THE SECOND FLOOR.
YOU HAVE *15 MINUTES* BEFORE THEIR NEXT ROUND.

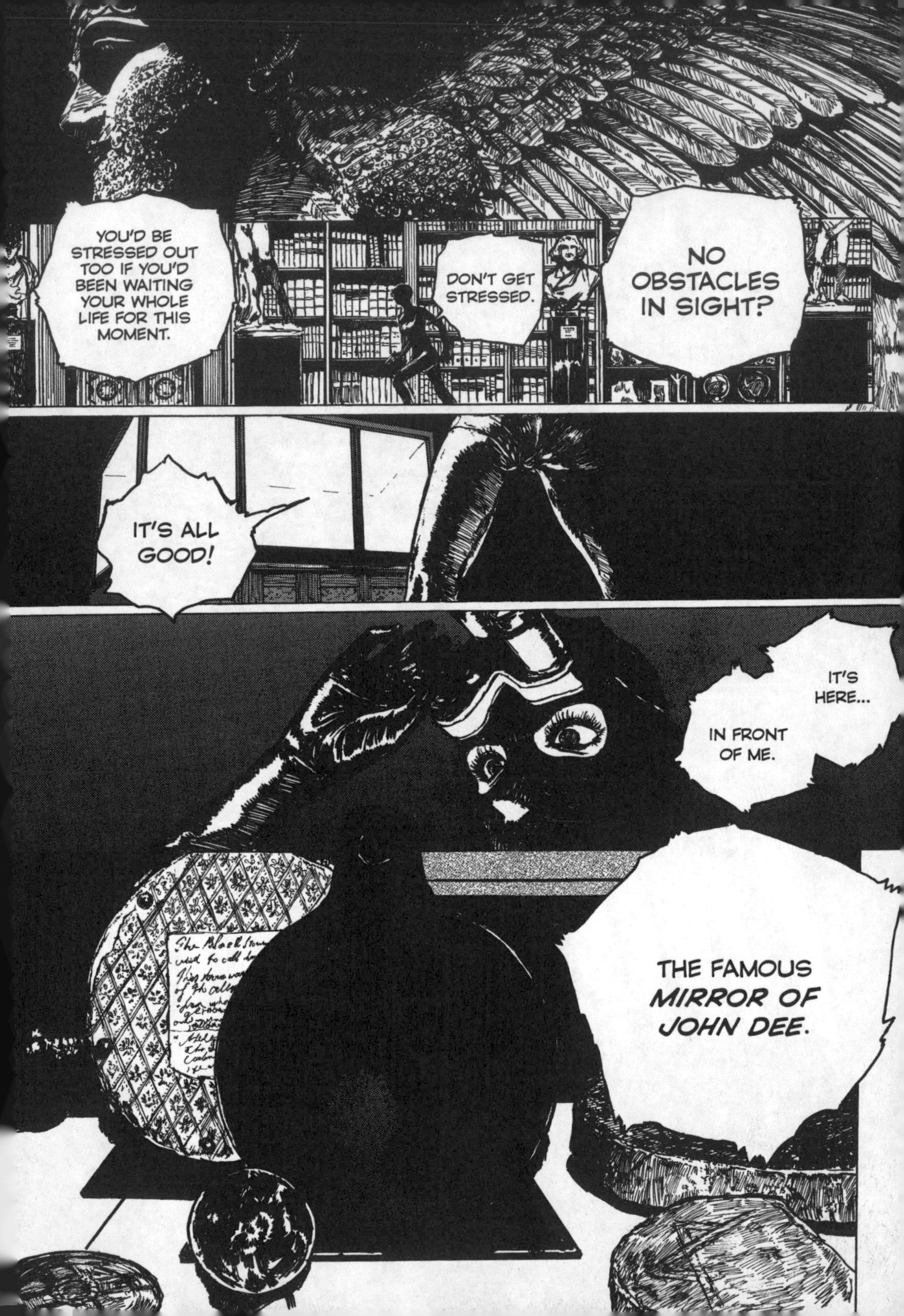
NO OBSTACLES IN SIGHT?
DON'T GET STRESSED.
YOU'D BE STRESSED OUT TOO IF YOU'D BEEN WAITING YOUR WHOLE LIFE FOR THIS MOMENT.
IT'S ALL GOOD!
IT'S HERE...
IN FRONT OF ME.
THE FAMOUS *MIRROR OF JOHN DEE*.

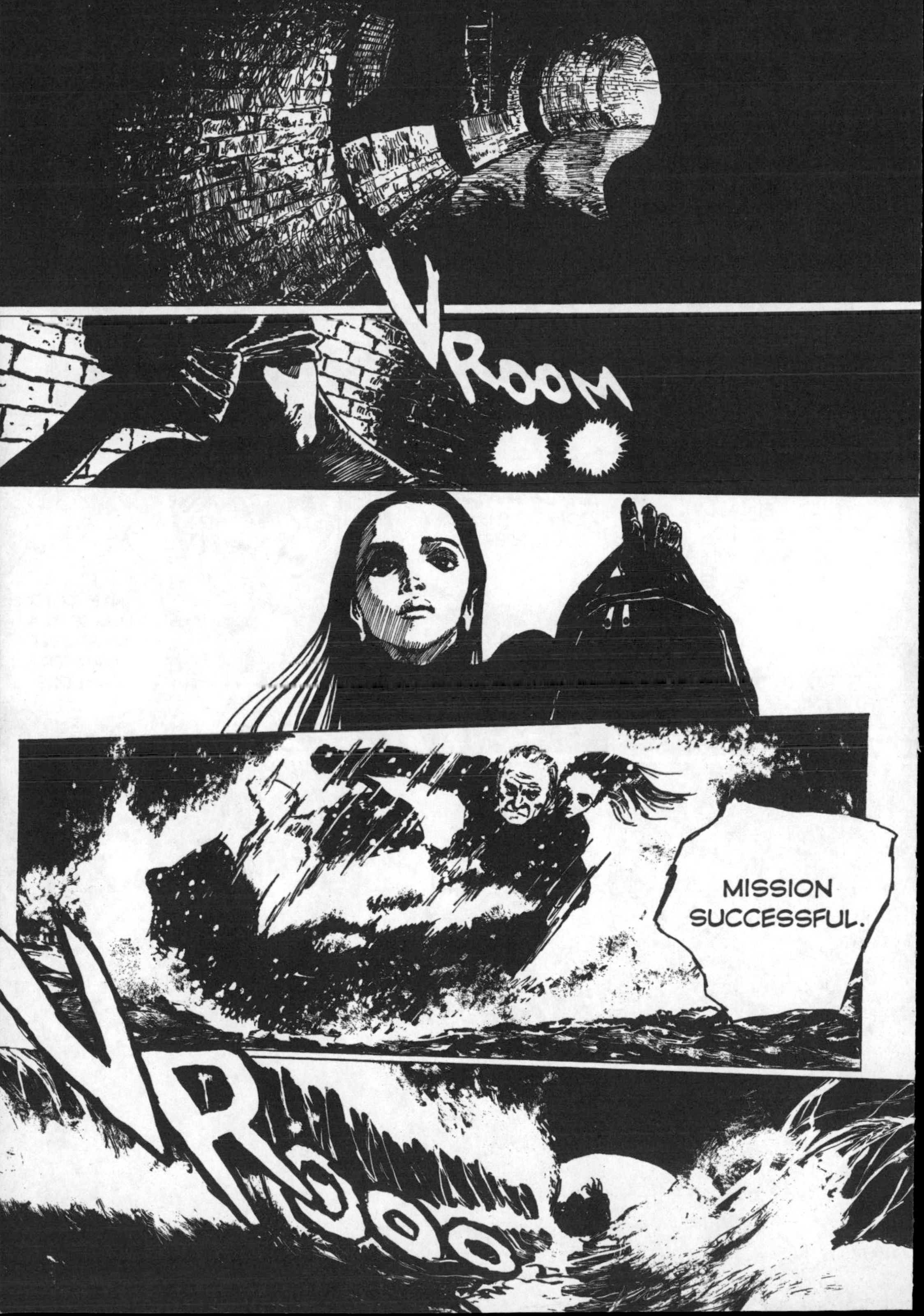
VROOM
MISSION SUCCESSFUL.
VROOOO

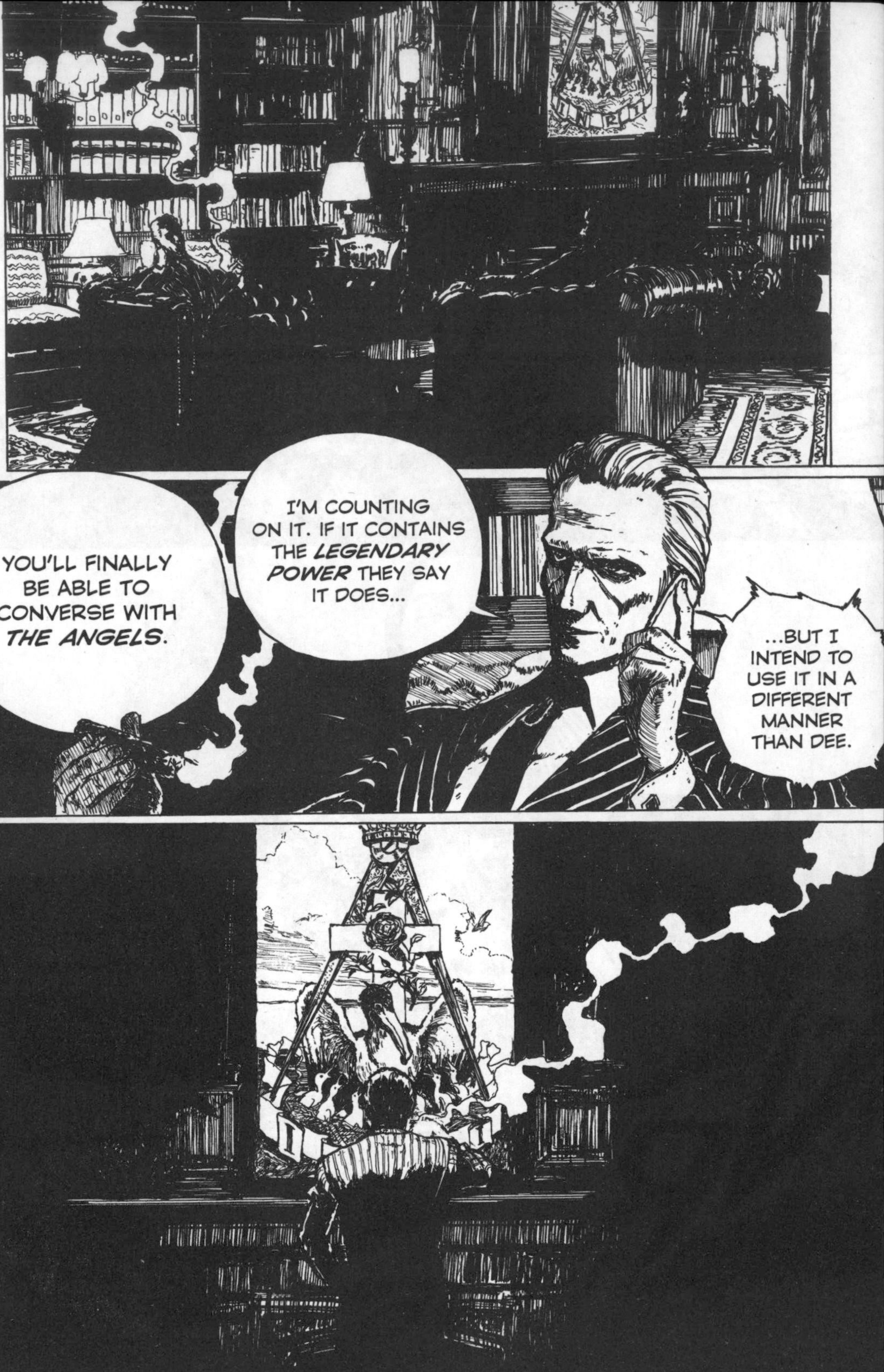
YOU'LL FINALLY BE ABLE TO CONVERSE WITH *THE ANGELS*.
I'M COUNTING ON IT. IF IT CONTAINS THE *LEGENDARY POWER* THEY SAY IT DOES...
...BUT I INTEND TO USE IT IN A DIFFERENT MANNER THAN DEE.

CHAPTER 1

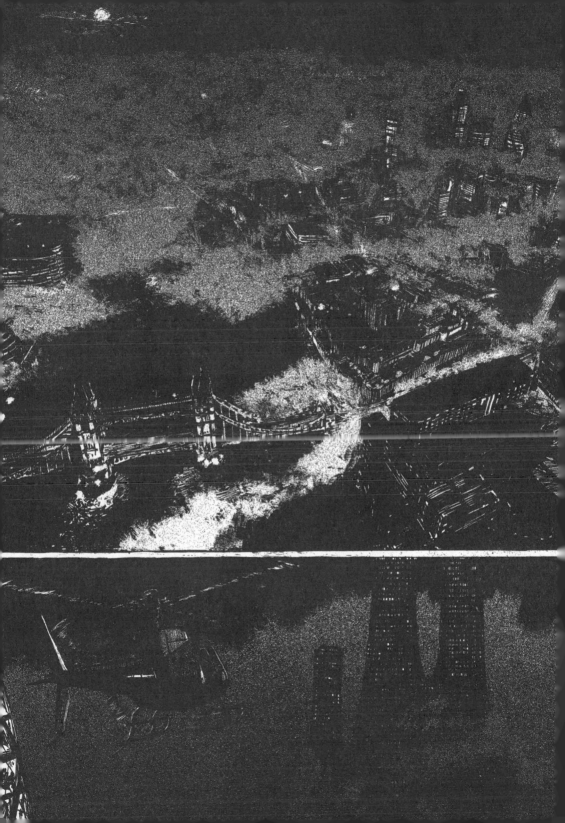

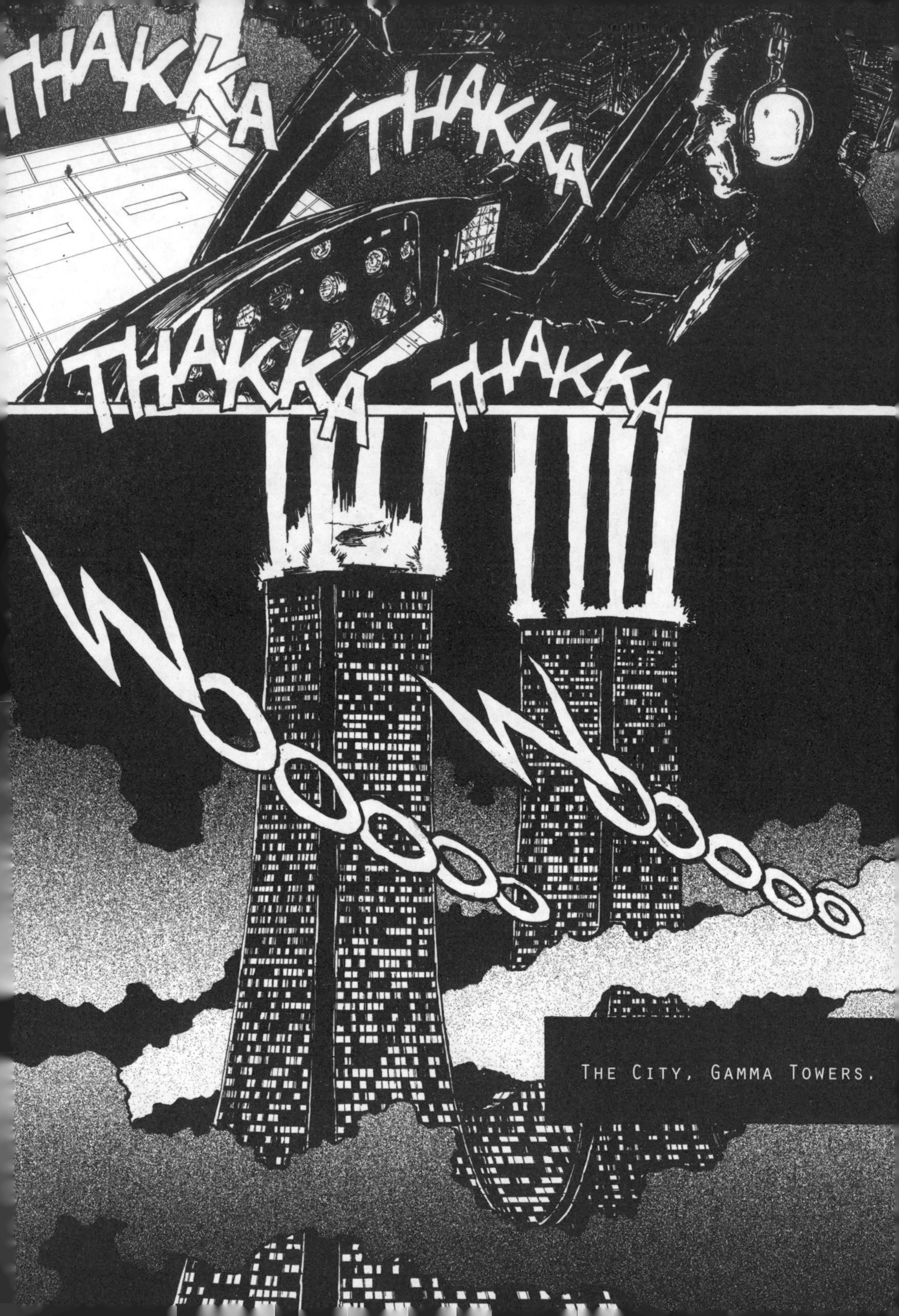
THAKKA
THAKKA
THAKKA
THAKKA
WOOOOOO
WOOOOOO
THE CITY, GAMMA TOWERS.

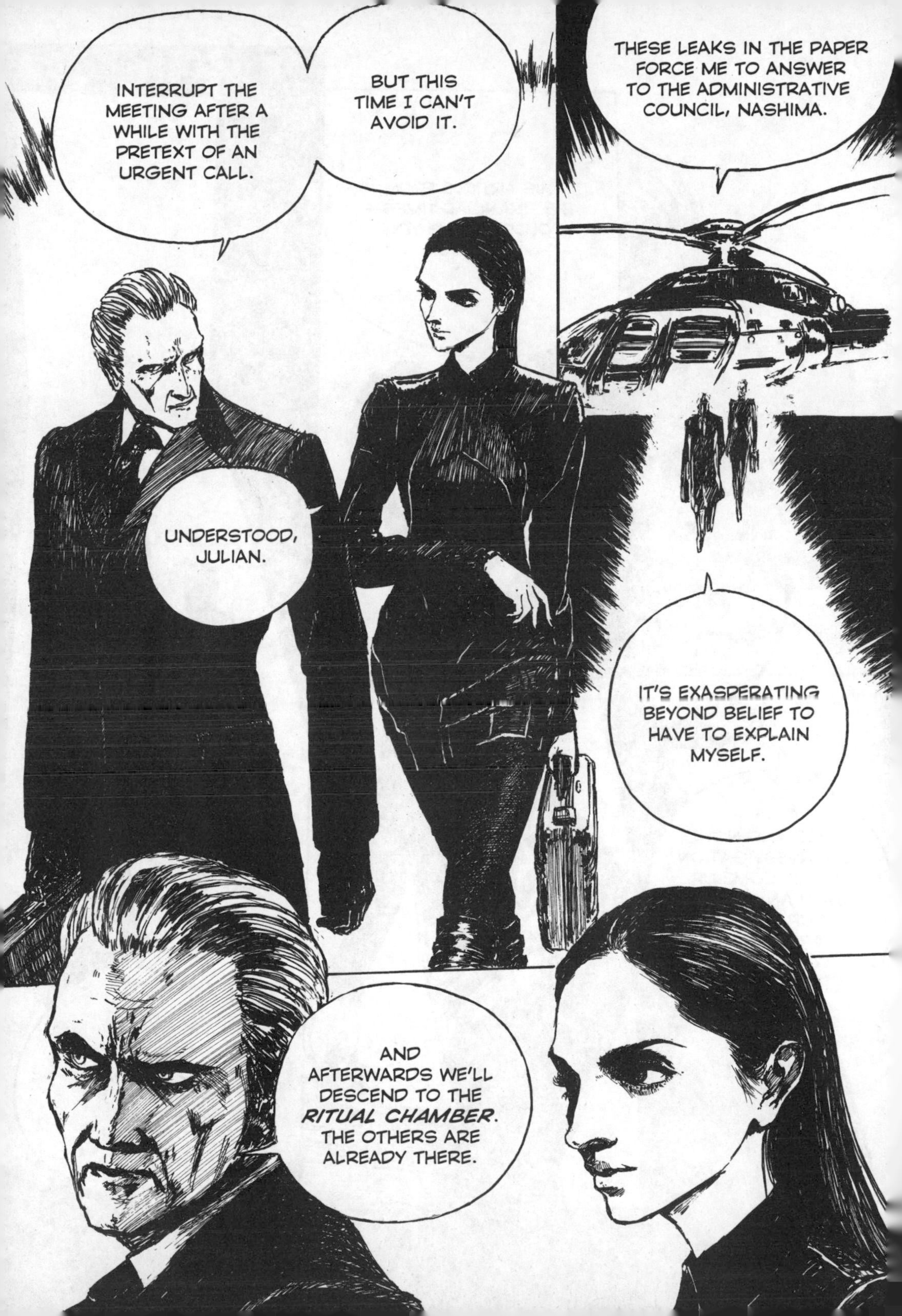
THESE LEAKS IN THE PAPER FORCE ME TO ANSWER TO THE ADMINISTRATIVE COUNCIL, NASHIMA.
IT'S EXASPERATING BEYOND BELIEF TO HAVE TO EXPLAIN MYSELF.
BUT THIS TIME I CAN'T AVOID IT.
INTERRUPT THE MEETING AFTER A WHILE WITH THE PRETEXT OF AN URGENT CALL.
UNDERSTOOD, JULIAN.
AND AFTERWARDS WE'LL DESCEND TO THE *RITUAL CHAMBER*. THE OTHERS ARE ALREADY THERE.

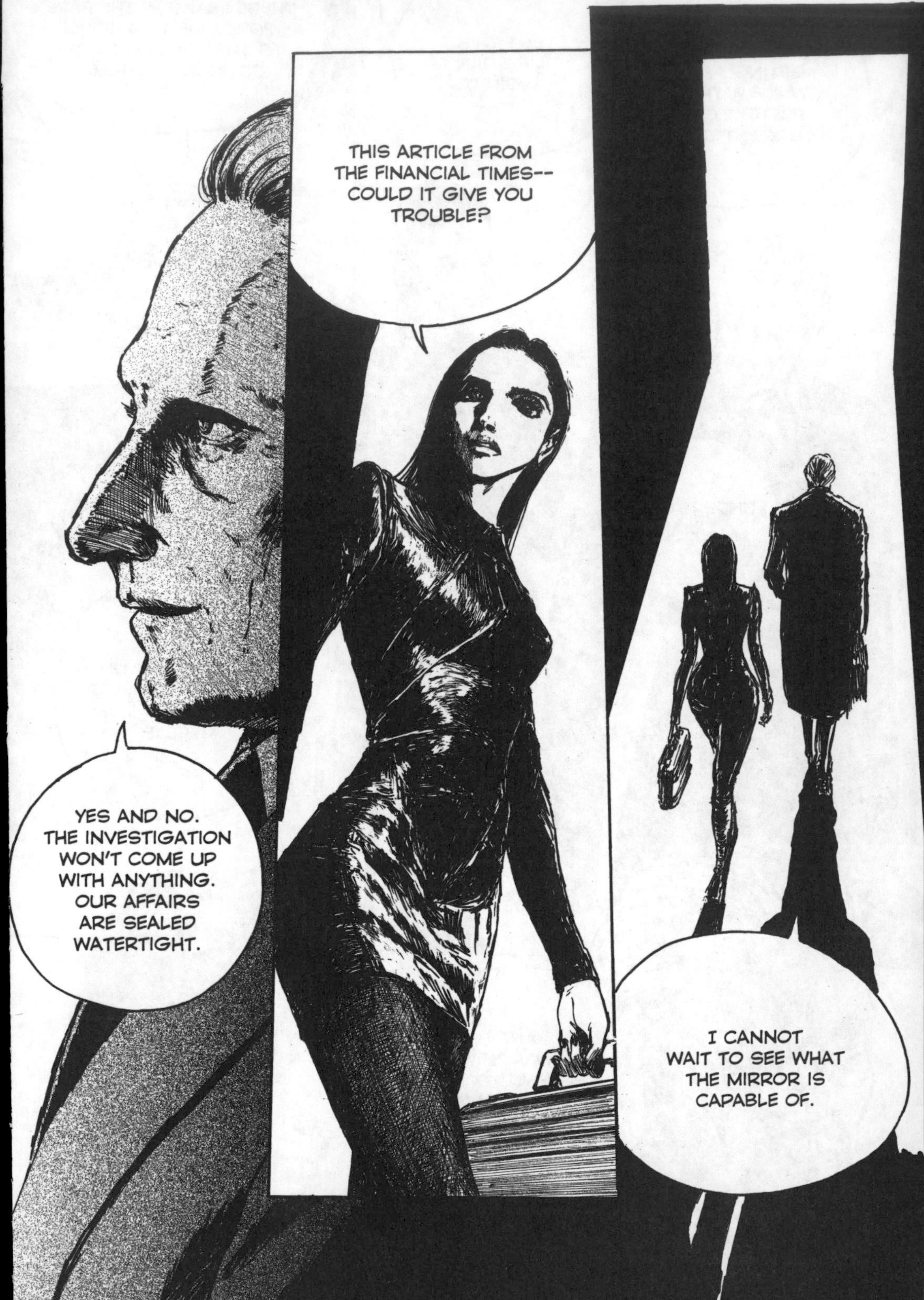
I CANNOT WAIT TO SEE WHAT THE MIRROR IS CAPABLE OF.
THIS ARTICLE FROM THE FINANCIAL TIMES-- COULD IT GIVE YOU TROUBLE?
YES AND NO. THE INVESTIGATION WON'T COME UP WITH ANYTHING. OUR AFFAIRS ARE SEALED WATERTIGHT.

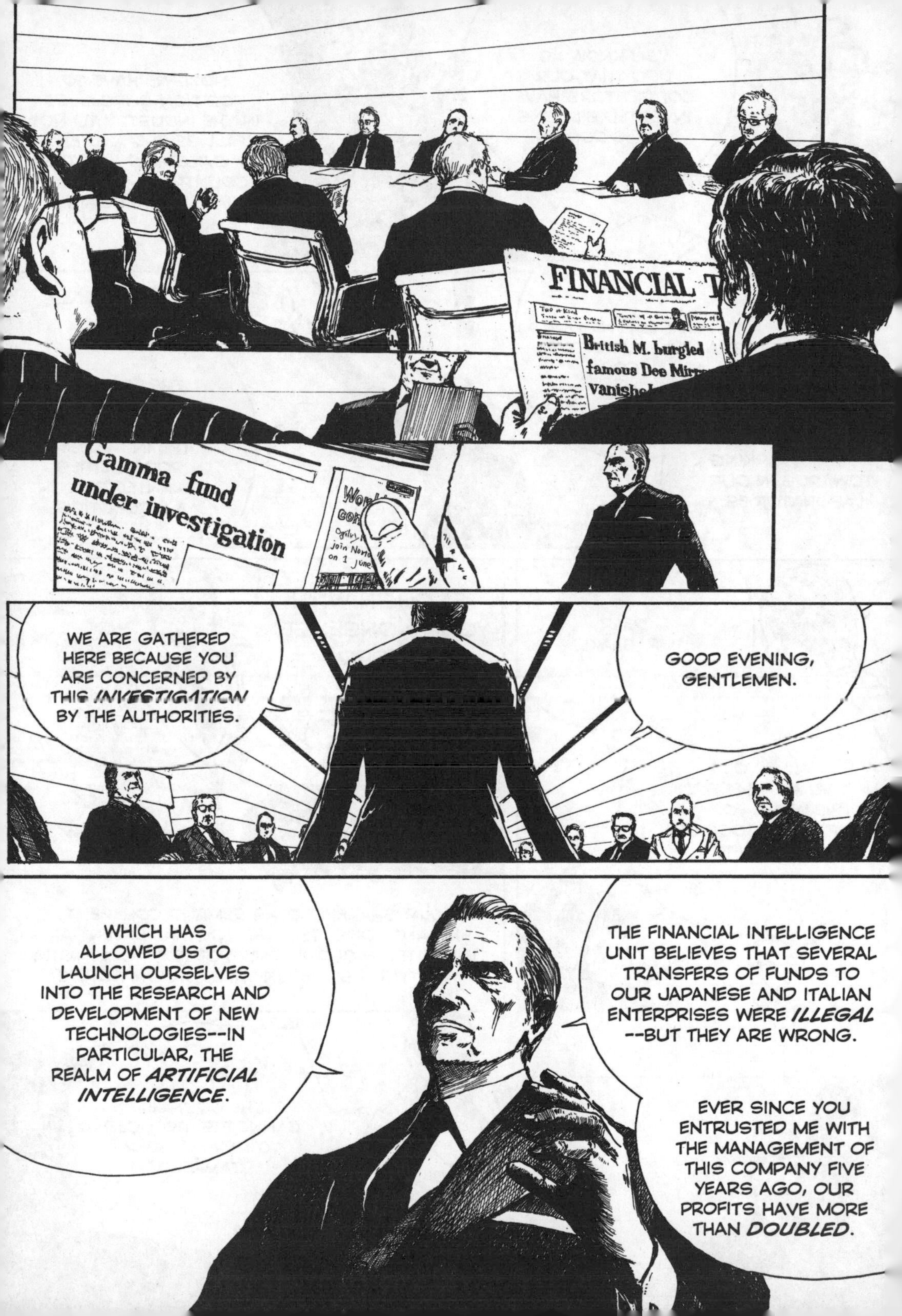
FINANCIAL
British M. burgled
Gamma fund under investigation
GOOD EVENING, GENTLEMEN.
WE ARE GATHERED HERE BECAUSE YOU ARE CONCERNED BY THIS *INVESTIGATION* BY THE AUTHORITIES.
THE FINANCIAL INTELLIGENCE UNIT BELIEVES THAT SEVERAL TRANSFERS OF FUNDS TO OUR JAPANESE AND ITALIAN ENTERPRISES WERE *ILLEGAL* --BUT THEY ARE WRONG.
EVER SINCE YOU ENTRUSTED ME WITH THE MANAGEMENT OF THIS COMPANY FIVE YEARS AGO, OUR PROFITS HAVE MORE THAN *DOUBLED*.
WHICH HAS ALLOWED US TO LAUNCH OURSELVES INTO THE RESEARCH AND DEVELOPMENT OF NEW TECHNOLOGIES--IN PARTICULAR, THE REALM OF *ARTIFICIAL INTELLIGENCE*.

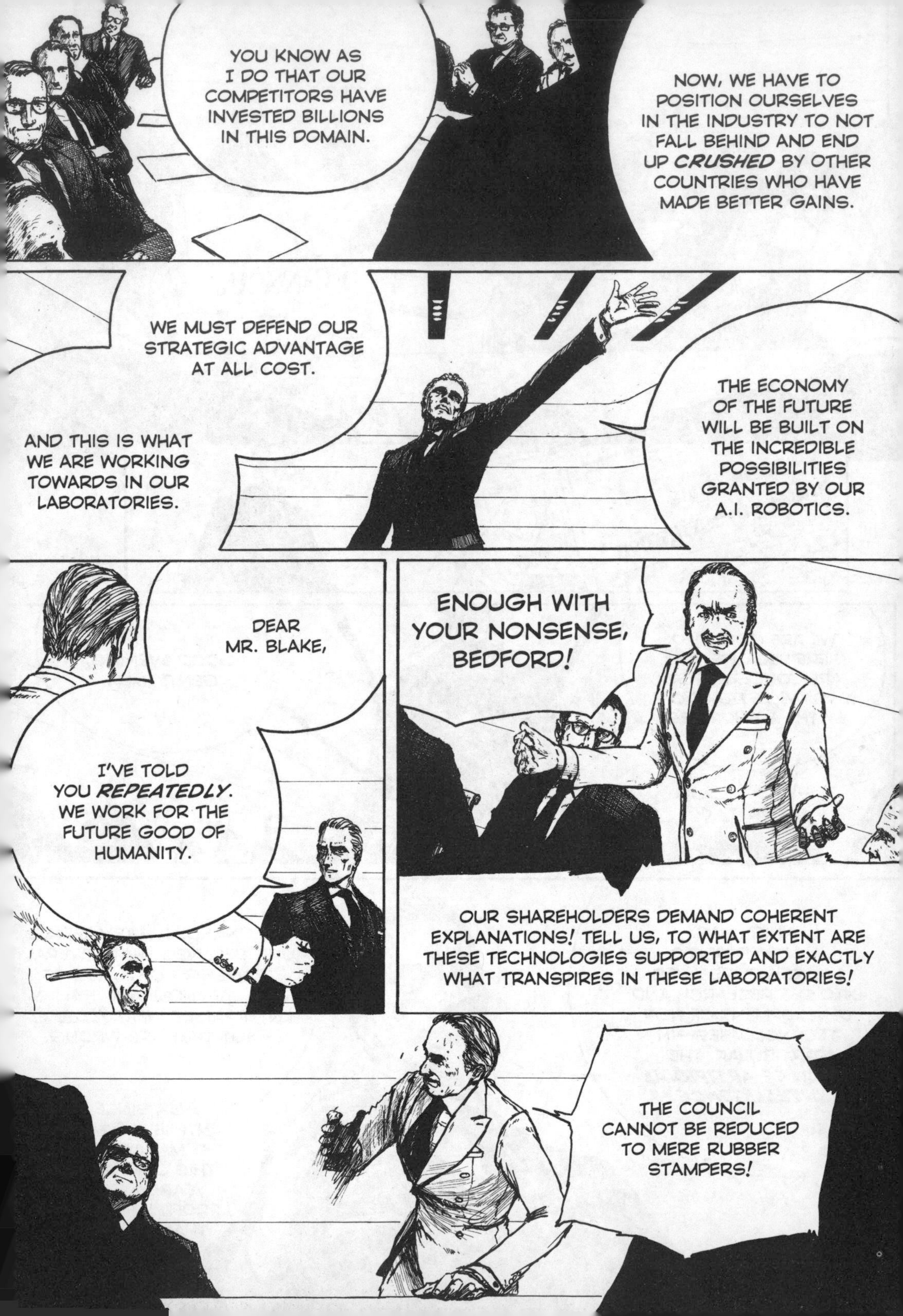
YOU KNOW AS I DO THAT OUR COMPETITORS HAVE INVESTED BILLIONS IN THIS DOMAIN.
NOW, WE HAVE TO POSITION OURSELVES IN THE INDUSTRY TO NOT FALL BEHIND AND END UP *CRUSHED* BY OTHER COUNTRIES WHO HAVE MADE BETTER GAINS.
WE MUST DEFEND OUR STRATEGIC ADVANTAGE AT ALL COST.
THE ECONOMY OF THE FUTURE WILL BE BUILT ON THE INCREDIBLE POSSIBILITIES GRANTED BY OUR A.I. ROBOTICS.
AND THIS IS WHAT WE ARE WORKING TOWARDS IN OUR LABORATORIES.
ENOUGH WITH YOUR NONSENSE, BEDFORD!
OUR SHAREHOLDERS DEMAND COHERENT EXPLANATIONS! TELL US, TO WHAT EXTENT ARE THESE TECHNOLOGIES SUPPORTED AND EXACTLY WHAT TRANSPIRES IN THESE LABORATORIES!
DEAR MR. BLAKE,
I'VE TOLD YOU *REPEATEDLY*. WE WORK FOR THE FUTURE GOOD OF HUMANITY.
THE COUNCIL CANNOT BE REDUCED TO MERE RUBBER STAMPERS!

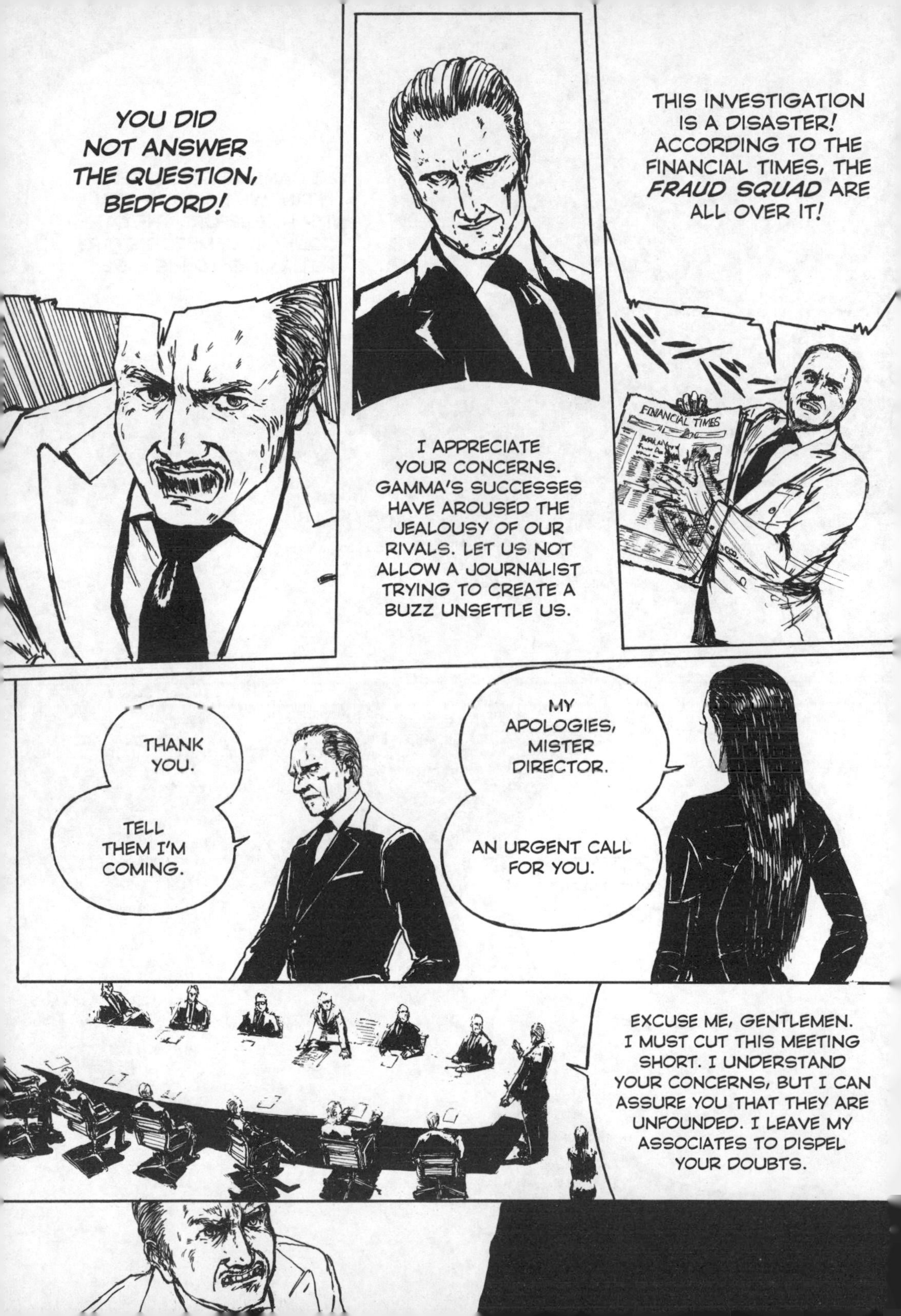
THIS INVESTIGATION IS A DISASTER! ACCORDING TO THE FINANCIAL TIMES, THE *FRAUD SQUAD* ARE ALL OVER IT!
FINANCIAL TIMES
I APPRECIATE YOUR CONCERNS. GAMMA'S SUCCESSES HAVE AROUSED THE JEALOUSY OF OUR RIVALS. LET US NOT ALLOW A JOURNALIST TRYING TO CREATE A BUZZ UNSETTLE US.
YOU DID NOT ANSWER THE QUESTION, BEDFORD!
MY APOLOGIES, MISTER DIRECTOR.
AN URGENT CALL FOR YOU.
THANK YOU.
TELL THEM I'M COMING.
EXCUSE ME, GENTLEMEN. I MUST CUT THIS MEETING SHORT. I UNDERSTAND YOUR CONCERNS, BUT I CAN ASSURE YOU THAT THEY ARE UNFOUNDED. I LEAVE MY ASSOCIATES TO DISPEL YOUR DOUBTS.

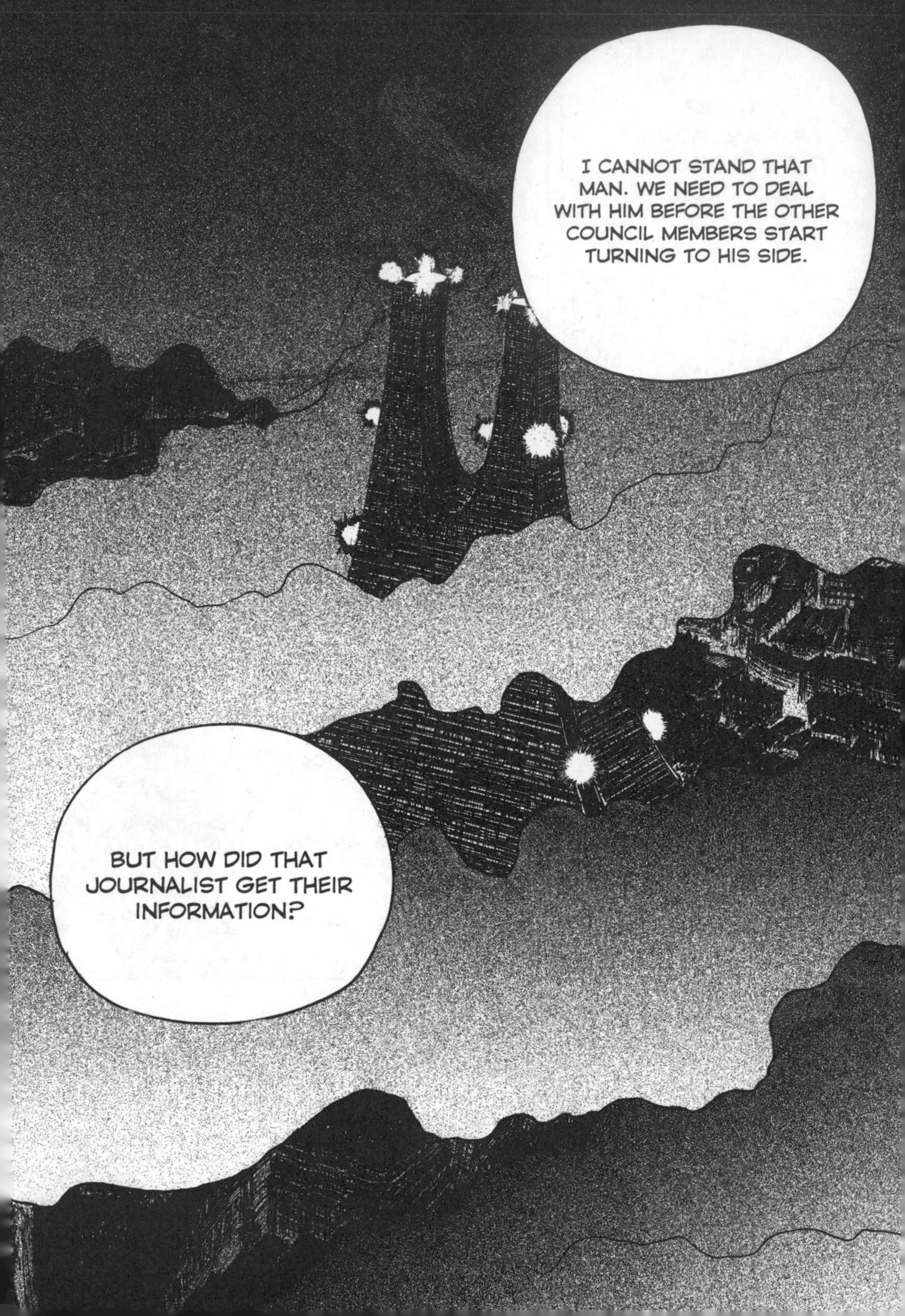
I CANNOT STAND THAT MAN. WE NEED TO DEAL WITH HIM BEFORE THE OTHER COUNCIL MEMBERS START TURNING TO HIS SIDE.
BUT HOW DID THAT JOURNALIST GET THEIR INFORMATION?

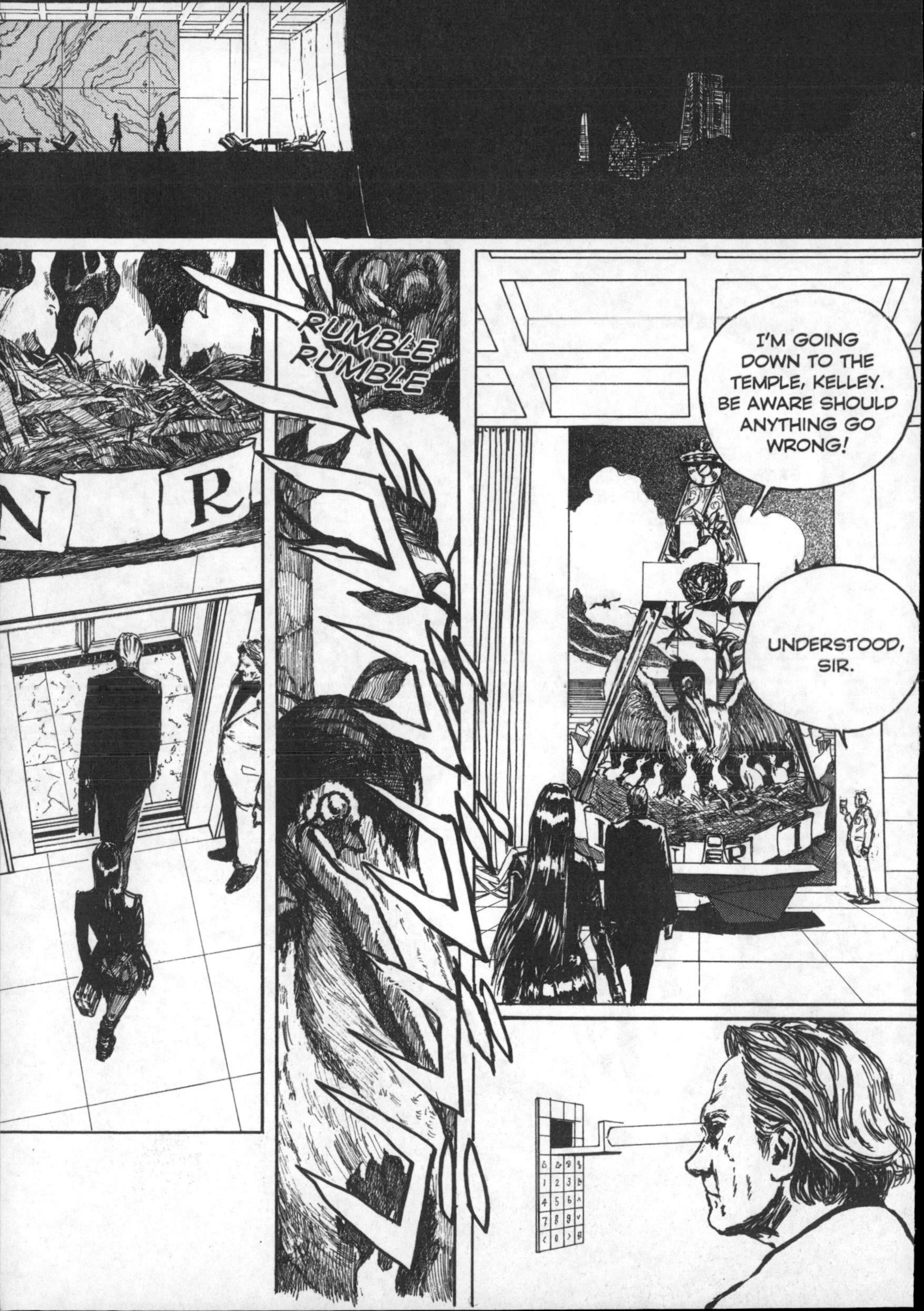
I'M GOING DOWN TO THE TEMPLE, KELLEY. BE AWARE SHOULD ANYTHING GO WRONG!
UNDERSTOOD, SIR.
RUMBLE RUMBLE

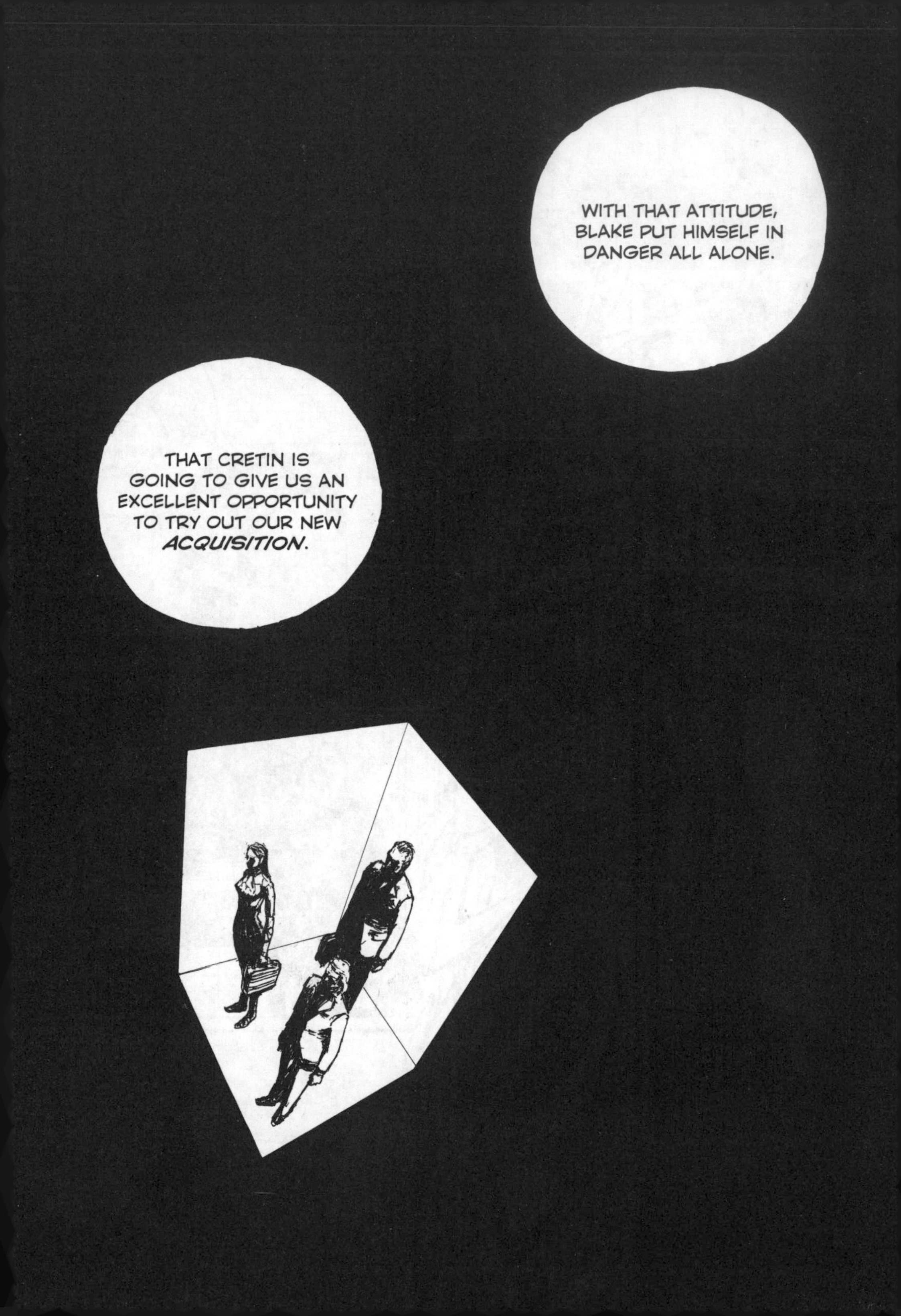
WITH THAT ATTITUDE, BLAKE PUT HIMSELF IN DANGER ALL ALONE.
THAT CRETIN IS GOING TO GIVE US AN EXCELLENT OPPORTUNITY TO TRY OUT OUR NEW *ACQUISITION*.

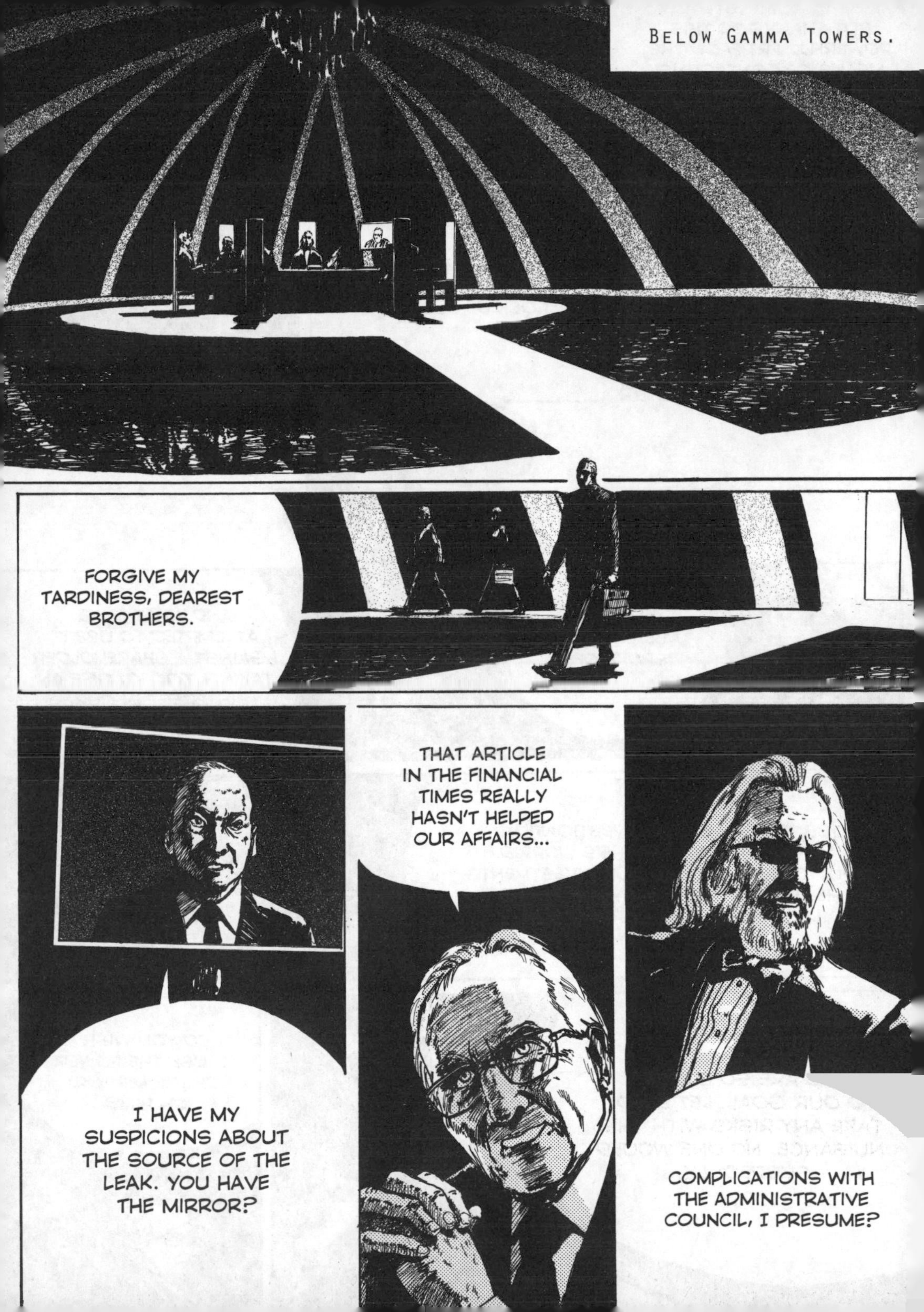
Below Gamma Towers.
FORGIVE MY TARDINESS, DEAREST BROTHERS.
COMPLICATIONS WITH THE ADMINISTRATIVE COUNCIL, I PRESUME?
THAT ARTICLE IN THE FINANCIAL TIMES REALLY HASN'T HELPED OUR AFFAIRS...
I HAVE MY SUSPICIONS ABOUT THE SOURCE OF THE LEAK. YOU HAVE THE MIRROR?

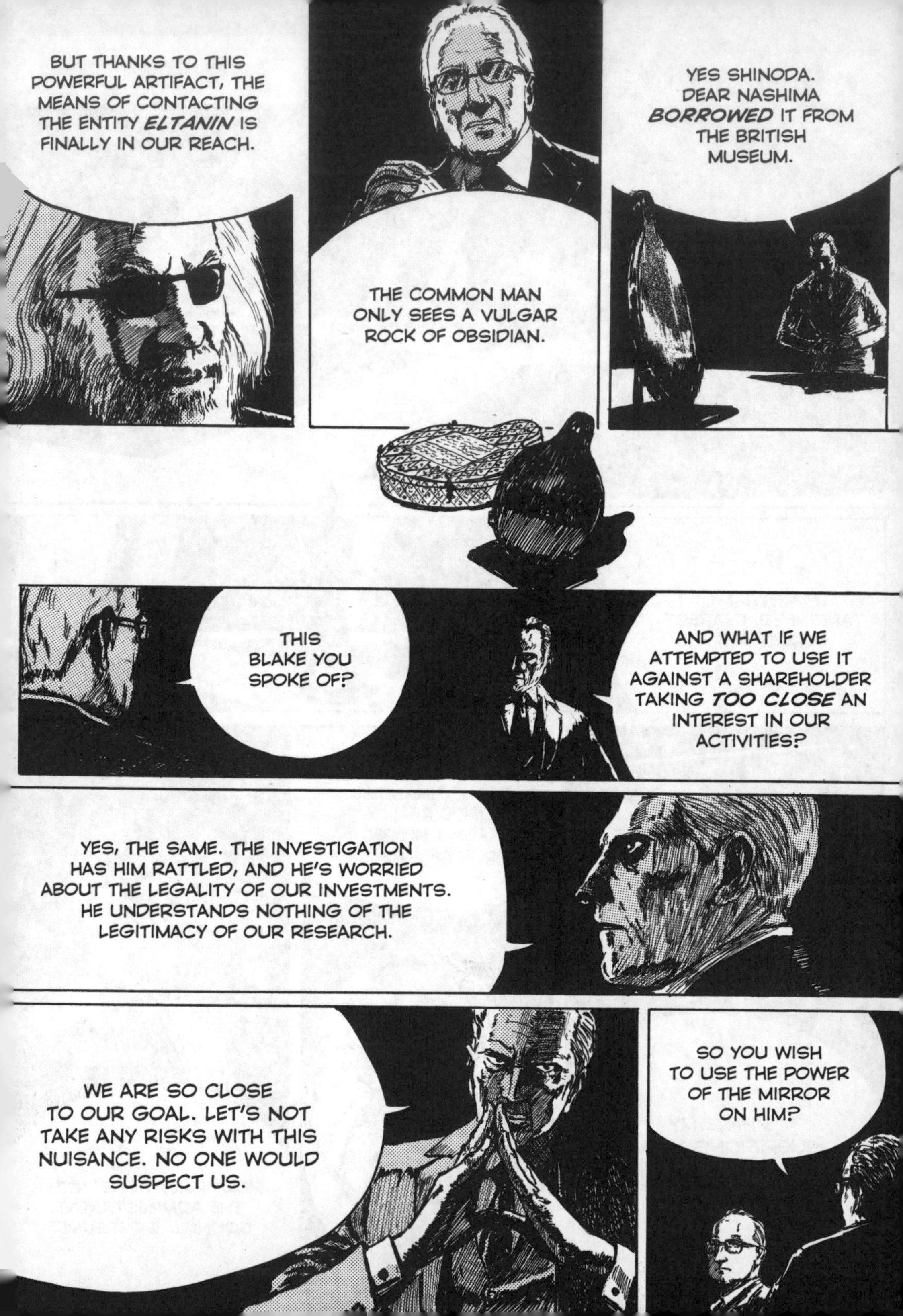
YES SHINODA. DEAR NASHIMA *BORROWED* IT FROM THE BRITISH MUSEUM.
THE COMMON MAN ONLY SEES A VULGAR ROCK OF OBSIDIAN.
BUT THANKS TO THIS POWERFUL ARTIFACT, THE MEANS OF CONTACTING THE ENTITY *ELTANIN* IS FINALLY IN OUR REACH.
AND WHAT IF WE ATTEMPTED TO USE IT AGAINST A SHAREHOLDER TAKING *TOO CLOSE* AN INTEREST IN OUR ACTIVITIES?
THIS BLAKE YOU SPOKE OF?
YES, THE SAME. THE INVESTIGATION HAS HIM RATTLED, AND HE'S WORRIED ABOUT THE LEGALITY OF OUR INVESTMENTS. HE UNDERSTANDS NOTHING OF THE LEGITIMACY OF OUR RESEARCH.
SO YOU WISH TO USE THE POWER OF THE MIRROR ON HIM?
WE ARE SO CLOSE TO OUR GOAL. LET'S NOT TAKE ANY RISKS WITH THIS NUISANCE. NO ONE WOULD SUSPECT US.

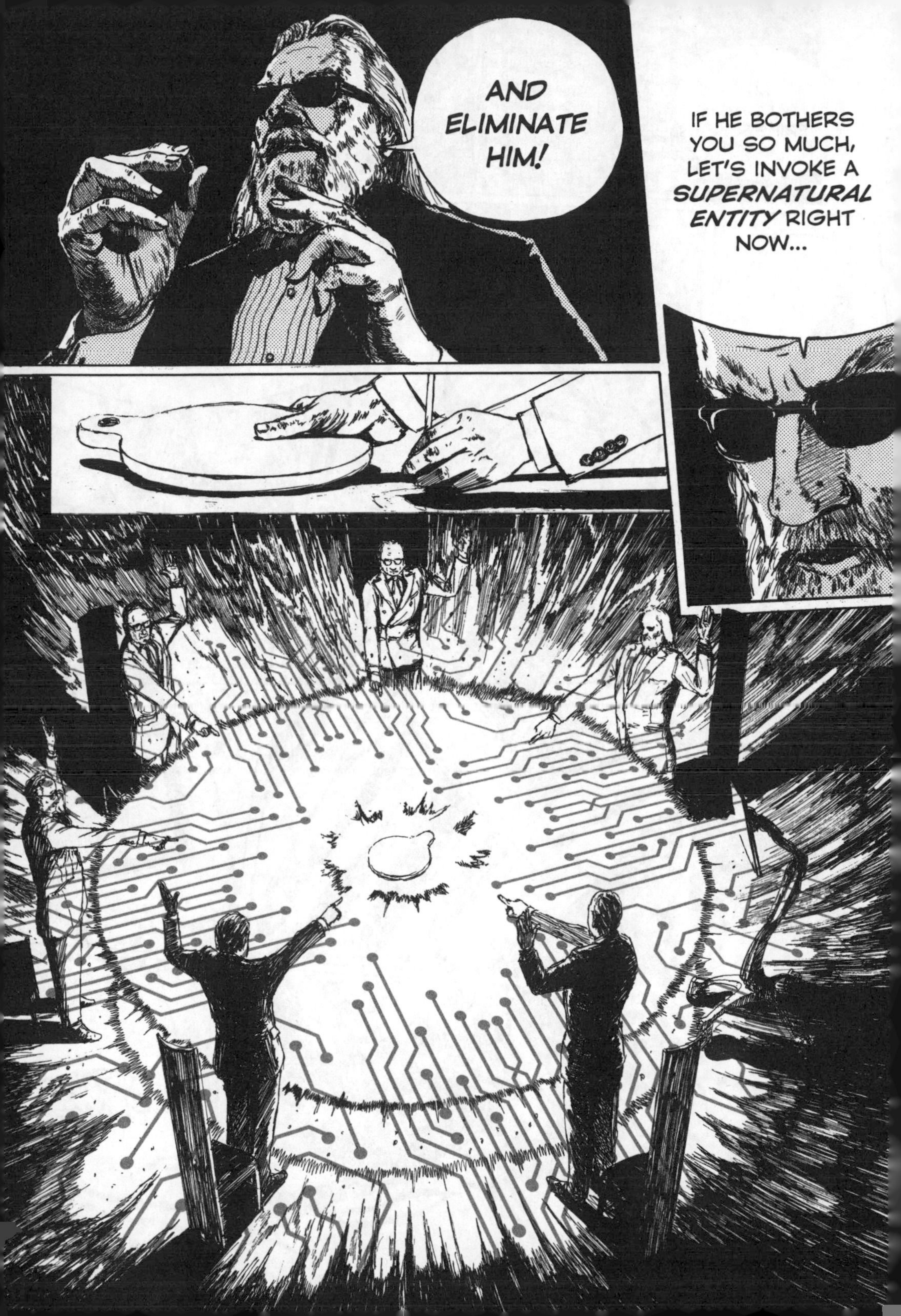
IF HE BOTHERS YOU SO MUCH, LET'S INVOKE A *SUPERNATURAL ENTITY* RIGHT NOW...
AND ELIMINATE HIM!

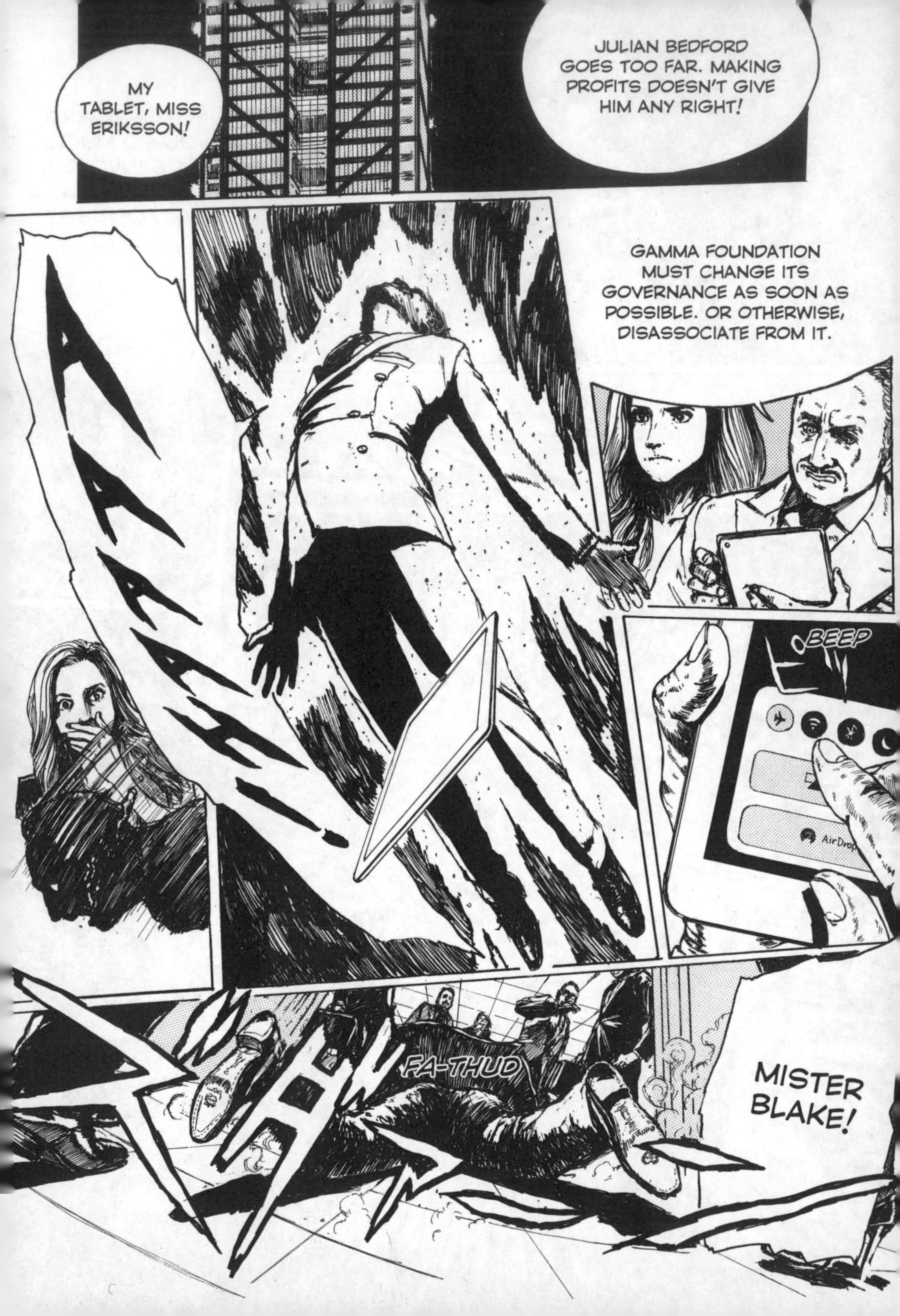
JULIAN BEDFORD GOES TOO FAR. MAKING PROFITS DOESN'T GIVE HIM ANY RIGHT!
MY TABLET, MISS ERIKSSON!
GAMMA FOUNDATION MUST CHANGE ITS GOVERNANCE AS SOON AS POSSIBLE. OR OTHERWISE, DISASSOCIATE FROM IT.
BEEP
AirDrop
AAAAH!
MISTER BLAKE!
FA-THUD

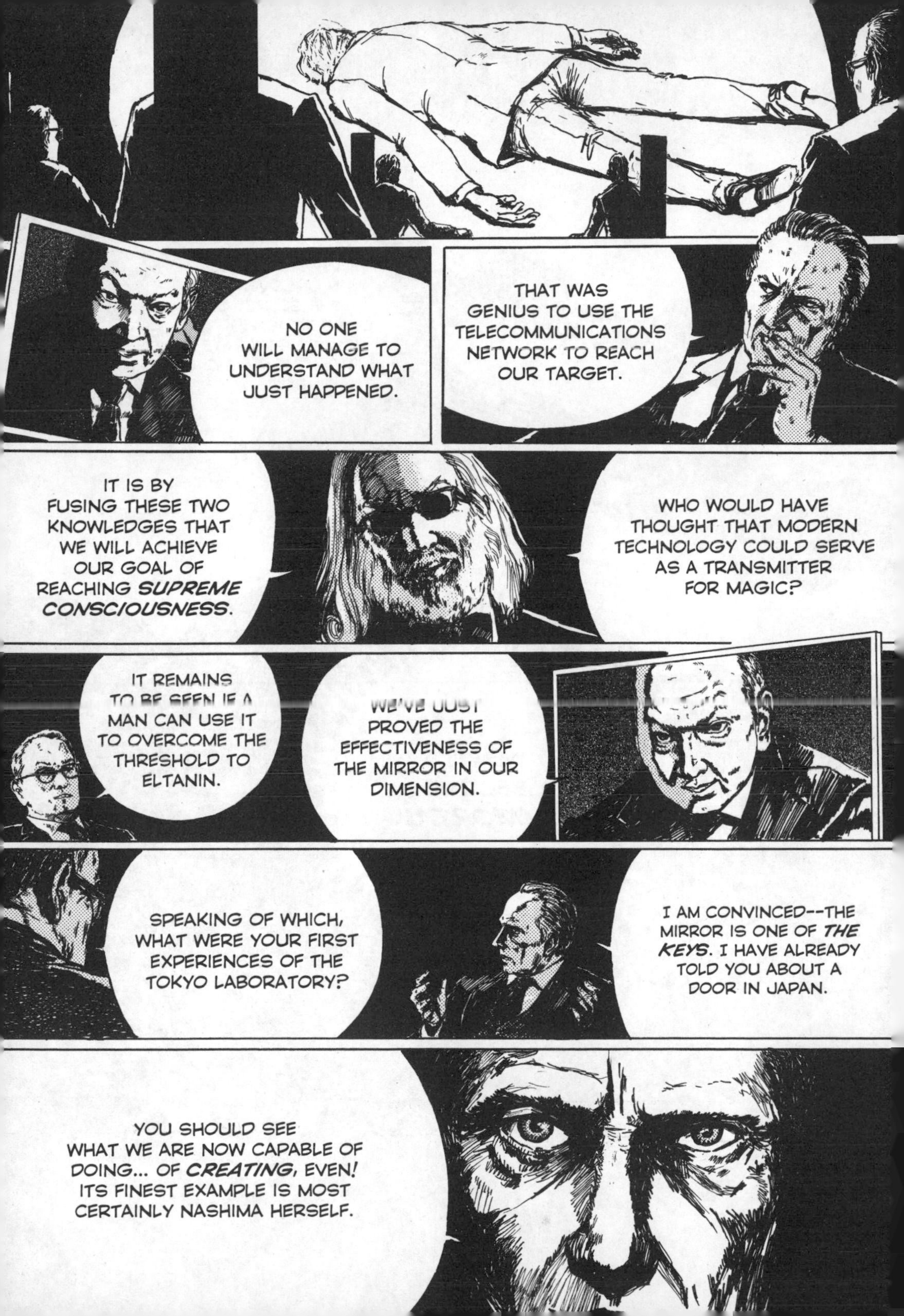
THAT WAS GENIUS TO USE THE TELECOMMUNICATIONS NETWORK TO REACH OUR TARGET.
NO ONE WILL MANAGE TO UNDERSTAND WHAT JUST HAPPENED.
WHO WOULD HAVE THOUGHT THAT MODERN TECHNOLOGY COULD SERVE AS A TRANSMITTER FOR MAGIC?
IT IS BY FUSING THESE TWO KNOWLEDGES THAT WE WILL ACHIEVE OUR GOAL OF REACHING *SUPREME CONSCIOUSNESS*.
WE'VE JUST PROVED THE EFFECTIVENESS OF THE MIRROR IN OUR DIMENSION.
IT REMAINS TO BE SEEN IF A MAN CAN USE IT TO OVERCOME THE THRESHOLD TO ELTANIN.
I AM CONVINCED--THE MIRROR IS ONE OF *THE KEYS*. I HAVE ALREADY TOLD YOU ABOUT A DOOR IN JAPAN.
SPEAKING OF WHICH, WHAT WERE YOUR FIRST EXPERIENCES OF THE TOKYO LABORATORY?
YOU SHOULD SEE WHAT WE ARE NOW CAPABLE OF DOING... OF *CREATING*, EVEN! ITS FINEST EXAMPLE IS MOST CERTAINLY NASHIMA HERSELF.

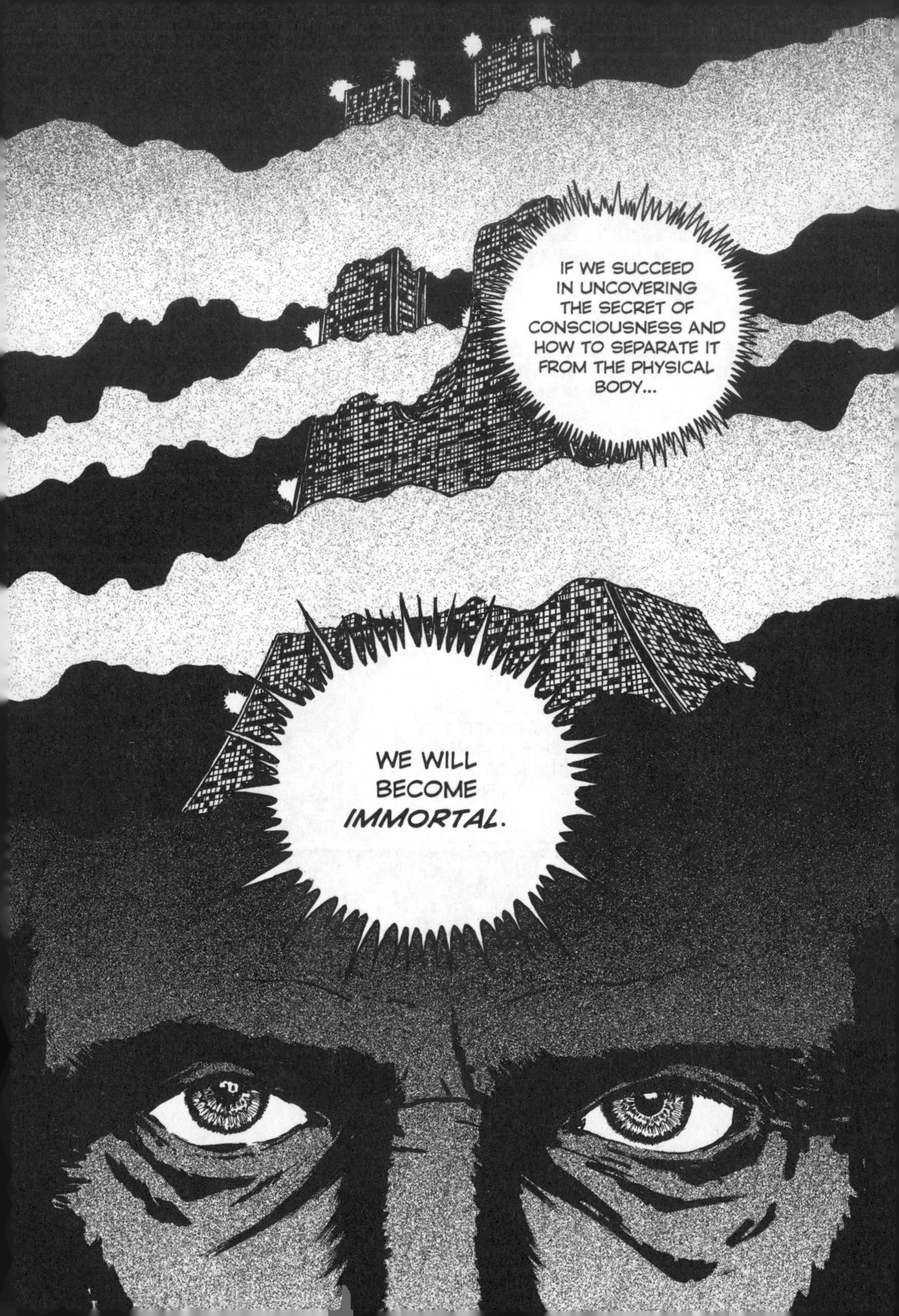
IF WE SUCCEED IN UNCOVERING THE SECRET OF CONSCIOUSNESS AND HOW TO SEPARATE IT FROM THE PHYSICAL BODY...
WE WILL BECOME *IMMORTAL*.

CHAPTER 2

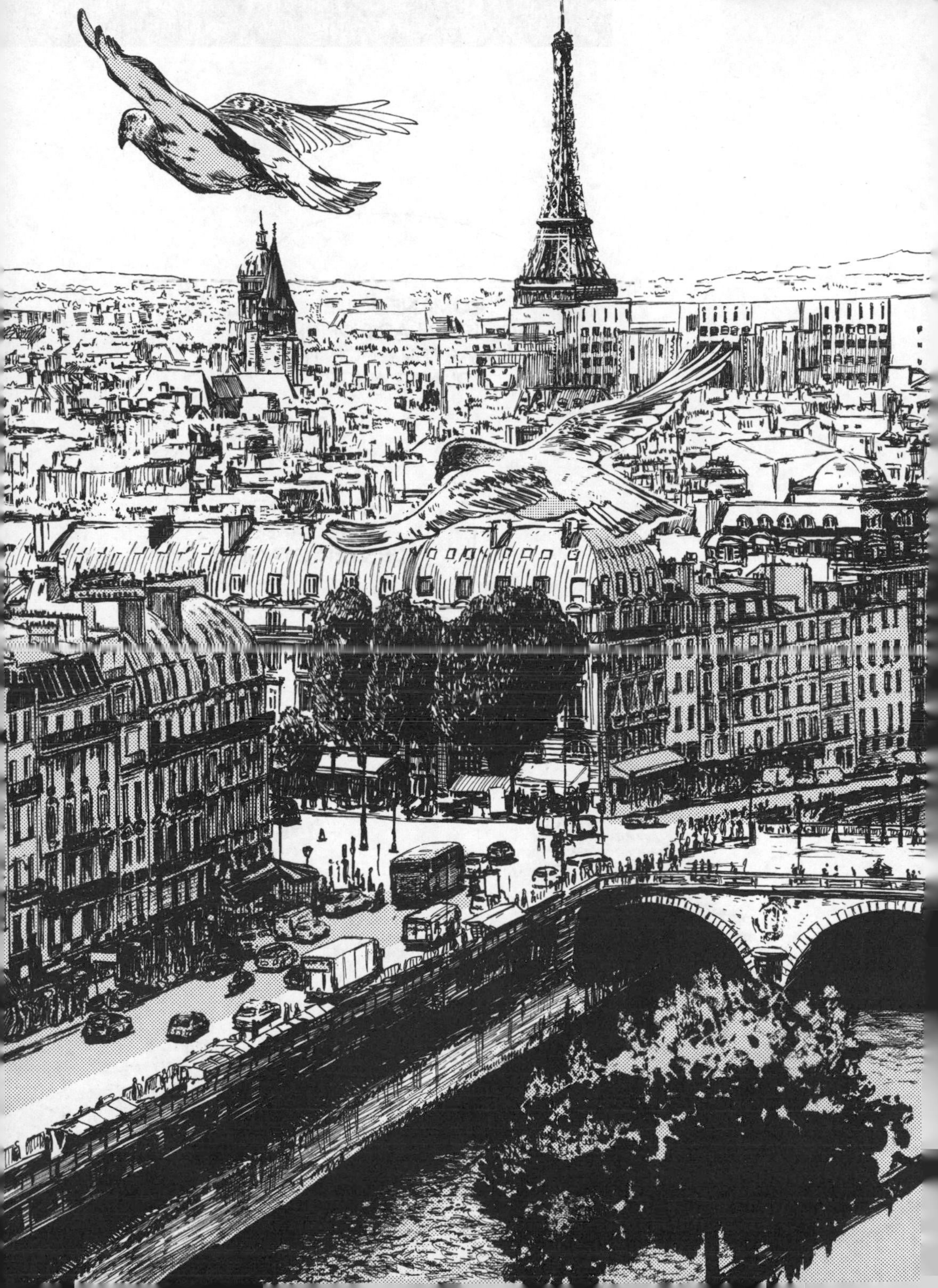

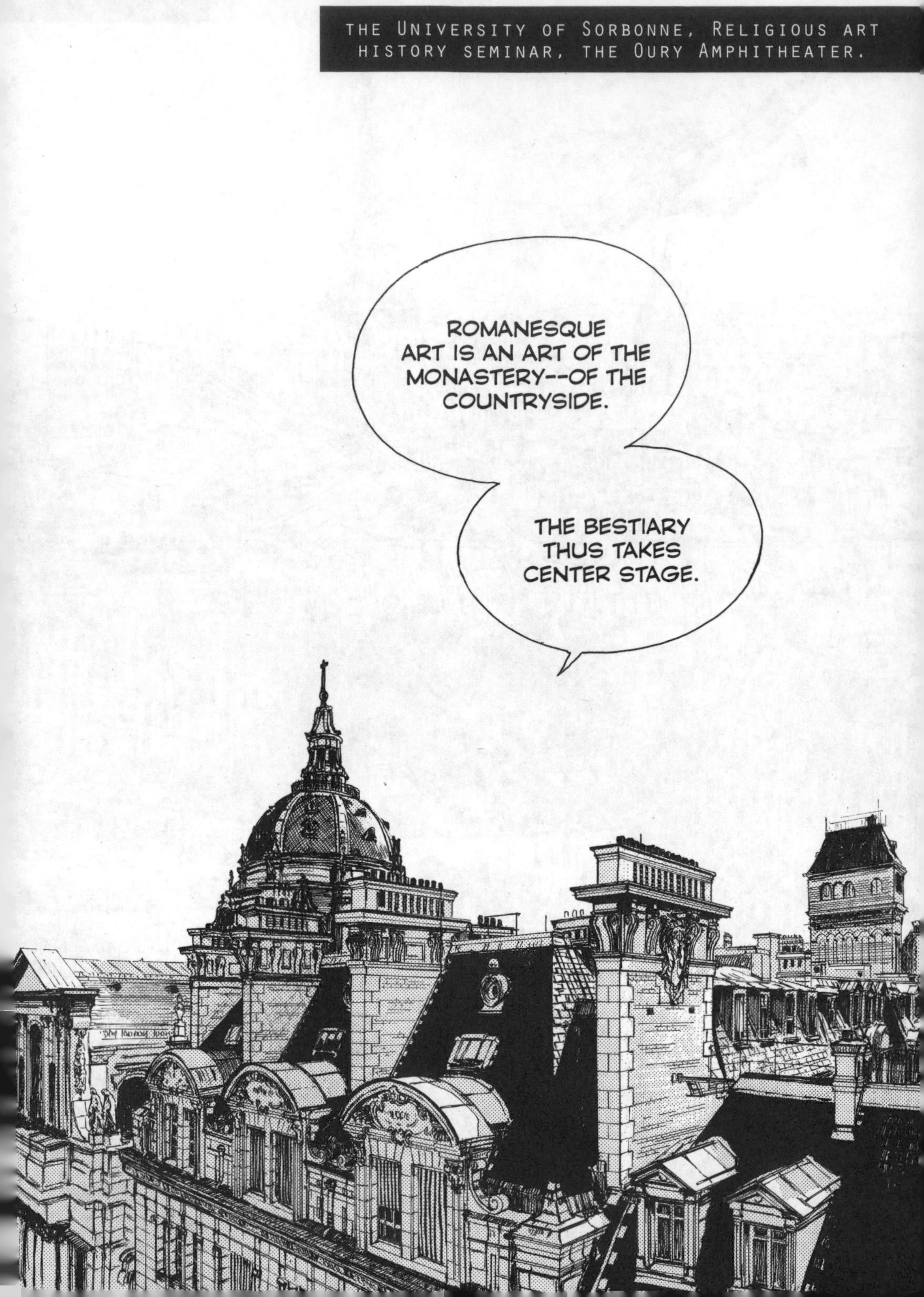
THE UNIVERSITY OF SORBONNE, RELIGIOUS ART HISTORY SEMINAR, THE OURY AMPHITHEATER.
ROMANESQUE ART IS AN ART OF THE MONASTERY--OF THE COUNTRYSIDE.
THE BESTIARY THUS TAKES CENTER STAGE.

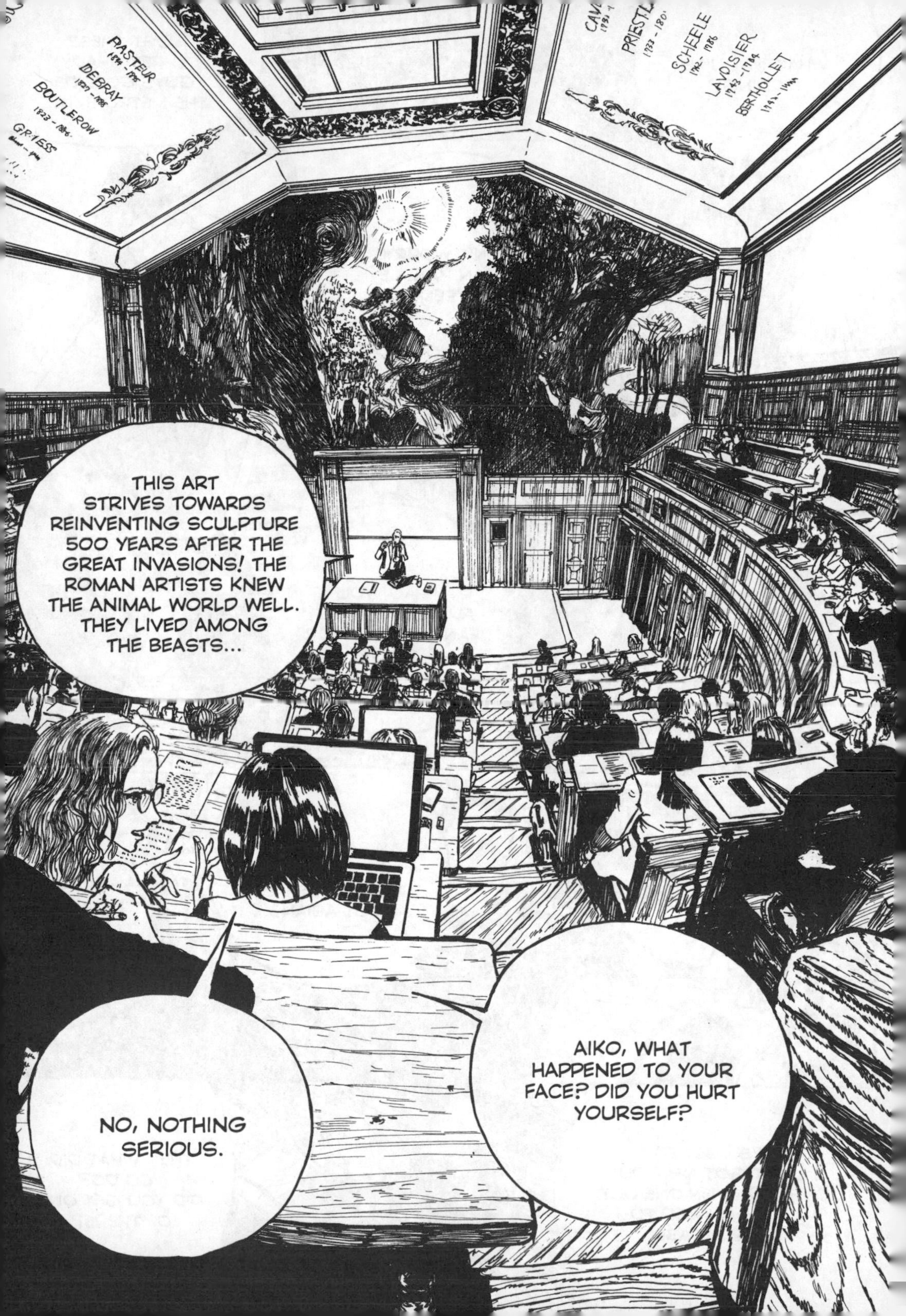
SCHEELE
BERTHOLLET
PASTEUR
DEBRAY
BOUTLEROW
GRIESS
THIS ART STRIVES TOWARDS REINVENTING SCULPTURE 500 YEARS AFTER THE GREAT INVASIONS! THE ROMAN ARTISTS KNEW THE ANIMAL WORLD WELL. THEY LIVED AMONG THE BEASTS...
AIKO, WHAT HAPPENED TO YOUR FACE? DID YOU HURT YOURSELF?
NO, NOTHING SERIOUS.

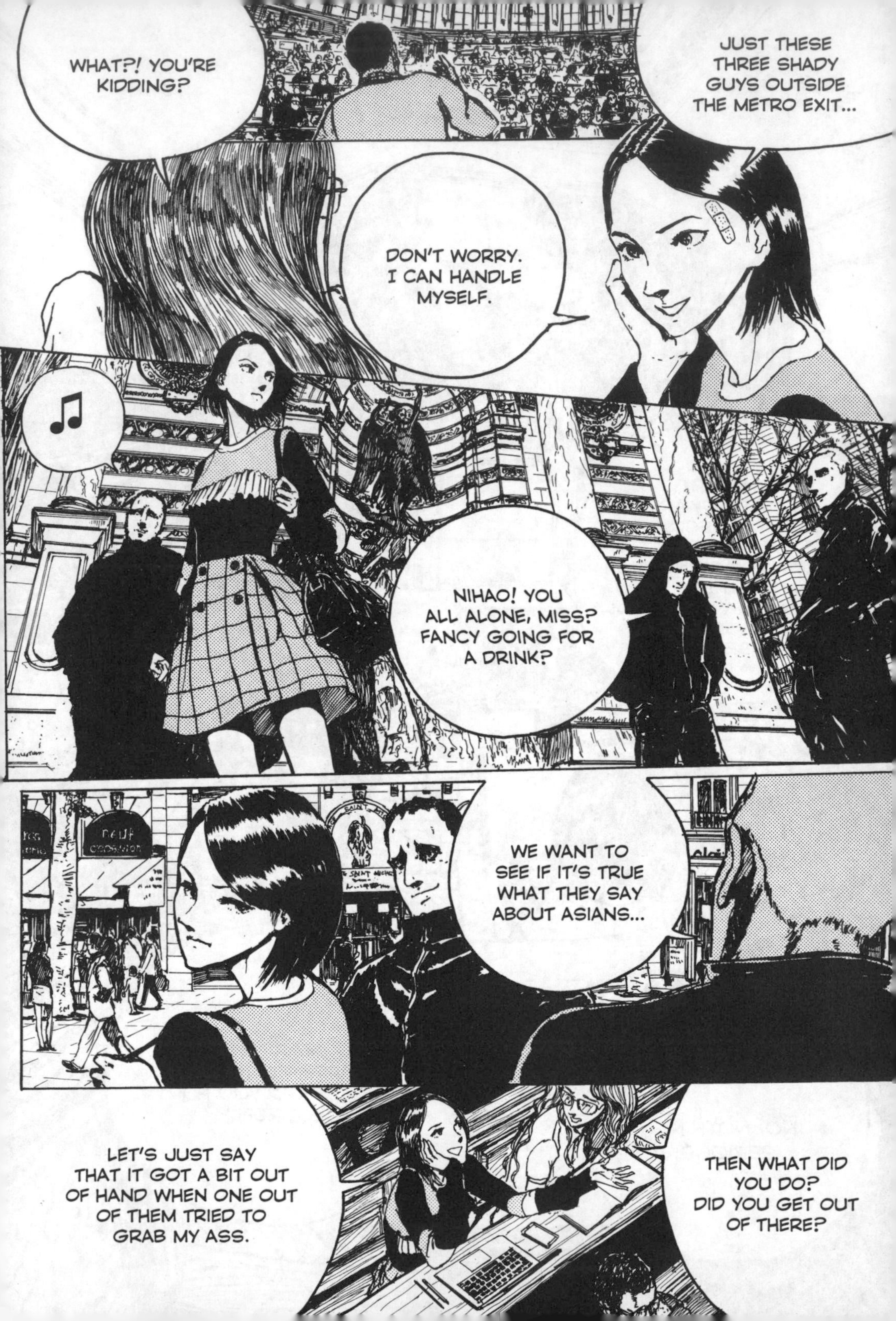
JUST THESE THREE SHADY GUYS OUTSIDE THE METRO EXIT...
WHAT?! YOU'RE KIDDING?
DON'T WORRY. I CAN HANDLE MYSELF.
NIHAO! YOU ALL ALONE, MISS? FANCY GOING FOR A DRINK?
WE WANT TO SEE IF IT'S TRUE WHAT THEY SAY ABOUT ASIANS...
THEN WHAT DID YOU DO? DID YOU GET OUT OF THERE?
LET'S JUST SAY THAT IT GOT A BIT OUT OF HAND WHEN ONE OUT OF THEM TRIED TO GRAB MY ASS.

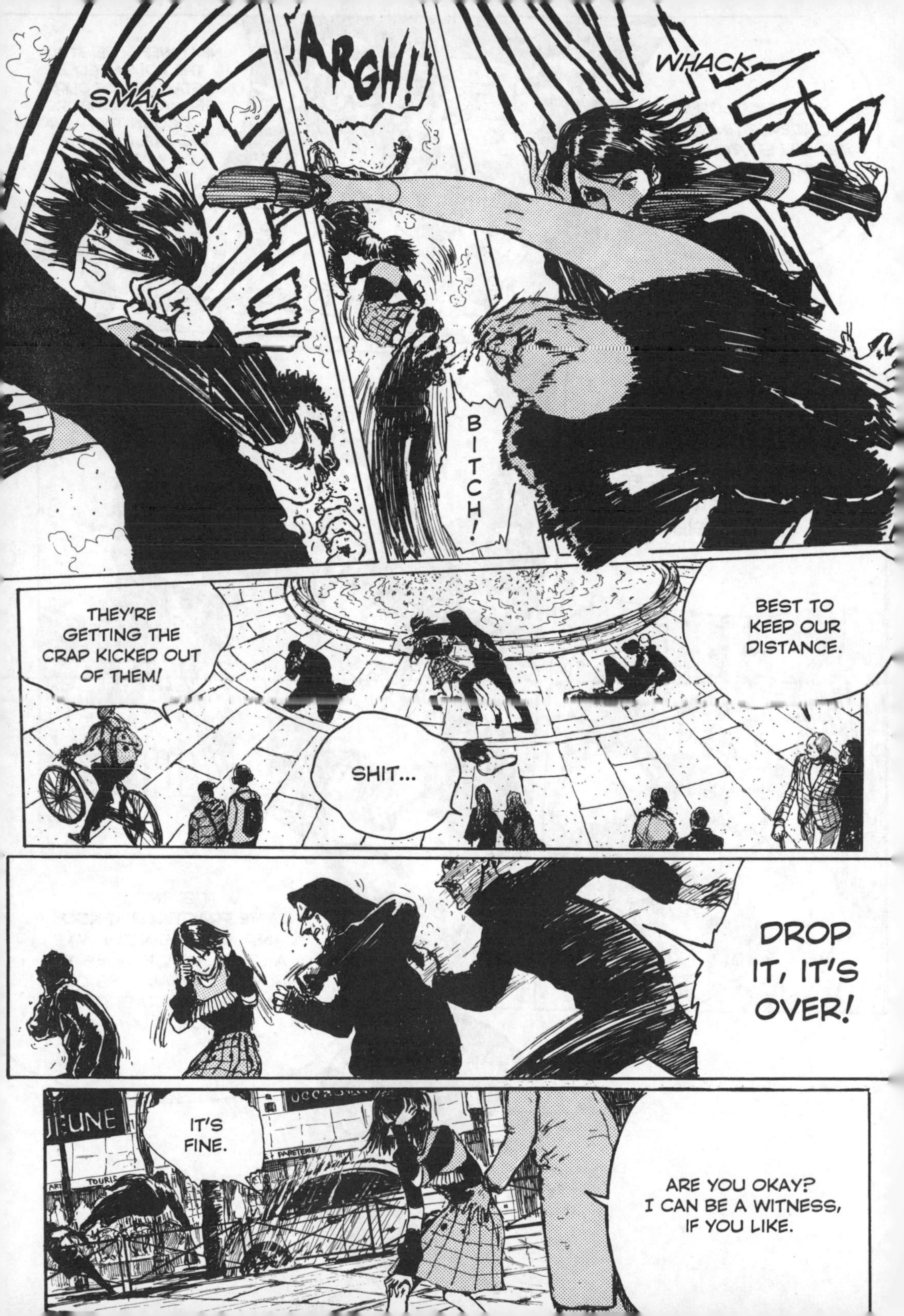
WHACK
BITCH!
ARGH!
SMAK
BEST TO KEEP OUR DISTANCE.
THEY'RE GETTING THE CRAP KICKED OUT OF THEM!
SHIT...
DROP IT, IT'S OVER!
ARE YOU OKAY? I CAN BE A WITNESS, IF YOU LIKE.
IT'S FINE.
JEUNE

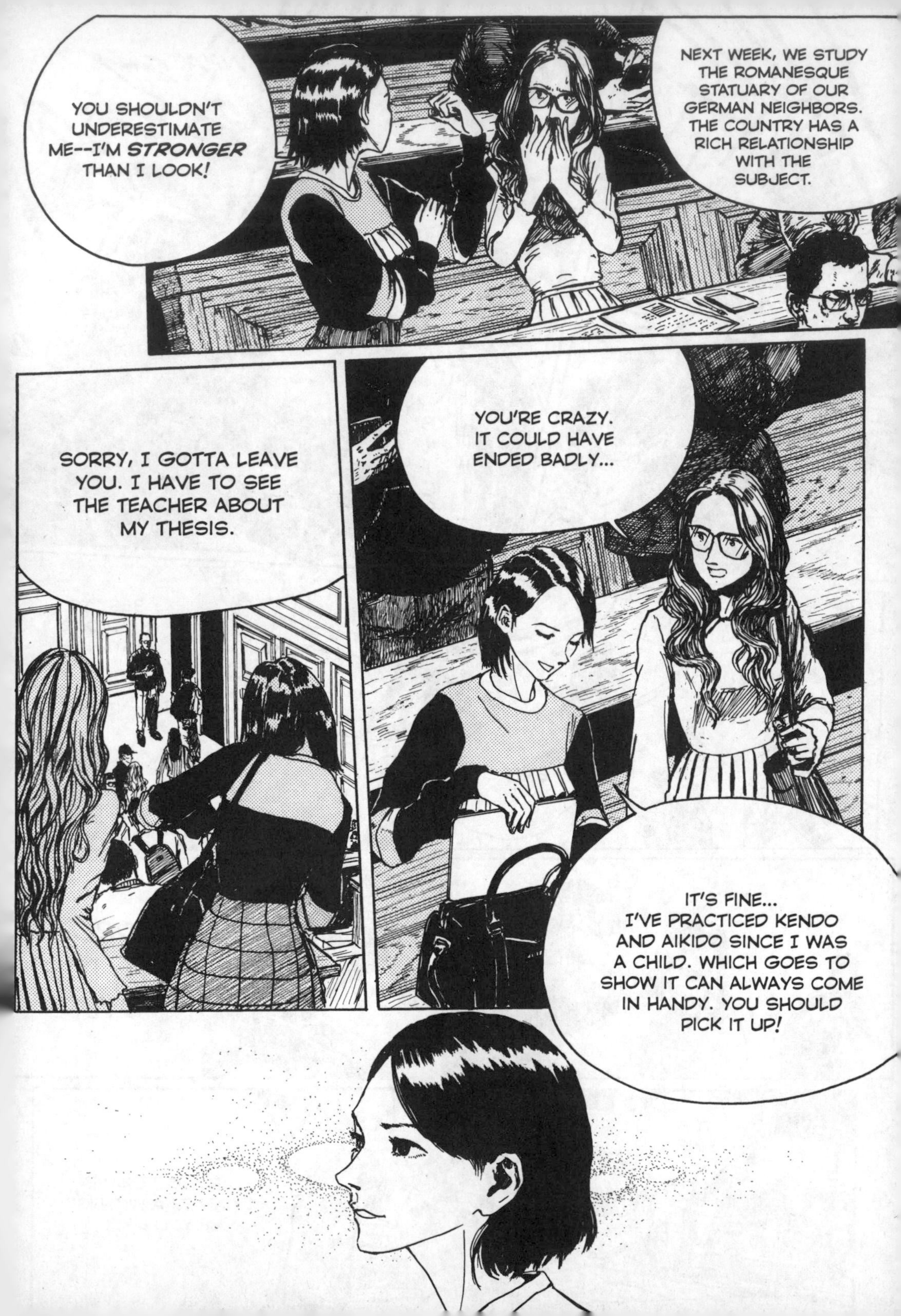
NEXT WEEK, WE STUDY THE ROMANESQUE STATUARY OF OUR GERMAN NEIGHBORS. THE COUNTRY HAS A RICH RELATIONSHIP WITH THE SUBJECT.
YOU SHOULDN'T UNDERESTIMATE ME--I'M *STRONGER* THAN I LOOK!
YOU'RE CRAZY. IT COULD HAVE ENDED BADLY...
IT'S FINE... I'VE PRACTICED KENDO AND AIKIDO SINCE I WAS A CHILD. WHICH GOES TO SHOW IT CAN ALWAYS COME IN HANDY. YOU SHOULD PICK IT UP!
SORRY, I GOTTA LEAVE YOU. I HAVE TO SEE THE TEACHER ABOUT MY THESIS.

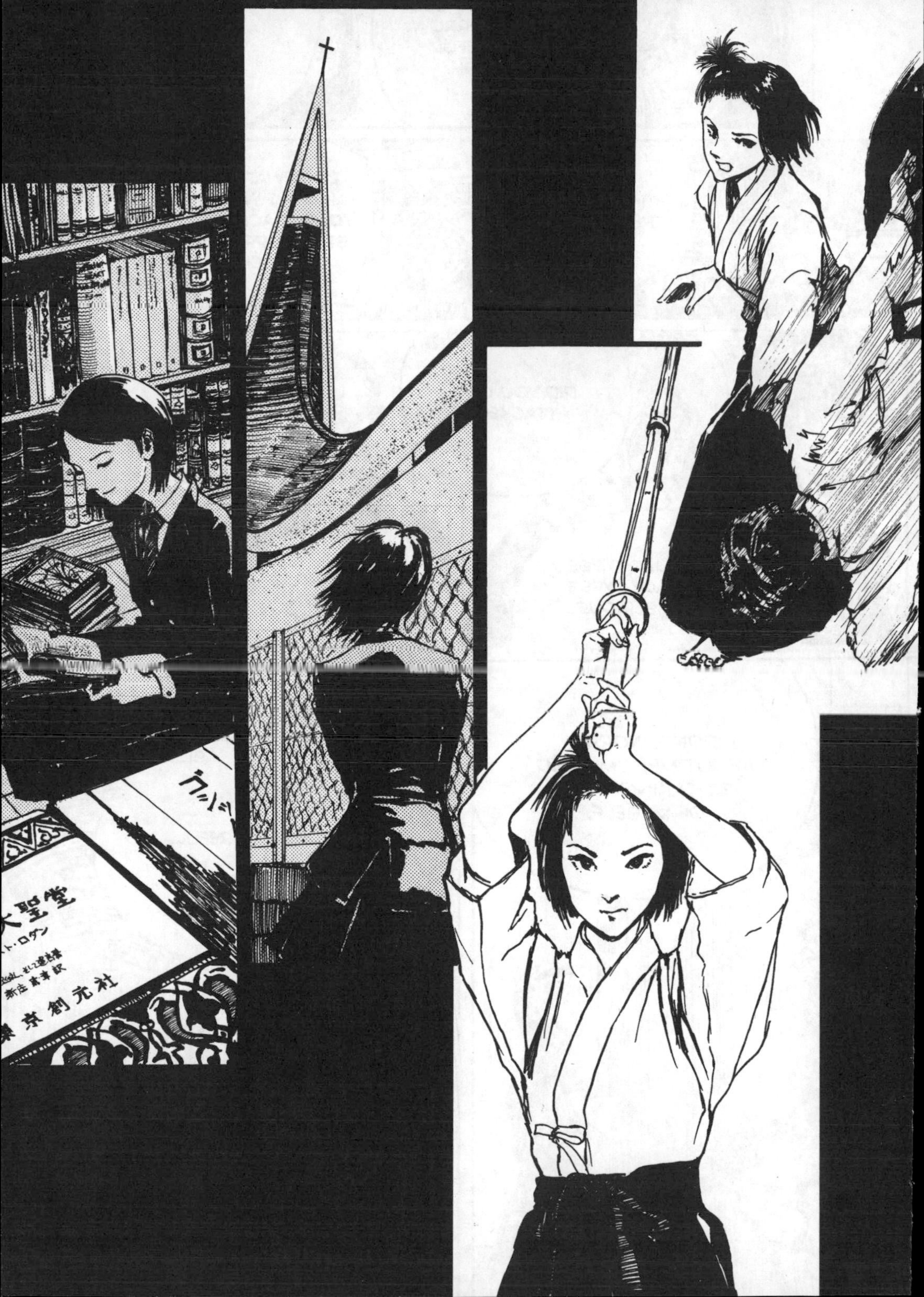
大聖堂
創元社

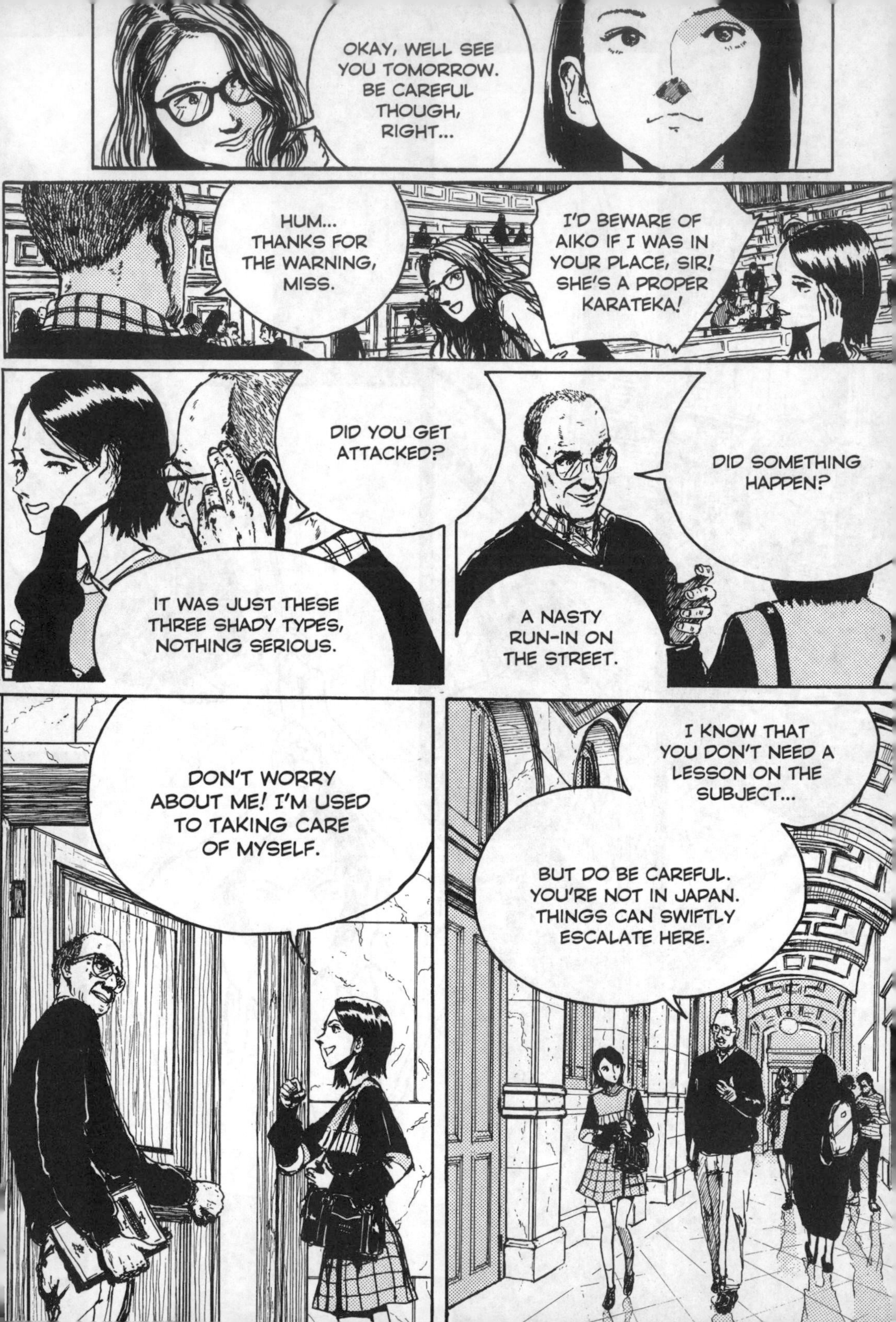
OKAY, WELL SEE YOU TOMORROW. BE CAREFUL THOUGH, RIGHT...
I'D BEWARE OF AIKO IF I WAS IN YOUR PLACE, SIR! SHE'S A PROPER KARATEKA!
HUM... THANKS FOR THE WARNING, MISS.
DID SOMETHING HAPPEN?
A NASTY RUN-IN ON THE STREET.
DID YOU GET ATTACKED?
IT WAS JUST THESE THREE SHADY TYPES, NOTHING SERIOUS.
I KNOW THAT YOU DON'T NEED A LESSON ON THE SUBJECT...
BUT DO BE CAREFUL. YOU'RE NOT IN JAPAN. THINGS CAN SWIFTLY ESCALATE HERE.
DON'T WORRY ABOUT ME! I'M USED TO TAKING CARE OF MYSELF.

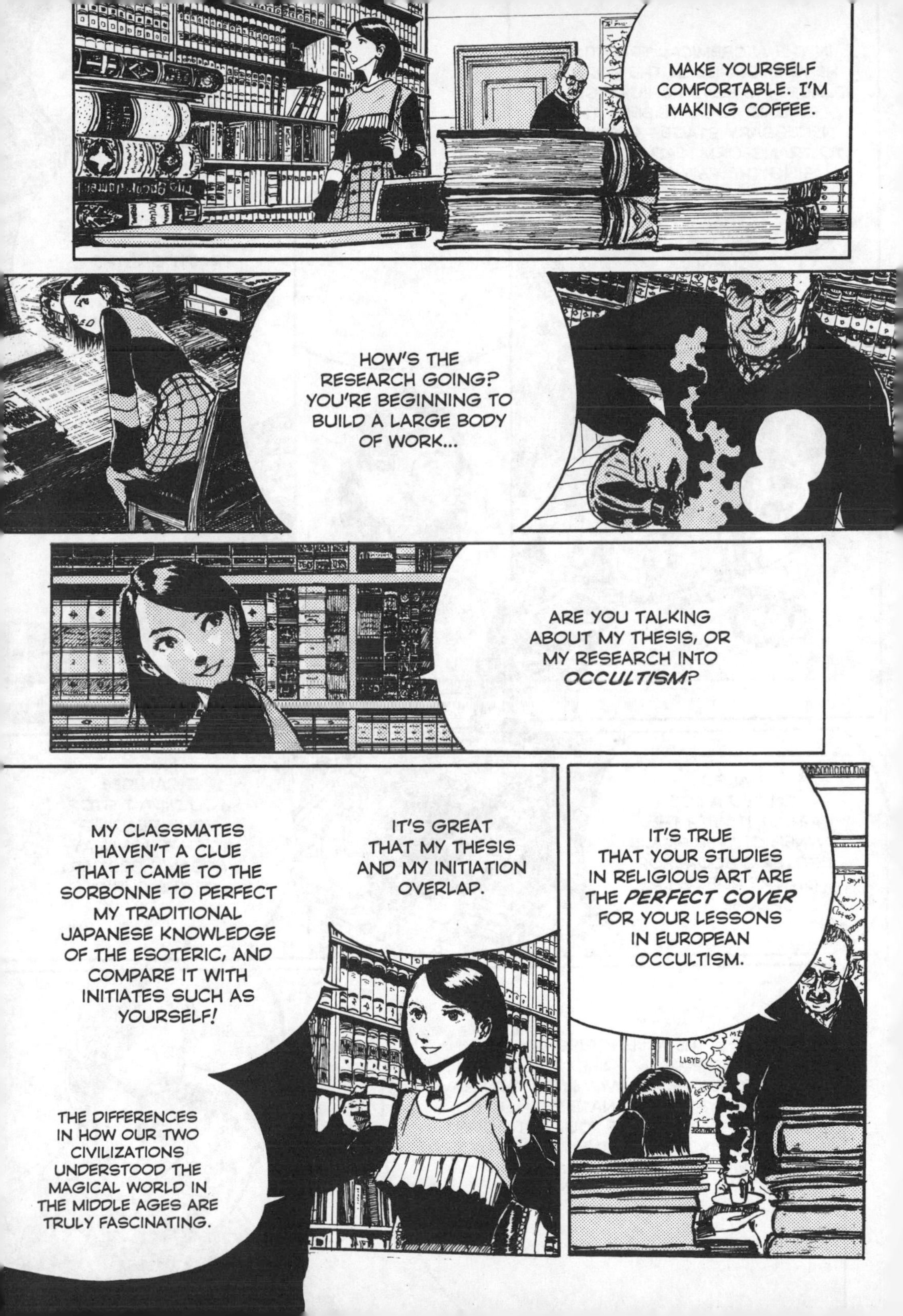
MAKE YOURSELF COMFORTABLE. I'M MAKING COFFEE.
HOW'S THE RESEARCH GOING? YOU'RE BEGINNING TO BUILD A LARGE BODY OF WORK...
ARE YOU TALKING ABOUT MY THESIS, OR MY RESEARCH INTO *OCCULTISM*?
IT'S TRUE THAT YOUR STUDIES IN RELIGIOUS ART ARE THE *PERFECT COVER* FOR YOUR LESSONS IN EUROPEAN OCCULTISM.
IT'S GREAT THAT MY THESIS AND MY INITIATION OVERLAP.
MY CLASSMATES HAVEN'T A CLUE THAT I CAME TO THE SORBONNE TO PERFECT MY TRADITIONAL JAPANESE KNOWLEDGE OF THE ESOTERIC, AND COMPARE IT WITH INITIATES SUCH AS YOURSELF!
THE DIFFERENCES IN HOW OUR TWO CIVILIZATIONS UNDERSTOOD THE MAGICAL WORLD IN THE MIDDLE AGES ARE TRULY FASCINATING.

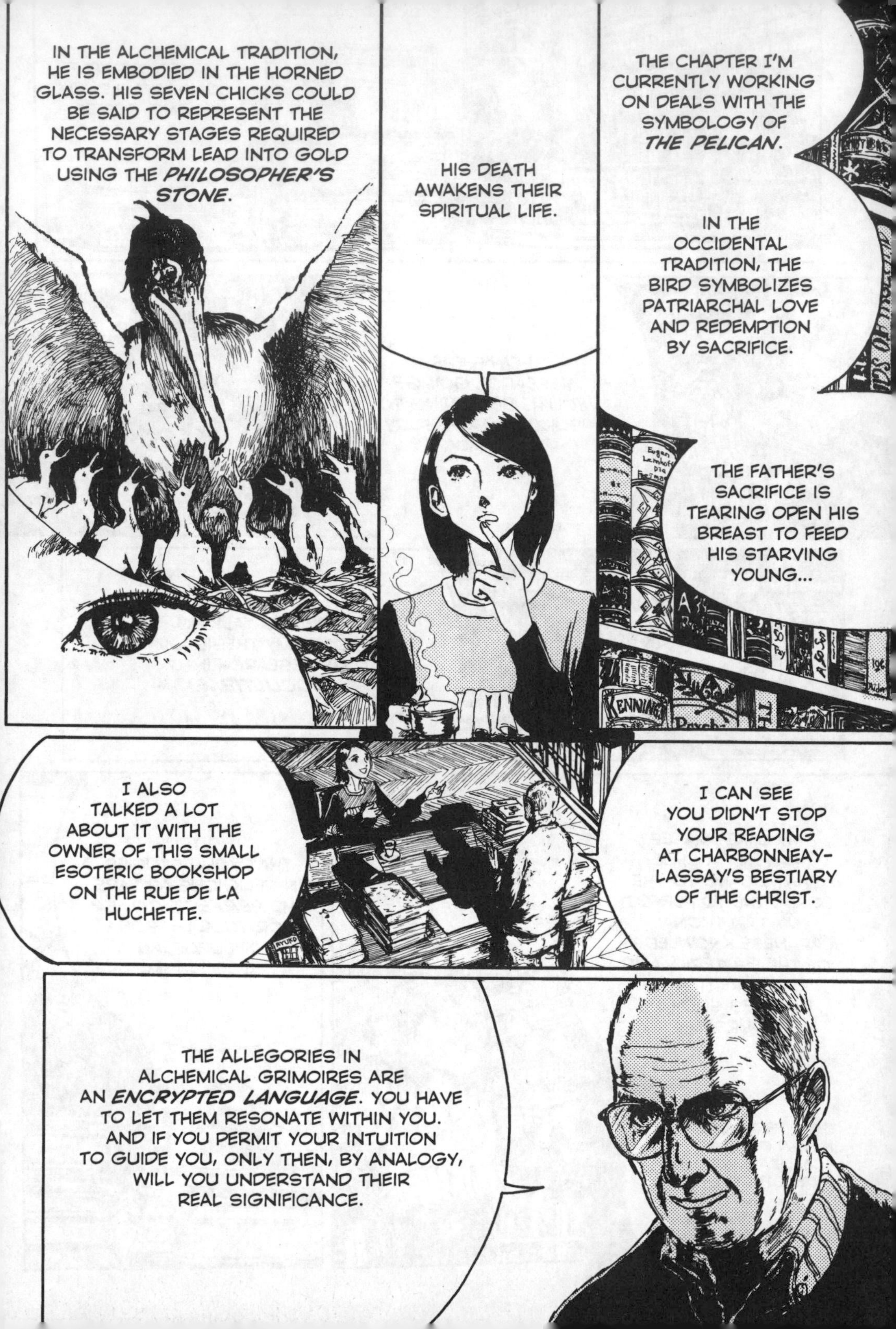
THE CHAPTER I'M CURRENTLY WORKING ON DEALS WITH THE SYMBOLOGY OF *THE PELICAN*.
IN THE OCCIDENTAL TRADITION, THE BIRD SYMBOLIZES PATRIARCHAL LOVE AND REDEMPTION BY SACRIFICE.
THE FATHER'S SACRIFICE IS TEARING OPEN HIS BREAST TO FEED HIS STARVING YOUNG...
HIS DEATH AWAKENS THEIR SPIRITUAL LIFE.
IN THE ALCHEMICAL TRADITION, HE IS EMBODIED IN THE HORNED GLASS. HIS SEVEN CHICKS COULD BE SAID TO REPRESENT THE NECESSARY STAGES REQUIRED TO TRANSFORM LEAD INTO GOLD USING THE *PHILOSOPHER'S STONE*.
I CAN SEE YOU DIDN'T STOP YOUR READING AT CHARBONNEAY-LASSAY'S BESTIARY OF THE CHRIST.
I ALSO TALKED A LOT ABOUT IT WITH THE OWNER OF THIS SMALL ESOTERIC BOOKSHOP ON THE RUE DE LA HUCHETTE.
THE ALLEGORIES IN ALCHEMICAL GRIMOIRES ARE AN *ENCRYPTED LANGUAGE*. YOU HAVE TO LET THEM RESONATE WITHIN YOU. AND IF YOU PERMIT YOUR INTUITION TO GUIDE YOU, ONLY THEN, BY ANALOGY, WILL YOU UNDERSTAND THEIR REAL SIGNIFICANCE.

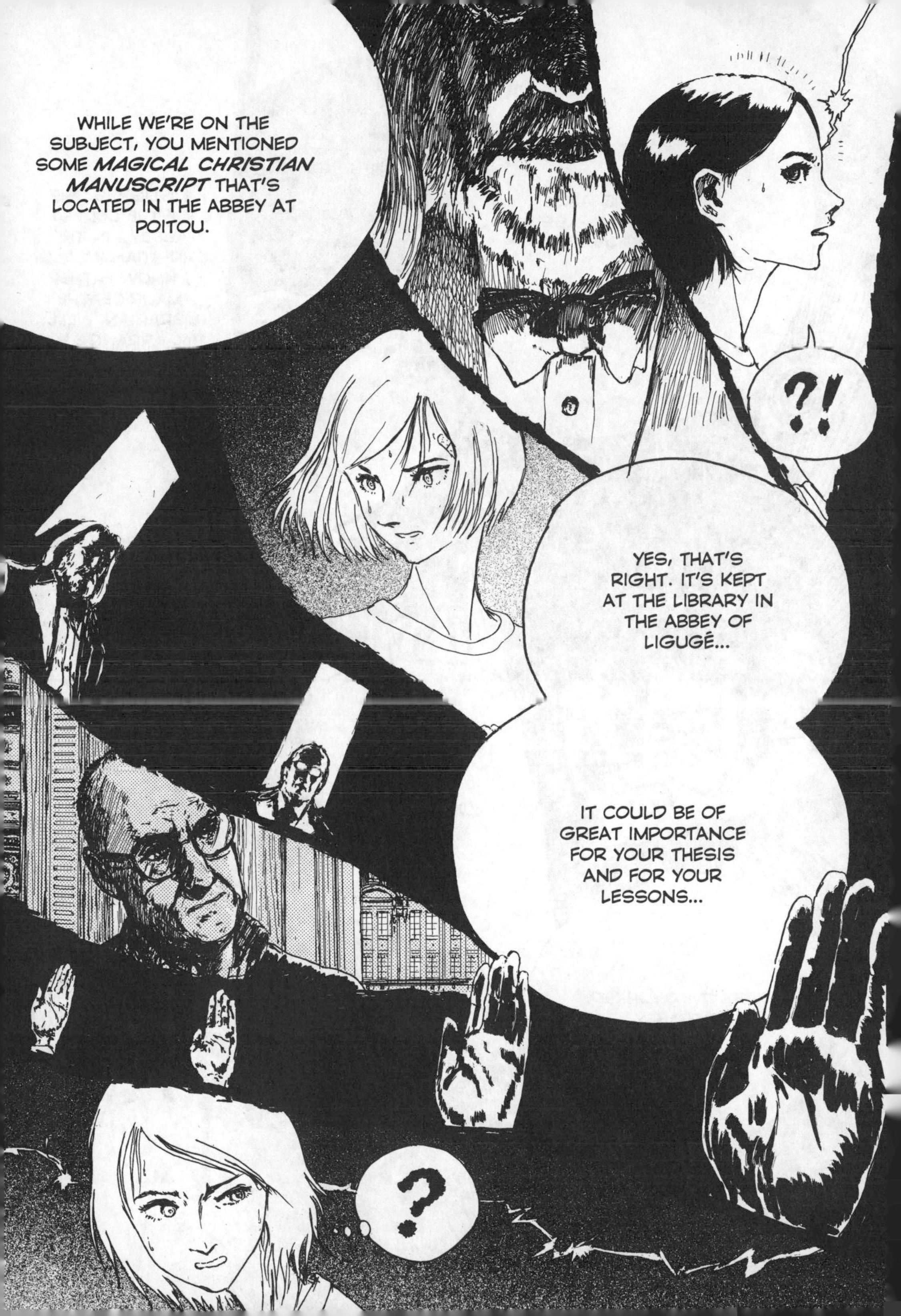
WHILE WE'RE ON THE SUBJECT, YOU MENTIONED SOME *MAGICAL CHRISTIAN MANUSCRIPT* THAT'S LOCATED IN THE ABBEY AT POITOU.
?!
YES, THAT'S RIGHT. IT'S KEPT AT THE LIBRARY IN THE ABBEY OF LIGUGÉ...
IT COULD BE OF GREAT IMPORTANCE FOR YOUR THESIS AND FOR YOUR LESSONS...
?

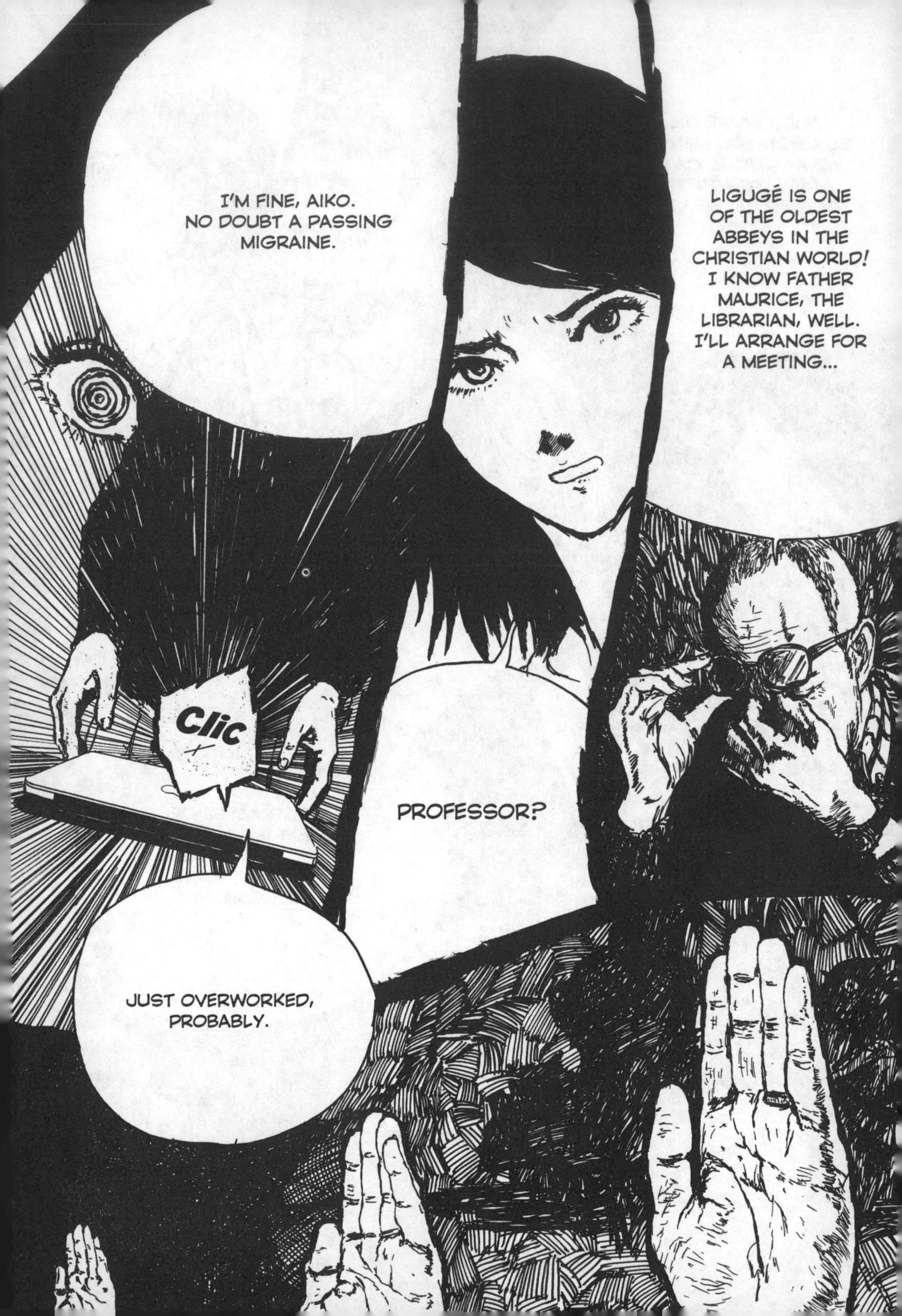
LIGUGÉ IS ONE OF THE OLDEST ABBEYS IN THE CHRISTIAN WORLD! I KNOW FATHER MAURICE, THE LIBRARIAN, WELL. I'LL ARRANGE FOR A MEETING...
I'M FINE, AIKO. NO DOUBT A PASSING MIGRAINE.
Clic
PROFESSOR?
JUST OVERWORKED, PROBABLY.

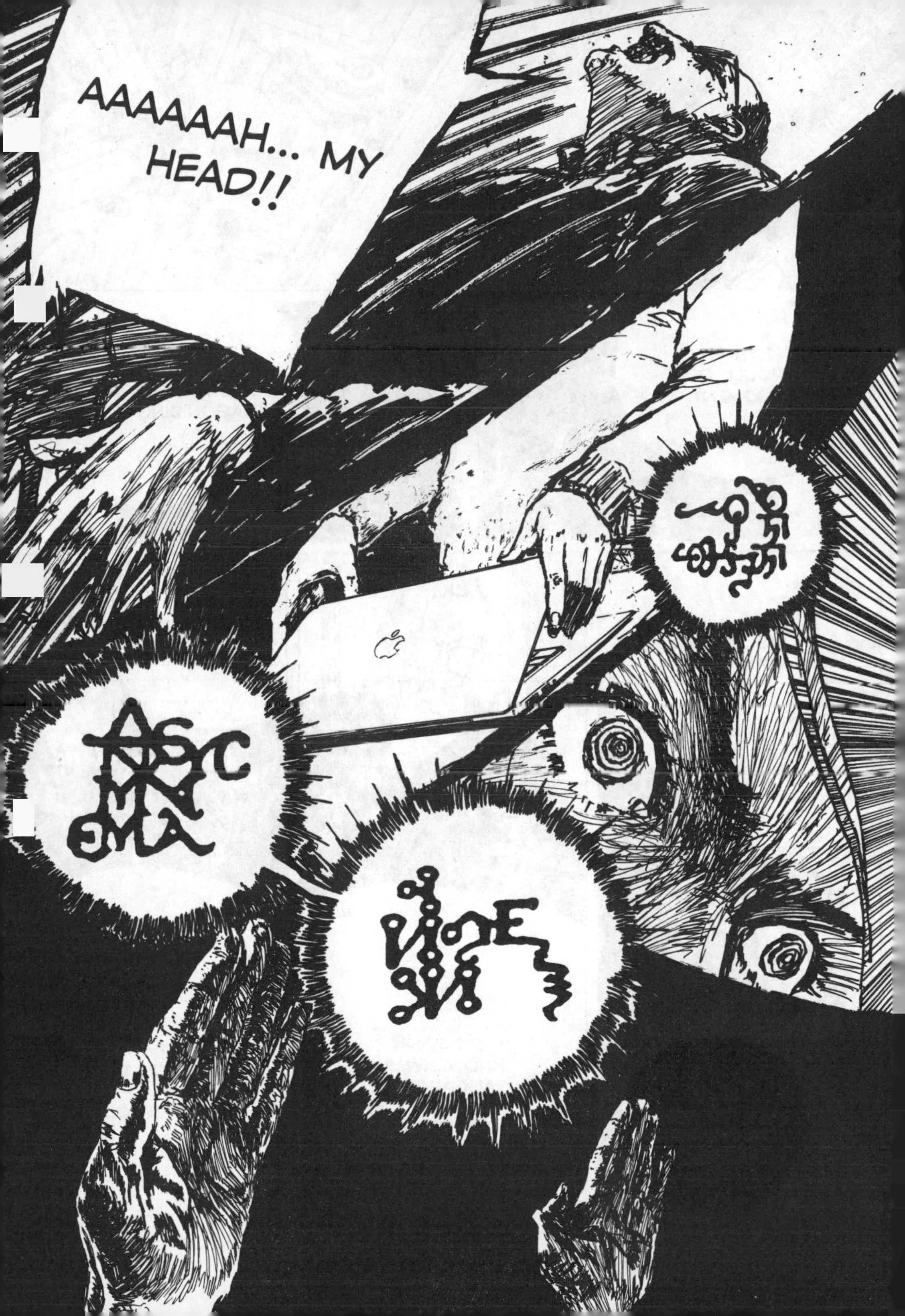
AAAAAAH... MY HEAD!!

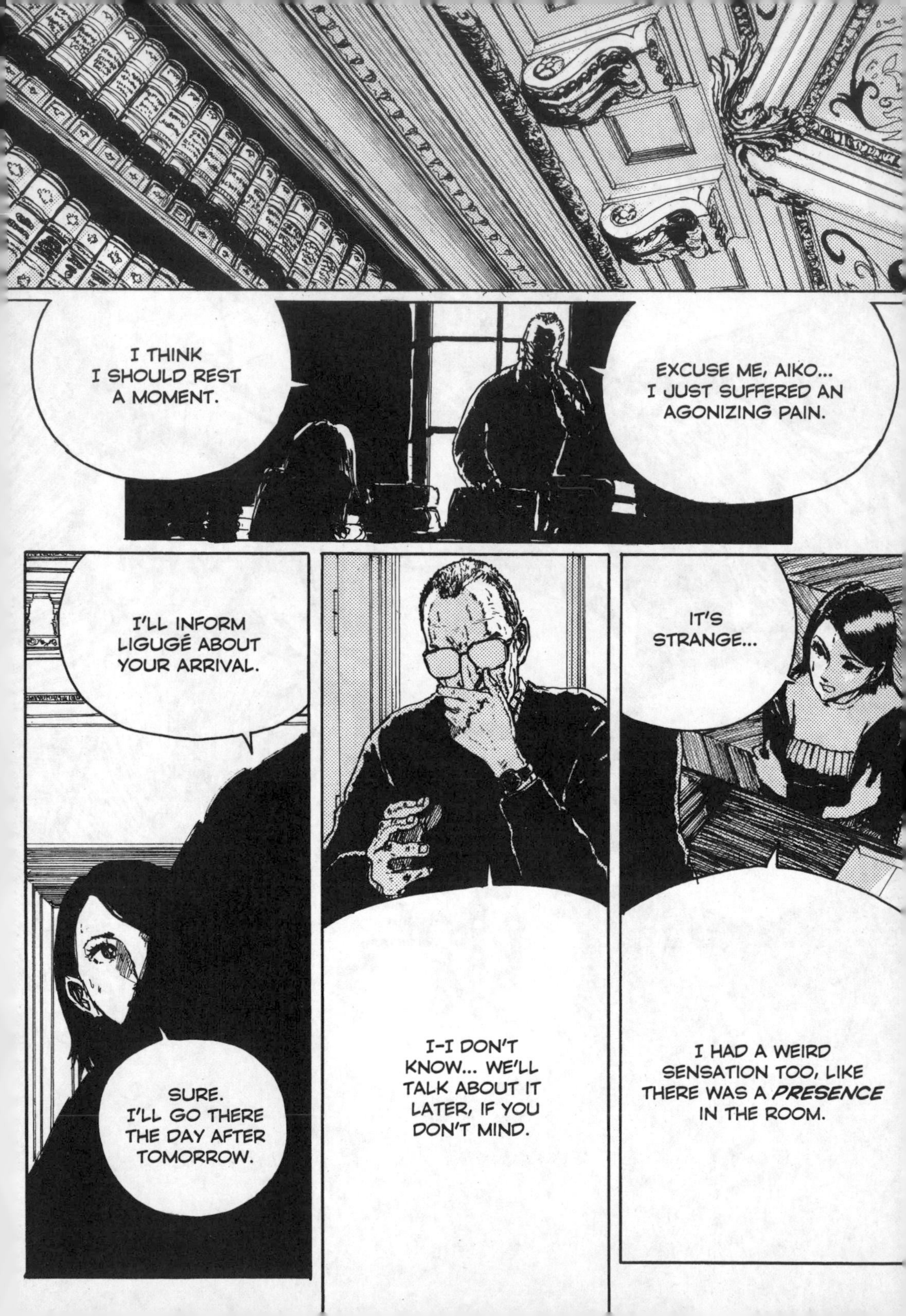
EXCUSE ME, AIKO... I JUST SUFFERED AN AGONIZING PAIN.
I THINK I SHOULD REST A MOMENT.
IT'S STRANGE...
I HAD A WEIRD SENSATION TOO, LIKE THERE WAS A *PRESENCE* IN THE ROOM.
I-I DON'T KNOW... WE'LL TALK ABOUT IT LATER, IF YOU DON'T MIND.
I'LL INFORM LIGUGÉ ABOUT YOUR ARRIVAL.
SURE. I'LL GO THERE THE DAY AFTER TOMORROW.

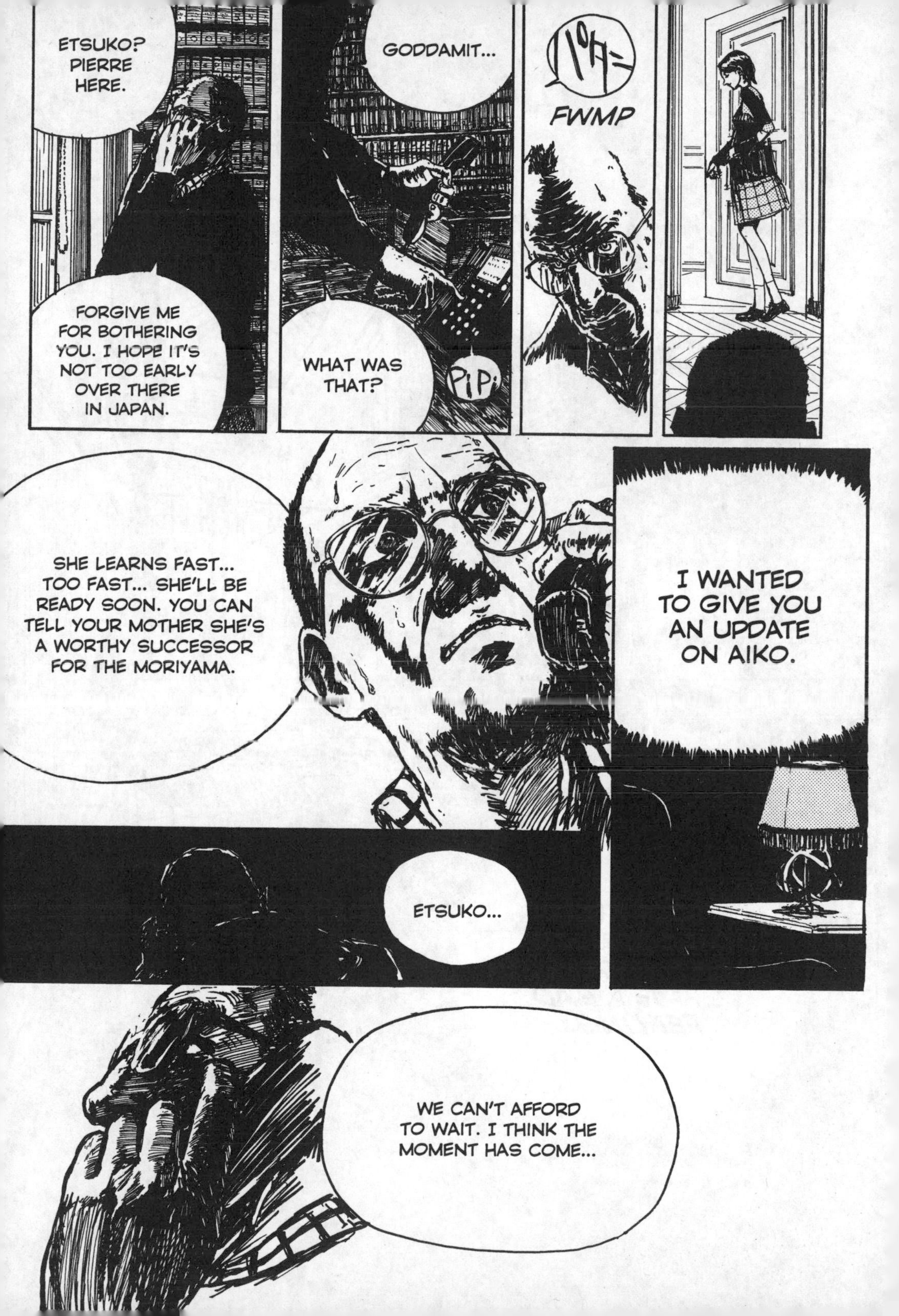
FWMP
GODDAMIT...
WHAT WAS THAT?
PiPi
ETSUKO? PIERRE HERE.
FORGIVE ME FOR BOTHERING YOU. I HOPE IT'S NOT TOO EARLY OVER THERE IN JAPAN.
I WANTED TO GIVE YOU AN UPDATE ON AIKO.
SHE LEARNS FAST... TOO FAST... SHE'LL BE READY SOON. YOU CAN TELL YOUR MOTHER SHE'S A WORTHY SUCCESSOR FOR THE MORIYAMA.
ETSUKO...
WE CAN'T AFFORD TO WAIT. I THINK THE MOMENT HAS COME...

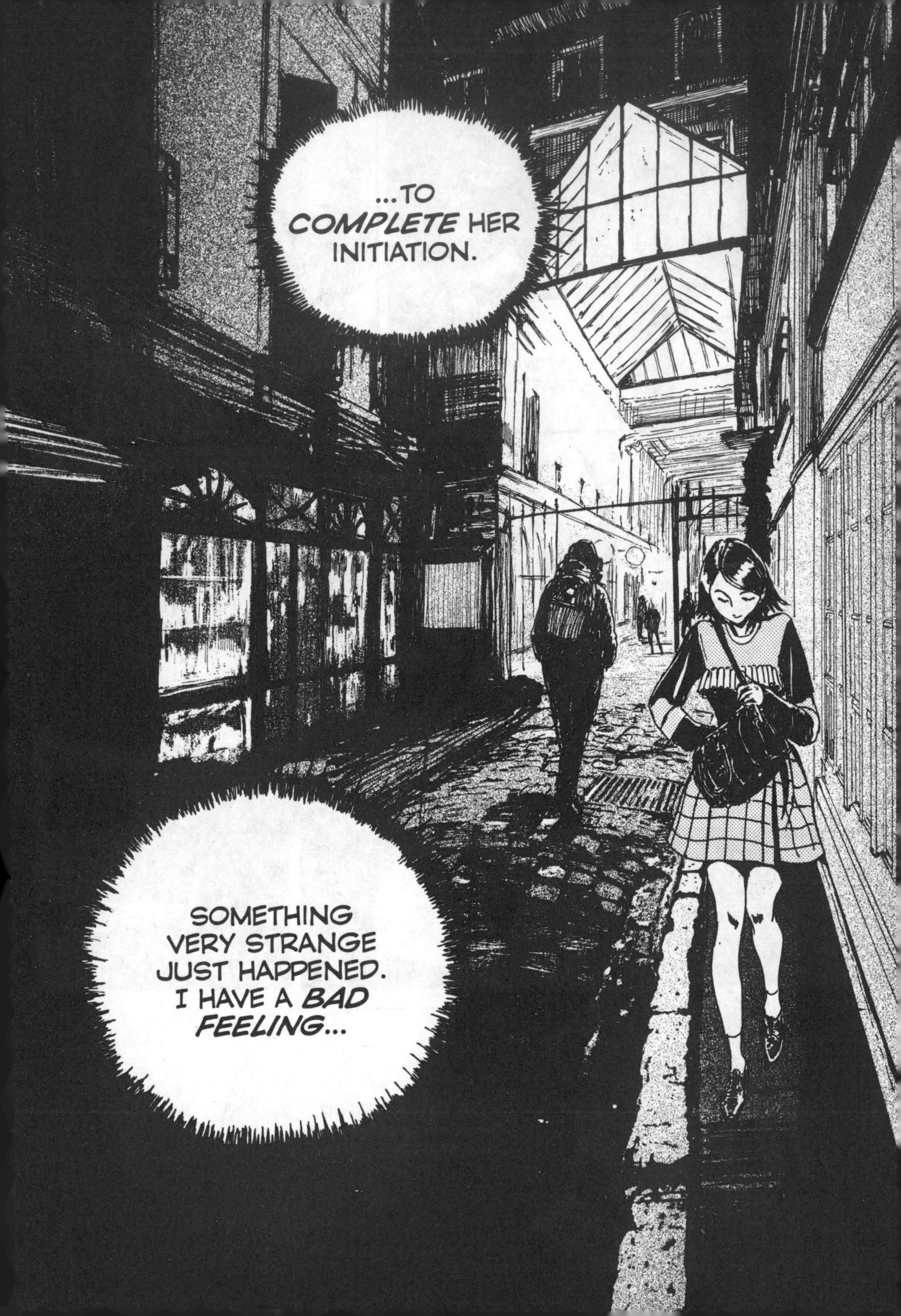
...TO *COMPLETE* HER INITIATION.
SOMETHING VERY STRANGE JUST HAPPENED. I HAVE A *BAD FEELING*...

CHAPTER 3

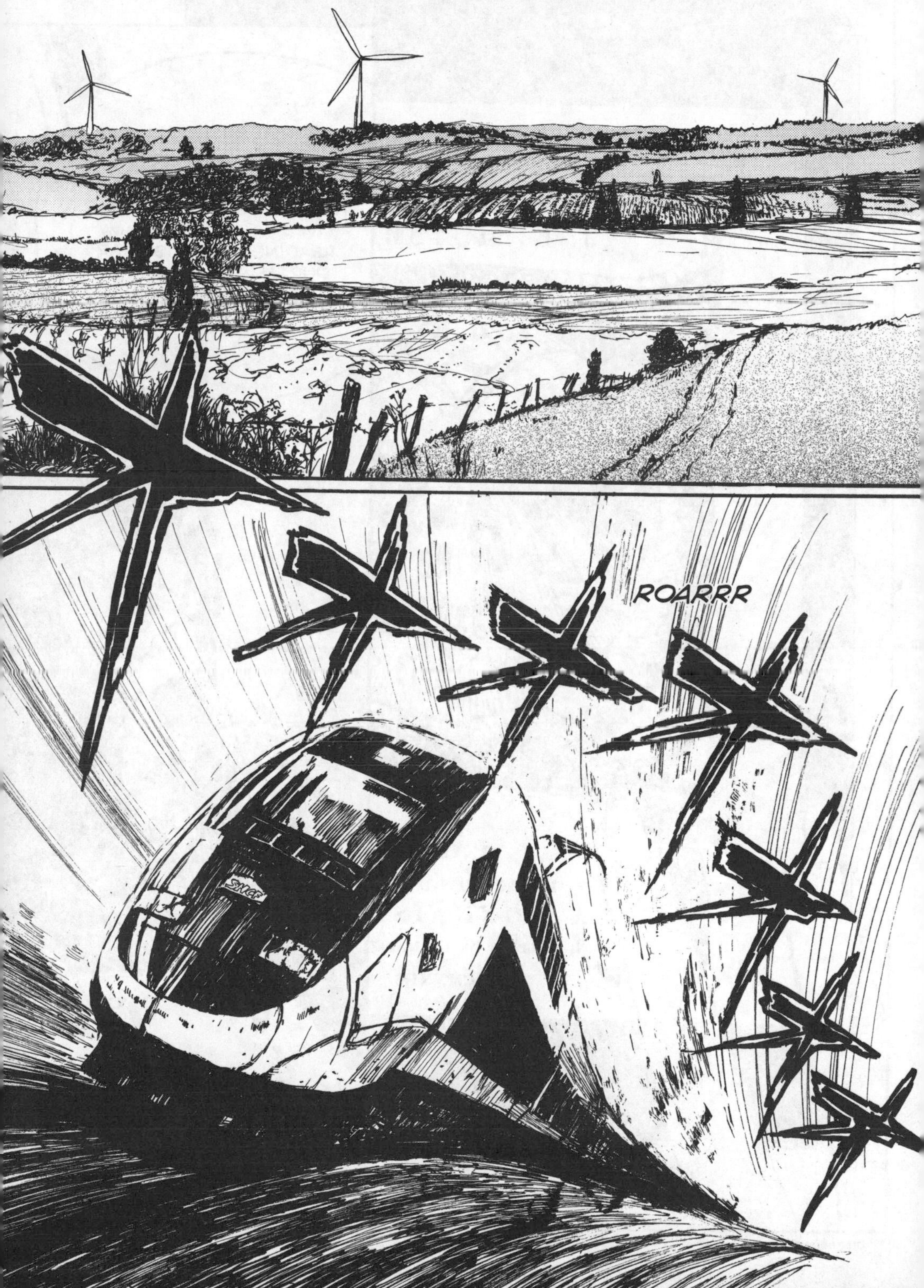
ROARRR
SNCF

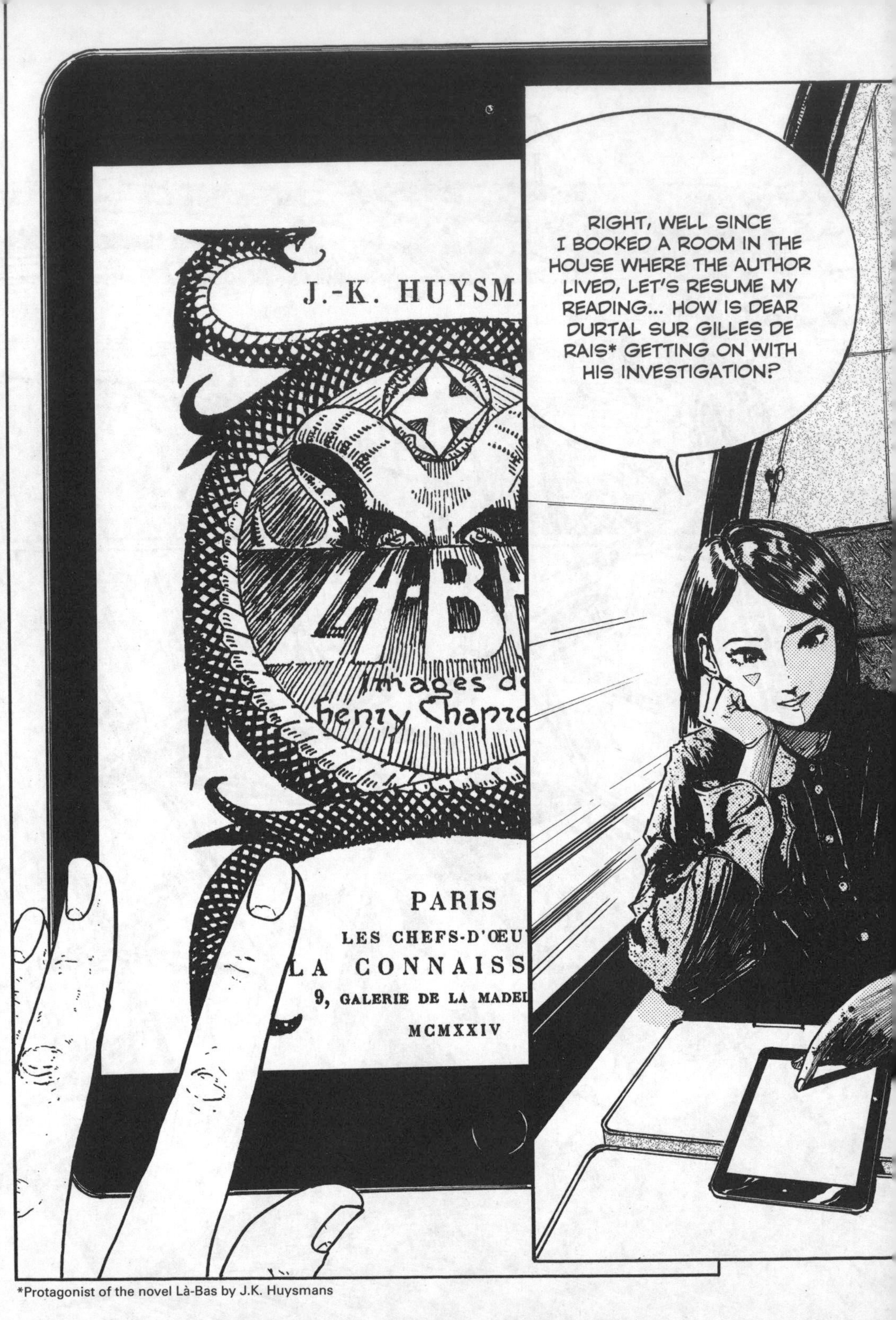
RIGHT, WELL SINCE I BOOKED A ROOM IN THE HOUSE WHERE THE AUTHOR LIVED, LET'S RESUME MY READING... HOW IS DEAR DURTAL SUR GILLES DE RAIS* GETTING ON WITH HIS INVESTIGATION?
PARIS
MCMXXIV

*Protagonist of the novel Là-Bas by J.K. Huysmans

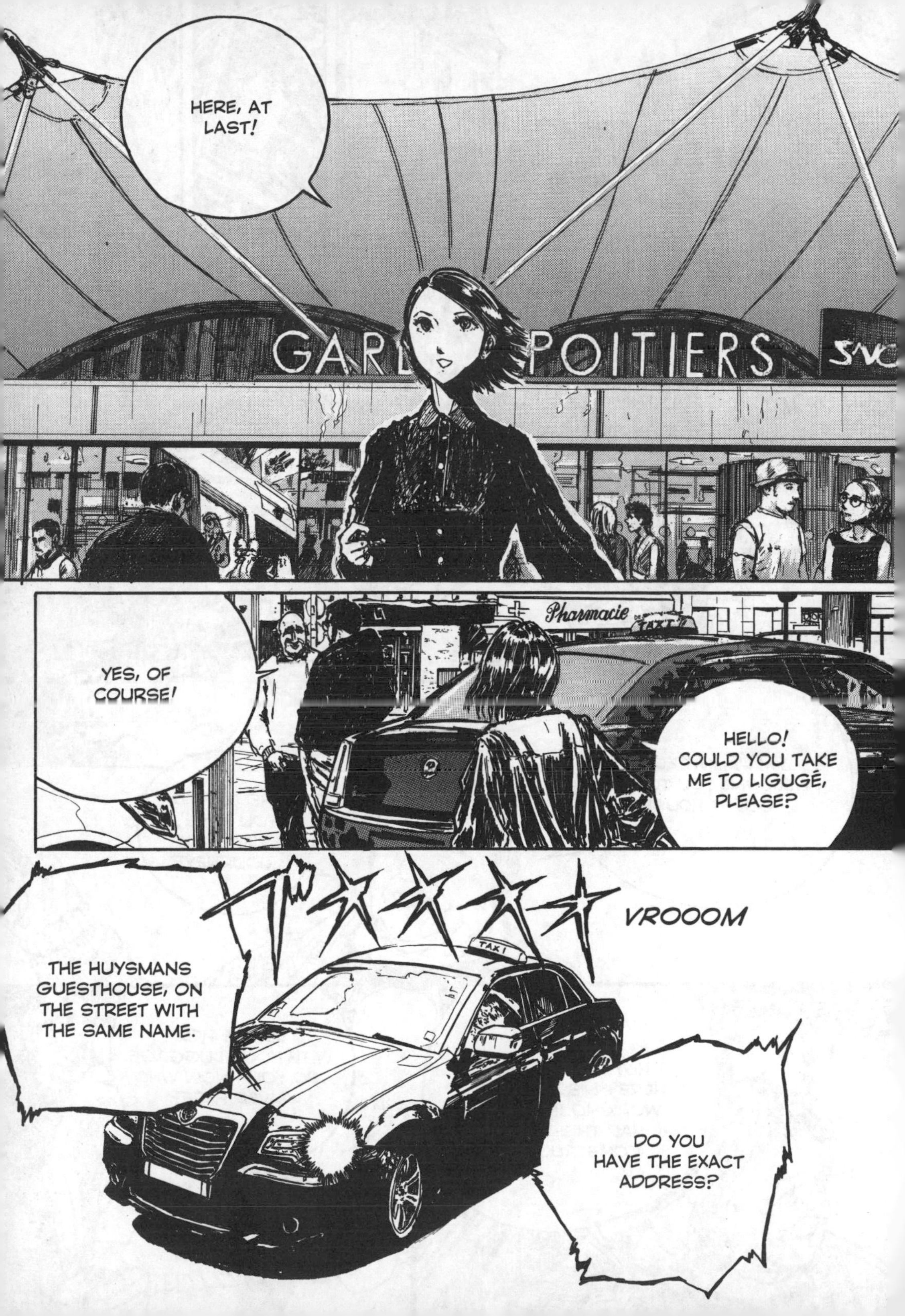
HERE, AT LAST!
POITIERS
Pharmacie
TAXI
HELLO! COULD YOU TAKE ME TO LIGUGÉ, PLEASE?
YES, OF COURSE!
VROOOM
TAXI
DO YOU HAVE THE EXACT ADDRESS?
THE HUYSMANS GUESTHOUSE, ON THE STREET WITH THE SAME NAME.

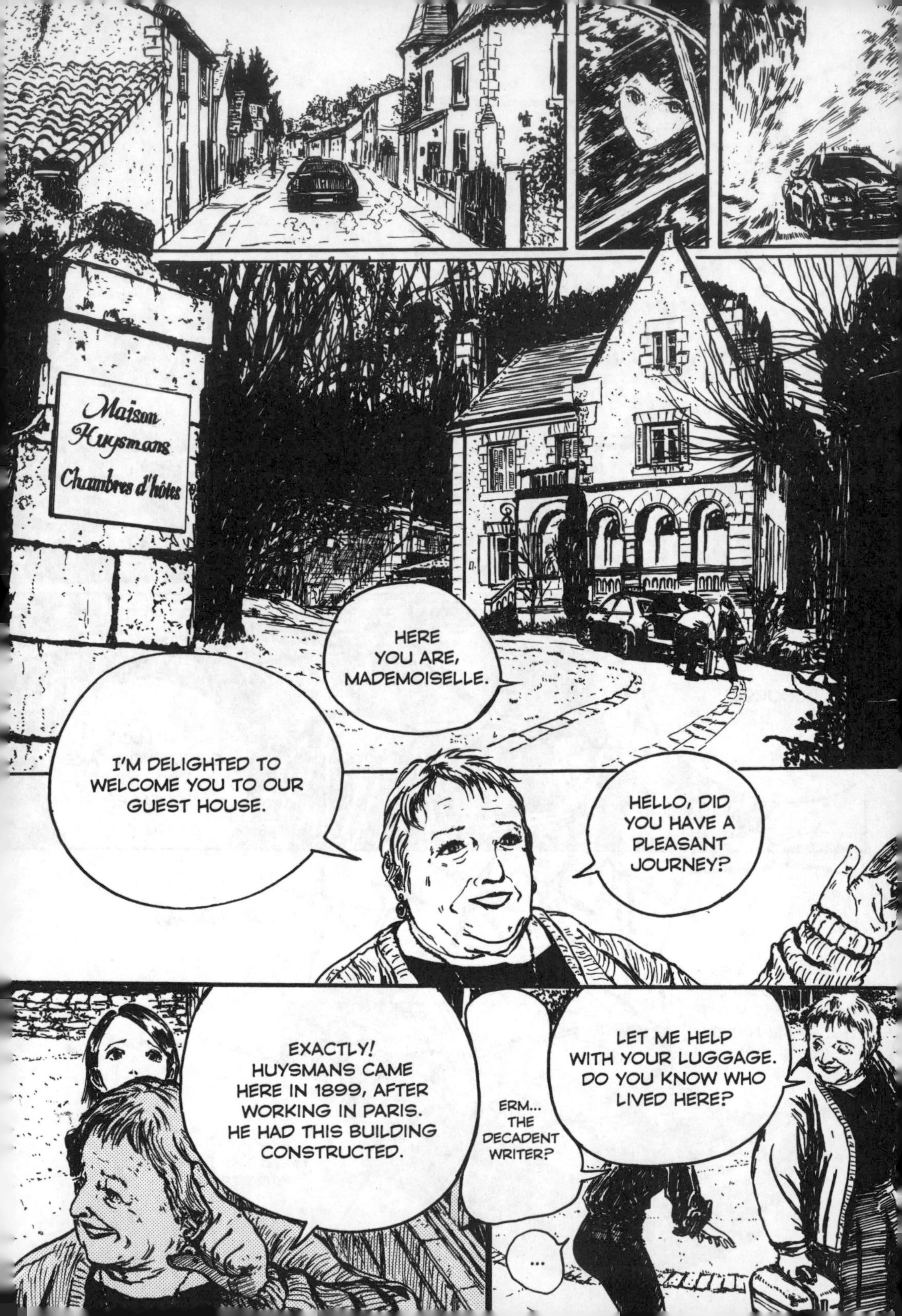
Maison Huysmans Chambres d'hôtes
HERE YOU ARE, MADEMOISELLE.
HELLO, DID YOU HAVE A PLEASANT JOURNEY?
I'M DELIGHTED TO WELCOME YOU TO OUR GUEST HOUSE.
LET ME HELP WITH YOUR LUGGAGE. DO YOU KNOW WHO LIVED HERE?
ERM... THE DECADENT WRITER?
...
EXACTLY! HUYSMANS CAME HERE IN 1899, AFTER WORKING IN PARIS. HE HAD THIS BUILDING CONSTRUCTED.

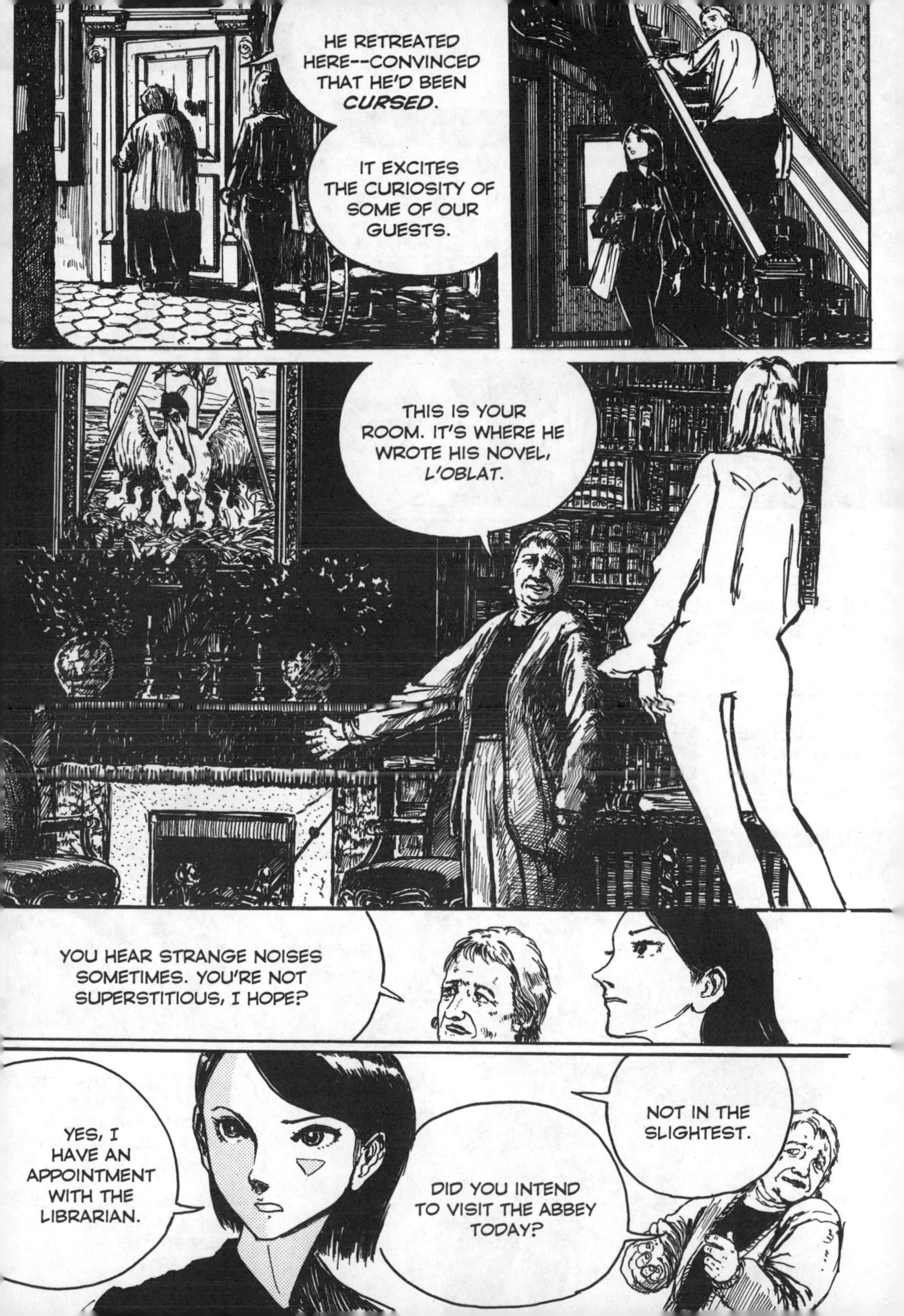
HE RETREATED HERE--CONVINCED THAT HE'D BEEN *CURSED*.
IT EXCITES THE CURIOSITY OF SOME OF OUR GUESTS.
THIS IS YOUR ROOM. IT'S WHERE HE WROTE HIS NOVEL, *L'OBLAT*.
YOU HEAR STRANGE NOISES SOMETIMES. YOU'RE NOT SUPERSTITIOUS, I HOPE?
NOT IN THE SLIGHTEST.
DID YOU INTEND TO VISIT THE ABBEY TODAY?
YES, I HAVE AN APPOINTMENT WITH THE LIBRARIAN.

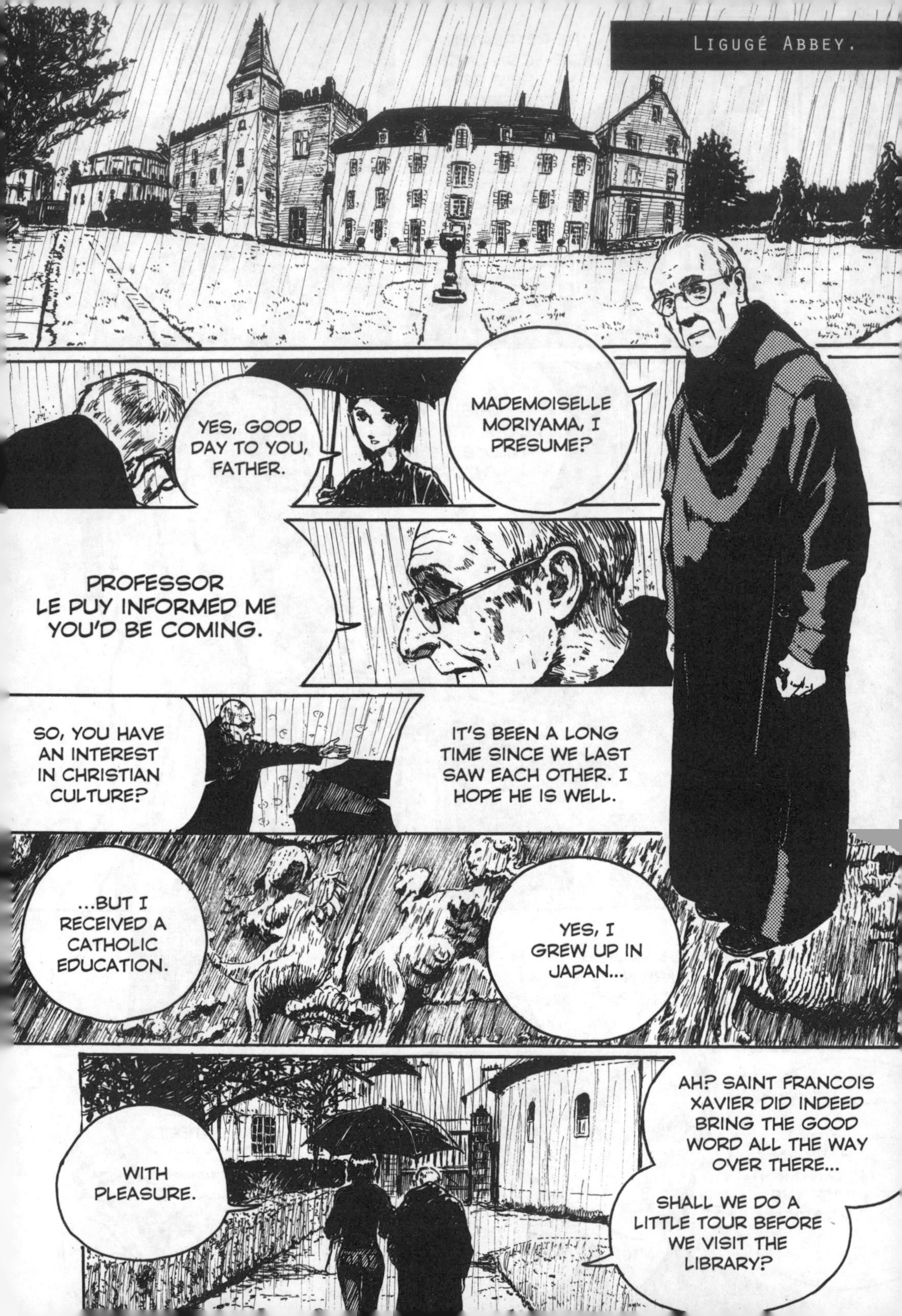
Ligugé Abbey.
MADEMOISELLE MORIYAMA, I PRESUME?
YES, GOOD DAY TO YOU, FATHER.
PROFESSOR LE PUY INFORMED ME YOU'D BE COMING.
IT'S BEEN A LONG TIME SINCE WE LAST SAW EACH OTHER. I HOPE HE IS WELL.
SO, YOU HAVE AN INTEREST IN CHRISTIAN CULTURE?
YES, I GREW UP IN JAPAN...
...BUT I RECEIVED A CATHOLIC EDUCATION.
AH? SAINT FRANCOIS XAVIER DID INDEED BRING THE GOOD WORD ALL THE WAY OVER THERE...
SHALL WE DO A LITTLE TOUR BEFORE WE VISIT THE LIBRARY?
WITH PLEASURE.

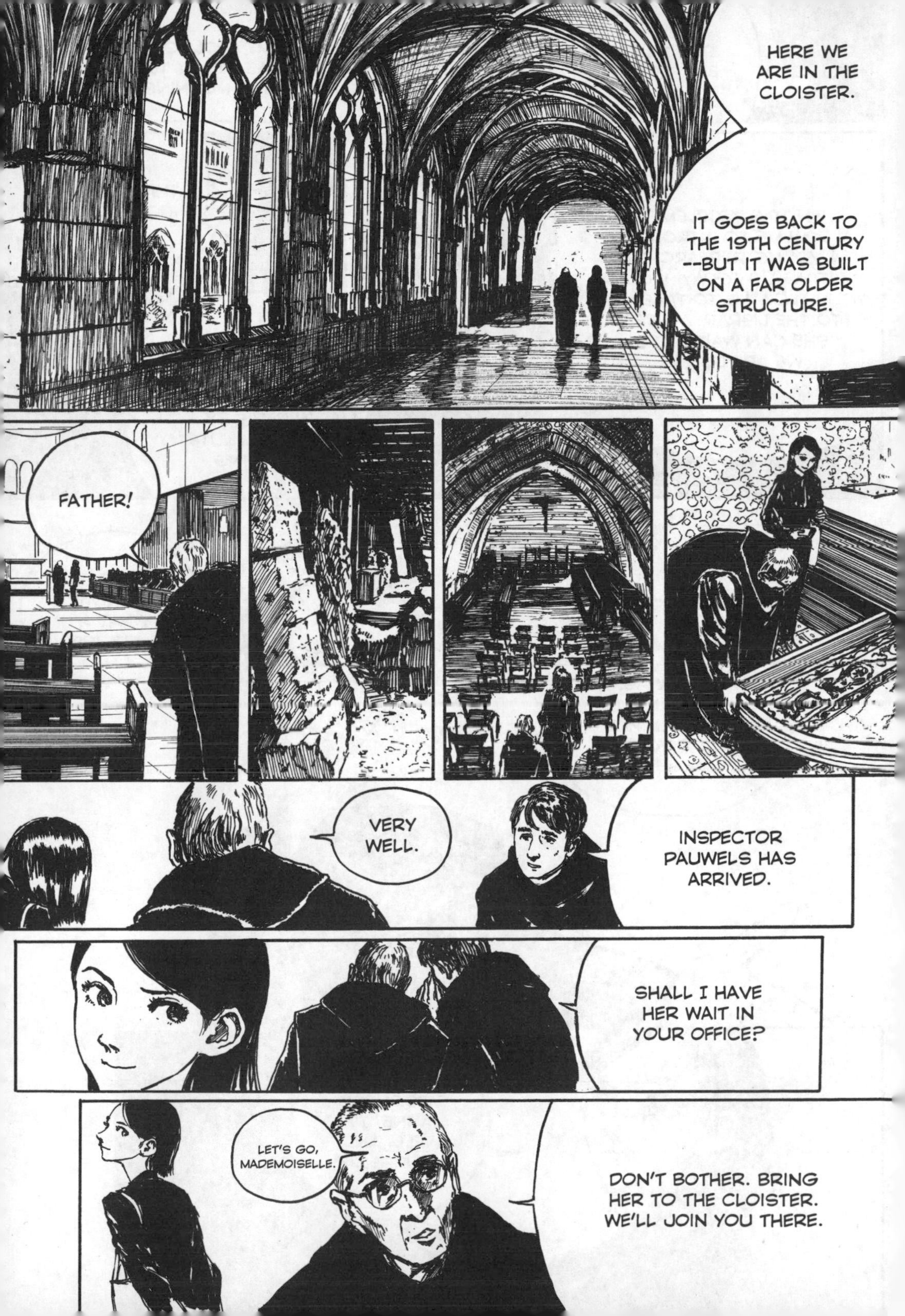
HERE WE ARE IN THE CLOISTER.
IT GOES BACK TO THE 19TH CENTURY --BUT IT WAS BUILT ON A FAR OLDER STRUCTURE.
FATHER!
INSPECTOR PAUWELS HAS ARRIVED.
VERY WELL.
SHALL I HAVE HER WAIT IN YOUR OFFICE?
DON'T BOTHER. BRING HER TO THE CLOISTER. WE'LL JOIN YOU THERE.
LET'S GO, MADEMOISELLE.

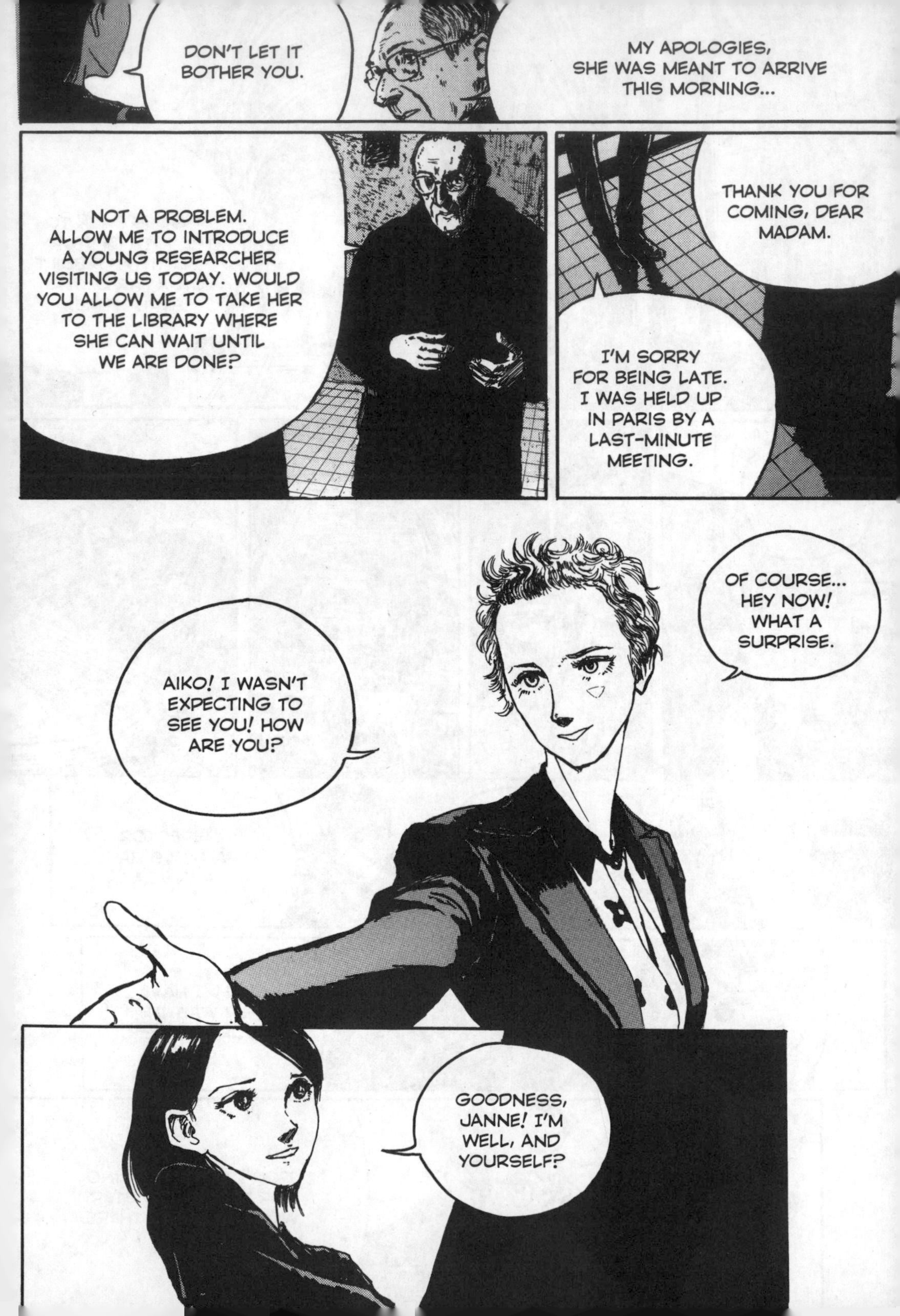
MY APOLOGIES, SHE WAS MEANT TO ARRIVE THIS MORNING...
DON'T LET IT BOTHER YOU.
THANK YOU FOR COMING, DEAR MADAM.
I'M SORRY FOR BEING LATE. I WAS HELD UP IN PARIS BY A LAST-MINUTE MEETING.
NOT A PROBLEM. ALLOW ME TO INTRODUCE A YOUNG RESEARCHER VISITING US TODAY. WOULD YOU ALLOW ME TO TAKE HER TO THE LIBRARY WHERE SHE CAN WAIT UNTIL WE ARE DONE?
OF COURSE... HEY NOW! WHAT A SURPRISE.
AIKO! I WASN'T EXPECTING TO SEE YOU! HOW ARE YOU?
GOODNESS, JANNE! I'M WELL, AND YOURSELF?

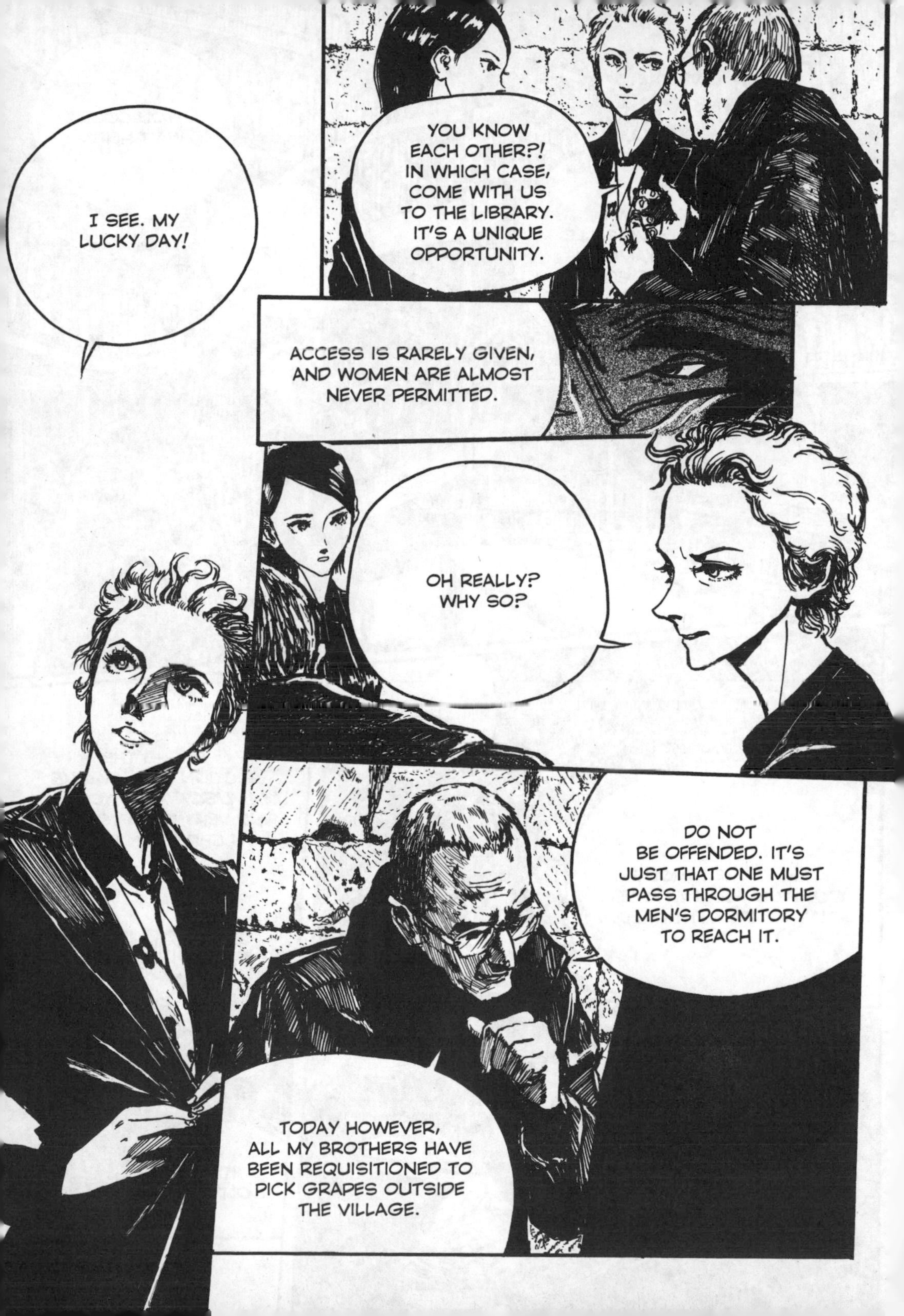
YOU KNOW EACH OTHER?! IN WHICH CASE, COME WITH US TO THE LIBRARY. IT'S A UNIQUE OPPORTUNITY.
ACCESS IS RARELY GIVEN, AND WOMEN ARE ALMOST NEVER PERMITTED.
OH REALLY? WHY SO?
DO NOT BE OFFENDED. IT'S JUST THAT ONE MUST PASS THROUGH THE MEN'S DORMITORY TO REACH IT.
TODAY HOWEVER, ALL MY BROTHERS HAVE BEEN REQUISITIONED TO PICK GRAPES OUTSIDE THE VILLAGE.
I SEE. MY LUCKY DAY!

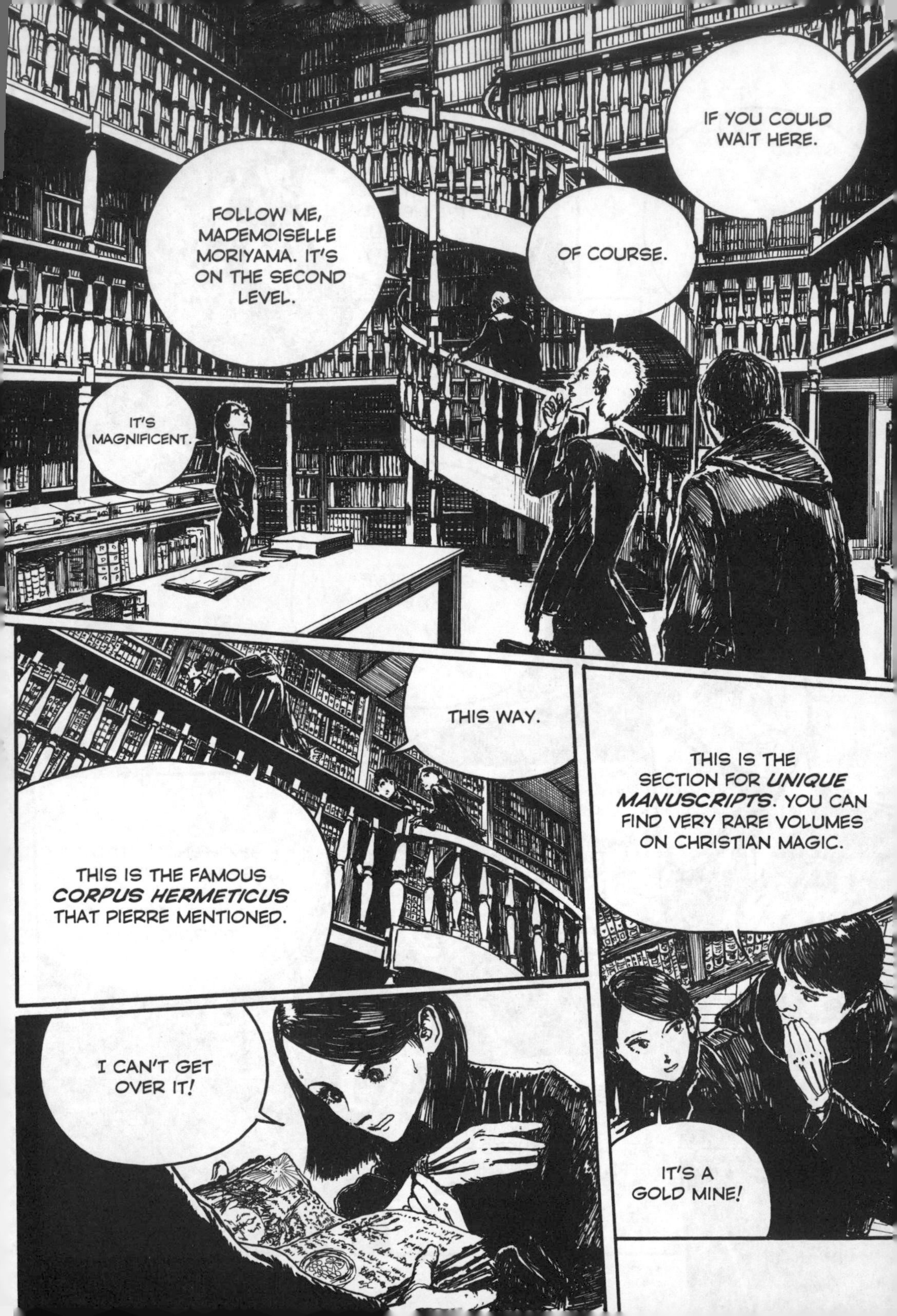
IF YOU COULD WAIT HERE.
OF COURSE.
FOLLOW ME, MADEMOISELLE MORIYAMA. IT'S ON THE SECOND LEVEL.
IT'S MAGNIFICENT.
THIS IS THE SECTION FOR *UNIQUE MANUSCRIPTS*. YOU CAN FIND VERY RARE VOLUMES ON CHRISTIAN MAGIC.
IT'S A GOLD MINE!
THIS WAY.
THIS IS THE FAMOUS *CORPUS HERMETICUS* THAT PIERRE MENTIONED.
I CAN'T GET OVER IT!

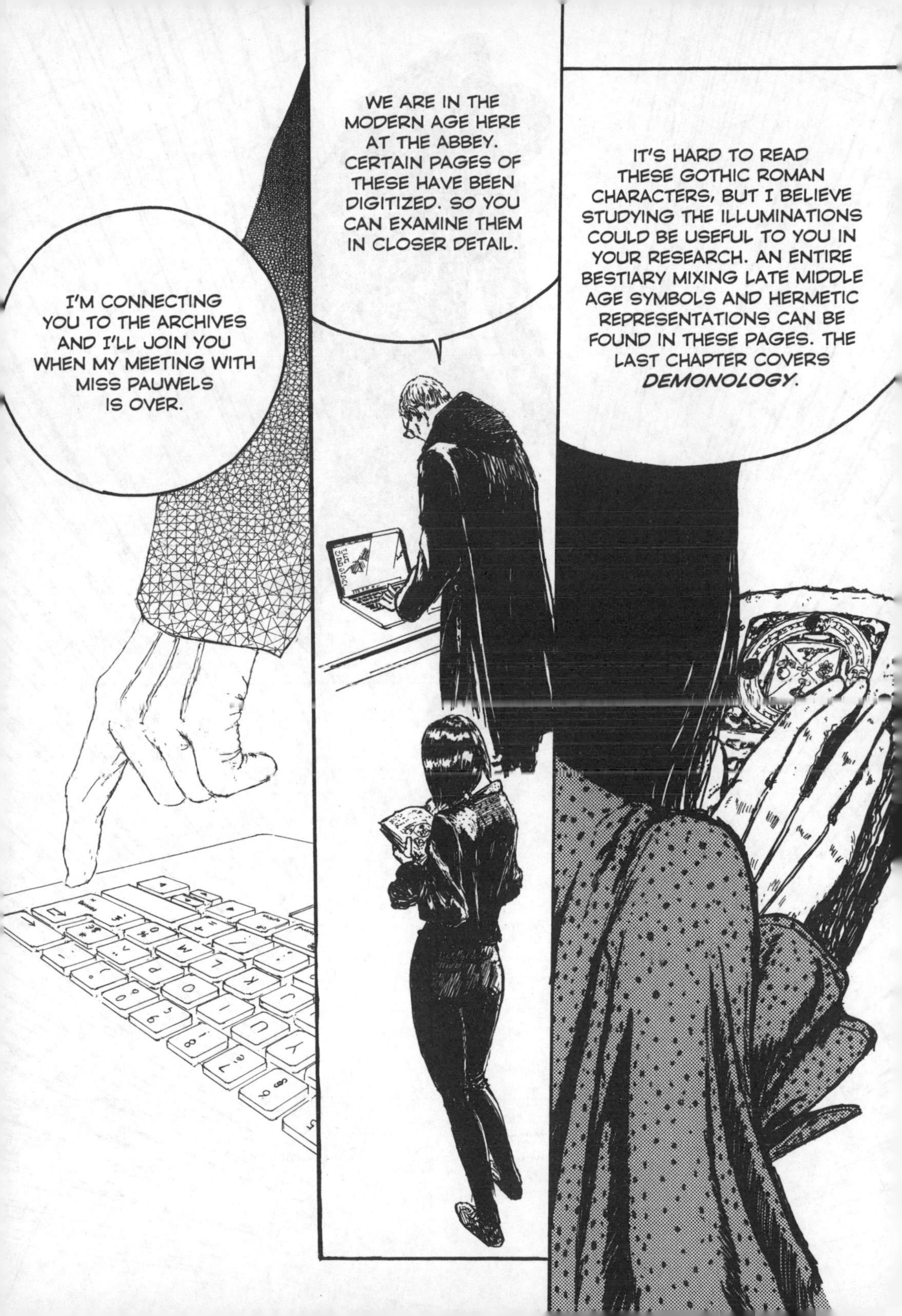
IT'S HARD TO READ THESE GOTHIC ROMAN CHARACTERS, BUT I BELIEVE STUDYING THE ILLUMINATIONS COULD BE USEFUL TO YOU IN YOUR RESEARCH. AN ENTIRE BESTIARY MIXING LATE MIDDLE AGE SYMBOLS AND HERMETIC REPRESENTATIONS CAN BE FOUND IN THESE PAGES. THE LAST CHAPTER COVERS *DEMONOLOGY*.
WE ARE IN THE MODERN AGE HERE AT THE ABBEY. CERTAIN PAGES OF THESE HAVE BEEN DIGITIZED. SO YOU CAN EXAMINE THEM IN CLOSER DETAIL.
I'M CONNECTING YOU TO THE ARCHIVES AND I'LL JOIN YOU WHEN MY MEETING WITH MISS PAUWELS IS OVER.

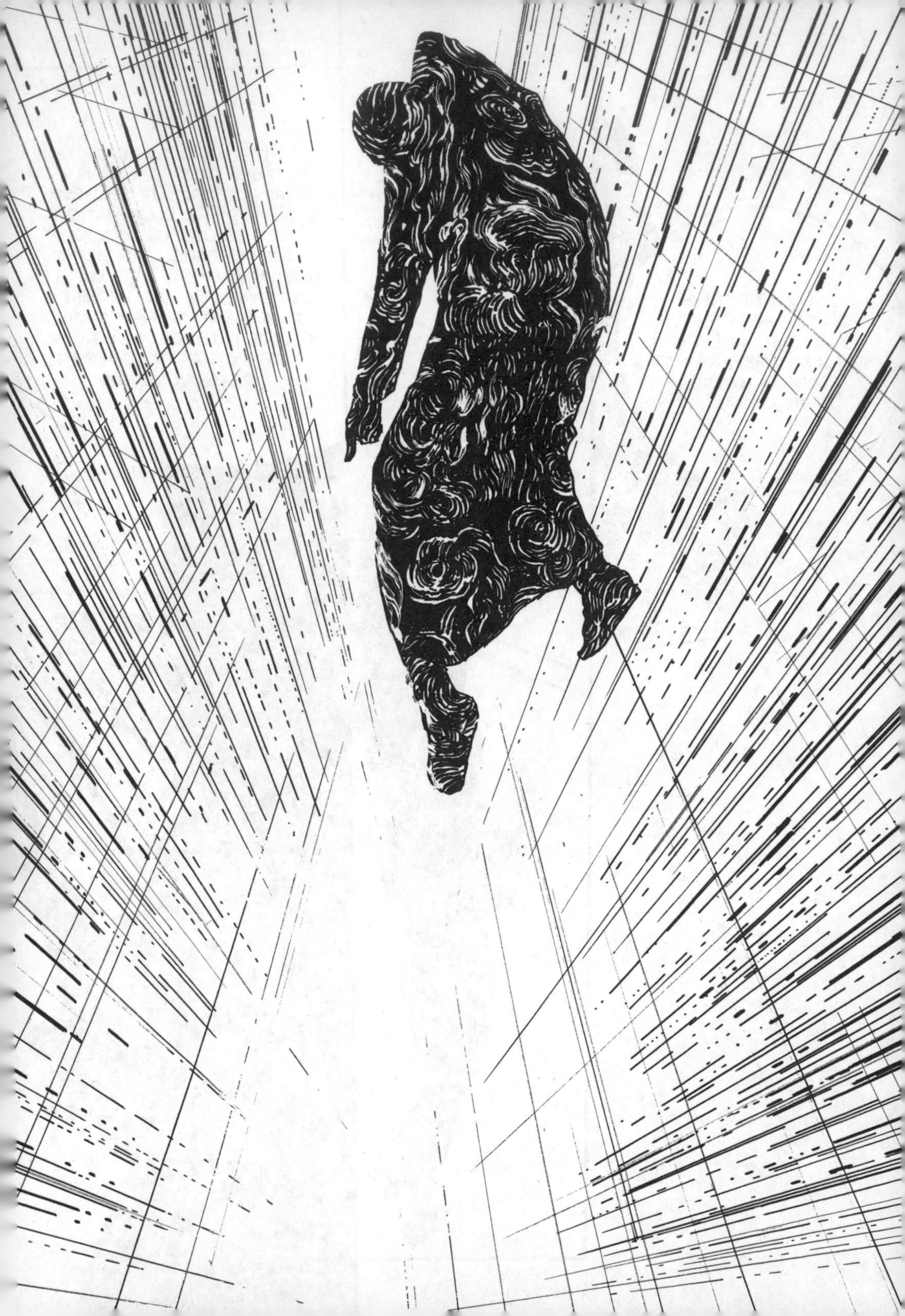

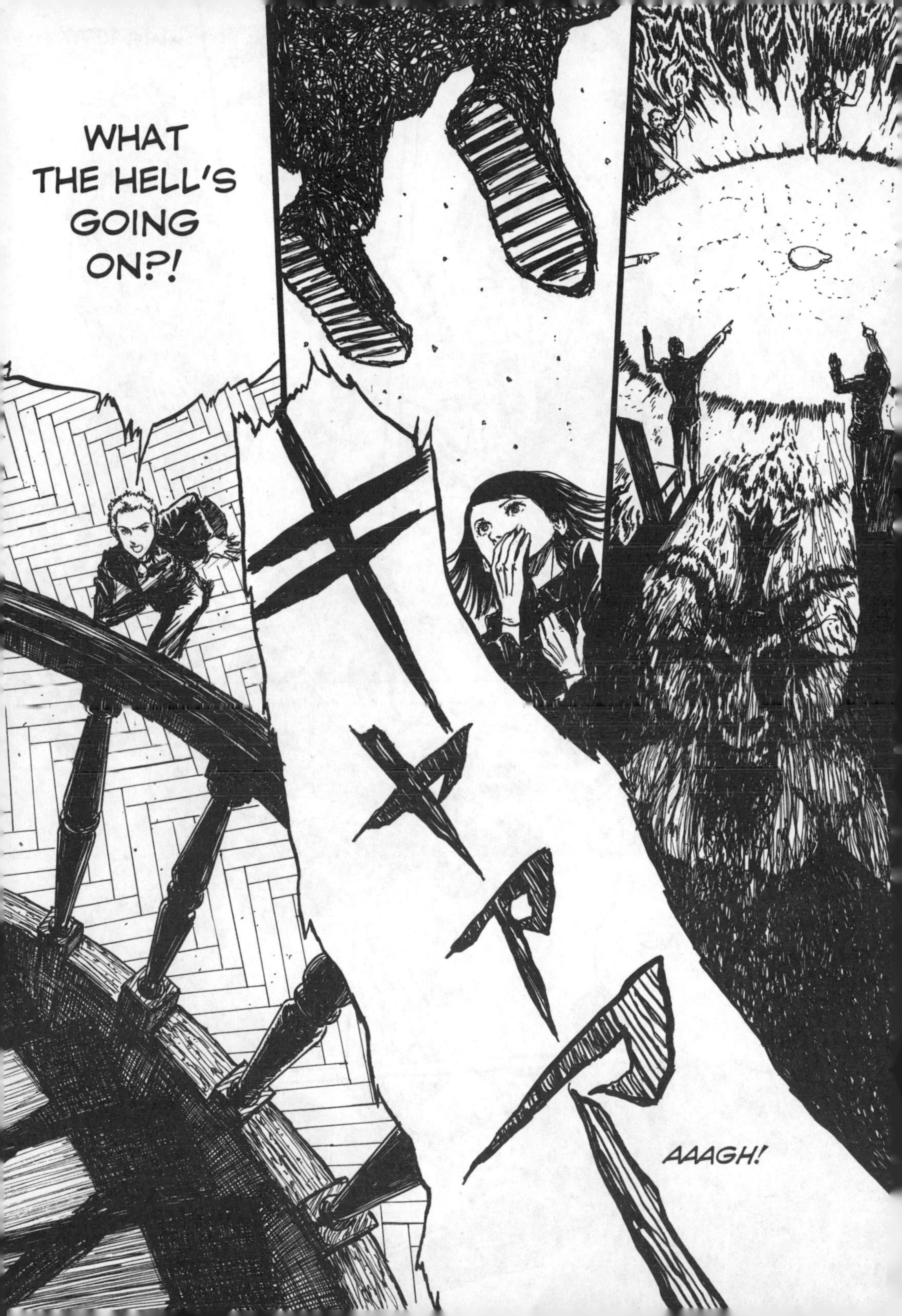
AAAGH!
WHAT THE HELL'S GOING ON?!

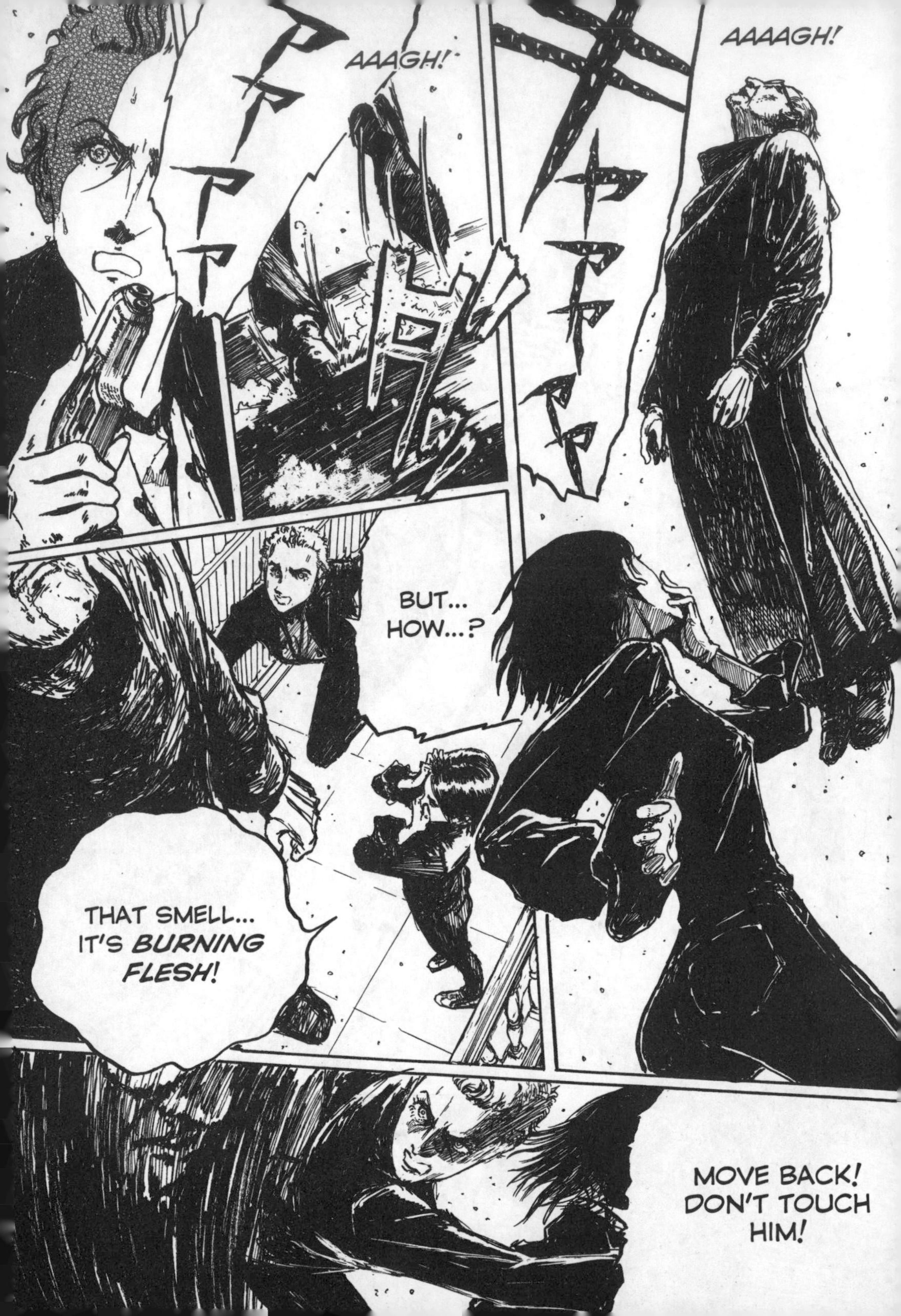
AAAAGH!
AAAGH!
BUT... HOW...?
THAT SMELL... IT'S BURNING FLESH!
MOVE BACK! DON'T TOUCH HIM!

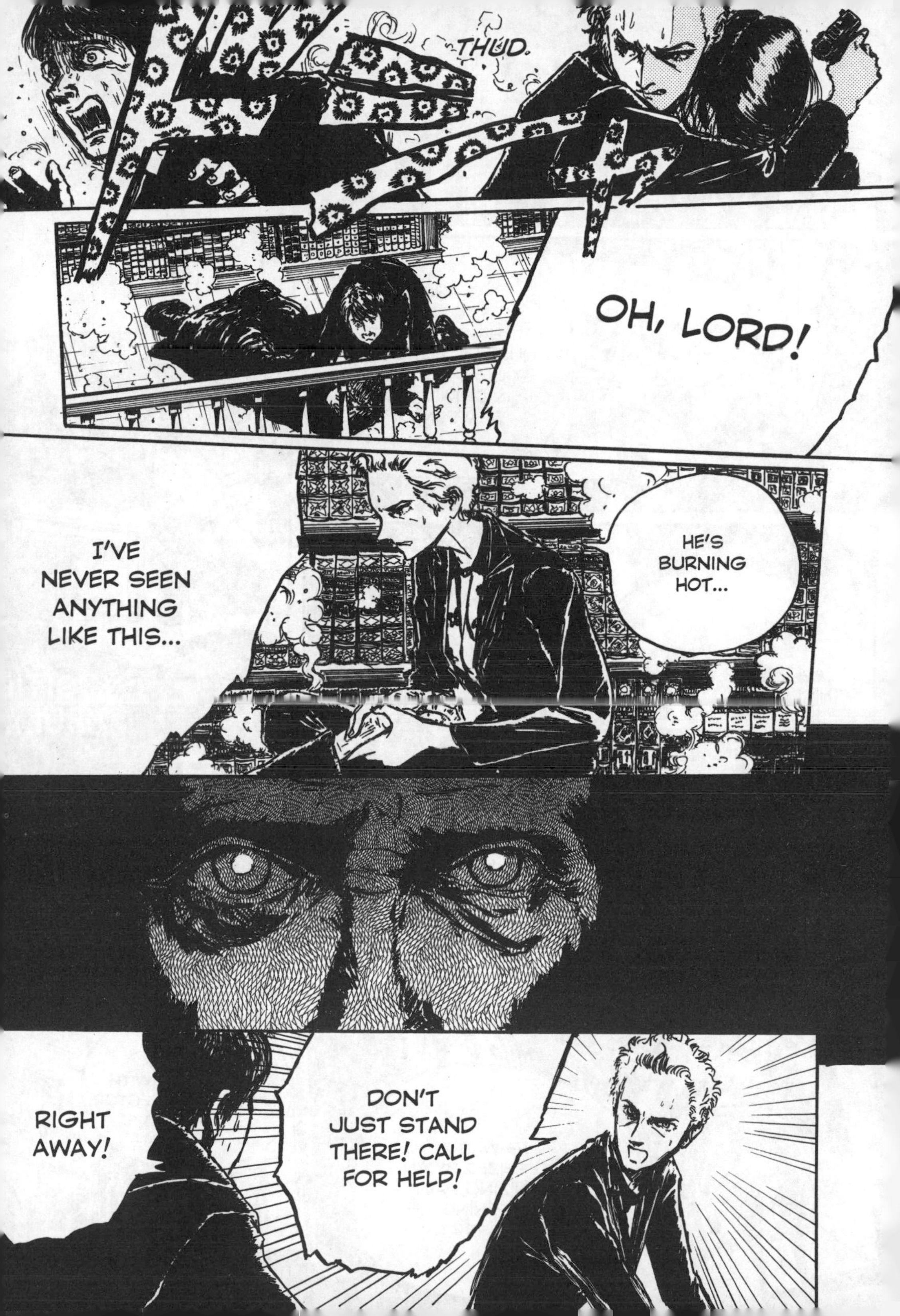
THUD.
OH, LORD!
HE'S BURNING HOT...
I'VE NEVER SEEN ANYTHING LIKE THIS...
DON'T JUST STAND THERE! CALL FOR HELP!
RIGHT AWAY!

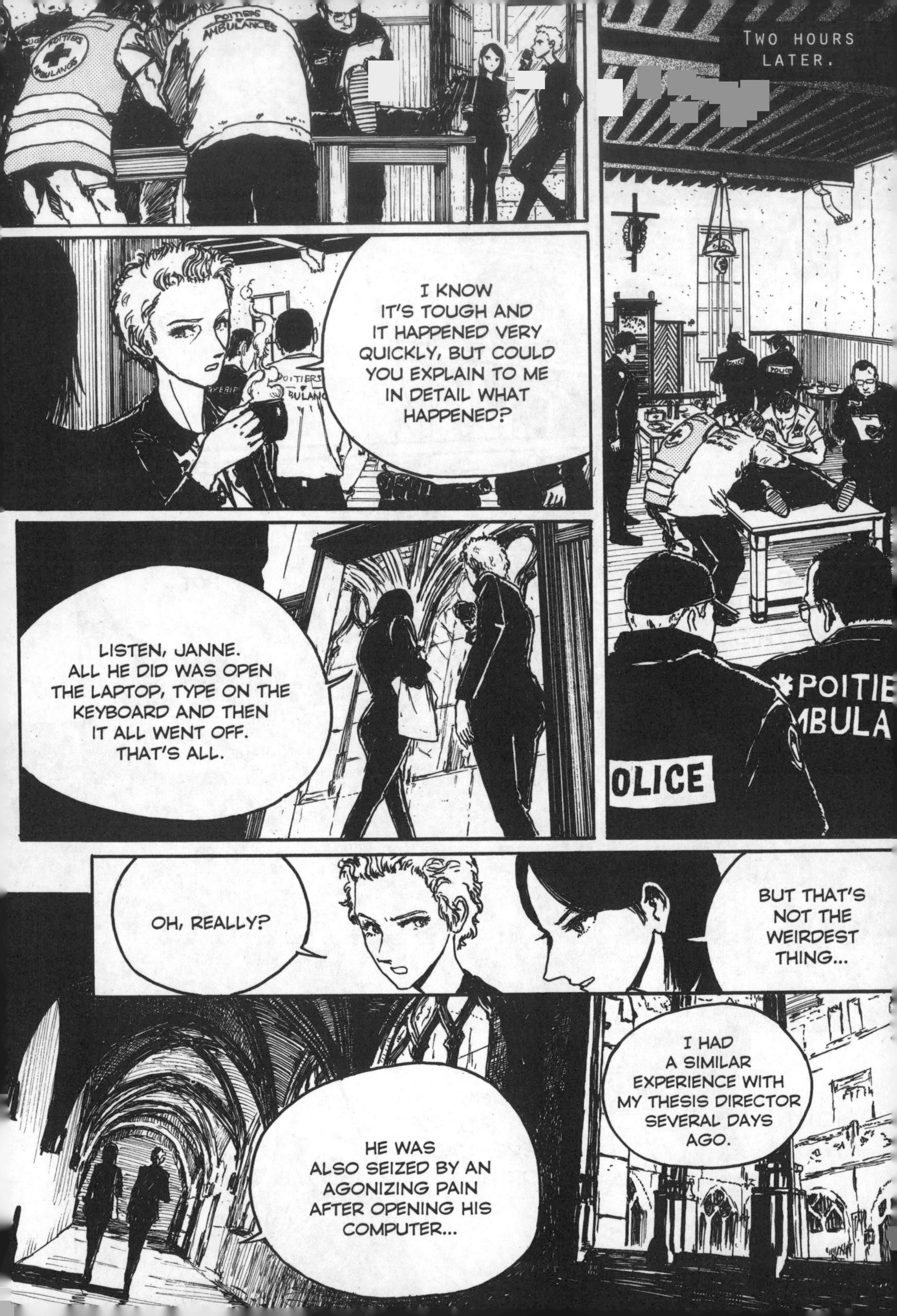
TWO HOURS LATER.
*POITIE
MBULA
OLICE
I KNOW IT'S TOUGH AND IT HAPPENED VERY QUICKLY, BUT COULD YOU EXPLAIN TO ME IN DETAIL WHAT HAPPENED?
LISTEN, JANNE. ALL HE DID WAS OPEN THE LAPTOP, TYPE ON THE KEYBOARD AND THEN IT ALL WENT OFF. THAT'S ALL.
BUT THAT'S NOT THE WEIRDEST THING...
OH, REALLY?
I HAD A SIMILAR EXPERIENCE WITH MY THESIS DIRECTOR SEVERAL DAYS AGO.
HE WAS ALSO SEIZED BY AN AGONIZING PAIN AFTER OPENING HIS COMPUTER...

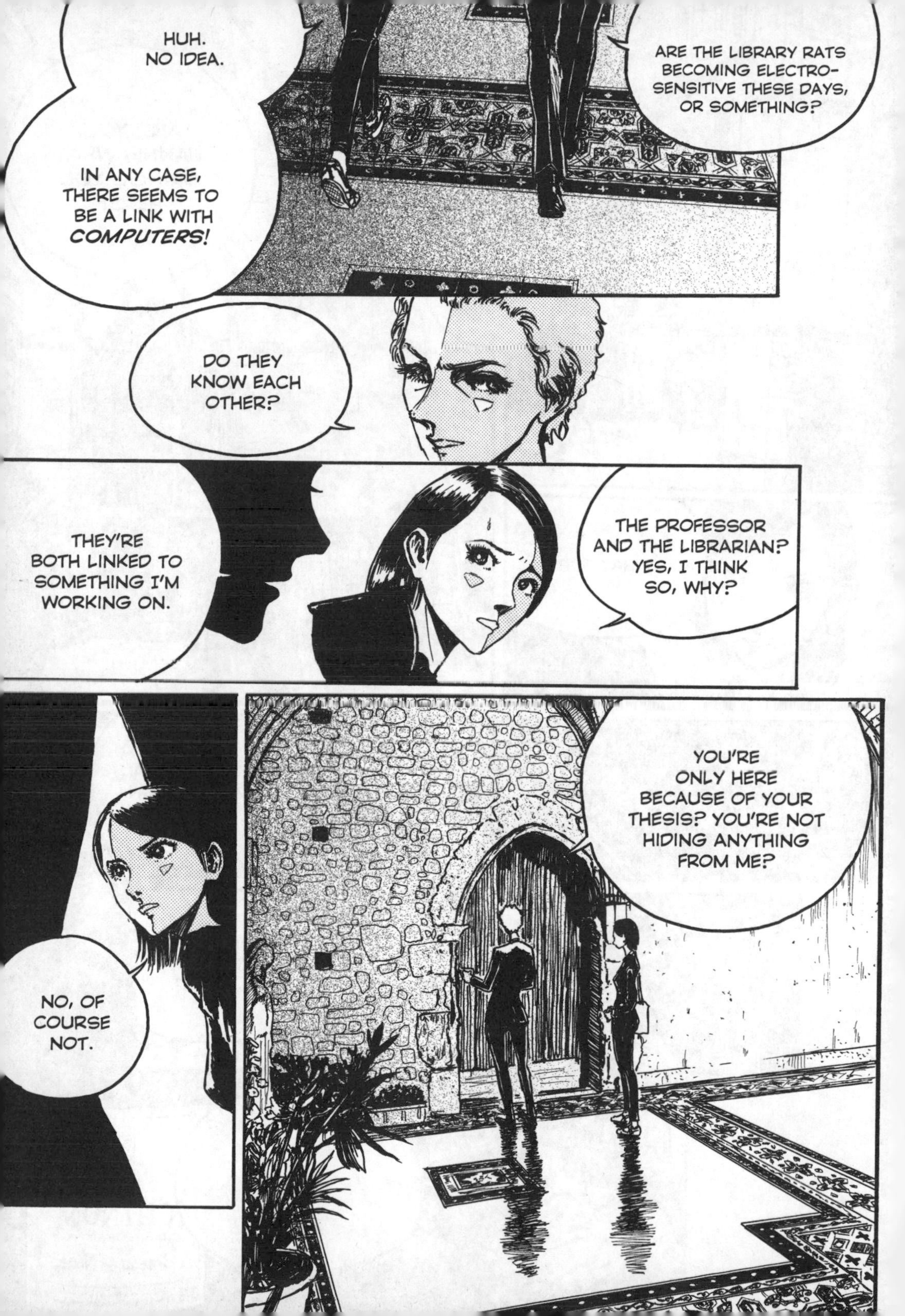
ARE THE LIBRARY RATS BECOMING ELECTRO-SENSITIVE THESE DAYS, OR SOMETHING?
HUH. NO IDEA.
IN ANY CASE, THERE SEEMS TO BE A LINK WITH *COMPUTERS*!
DO THEY KNOW EACH OTHER?
THE PROFESSOR AND THE LIBRARIAN? YES, I THINK SO, WHY?
THEY'RE BOTH LINKED TO SOMETHING I'M WORKING ON.
YOU'RE ONLY HERE BECAUSE OF YOUR THESIS? YOU'RE NOT HIDING ANYTHING FROM ME?
NO, OF COURSE NOT.

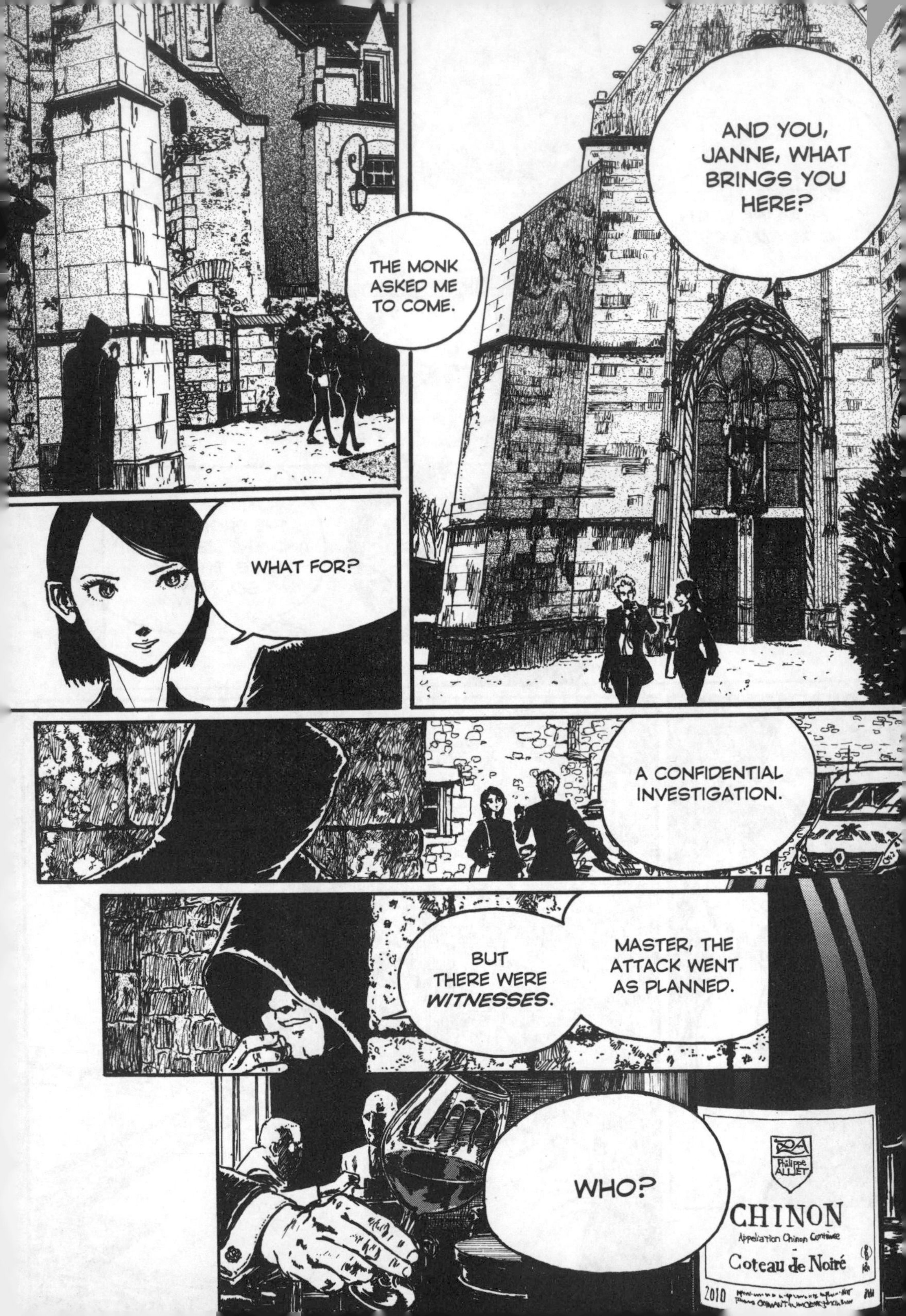
AND YOU, JANNE, WHAT BRINGS YOU HERE?
THE MONK ASKED ME TO COME.
WHAT FOR?
A CONFIDENTIAL INVESTIGATION.
MASTER, THE ATTACK WENT AS PLANNED.
BUT THERE WERE *WITNESSES*.
WHO?
Philippe ALLIET
CHINON
Coteau de Noiré
2010

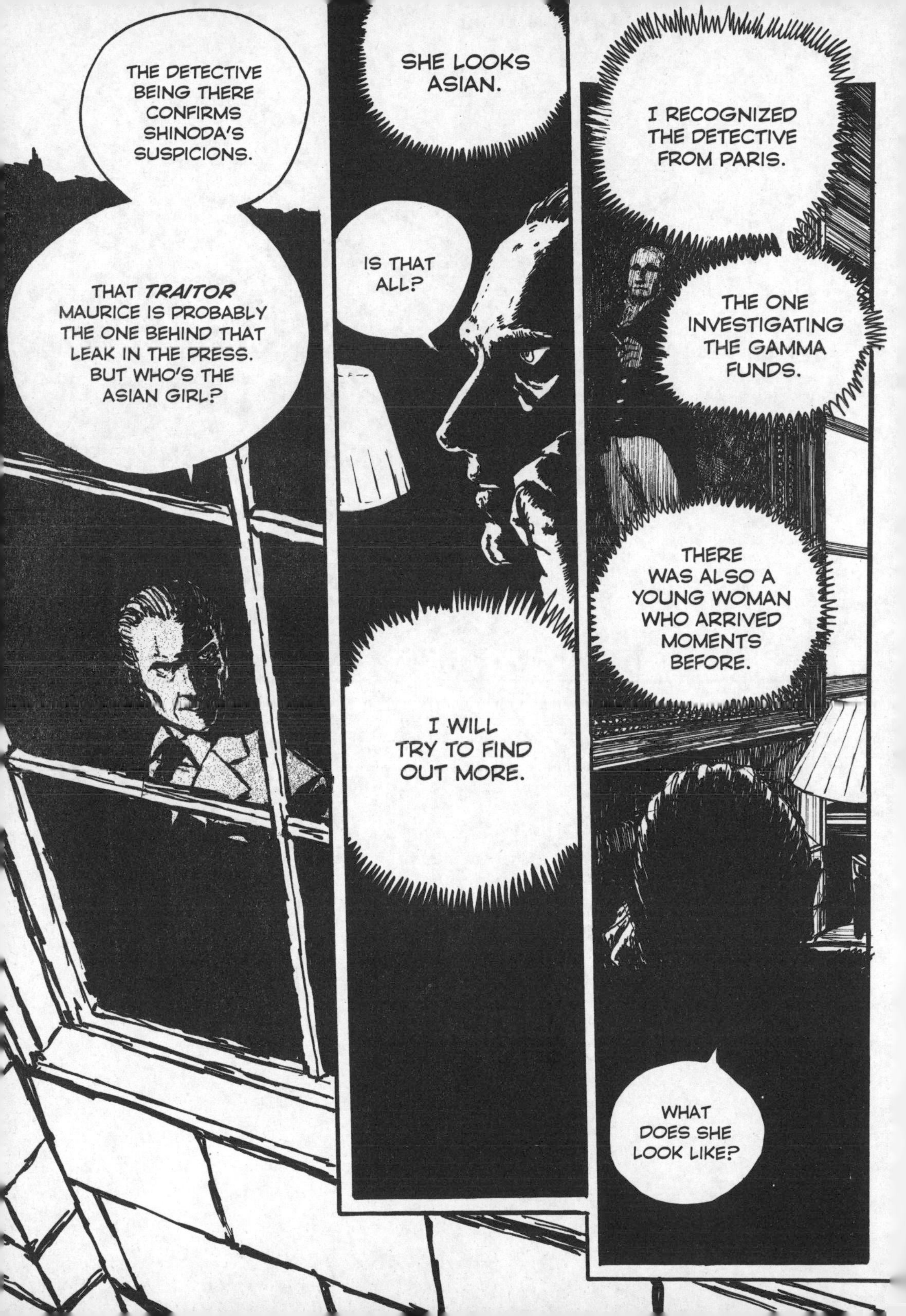
I RECOGNIZED THE DETECTIVE FROM PARIS.
THE ONE INVESTIGATING THE GAMMA FUNDS.
THERE WAS ALSO A YOUNG WOMAN WHO ARRIVED MOMENTS BEFORE.
WHAT DOES SHE LOOK LIKE?
SHE LOOKS ASIAN.
IS THAT ALL?
I WILL TRY TO FIND OUT MORE.
THE DETECTIVE BEING THERE CONFIRMS SHINODA'S SUSPICIONS.
THAT *TRAITOR* MAURICE IS PROBABLY THE ONE BEHIND THAT LEAK IN THE PRESS. BUT WHO'S THE ASIAN GIRL?

CHAPTER 4

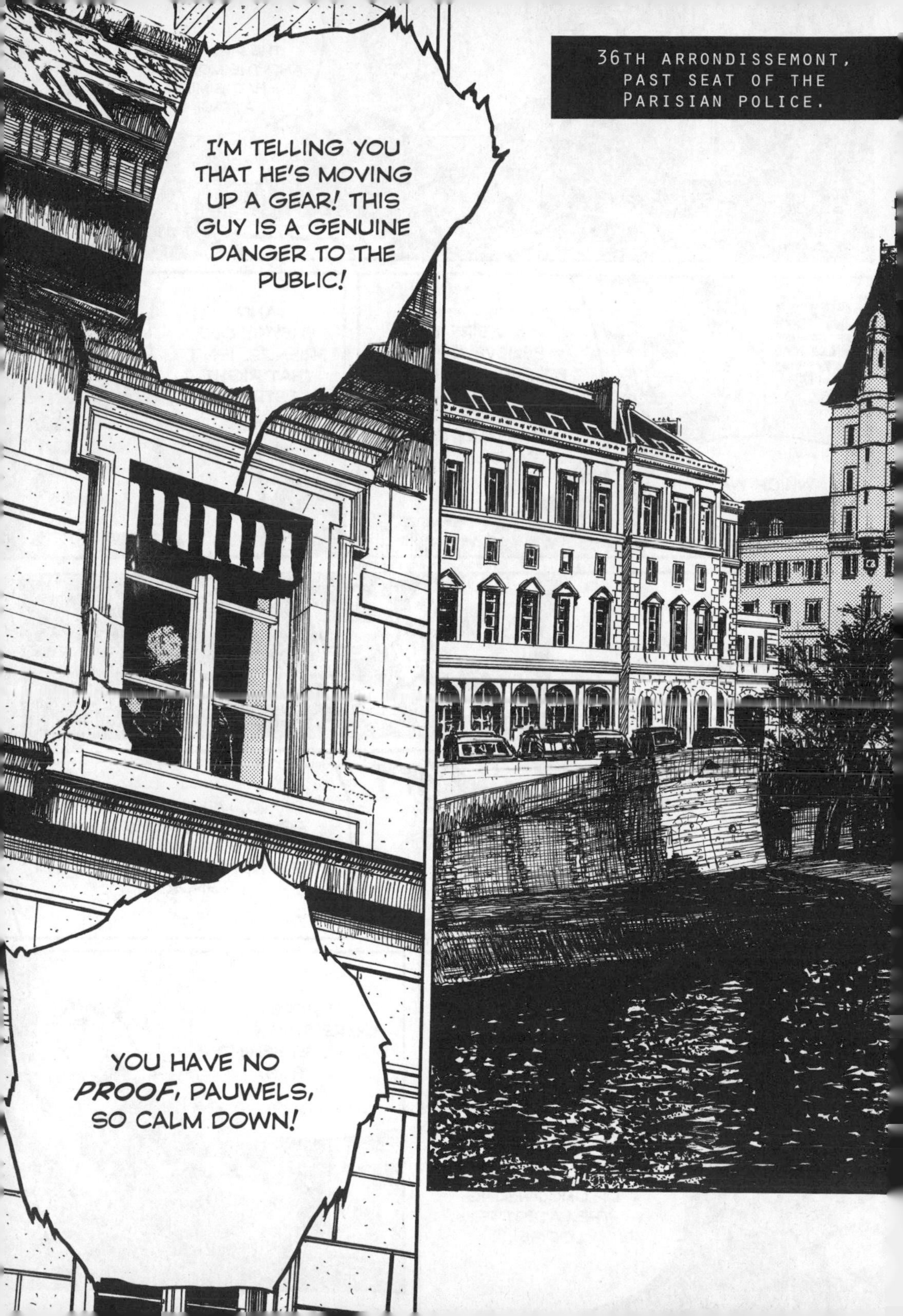
36TH ARRONDISSEMONT, PAST SEAT OF THE PARISIAN POLICE.
I'M TELLING YOU THAT HE'S MOVING UP A GEAR! THIS GUY IS A GENUINE DANGER TO THE PUBLIC!
YOU HAVE NO PROOF, PAUWELS, SO CALM DOWN!

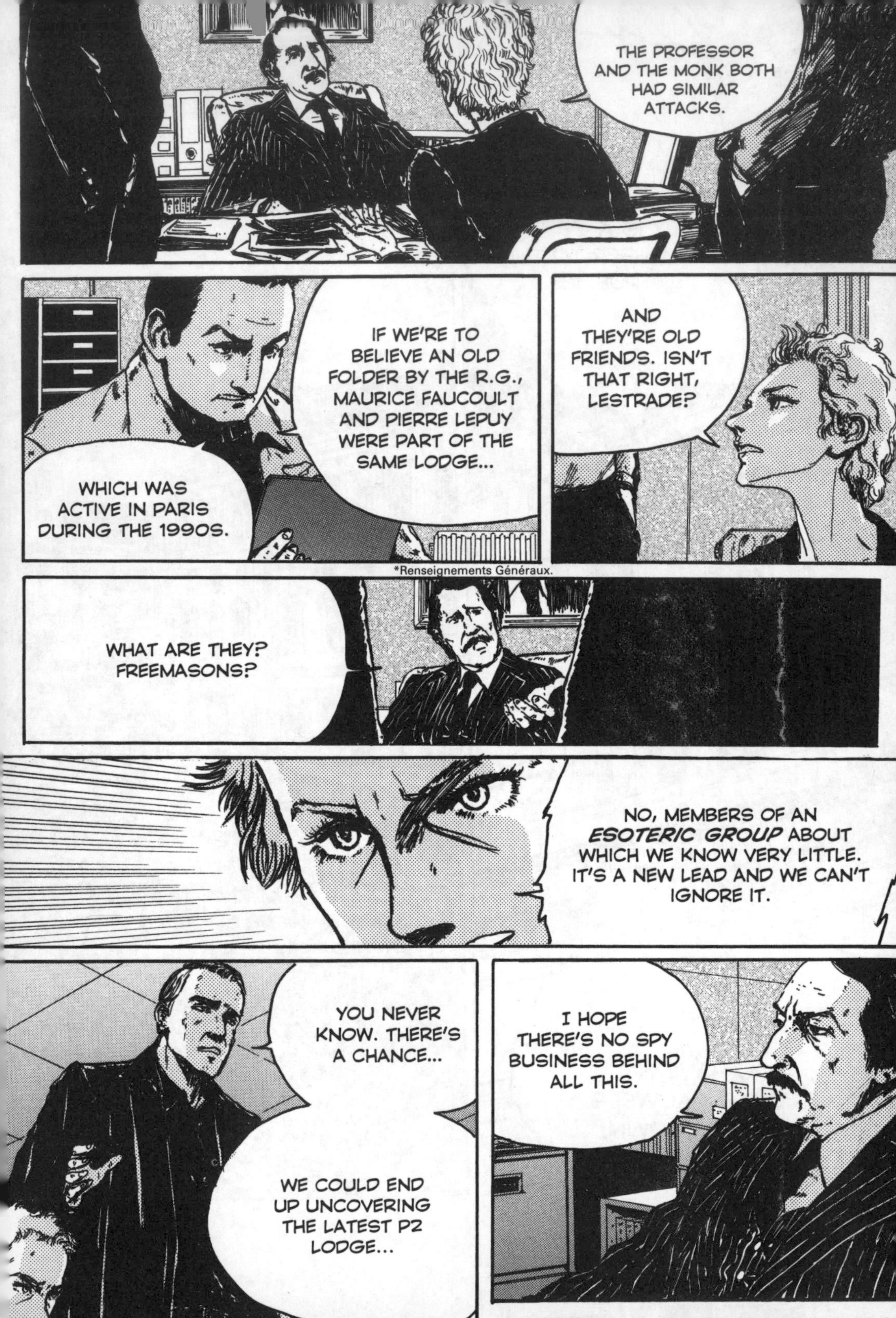
THE PROFESSOR AND THE MONK BOTH HAD SIMILAR ATTACKS.
AND THEY'RE OLD FRIENDS. ISN'T THAT RIGHT, LESTRADE?
IF WE'RE TO BELIEVE AN OLD FOLDER BY THE R.G., MAURICE FAUCOULT AND PIERRE LEPUY WERE PART OF THE SAME LODGE...
WHICH WAS ACTIVE IN PARIS DURING THE 1990S.
*Renseignements Généraux.
WHAT ARE THEY? FREEMASONS?
NO, MEMBERS OF AN *ESOTERIC GROUP* ABOUT WHICH WE KNOW VERY LITTLE. IT'S A NEW LEAD AND WE CAN'T IGNORE IT.
I HOPE THERE'S NO SPY BUSINESS BEHIND ALL THIS.
YOU NEVER KNOW. THERE'S A CHANCE...
WE COULD END UP UNCOVERING THE LATEST P2 LODGE...

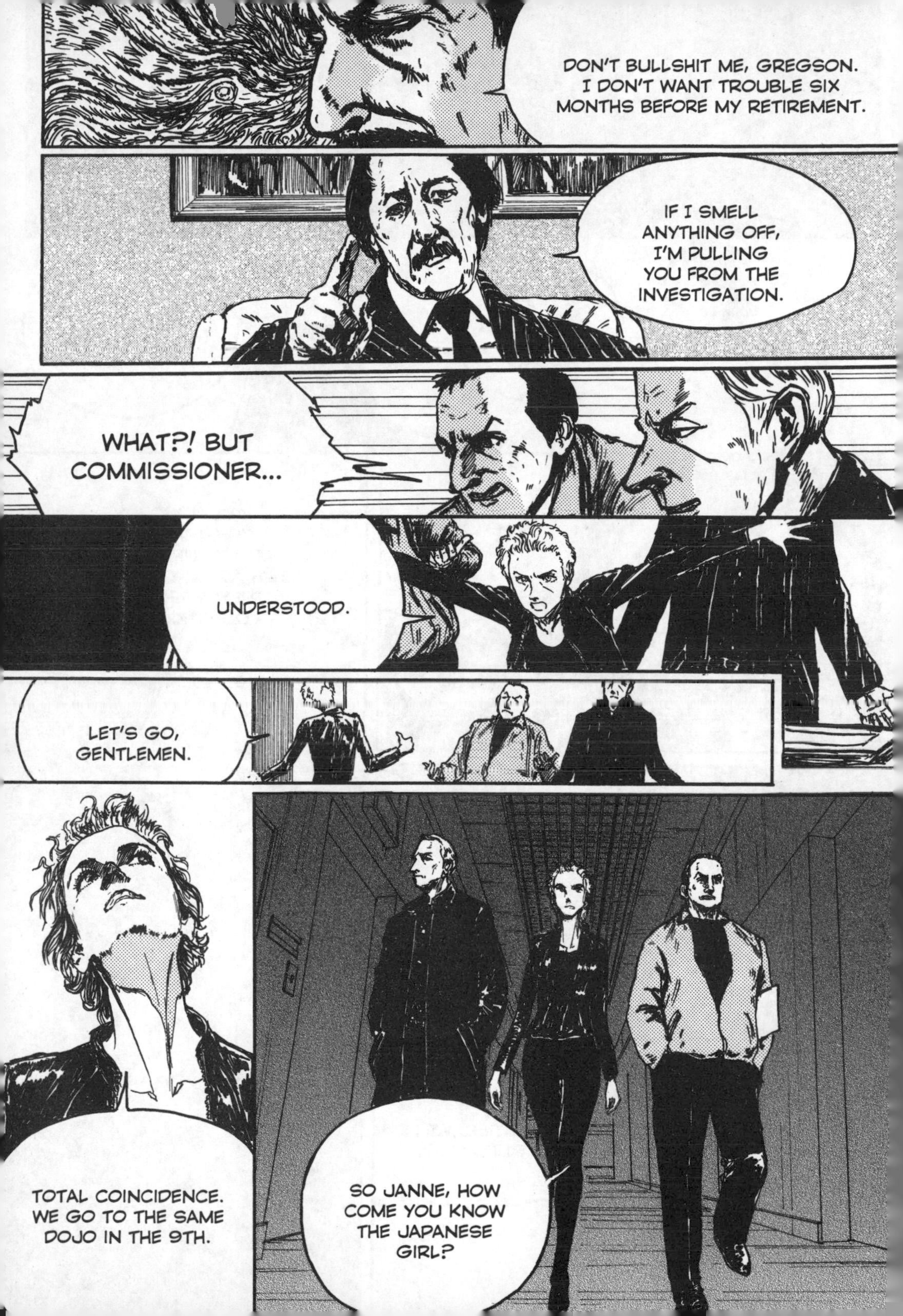
DON'T BULLSHIT ME, GREGSON. I DON'T WANT TROUBLE SIX MONTHS BEFORE MY RETIREMENT.
IF I SMELL ANYTHING OFF, I'M PULLING YOU FROM THE INVESTIGATION.
WHAT?! BUT COMMISSIONER...
UNDERSTOOD.
LET'S GO, GENTLEMEN.
SO JANNE, HOW COME YOU KNOW THE JAPANESE GIRL?
TOTAL COINCIDENCE. WE GO TO THE SAME DOJO IN THE 9TH.

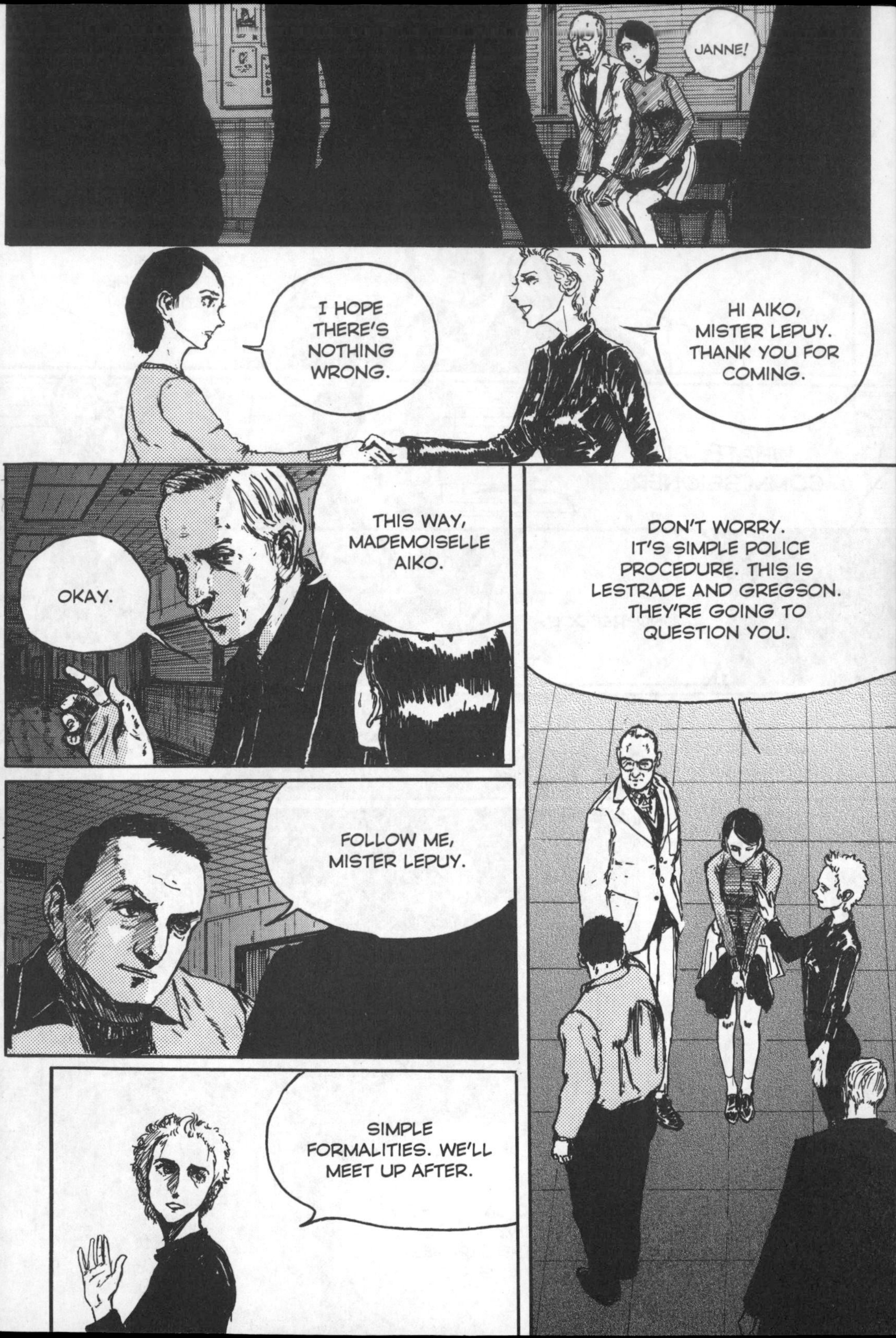
JANNE!
HI AIKO, MISTER LEPUY. THANK YOU FOR COMING.
I HOPE THERE'S NOTHING WRONG.
DON'T WORRY. IT'S SIMPLE POLICE PROCEDURE. THIS IS LESTRADE AND GREGSON. THEY'RE GOING TO QUESTION YOU.
THIS WAY, MADEMOISELLE AIKO.
OKAY.
FOLLOW ME, MISTER LEPUY.
SIMPLE FORMALITIES. WE'LL MEET UP AFTER.

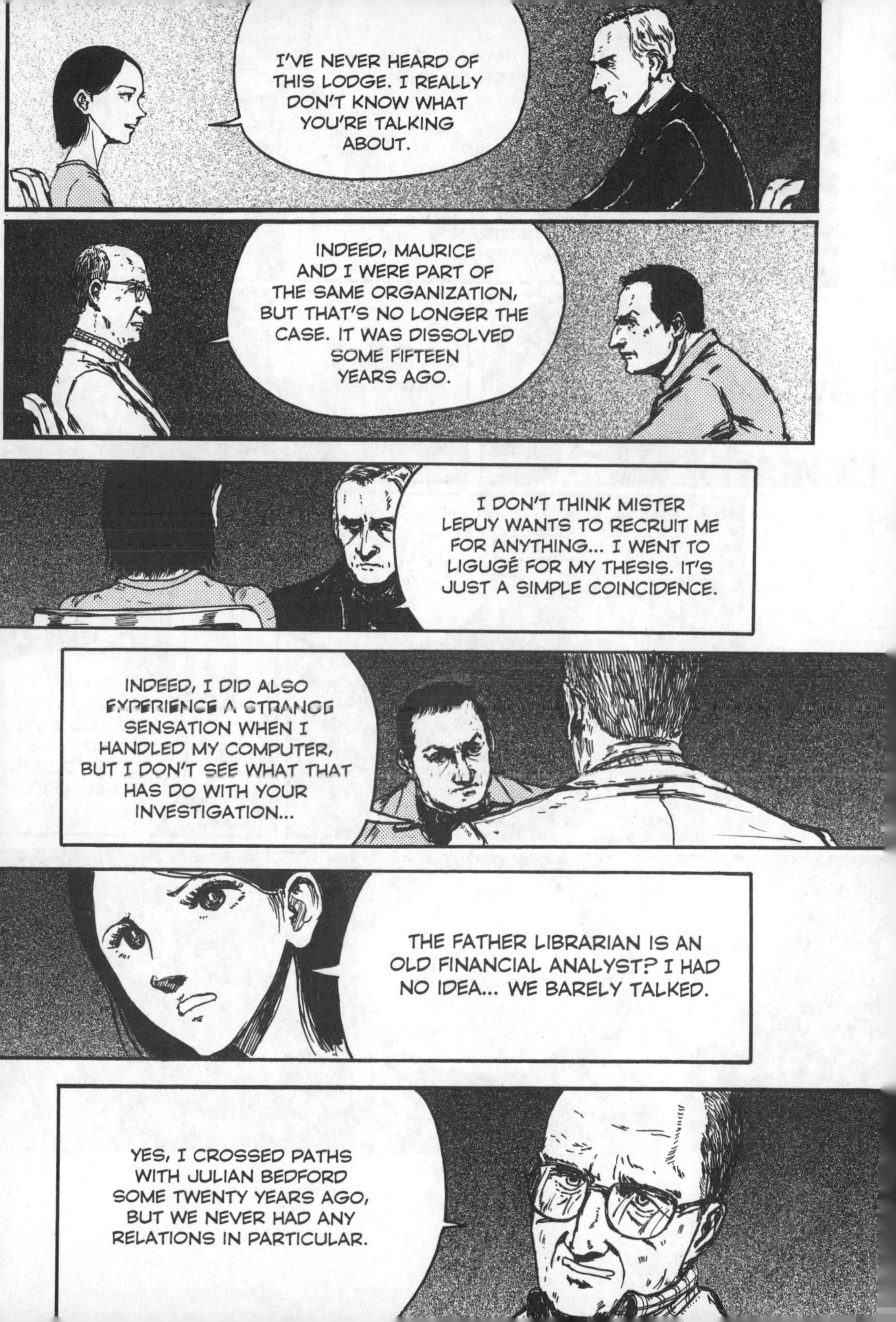
I'VE NEVER HEARD OF THIS LODGE. I REALLY DON'T KNOW WHAT YOU'RE TALKING ABOUT.
INDEED, MAURICE AND I WERE PART OF THE SAME ORGANIZATION, BUT THAT'S NO LONGER THE CASE. IT WAS DISSOLVED SOME FIFTEEN YEARS AGO.
I DON'T THINK MISTER LEPUY WANTS TO RECRUIT ME FOR ANYTHING... I WENT TO LIGUGÉ FOR MY THESIS. IT'S JUST A SIMPLE COINCIDENCE.
INDEED, I DID ALSO EXPERIENCE A STRANGE SENSATION WHEN I HANDLED MY COMPUTER, BUT I DON'T SEE WHAT THAT HAS DO WITH YOUR INVESTIGATION...
THE FATHER LIBRARIAN IS AN OLD FINANCIAL ANALYST? I HAD NO IDEA... WE BARELY TALKED.
YES, I CROSSED PATHS WITH JULIAN BEDFORD SOME TWENTY YEARS AGO, BUT WE NEVER HAD ANY RELATIONS IN PARTICULAR.

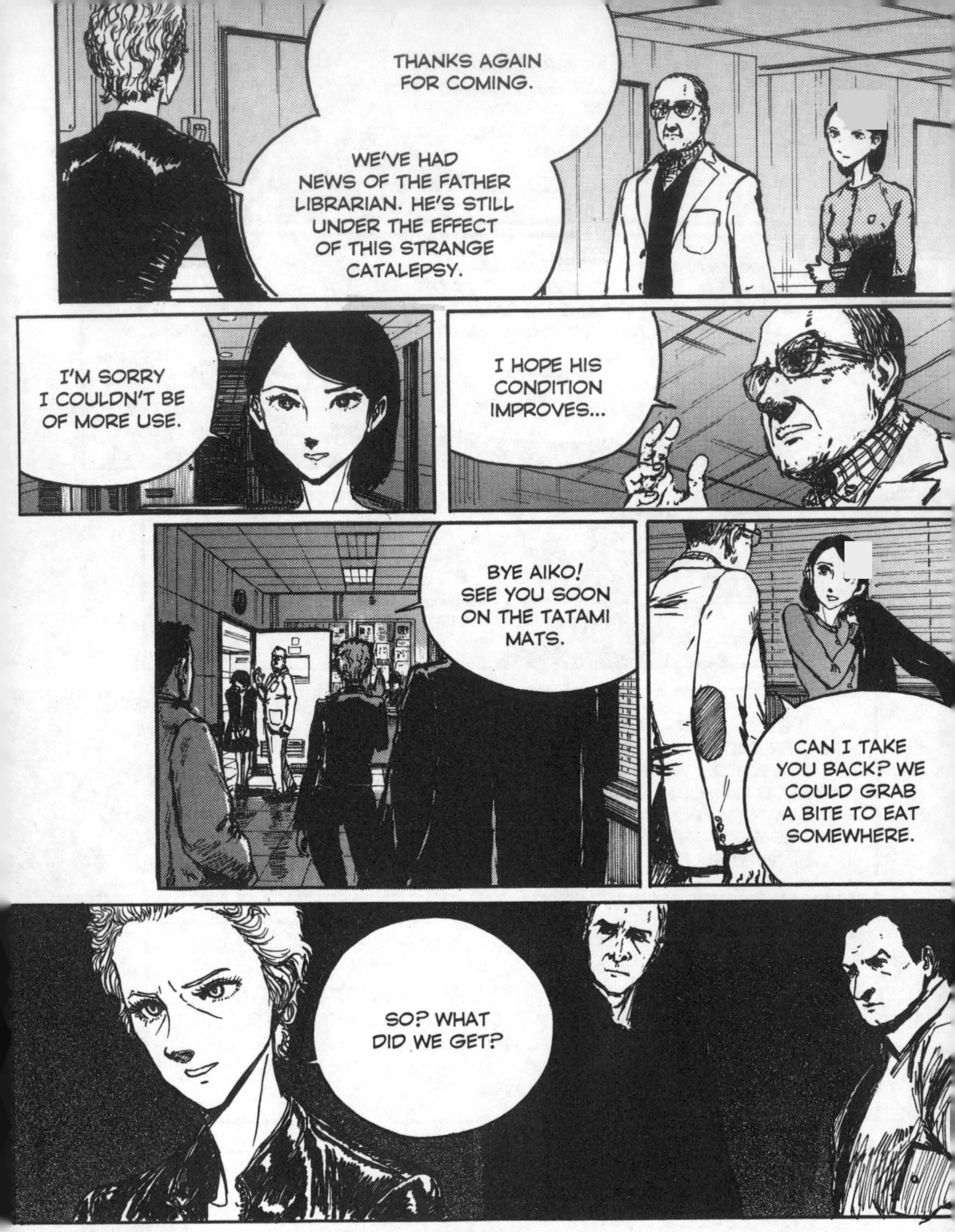
THANKS AGAIN FOR COMING.
WE'VE HAD NEWS OF THE FATHER LIBRARIAN. HE'S STILL UNDER THE EFFECT OF THIS STRANGE CATALEPSY.
I HOPE HIS CONDITION IMPROVES...
I'M SORRY I COULDN'T BE OF MORE USE.
CAN I TAKE YOU BACK? WE COULD GRAB A BITE TO EAT SOMEWHERE.
BYE AIKO! SEE YOU SOON ON THE TATAMI MATS.
SO? WHAT DID WE GET?

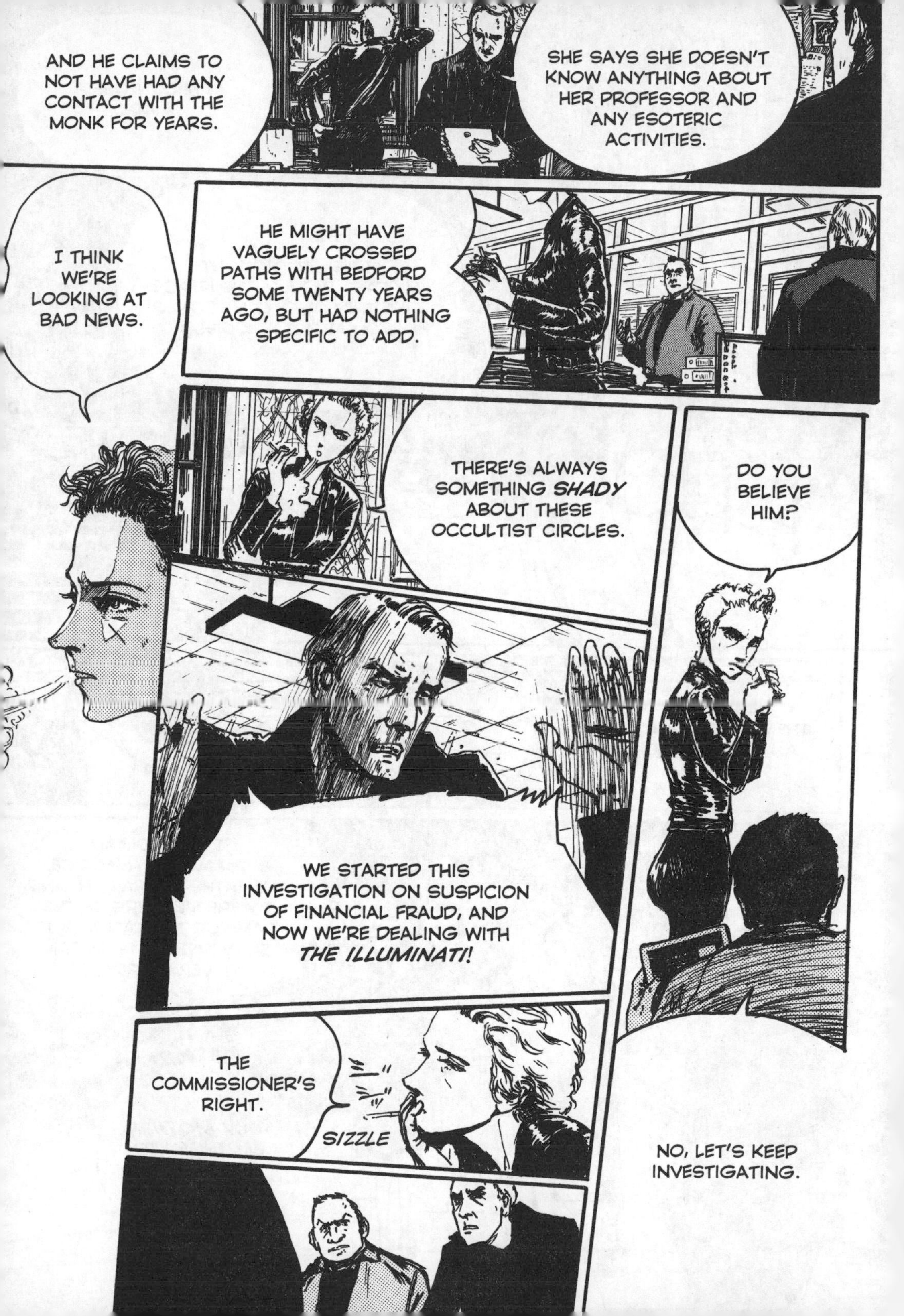
SHE SAYS SHE DOESN'T KNOW ANYTHING ABOUT HER PROFESSOR AND ANY ESOTERIC ACTIVITIES.
AND HE CLAIMS TO NOT HAVE HAD ANY CONTACT WITH THE MONK FOR YEARS.
HE MIGHT HAVE VAGUELY CROSSED PATHS WITH BEDFORD SOME TWENTY YEARS AGO, BUT HAD NOTHING SPECIFIC TO ADD.
I THINK WE'RE LOOKING AT BAD NEWS.
DO YOU BELIEVE HIM?
NO, LET'S KEEP INVESTIGATING.
THERE'S ALWAYS SOMETHING *SHADY* ABOUT THESE OCCULTIST CIRCLES.
WE STARTED THIS INVESTIGATION ON SUSPICION OF FINANCIAL FRAUD, AND NOW WE'RE DEALING WITH *THE ILLUMINATI*!
THE COMMISSIONER'S RIGHT.
SIZZLE

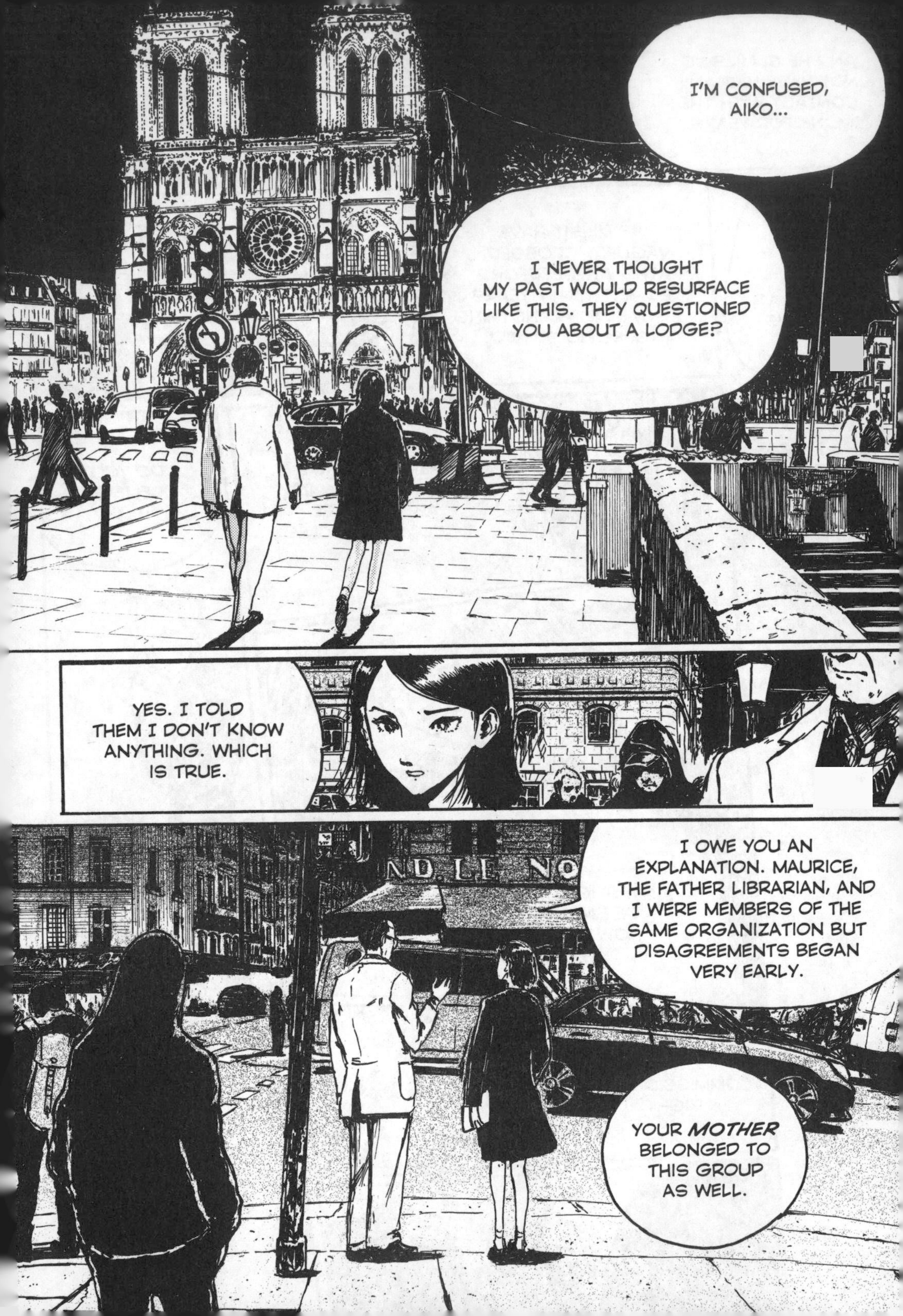
I'M CONFUSED, AIKO...
I NEVER THOUGHT MY PAST WOULD RESURFACE LIKE THIS. THEY QUESTIONED YOU ABOUT A LODGE?
YES. I TOLD THEM I DON'T KNOW ANYTHING. WHICH IS TRUE.
I OWE YOU AN EXPLANATION. MAURICE, THE FATHER LIBRARIAN, AND I WERE MEMBERS OF THE SAME ORGANIZATION BUT DISAGREEMENTS BEGAN VERY EARLY.
YOUR *MOTHER* BELONGED TO THIS GROUP AS WELL.

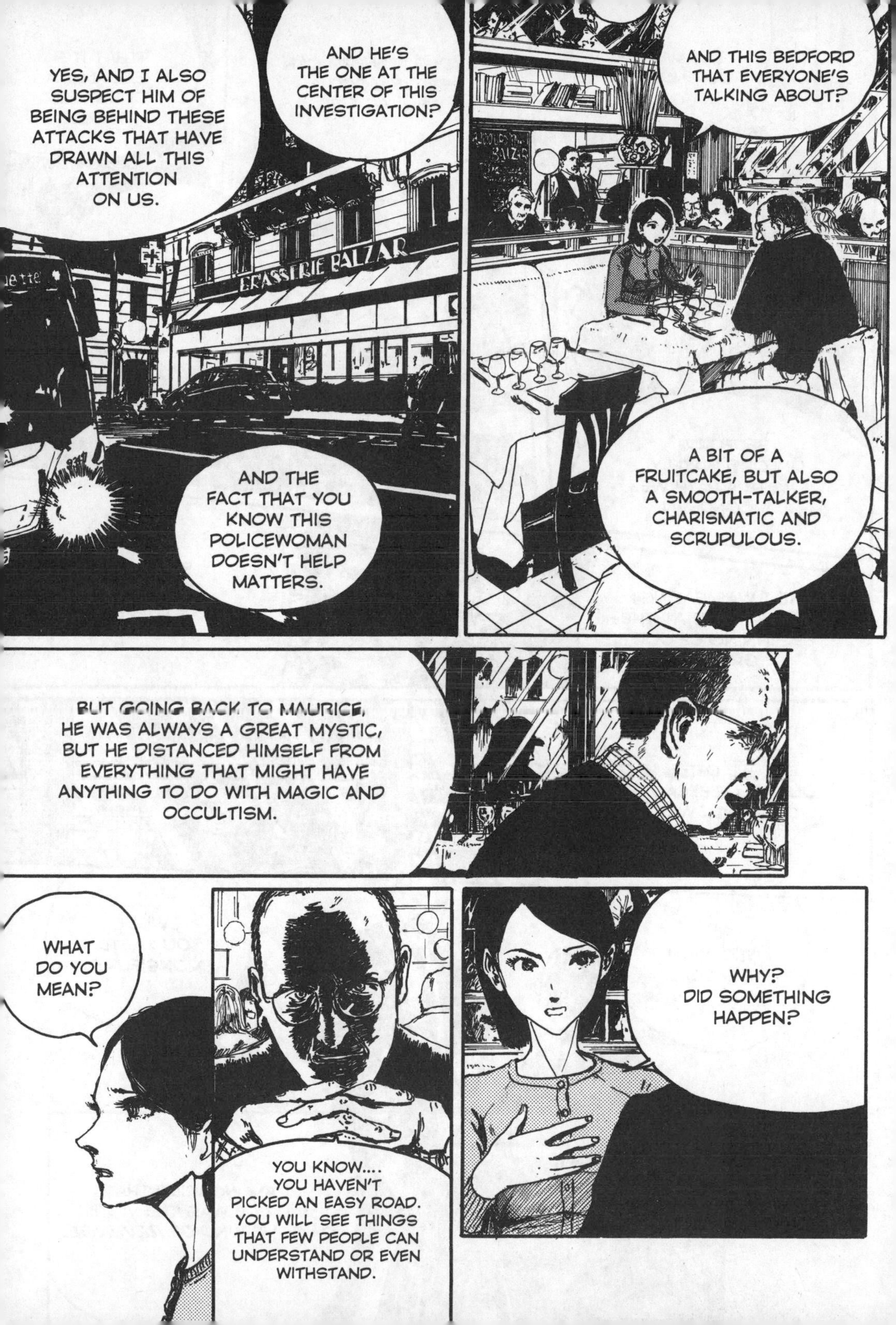
AND THIS BEDFORD THAT EVERYONE'S TALKING ABOUT?
A BIT OF A FRUITCAKE, BUT ALSO A SMOOTH-TALKER, CHARISMATIC AND SCRUPULOUS.
AND HE'S THE ONE AT THE CENTER OF THIS INVESTIGATION?
YES, AND I ALSO SUSPECT HIM OF BEING BEHIND THESE ATTACKS THAT HAVE DRAWN ALL THIS ATTENTION ON US.
BRASSERIE BALZAR
AND THE FACT THAT YOU KNOW THIS POLICEWOMAN DOESN'T HELP MATTERS.
BUT GOING BACK TO MAURICE, HE WAS ALWAYS A GREAT MYSTIC, BUT HE DISTANCED HIMSELF FROM EVERYTHING THAT MIGHT HAVE ANYTHING TO DO WITH MAGIC AND OCCULTISM.
WHY? DID SOMETHING HAPPEN?
YOU KNOW.... YOU HAVEN'T PICKED AN EASY ROAD. YOU WILL SEE THINGS THAT FEW PEOPLE CAN UNDERSTAND OR EVEN WITHSTAND.
WHAT DO YOU MEAN?

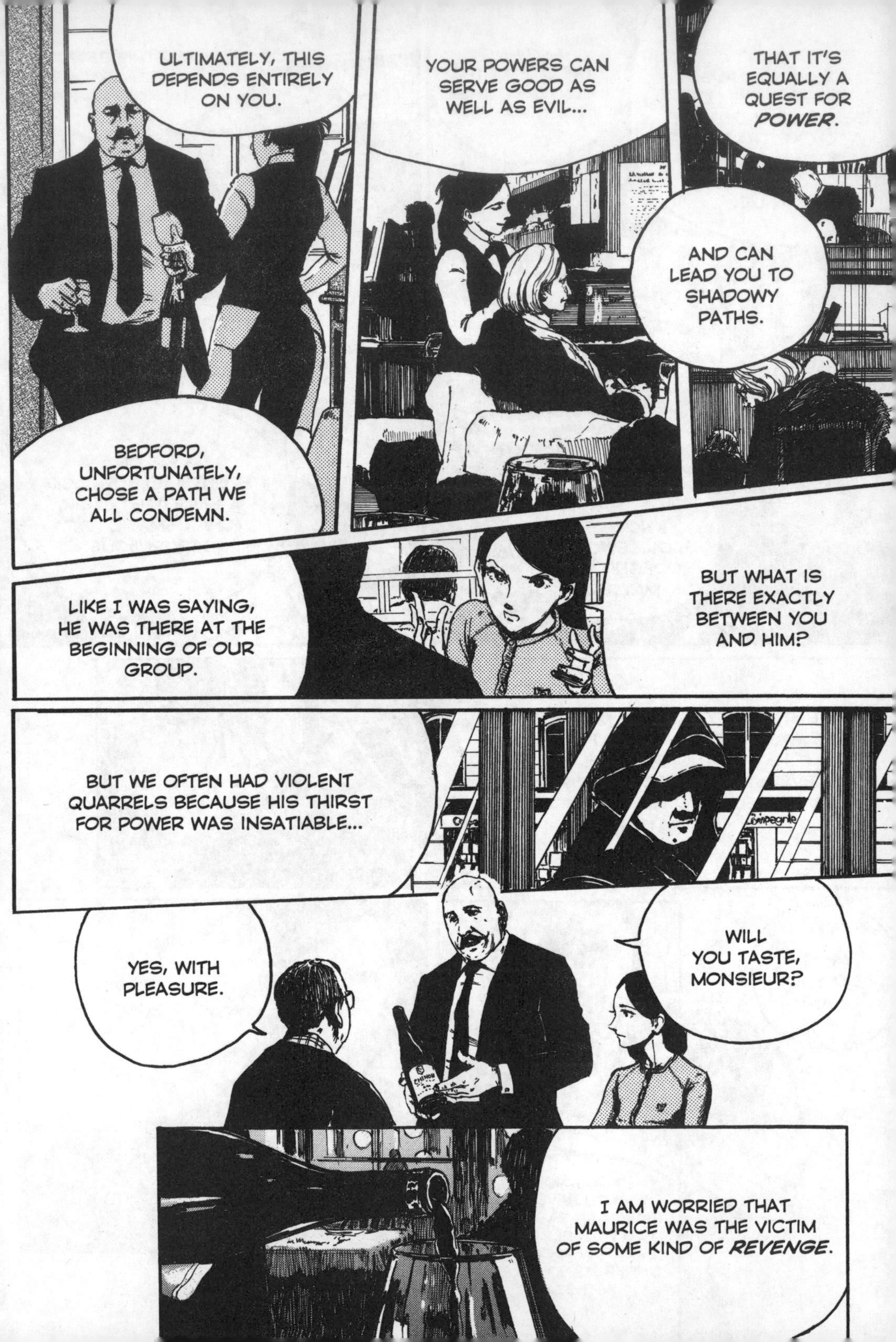
THAT IT'S EQUALLY A QUEST FOR *POWER*.
AND CAN LEAD YOU TO SHADOWY PATHS.
YOUR POWERS CAN SERVE GOOD AS WELL AS EVIL...
ULTIMATELY, THIS DEPENDS ENTIRELY ON YOU.
BEDFORD, UNFORTUNATELY, CHOSE A PATH WE ALL CONDEMN.
BUT WHAT IS THERE EXACTLY BETWEEN YOU AND HIM?
LIKE I WAS SAYING, HE WAS THERE AT THE BEGINNING OF OUR GROUP.
BUT WE OFTEN HAD VIOLENT QUARRELS BECAUSE HIS THIRST FOR POWER WAS INSATIABLE...
WILL YOU TASTE, MONSIEUR?
YES, WITH PLEASURE.
I AM WORRIED THAT MAURICE WAS THE VICTIM OF SOME KIND OF *REVENGE*.

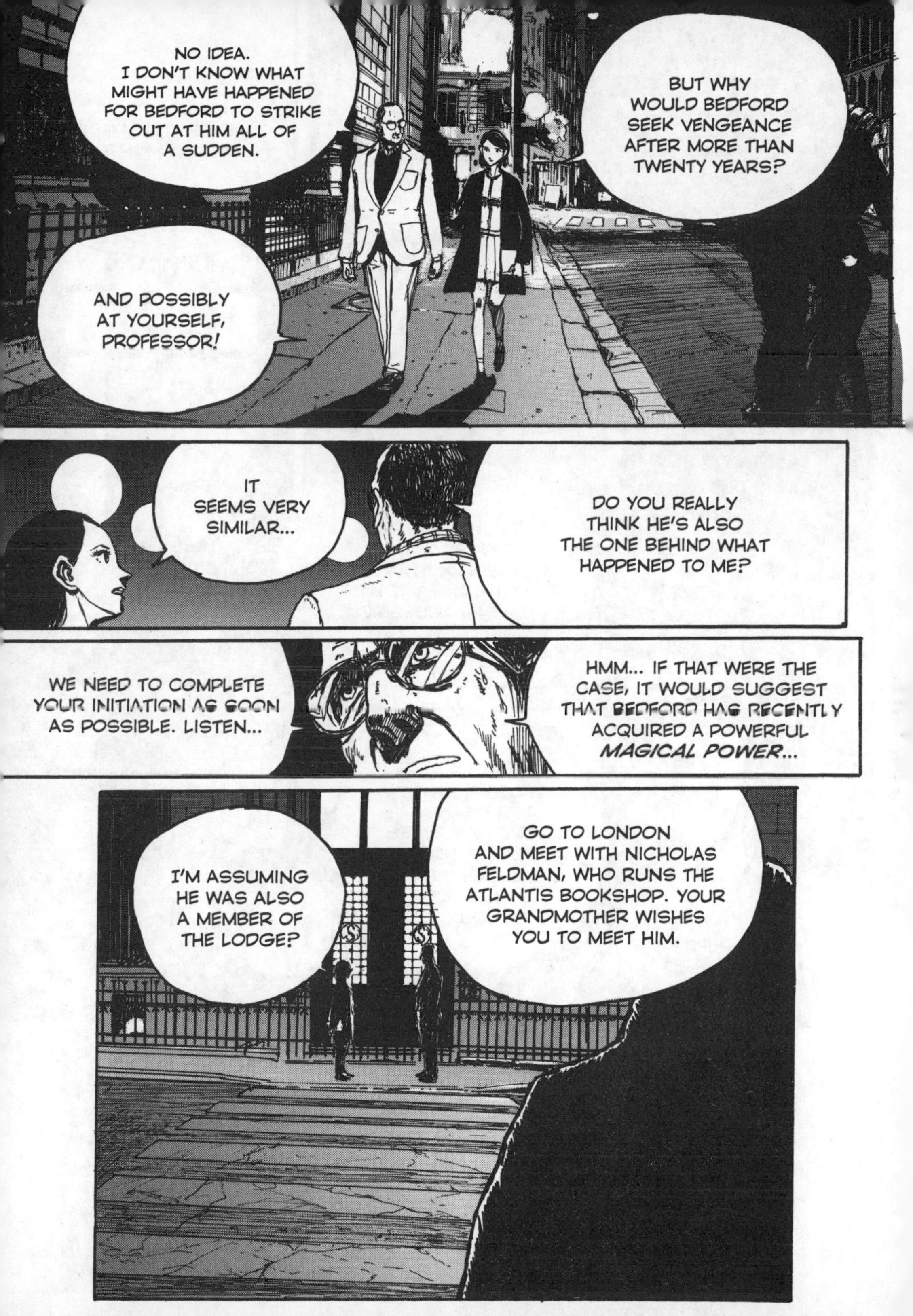
BUT WHY WOULD BEDFORD SEEK VENGEANCE AFTER MORE THAN TWENTY YEARS?
NO IDEA. I DON'T KNOW WHAT MIGHT HAVE HAPPENED FOR BEDFORD TO STRIKE OUT AT HIM ALL OF A SUDDEN.
AND POSSIBLY AT YOURSELF, PROFESSOR!
DO YOU REALLY THINK HE'S ALSO THE ONE BEHIND WHAT HAPPENED TO ME?
IT SEEMS VERY SIMILAR...
HMM... IF THAT WERE THE CASE, IT WOULD SUGGEST THAT BEDFORD HAS RECENTLY ACQUIRED A POWERFUL *MAGICAL POWER*...
WE NEED TO COMPLETE YOUR INITIATION AS SOON AS POSSIBLE. LISTEN...
GO TO LONDON AND MEET WITH NICHOLAS FELDMAN, WHO RUNS THE ATLANTIS BOOKSHOP. YOUR GRANDMOTHER WISHES YOU TO MEET HIM.
I'M ASSUMING HE WAS ALSO A MEMBER OF THE LODGE?

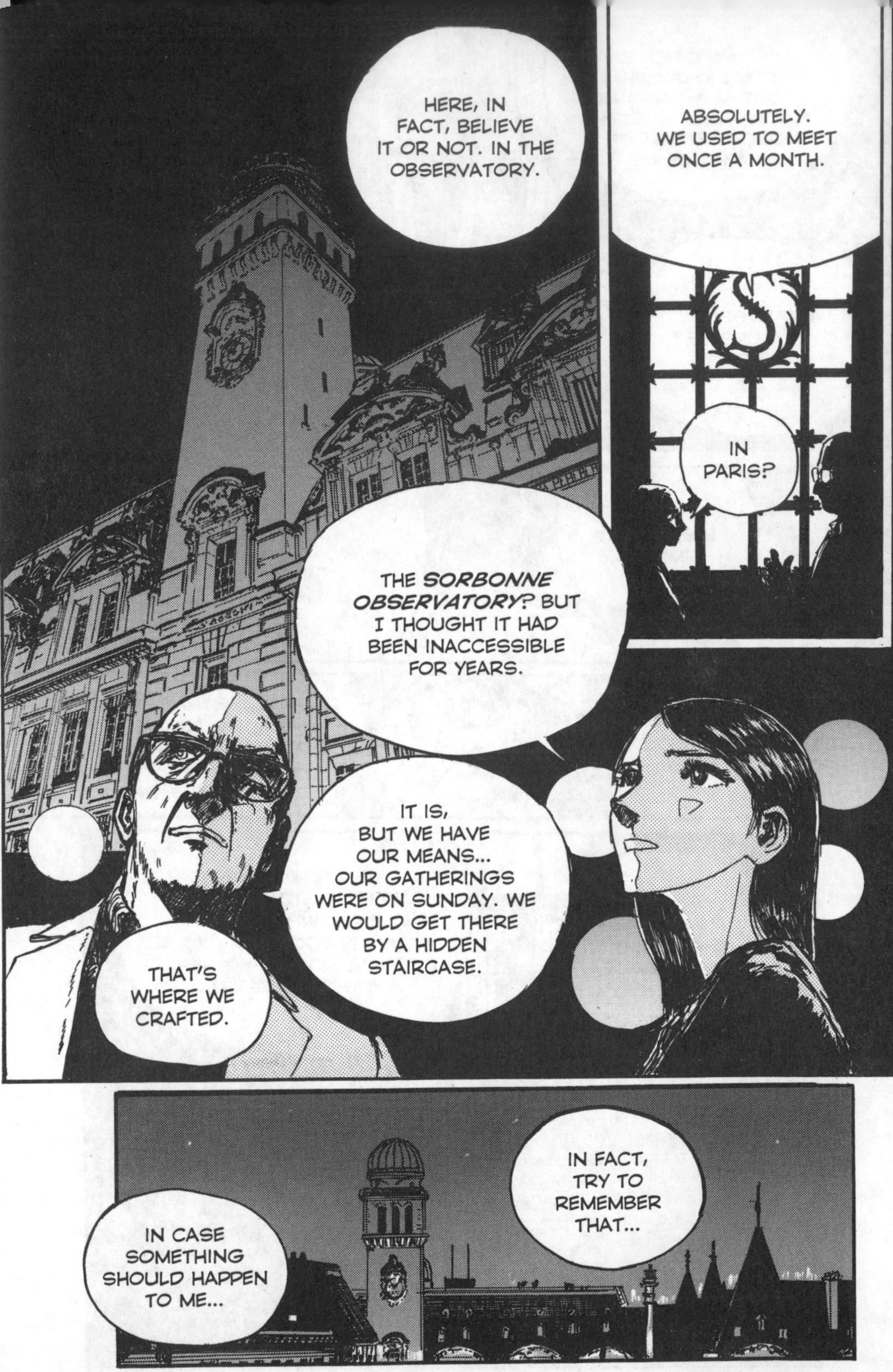
ABSOLUTELY. WE USED TO MEET ONCE A MONTH.
IN PARIS?
HERE, IN FACT, BELIEVE IT OR NOT. IN THE OBSERVATORY.
THE *SORBONNE OBSERVATORY?* BUT I THOUGHT IT HAD BEEN INACCESSIBLE FOR YEARS.
IT IS, BUT WE HAVE OUR MEANS... OUR GATHERINGS WERE ON SUNDAY. WE WOULD GET THERE BY A HIDDEN STAIRCASE.
THAT'S WHERE WE CRAFTED.
IN FACT, TRY TO REMEMBER THAT...
IN CASE SOMETHING SHOULD HAPPEN TO ME...

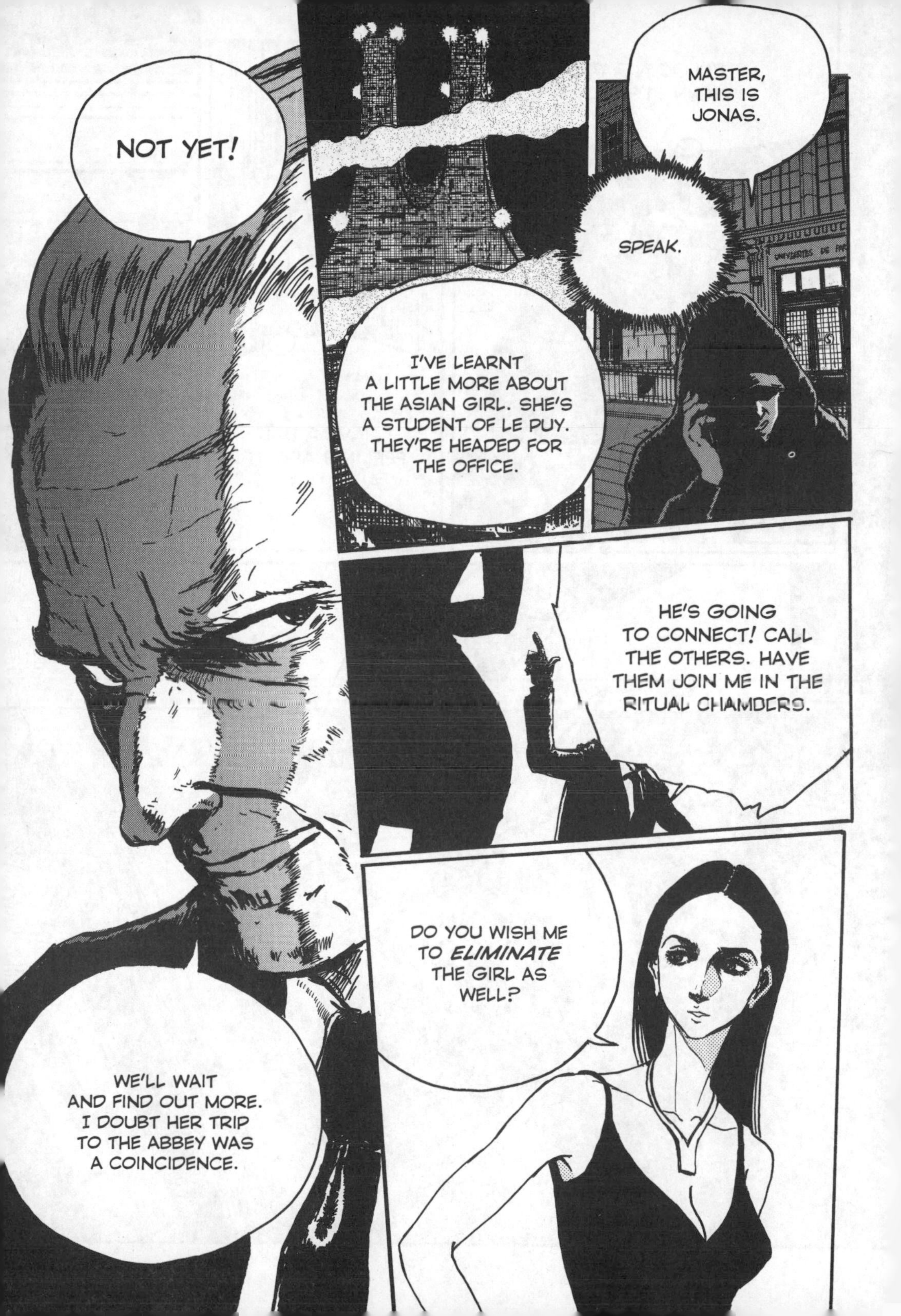
MASTER, THIS IS JONAS.
SPEAK.
I'VE LEARNT A LITTLE MORE ABOUT THE ASIAN GIRL. SHE'S A STUDENT OF LE PUY. THEY'RE HEADED FOR THE OFFICE.
HE'S GOING TO CONNECT! CALL THE OTHERS. HAVE THEM JOIN ME IN THE RITUAL CHAMBERS.
DO YOU WISH ME TO *ELIMINATE* THE GIRL AS WELL?
NOT YET!
WE'LL WAIT AND FIND OUT MORE. I DOUBT HER TRIP TO THE ABBEY WAS A COINCIDENCE.

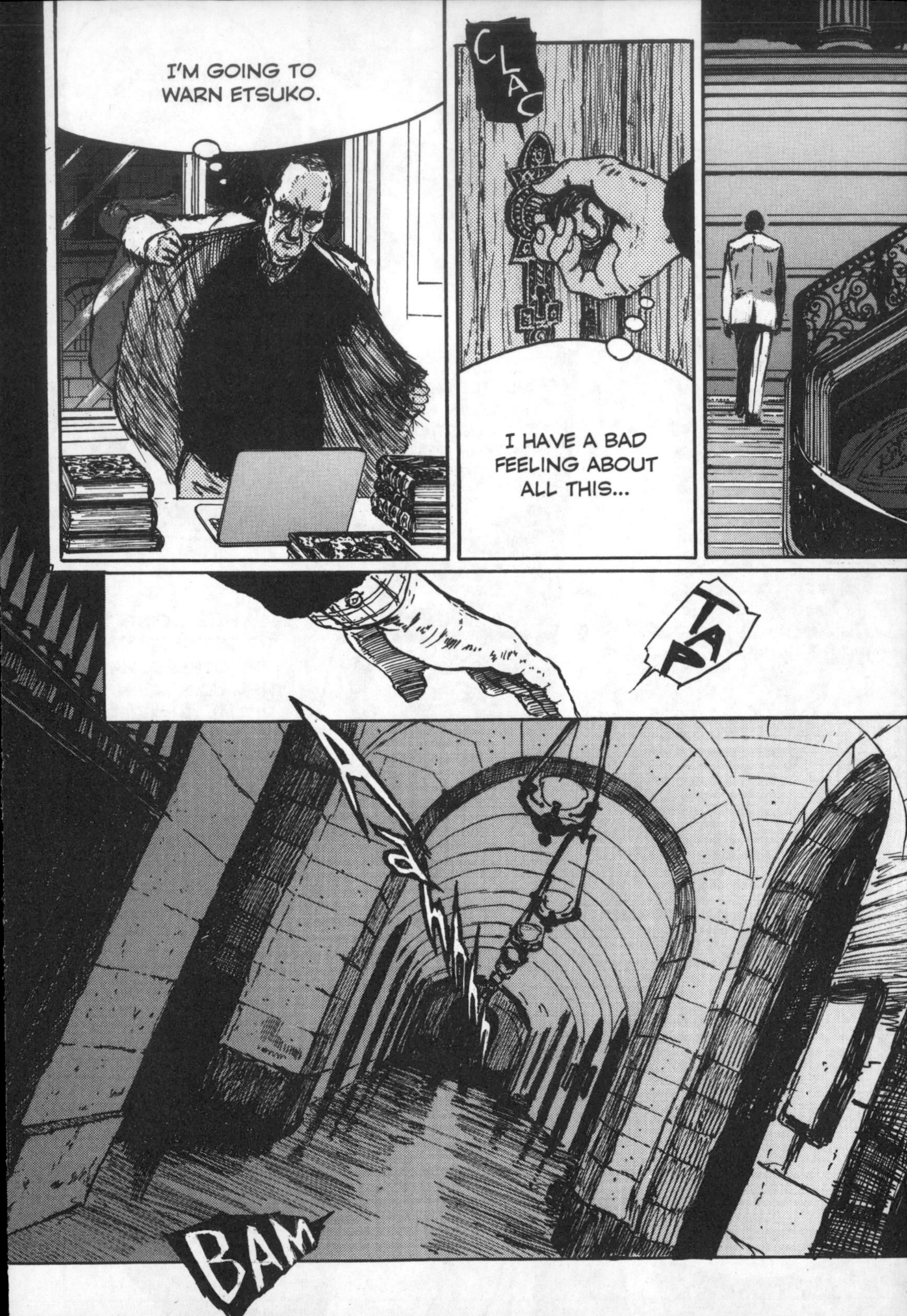
CLAC
I HAVE A BAD FEELING ABOUT ALL THIS...
I'M GOING TO WARN ETSUKO.
TAP
BAM

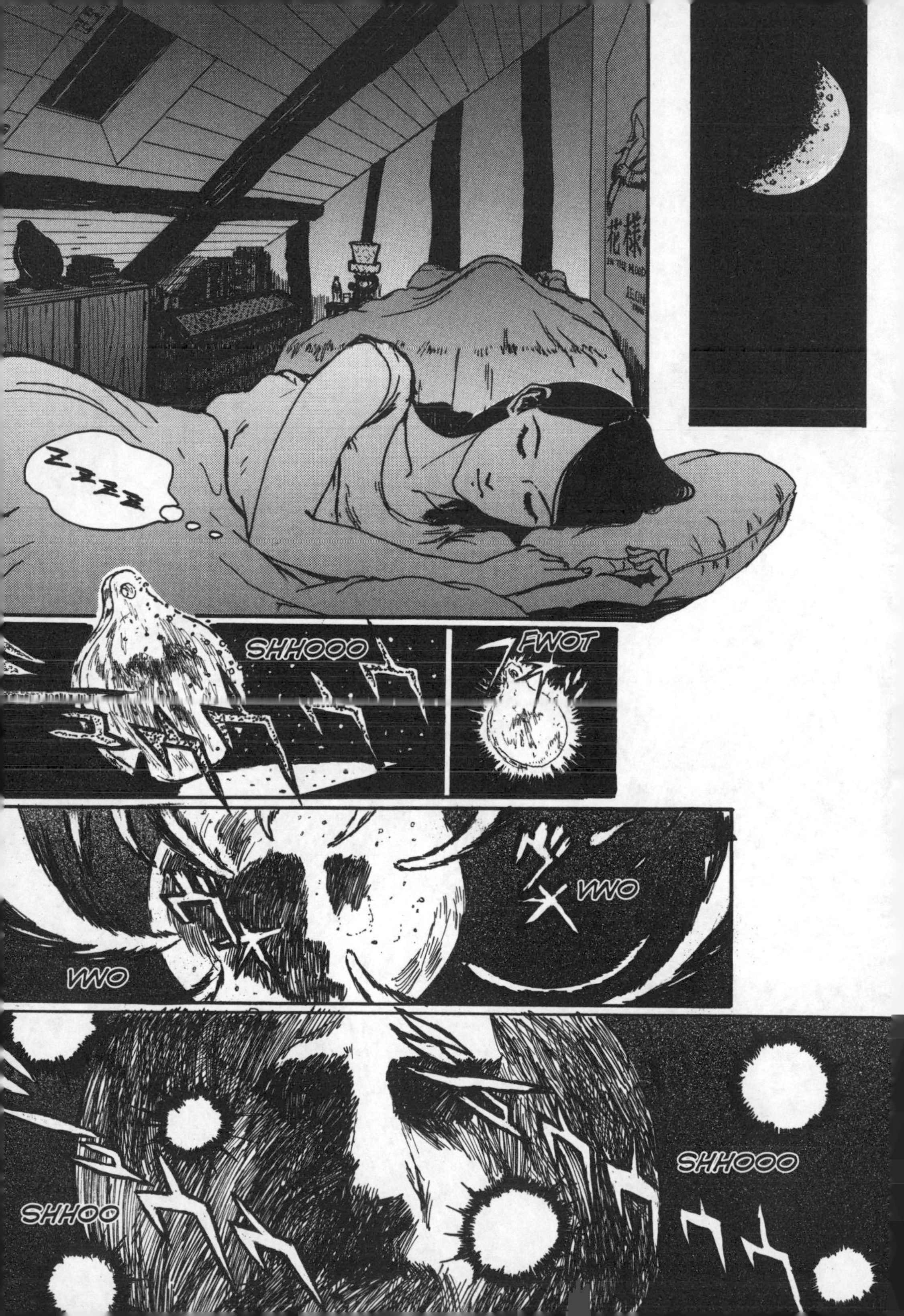
ZZZZ
FWOT
SHHOOO
VWO
VWO
SHHOOO
SHHOO

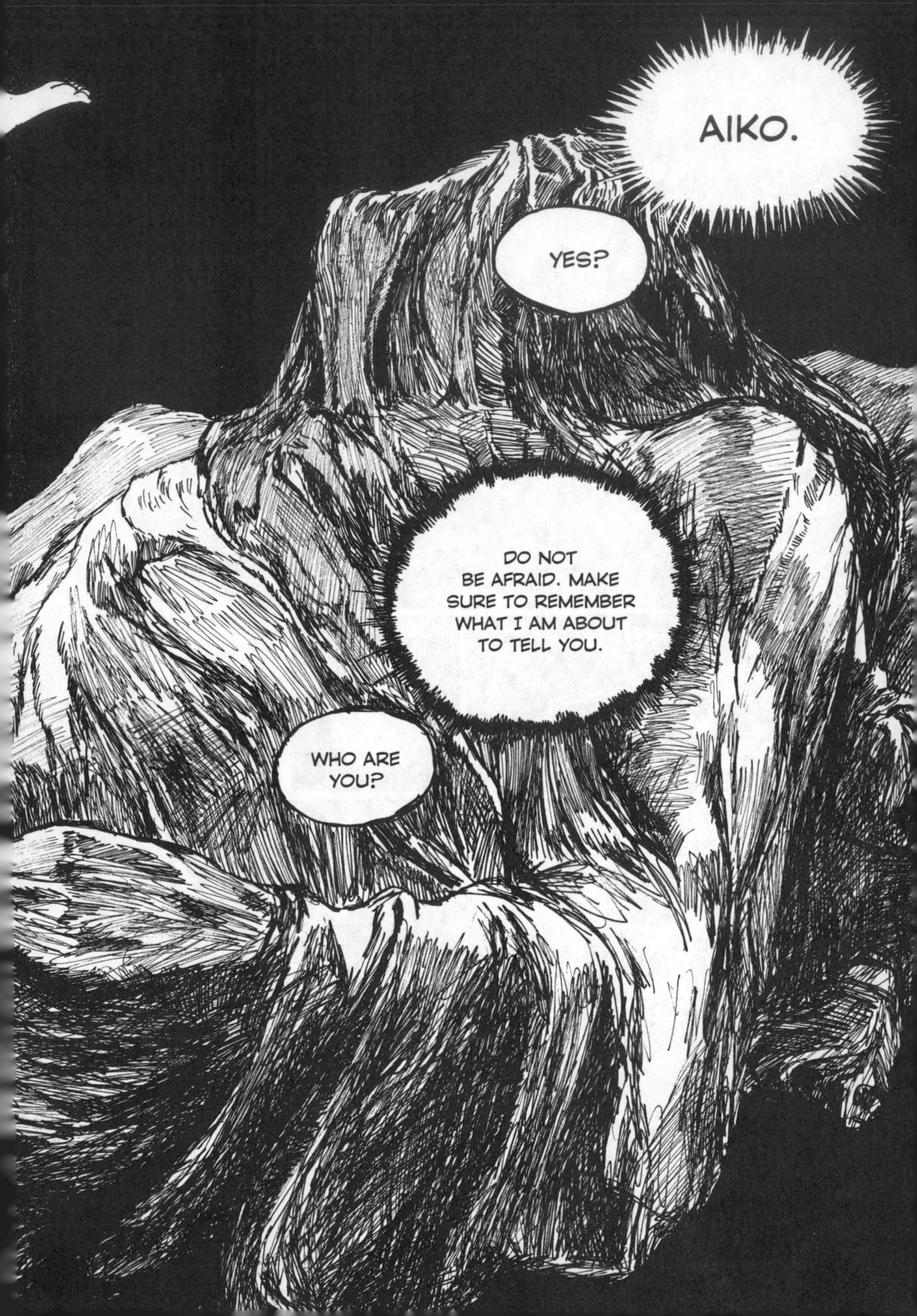
AIKO.
YES?
DO NOT BE AFRAID. MAKE SURE TO REMEMBER WHAT I AM ABOUT TO TELL YOU.
WHO ARE YOU?

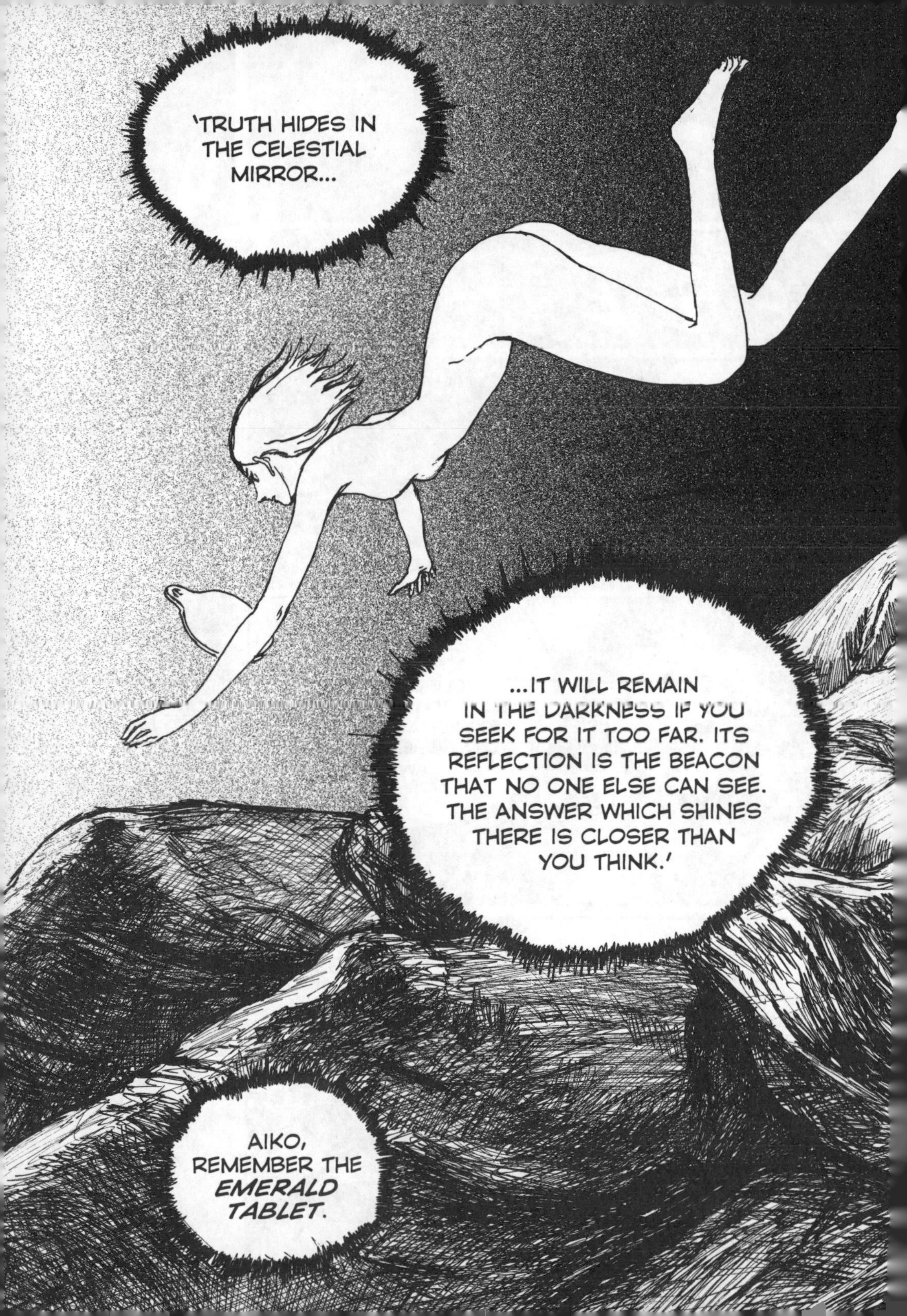
'TRUTH HIDES IN THE CELESTIAL MIRROR...
...IT WILL REMAIN IN THE DARKNESS IF YOU SEEK FOR IT TOO FAR. ITS REFLECTION IS THE BEACON THAT NO ONE ELSE CAN SEE. THE ANSWER WHICH SHINES THERE IS CLOSER THAN YOU THINK.'
AIKO, REMEMBER THE *EMERALD TABLET*.

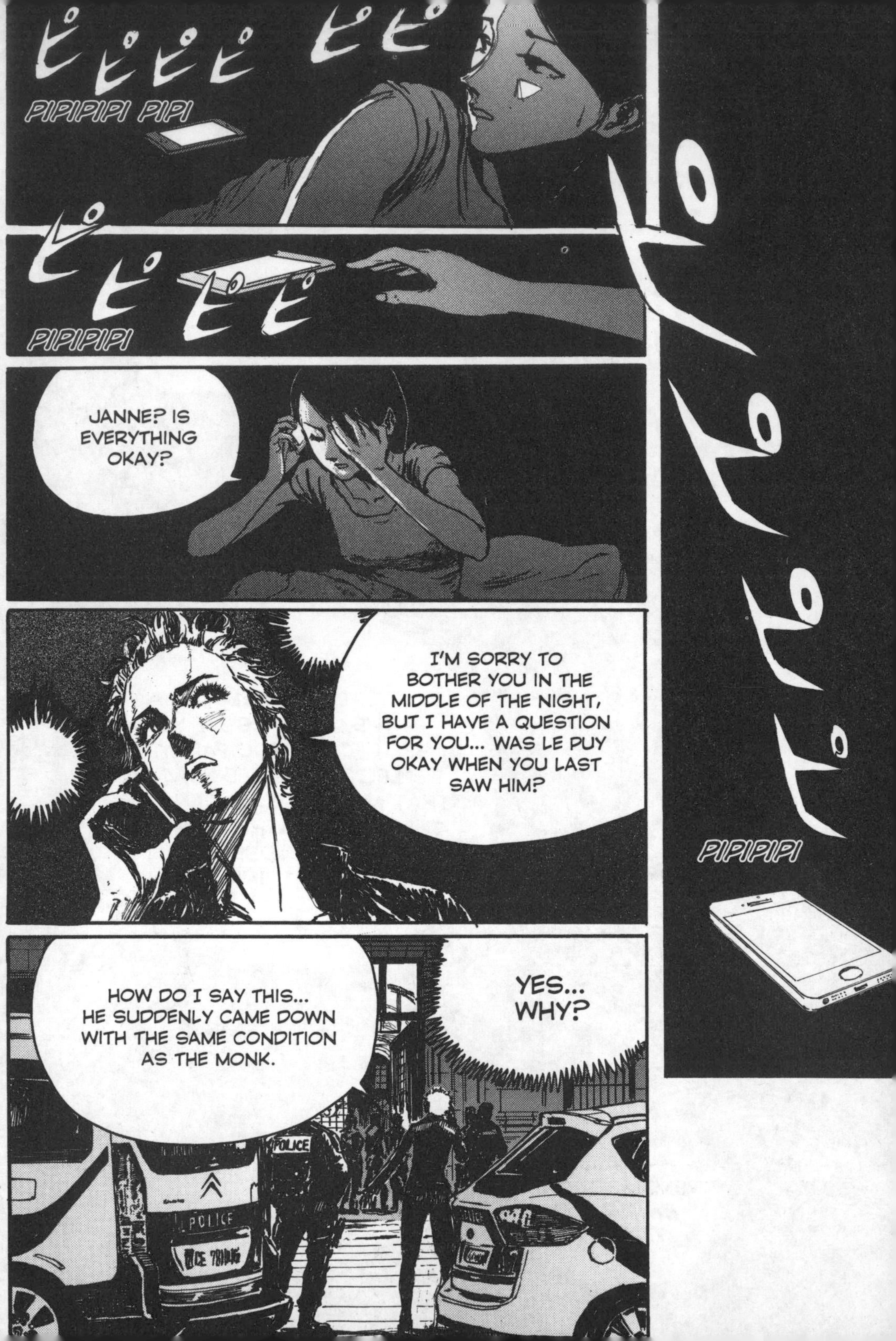
PIPIPIPI
PIPIPIPI PIPI
PIPIPIPI
JANNE? IS EVERYTHING OKAY?
I'M SORRY TO BOTHER YOU IN THE MIDDLE OF THE NIGHT, BUT I HAVE A QUESTION FOR YOU... WAS LE PUY OKAY WHEN YOU LAST SAW HIM?
YES... WHY?
HOW DO I SAY THIS... HE SUDDENLY CAME DOWN WITH THE SAME CONDITION AS THE MONK.
POLICE
POLICE

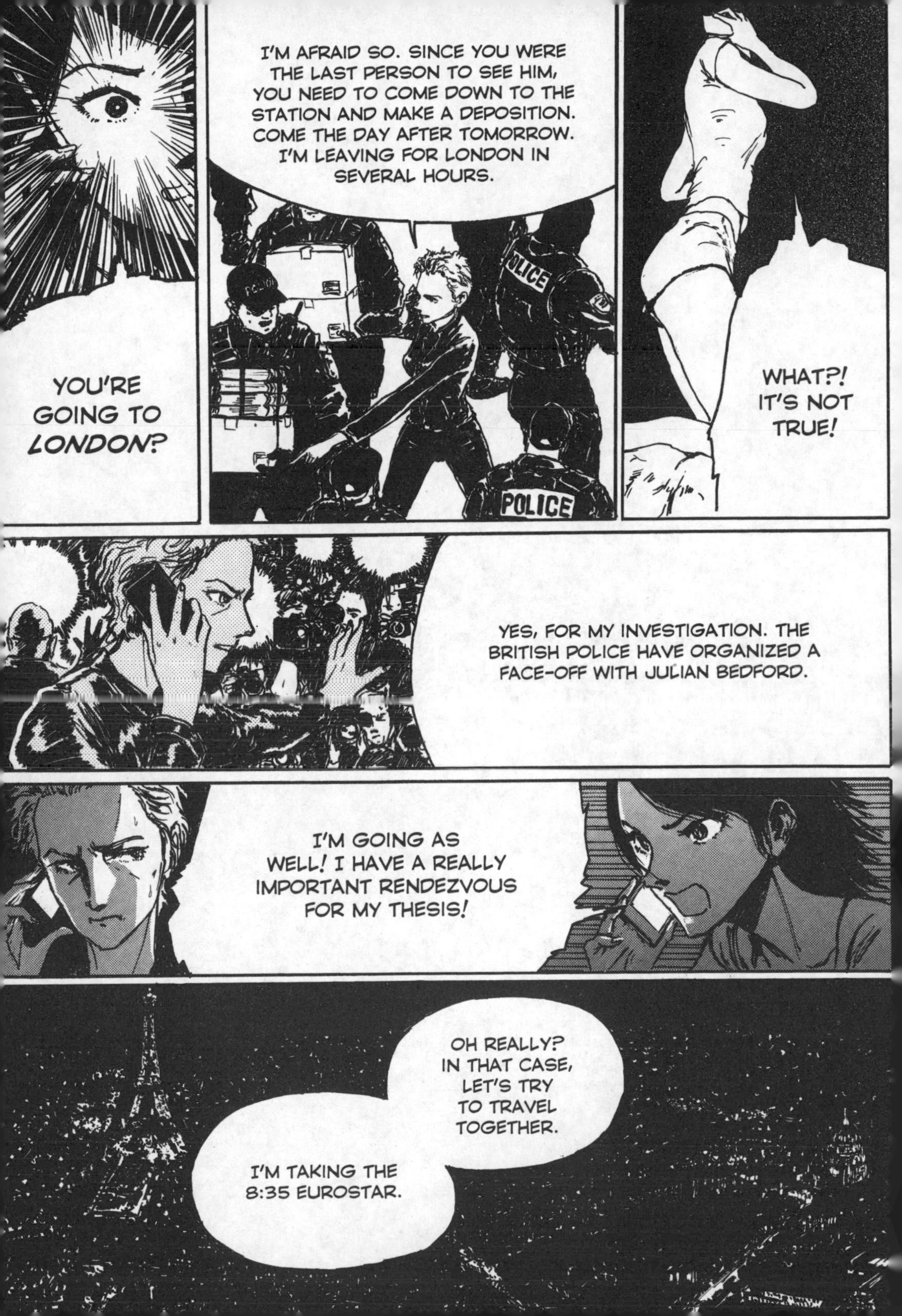
WHAT?! IT'S NOT TRUE!
I'M AFRAID SO. SINCE YOU WERE THE LAST PERSON TO SEE HIM, YOU NEED TO COME DOWN TO THE STATION AND MAKE A DEPOSITION. COME THE DAY AFTER TOMORROW. I'M LEAVING FOR LONDON IN SEVERAL HOURS.
POLICE
POLICE
YOU'RE GOING TO *LONDON*?
YES, FOR MY INVESTIGATION. THE BRITISH POLICE HAVE ORGANIZED A FACE-OFF WITH JULIAN BEDFORD.
I'M GOING AS WELL! I HAVE A REALLY IMPORTANT RENDEZVOUS FOR MY THESIS!
OH REALLY? IN THAT CASE, LET'S TRY TO TRAVEL TOGETHER.
I'M TAKING THE 8:35 EUROSTAR.

CHAPTER 5

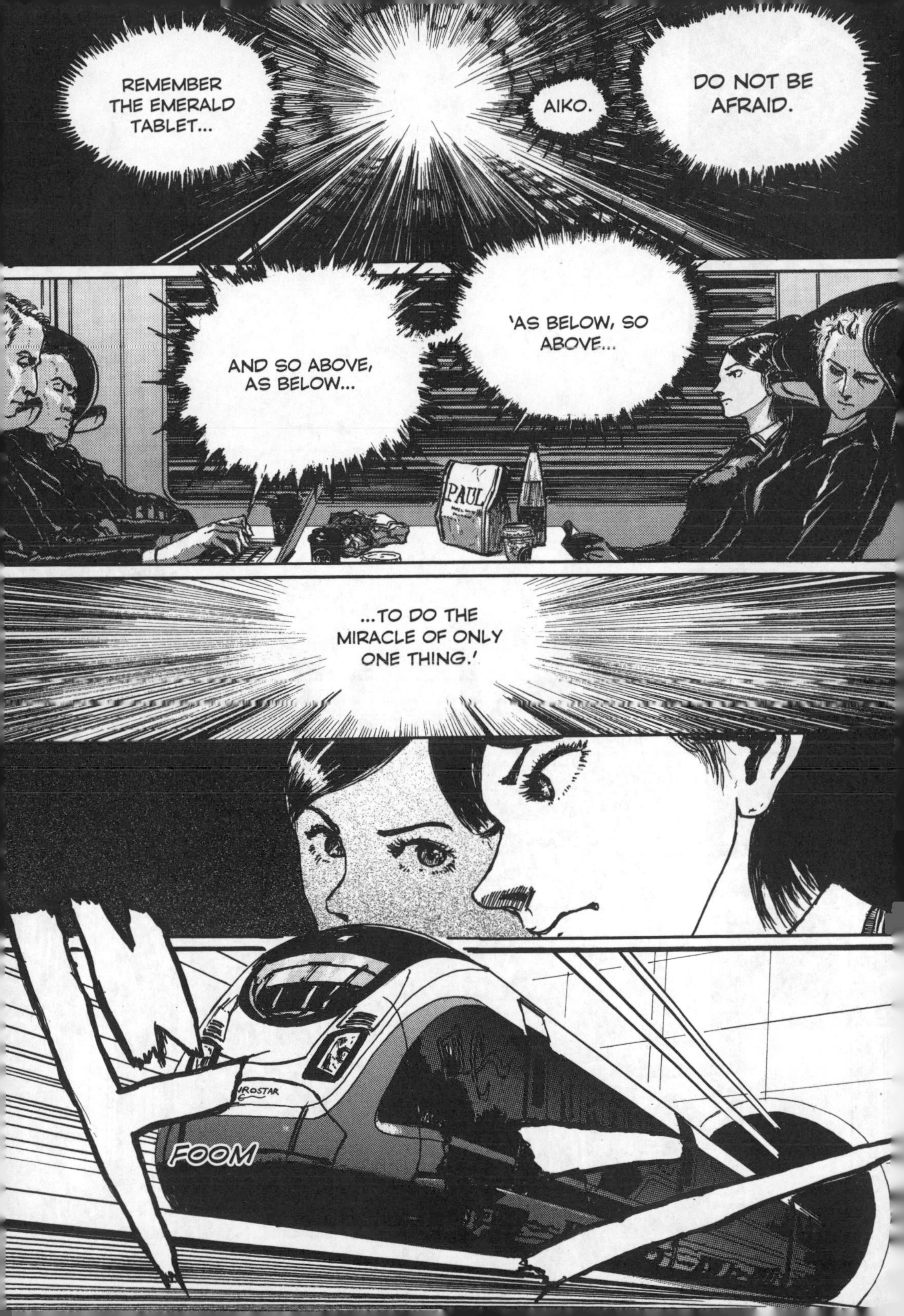
DO NOT BE AFRAID.
AIKO.
REMEMBER THE EMERALD TABLET...
'AS BELOW, SO ABOVE...
AND SO ABOVE, AS BELOW...
PAUL
...TO DO THE MIRACLE OF ONLY ONE THING.'
FOOM

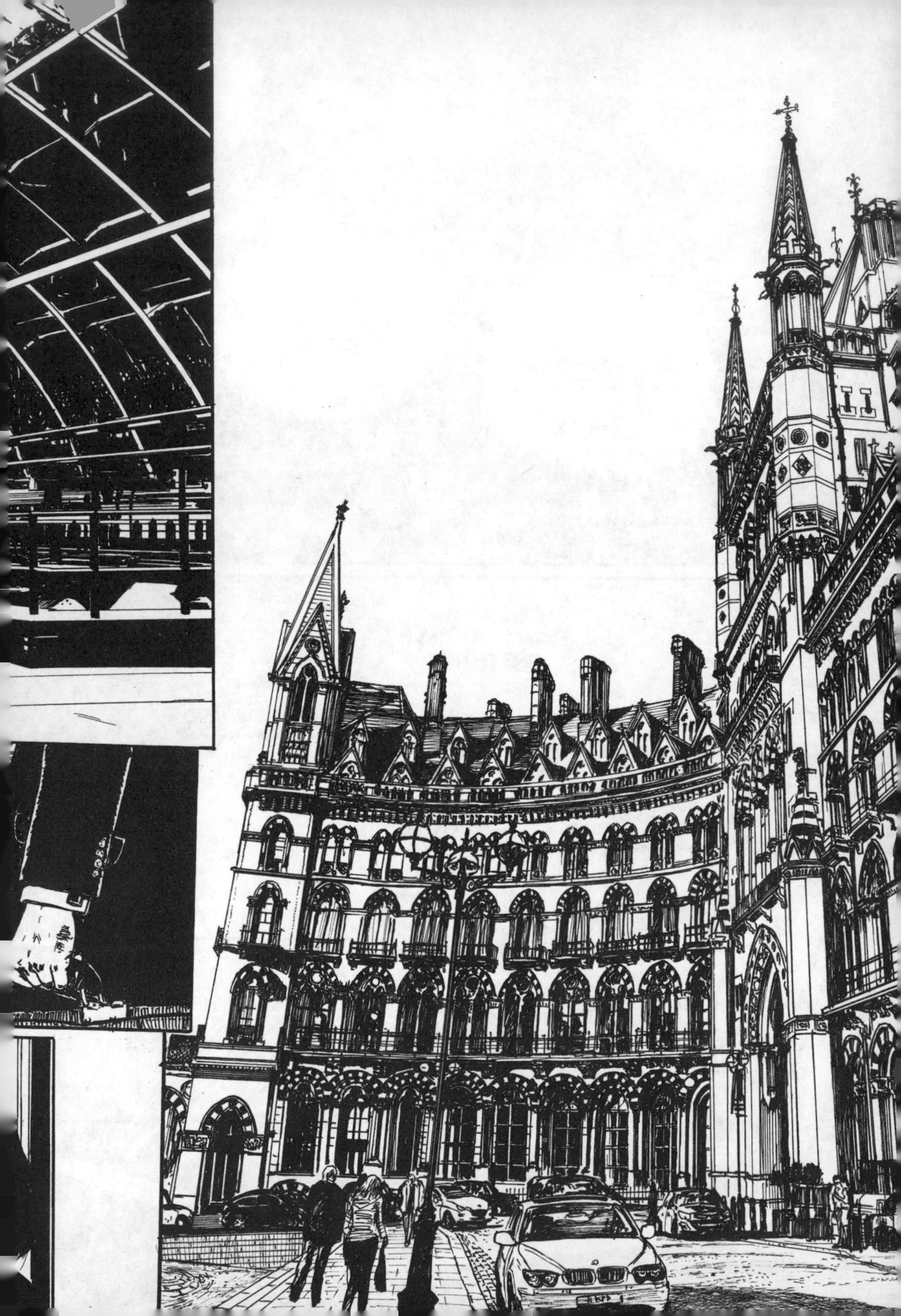

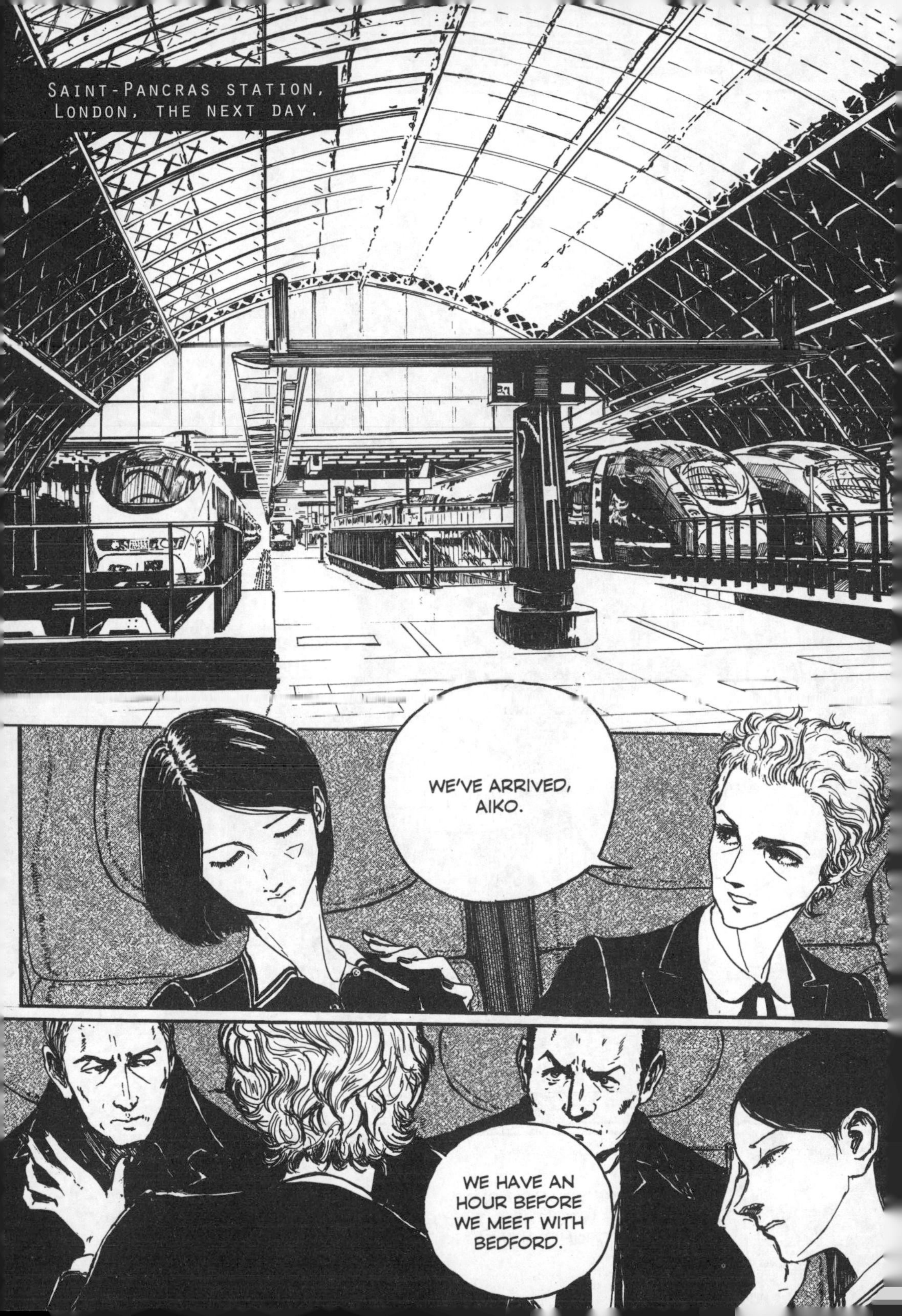
Saint-Pancras station, London, the next day.
WE'VE ARRIVED, AIKO.
WE HAVE AN HOUR BEFORE WE MEET WITH BEDFORD.

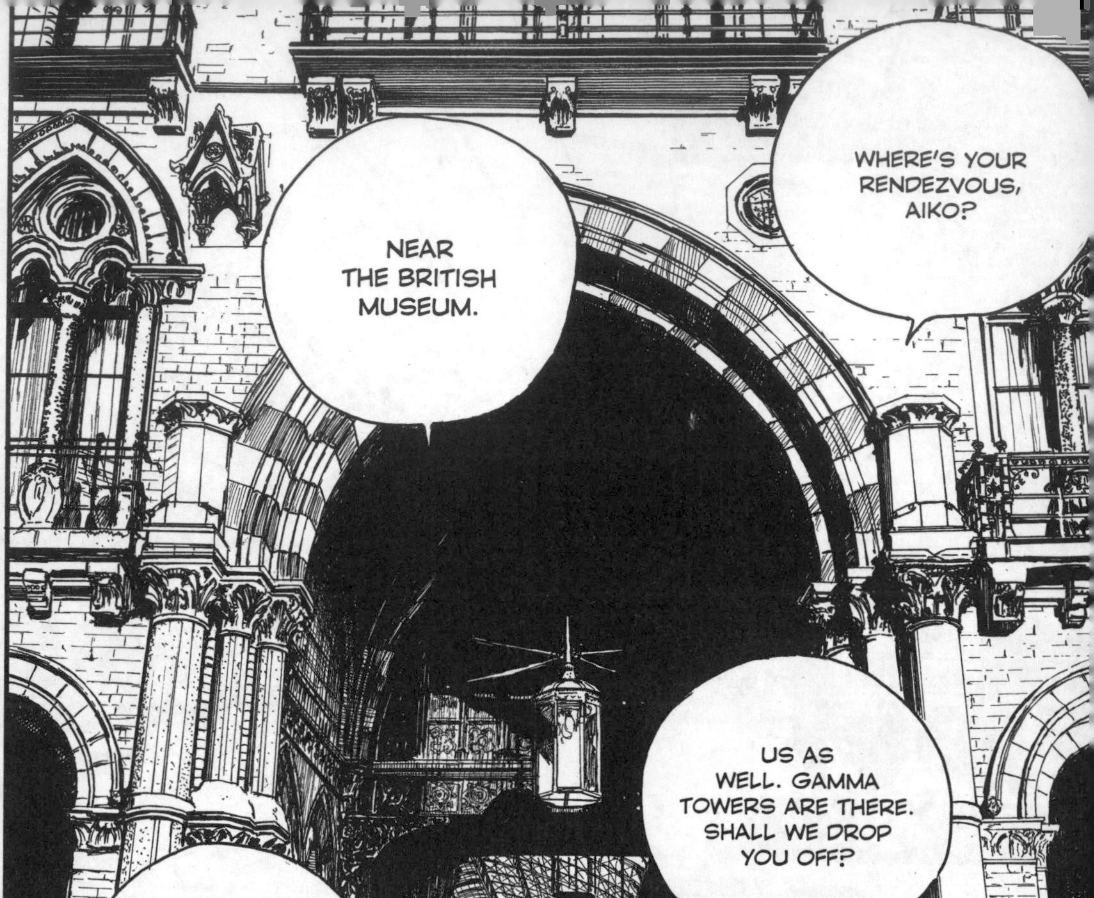
WHERE'S YOUR RENDEZVOUS, AIKO?
NEAR THE BRITISH MUSEUM.
US AS WELL. GAMMA TOWERS ARE THERE. SHALL WE DROP YOU OFF?
THANKS, WE'LL MEET UP AFTER.
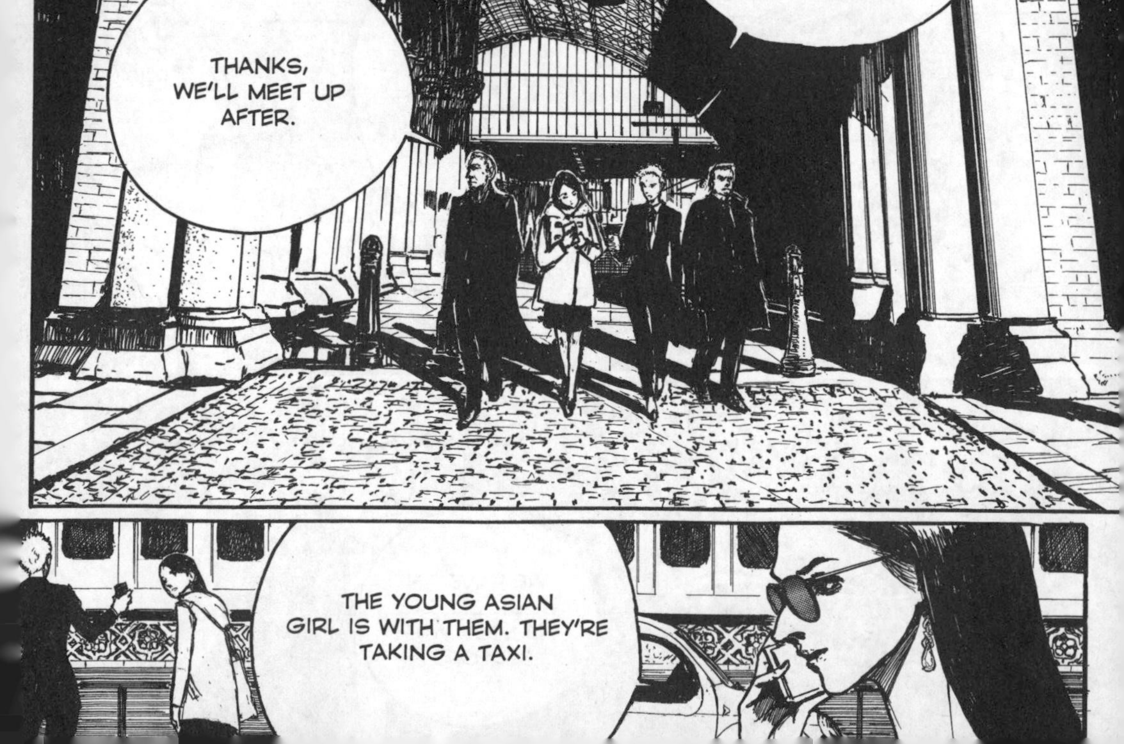
THE YOUNG ASIAN GIRL IS WITH THEM. THEY'RE TAKING A TAXI.

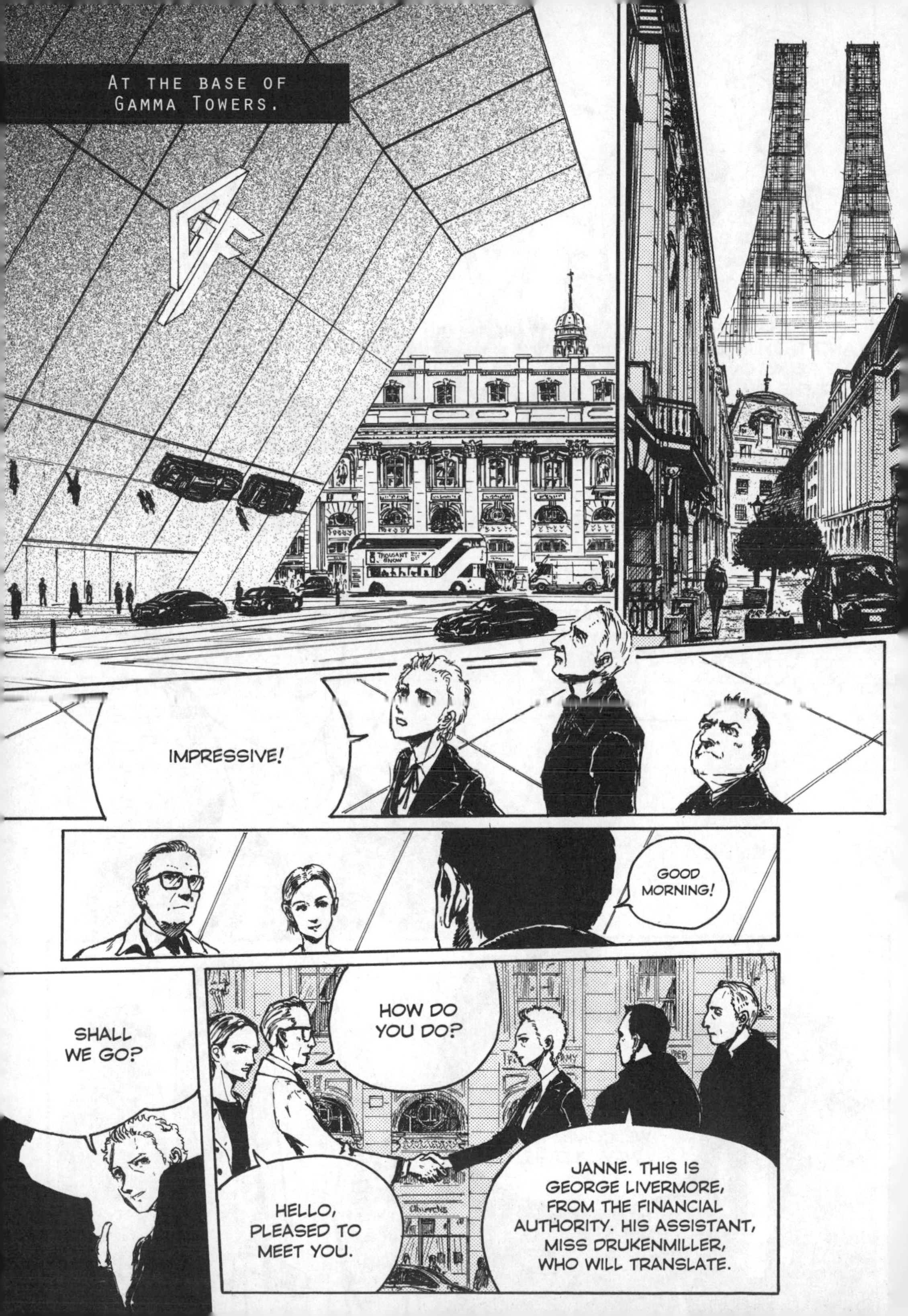
At the base of Gamma Towers.
IMPRESSIVE!
GOOD MORNING!
HOW DO YOU DO?
JANNE. THIS IS GEORGE LIVERMORE, FROM THE FINANCIAL AUTHORITY. HIS ASSISTANT, MISS DRUKENMILLER, WHO WILL TRANSLATE.
HELLO, PLEASED TO MEET YOU.
SHALL WE GO?

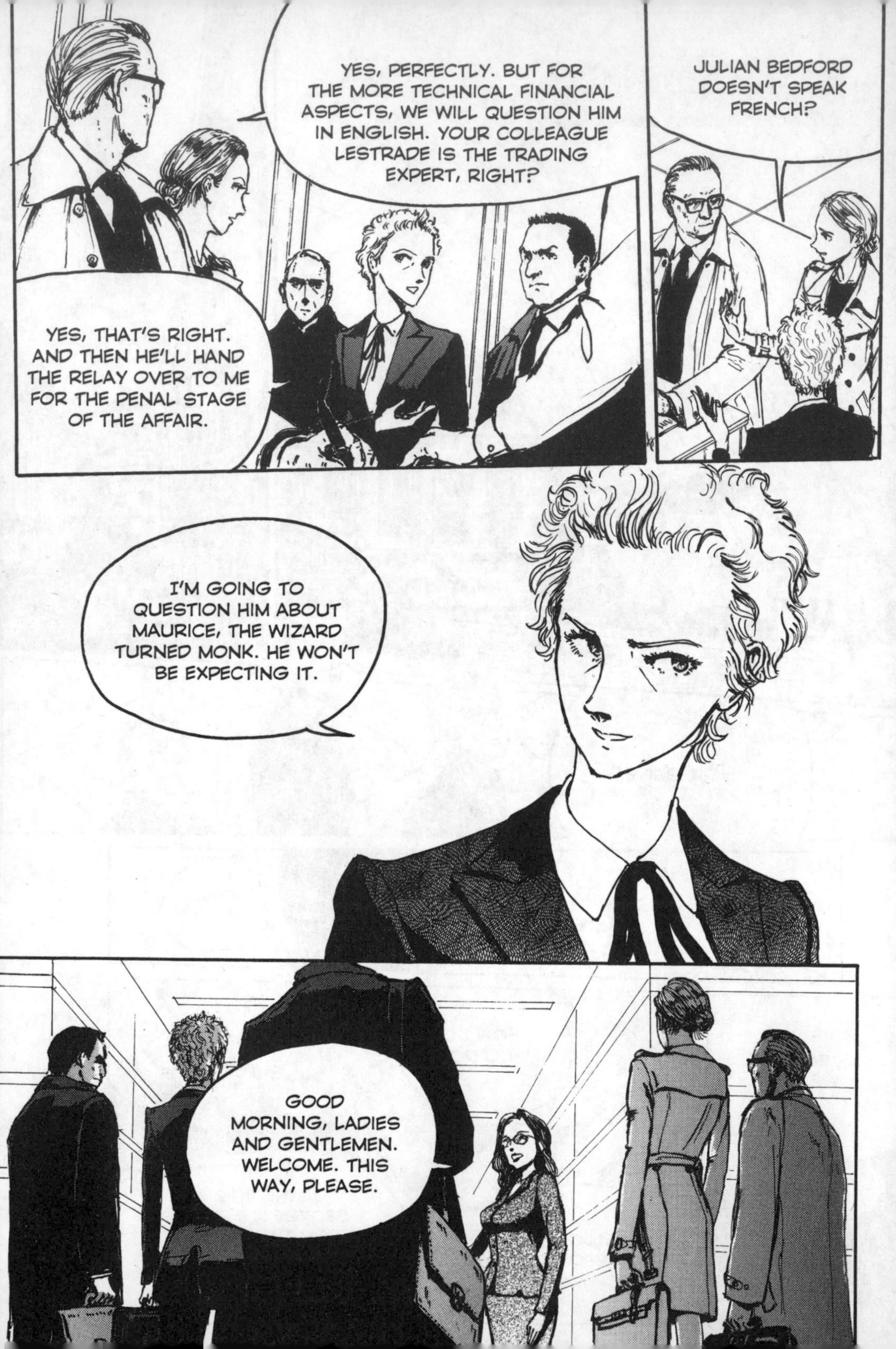
JULIAN BEDFORD DOESN'T SPEAK FRENCH?
YES, PERFECTLY. BUT FOR THE MORE TECHNICAL FINANCIAL ASPECTS, WE WILL QUESTION HIM IN ENGLISH. YOUR COLLEAGUE LESTRADE IS THE TRADING EXPERT, RIGHT?
YES, THAT'S RIGHT. AND THEN HE'LL HAND THE RELAY OVER TO ME FOR THE PENAL STAGE OF THE AFFAIR.
I'M GOING TO QUESTION HIM ABOUT MAURICE, THE WIZARD TURNED MONK. HE WON'T BE EXPECTING IT.
GOOD MORNING, LADIES AND GENTLEMEN. WELCOME. THIS WAY, PLEASE.

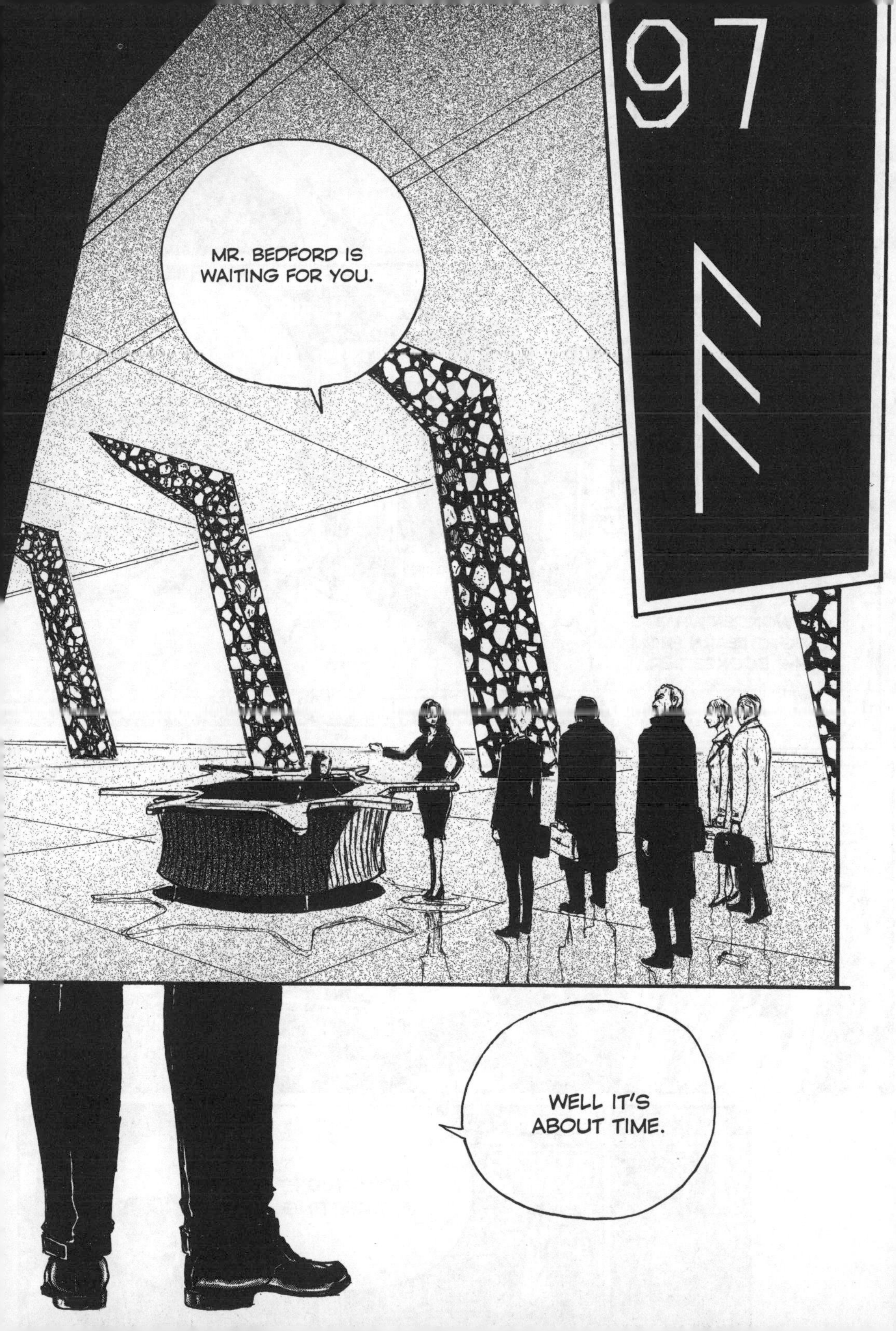
97
MR. BEDFORD IS WAITING FOR YOU.
WELL IT'S ABOUT TIME.

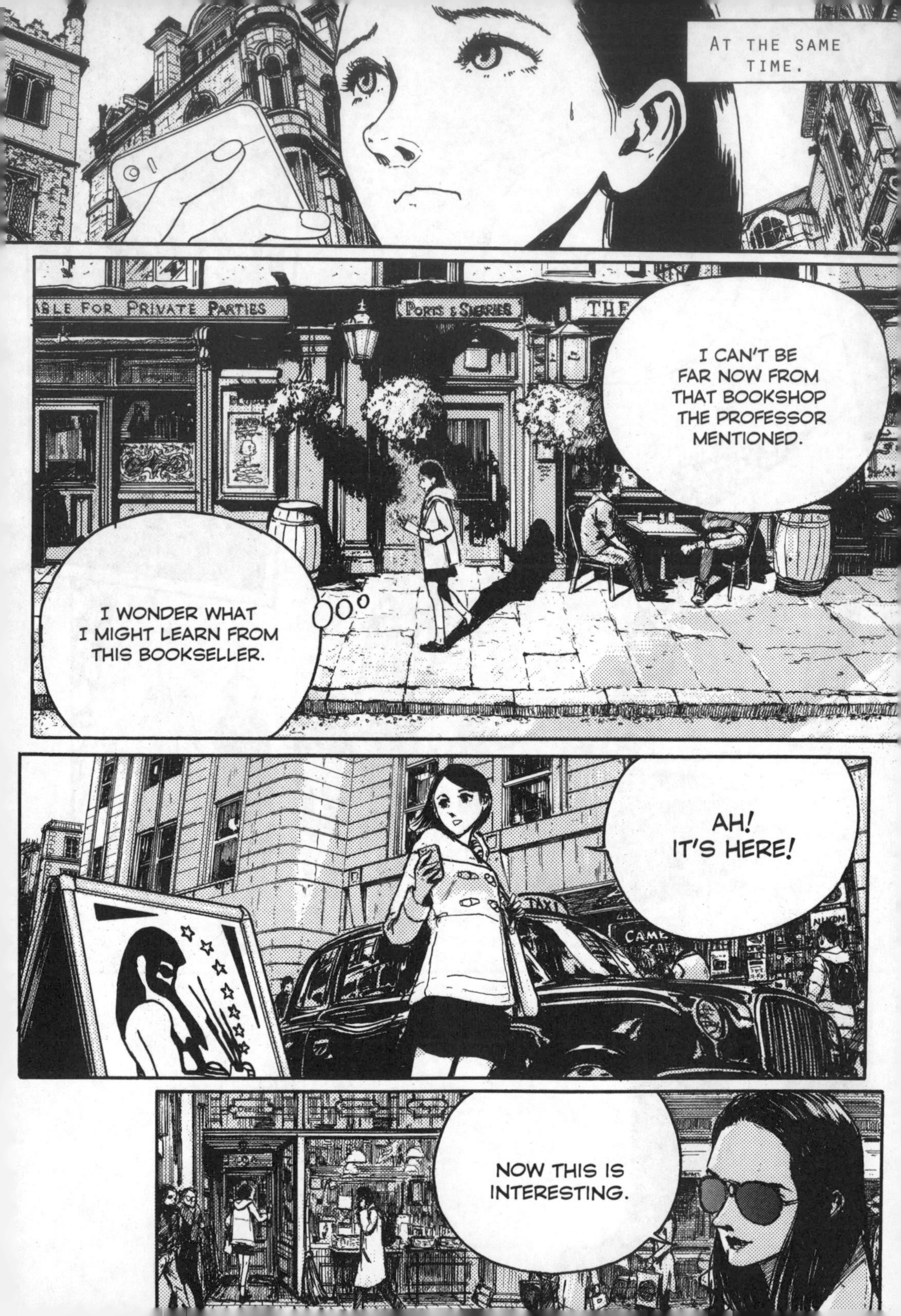
At the same time.
I CAN'T BE FAR NOW FROM THAT BOOKSHOP THE PROFESSOR MENTIONED.
I WONDER WHAT I MIGHT LEARN FROM THIS BOOKSELLER.
AH! IT'S HERE!
NOW THIS IS INTERESTING.

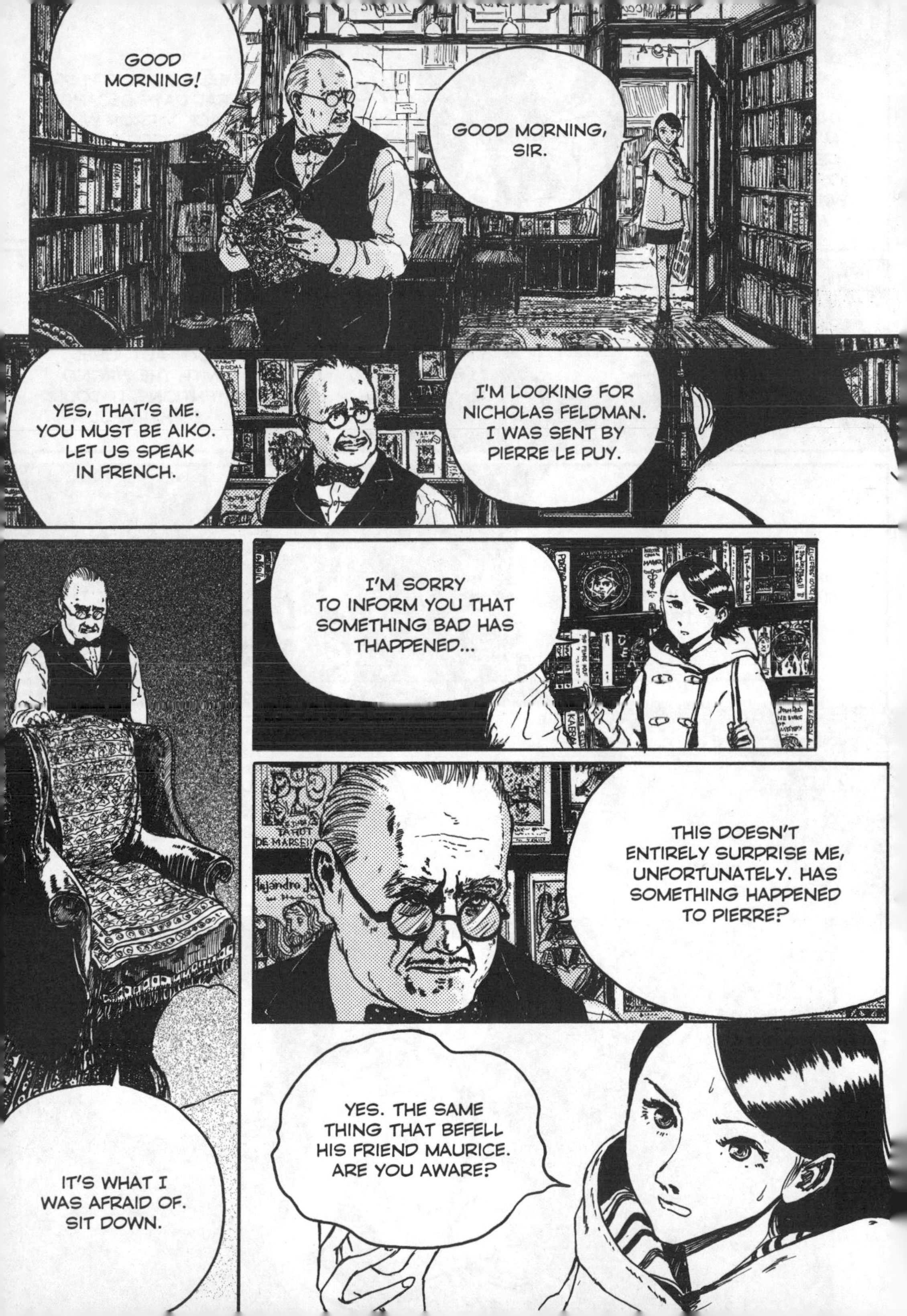

GOOD MORNING, SIR.
GOOD MORNING!
I'M LOOKING FOR NICHOLAS FELDMAN. I WAS SENT BY PIERRE LE PUY.
YES, THAT'S ME. YOU MUST BE AIKO. LET US SPEAK IN FRENCH.
I'M SORRY TO INFORM YOU THAT SOMETHING BAD HAS THAPPENED...
THIS DOESN'T ENTIRELY SURPRISE ME, UNFORTUNATELY. HAS SOMETHING HAPPENED TO PIERRE?
YES. THE SAME THING THAT BEFELL HIS FRIEND MAURICE. ARE YOU AWARE?
IT'S WHAT I WAS AFRAID OF. SIT DOWN.

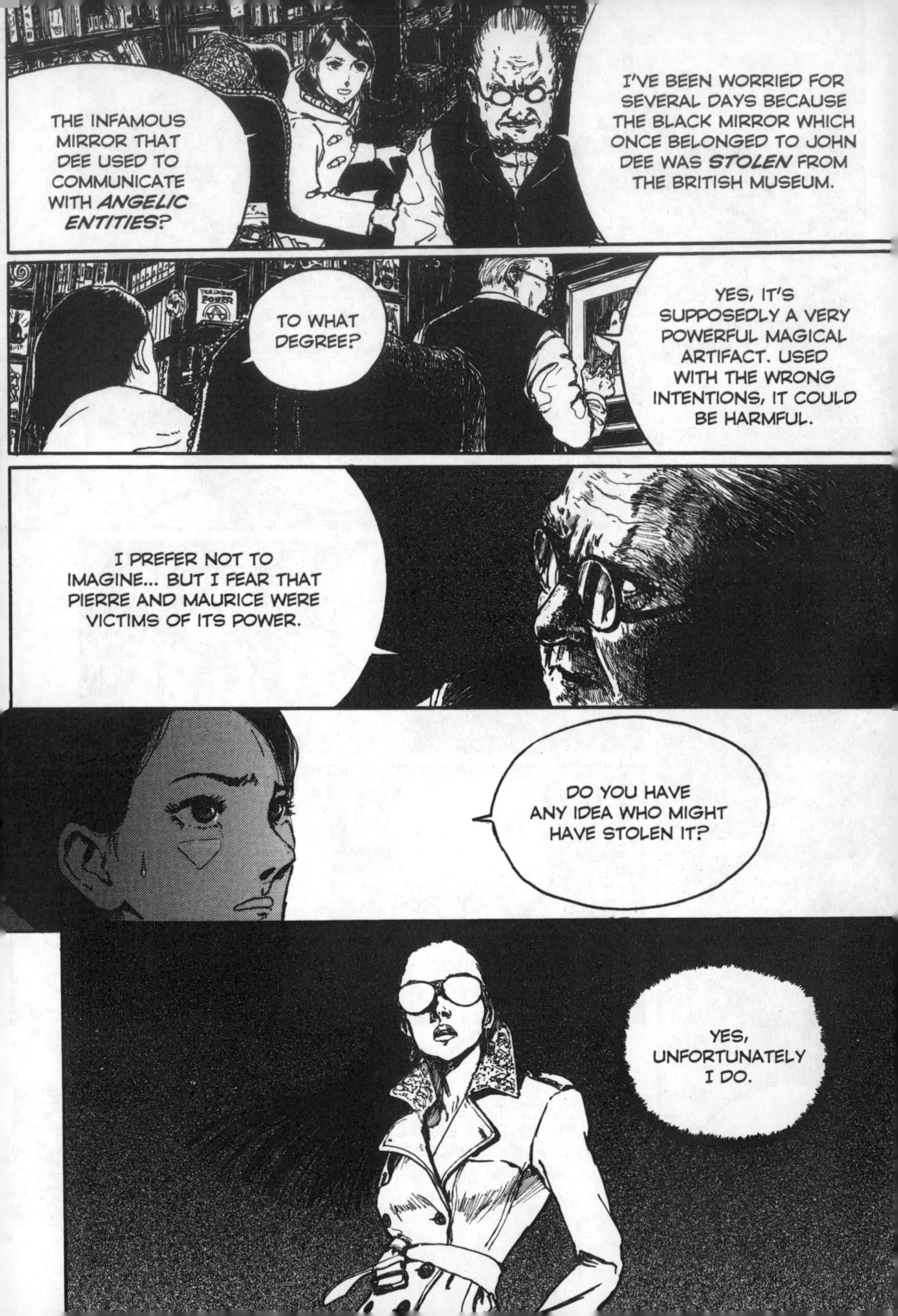
I'VE BEEN WORRIED FOR SEVERAL DAYS BECAUSE THE BLACK MIRROR WHICH ONCE BELONGED TO JOHN DEE WAS *STOLEN* FROM THE BRITISH MUSEUM.
THE INFAMOUS MIRROR THAT DEE USED TO COMMUNICATE WITH *ANGELIC ENTITIES*?
YES, IT'S SUPPOSEDLY A VERY POWERFUL MAGICAL ARTIFACT. USED WITH THE WRONG INTENTIONS, IT COULD BE HARMFUL.
TO WHAT DEGREE?
I PREFER NOT TO IMAGINE... BUT I FEAR THAT PIERRE AND MAURICE WERE VICTIMS OF ITS POWER.
DO YOU HAVE ANY IDEA WHO MIGHT HAVE STOLEN IT?
YES, UNFORTUNATELY I DO.

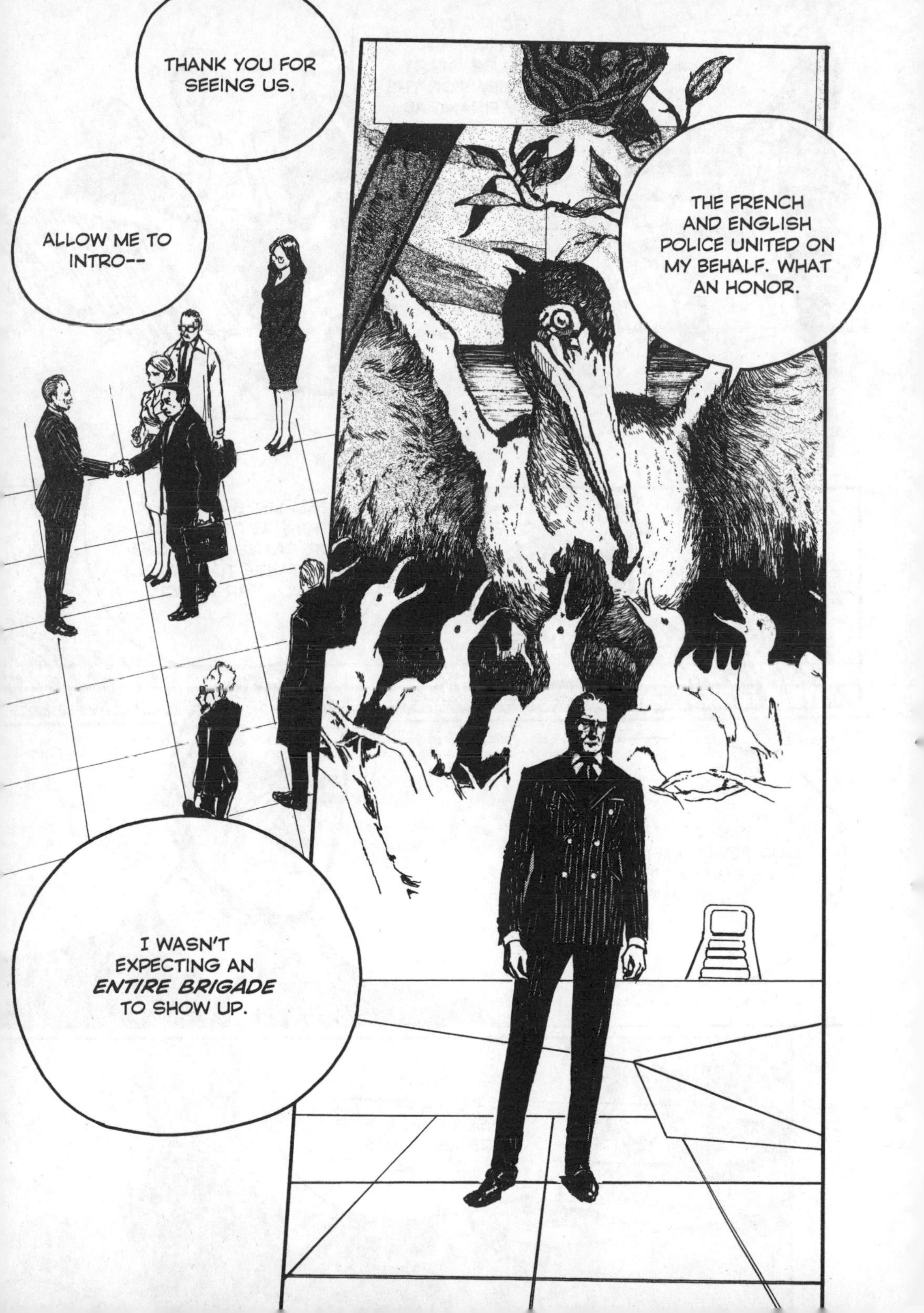
THANK YOU FOR SEEING US.
ALLOW ME TO INTRO--
THE FRENCH AND ENGLISH POLICE UNITED ON MY BEHALF. WHAT AN HONOR.
I WASN'T EXPECTING AN *ENTIRE BRIGADE* TO SHOW UP.

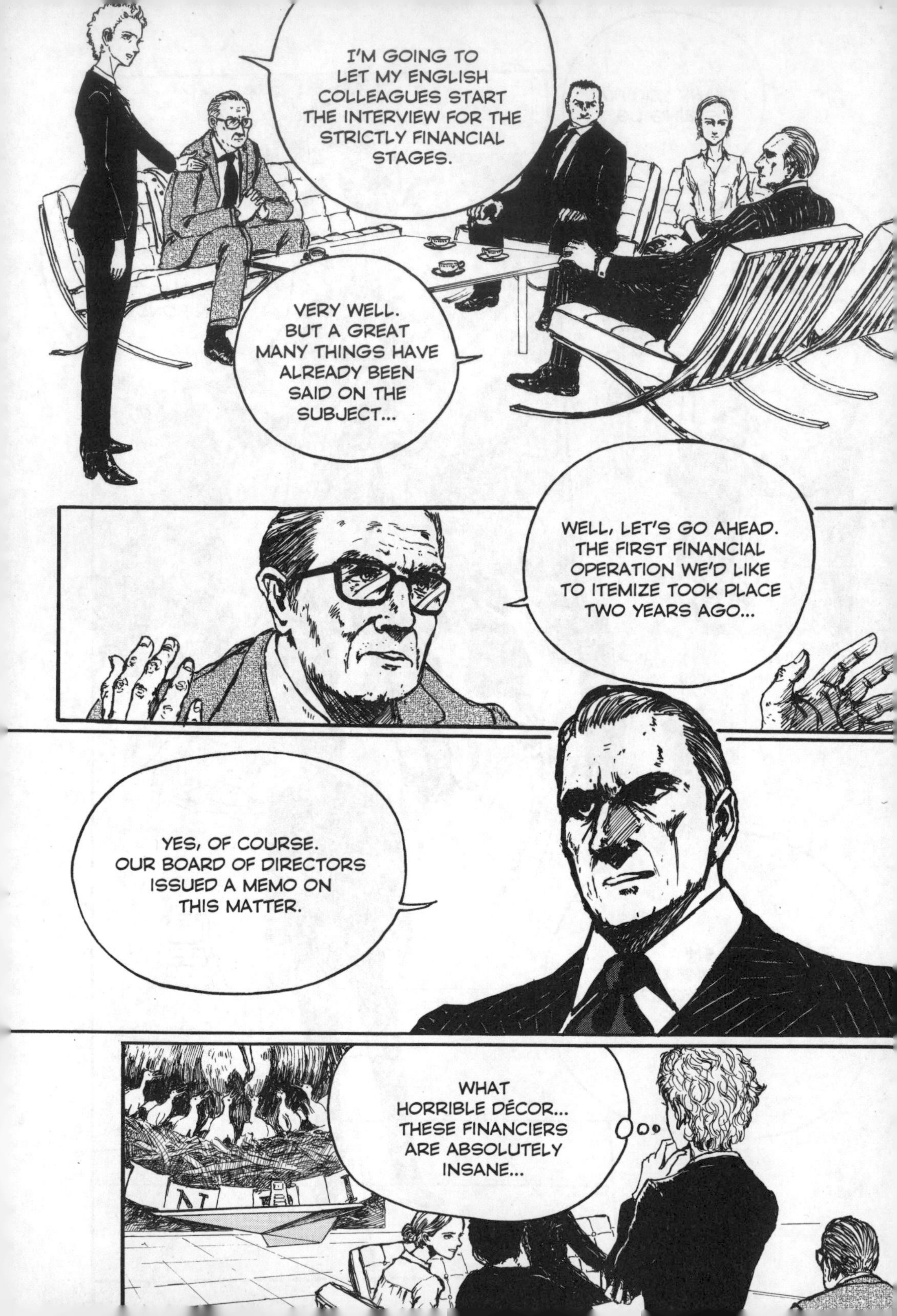
I'M GOING TO LET MY ENGLISH COLLEAGUES START THE INTERVIEW FOR THE STRICTLY FINANCIAL STAGES.
VERY WELL. BUT A GREAT MANY THINGS HAVE ALREADY BEEN SAID ON THE SUBJECT...
WELL, LET'S GO AHEAD. THE FIRST FINANCIAL OPERATION WE'D LIKE TO ITEMIZE TOOK PLACE TWO YEARS AGO...
YES, OF COURSE. OUR BOARD OF DIRECTORS ISSUED A MEMO ON THIS MATTER.
WHAT HORRIBLE DÉCOR... THESE FINANCIERS ARE ABSOLUTELY INSANE...

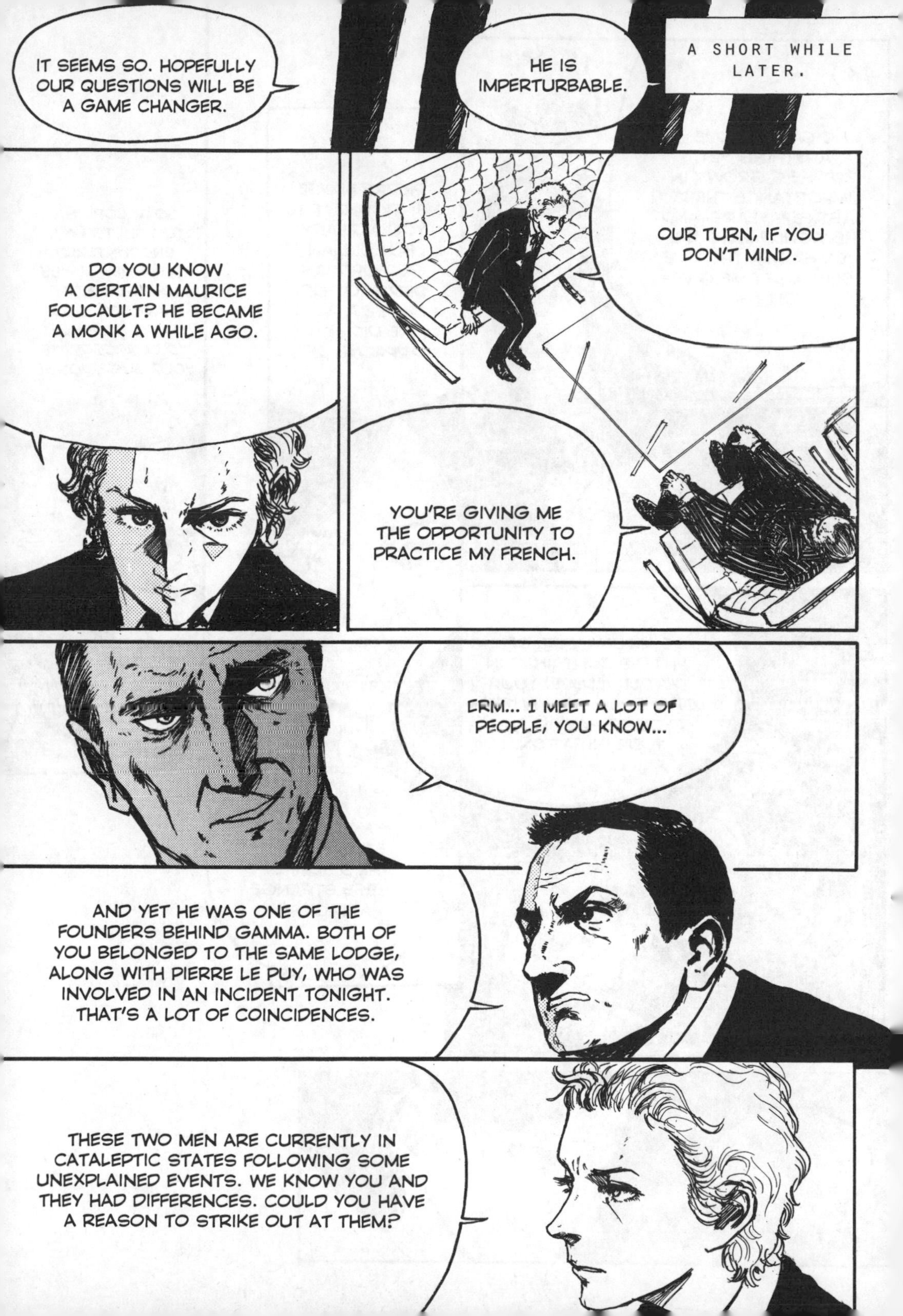
A SHORT WHILE LATER.
HE IS IMPERTURBABLE.
IT SEEMS SO. HOPEFULLY OUR QUESTIONS WILL BE A GAME CHANGER.
OUR TURN, IF YOU DON'T MIND.
YOU'RE GIVING ME THE OPPORTUNITY TO PRACTICE MY FRENCH.
DO YOU KNOW A CERTAIN MAURICE FOUCAULT? HE BECAME A MONK A WHILE AGO.
ERM... I MEET A LOT OF PEOPLE, YOU KNOW...
AND YET HE WAS ONE OF THE FOUNDERS BEHIND GAMMA. BOTH OF YOU BELONGED TO THE SAME LODGE, ALONG WITH PIERRE LE PUY, WHO WAS INVOLVED IN AN INCIDENT TONIGHT. THAT'S A LOT OF COINCIDENCES.
THESE TWO MEN ARE CURRENTLY IN CATALEPTIC STATES FOLLOWING SOME UNEXPLAINED EVENTS. WE KNOW YOU AND THEY HAD DIFFERENCES. COULD YOU HAVE A REASON TO STRIKE OUT AT THEM?

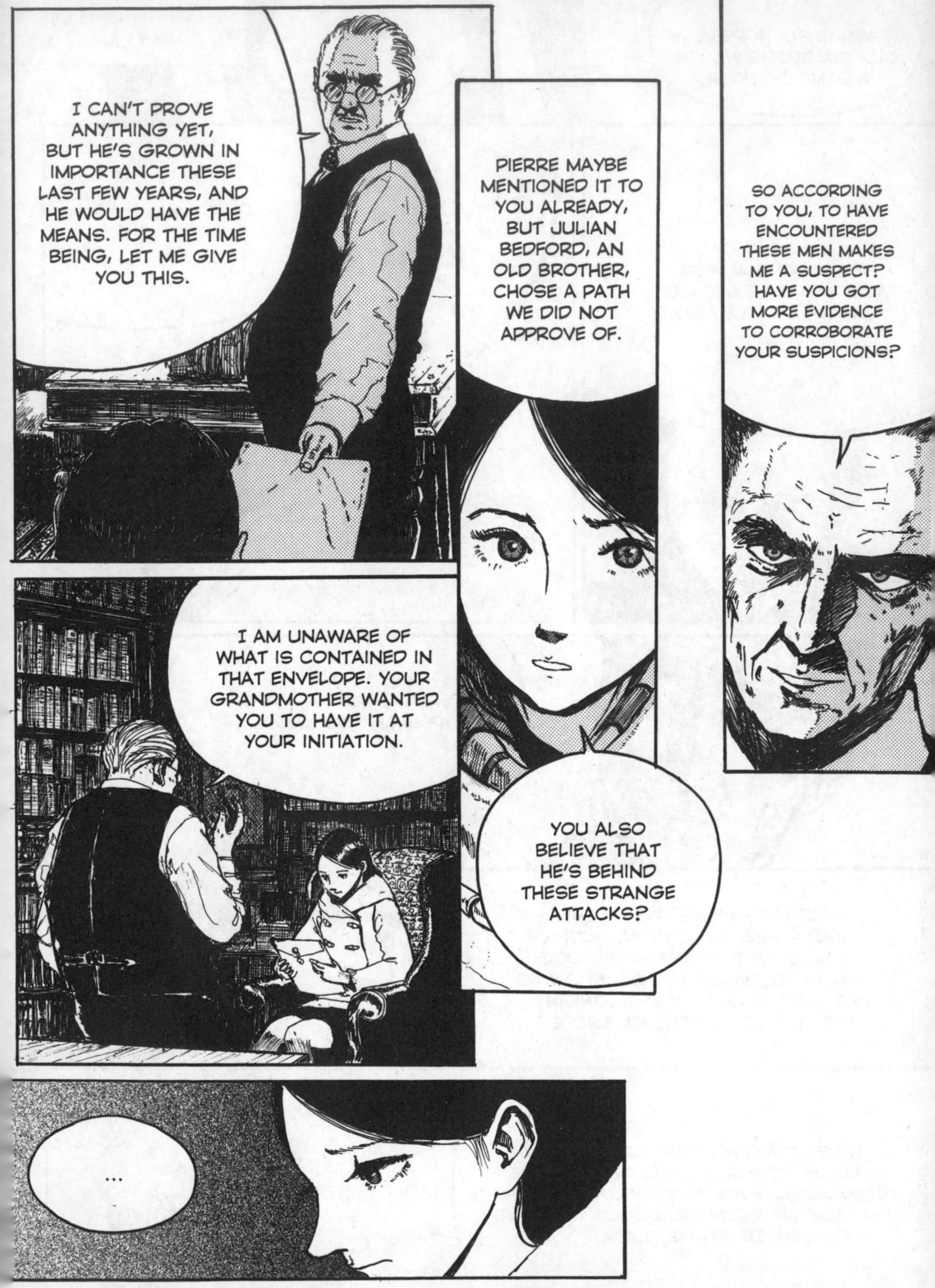
SO ACCORDING TO YOU, TO HAVE ENCOUNTERED THESE MEN MAKES ME A SUSPECT? HAVE YOU GOT MORE EVIDENCE TO CORROBORATE YOUR SUSPICIONS?
PIERRE MAYBE MENTIONED IT TO YOU ALREADY, BUT JULIAN BEDFORD, AN OLD BROTHER, CHOSE A PATH WE DID NOT APPROVE OF.
YOU ALSO BELIEVE THAT HE'S BEHIND THESE STRANGE ATTACKS?
I CAN'T PROVE ANYTHING YET, BUT HE'S GROWN IN IMPORTANCE THESE LAST FEW YEARS, AND HE WOULD HAVE THE MEANS. FOR THE TIME BEING, LET ME GIVE YOU THIS.
I AM UNAWARE OF WHAT IS CONTAINED IN THAT ENVELOPE. YOUR GRANDMOTHER WANTED YOU TO HAVE IT AT YOUR INITIATION.
...

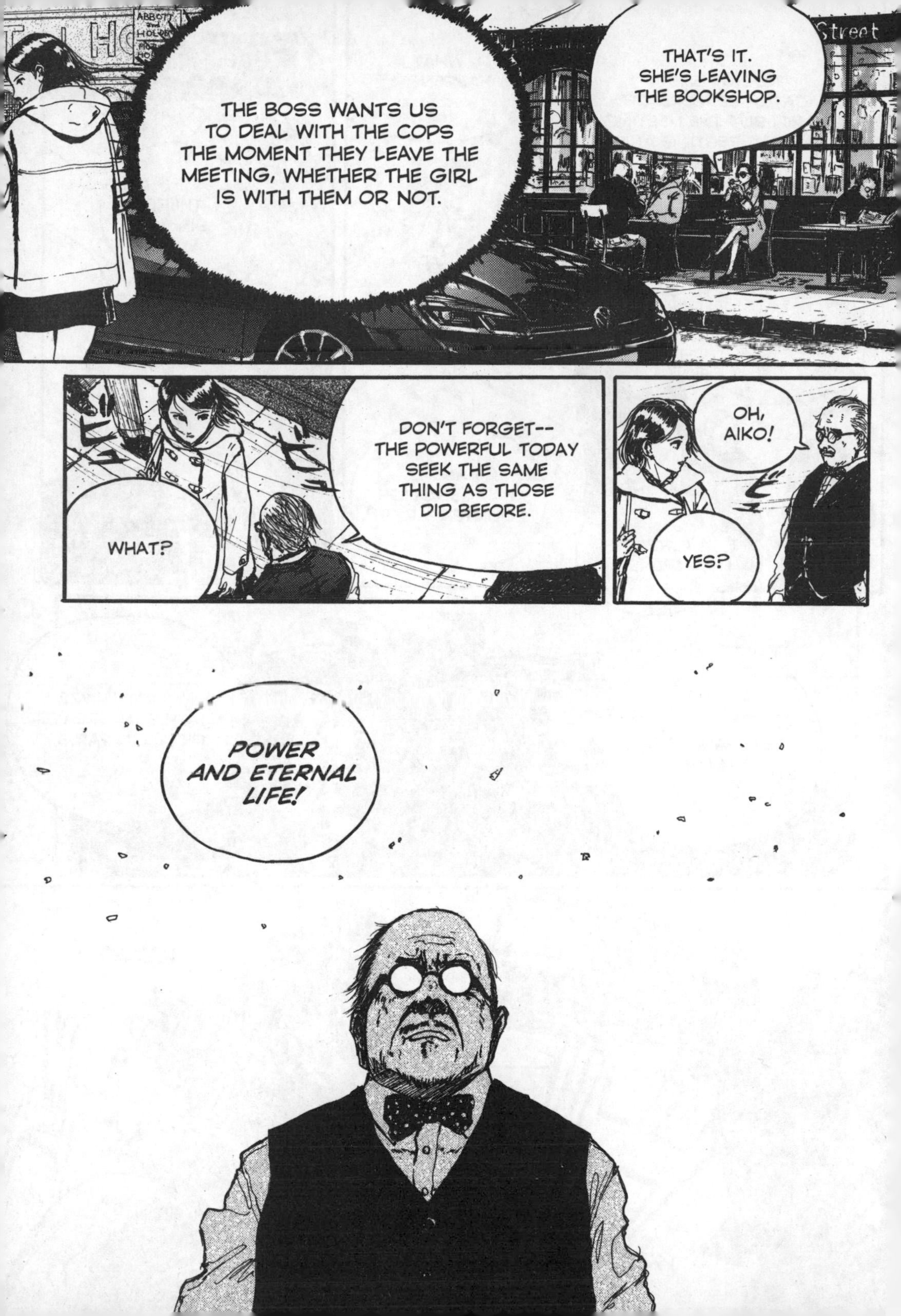
Street
THAT'S IT. SHE'S LEAVING THE BOOKSHOP.
THE BOSS WANTS US TO DEAL WITH THE COPS THE MOMENT THEY LEAVE THE MEETING, WHETHER THE GIRL IS WITH THEM OR NOT.
OH, AIKO!
YES?
DON'T FORGET-- THE POWERFUL TODAY SEEK THE SAME THING AS THOSE DID BEFORE.
WHAT?
POWER AND ETERNAL LIFE!

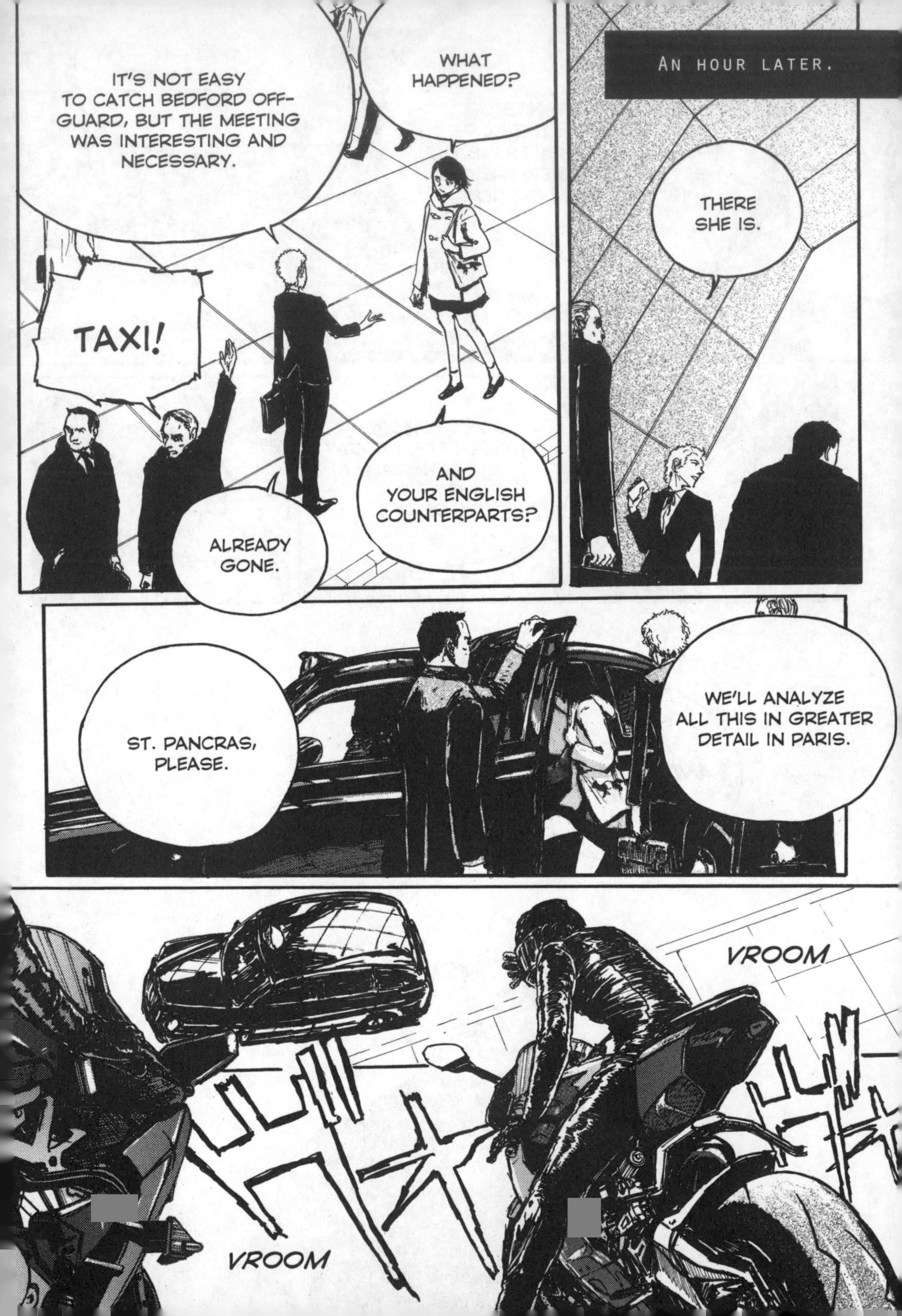
AN HOUR LATER.
THERE SHE IS.
WHAT HAPPENED?
IT'S NOT EASY TO CATCH BEDFORD OFF-GUARD, BUT THE MEETING WAS INTERESTING AND NECESSARY.
TAXI!
AND YOUR ENGLISH COUNTERPARTS?
ALREADY GONE.
WE'LL ANALYZE ALL THIS IN GREATER DETAIL IN PARIS.
ST. PANCRAS, PLEASE.
VROOM
VROOM

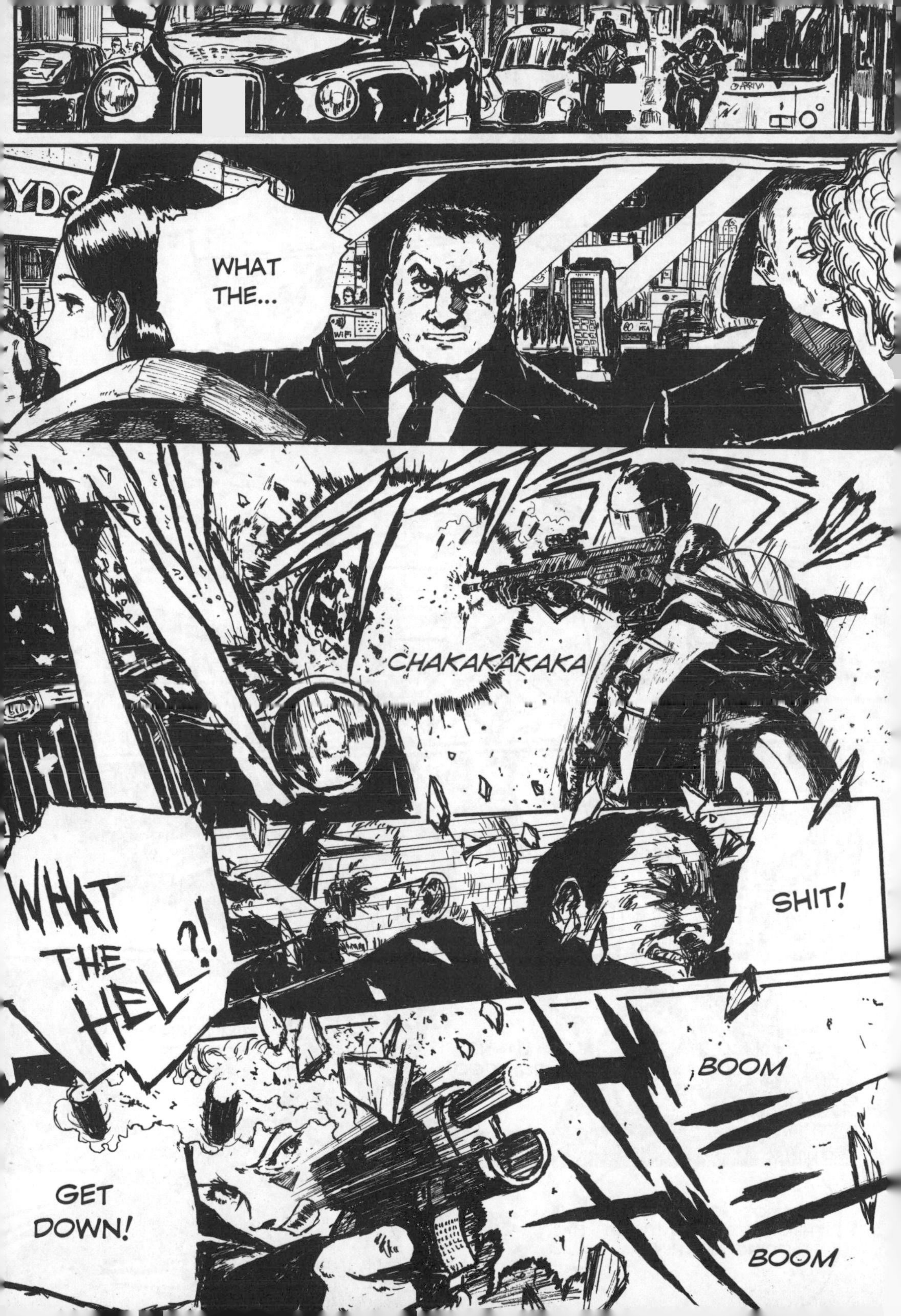
WHAT THE...
CHAKAKAKAKA
SHIT!
WHAT THE HELL?!
BOOM
BOOM
GET DOWN!

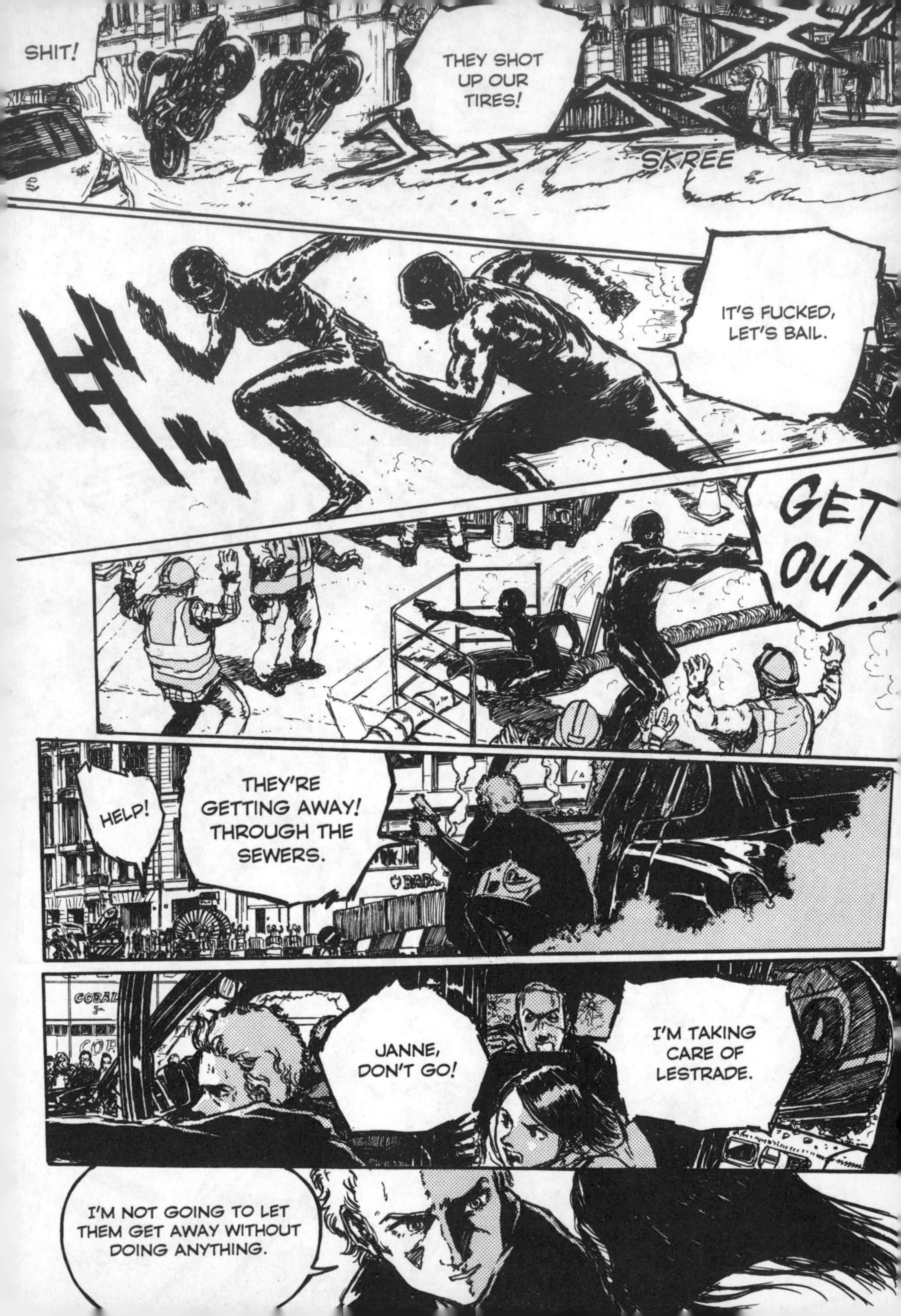
THEY SHOT UP OUR TIRES!
SHIT!
SKREE
IT'S FUCKED, LET'S BAIL.
GET OUT!
THEY'RE GETTING AWAY! THROUGH THE SEWERS.
HELP!
I'M TAKING CARE OF LESTRADE.
JANNE, DON'T GO!
I'M NOT GOING TO LET THEM GET AWAY WITHOUT DOING ANYTHING.

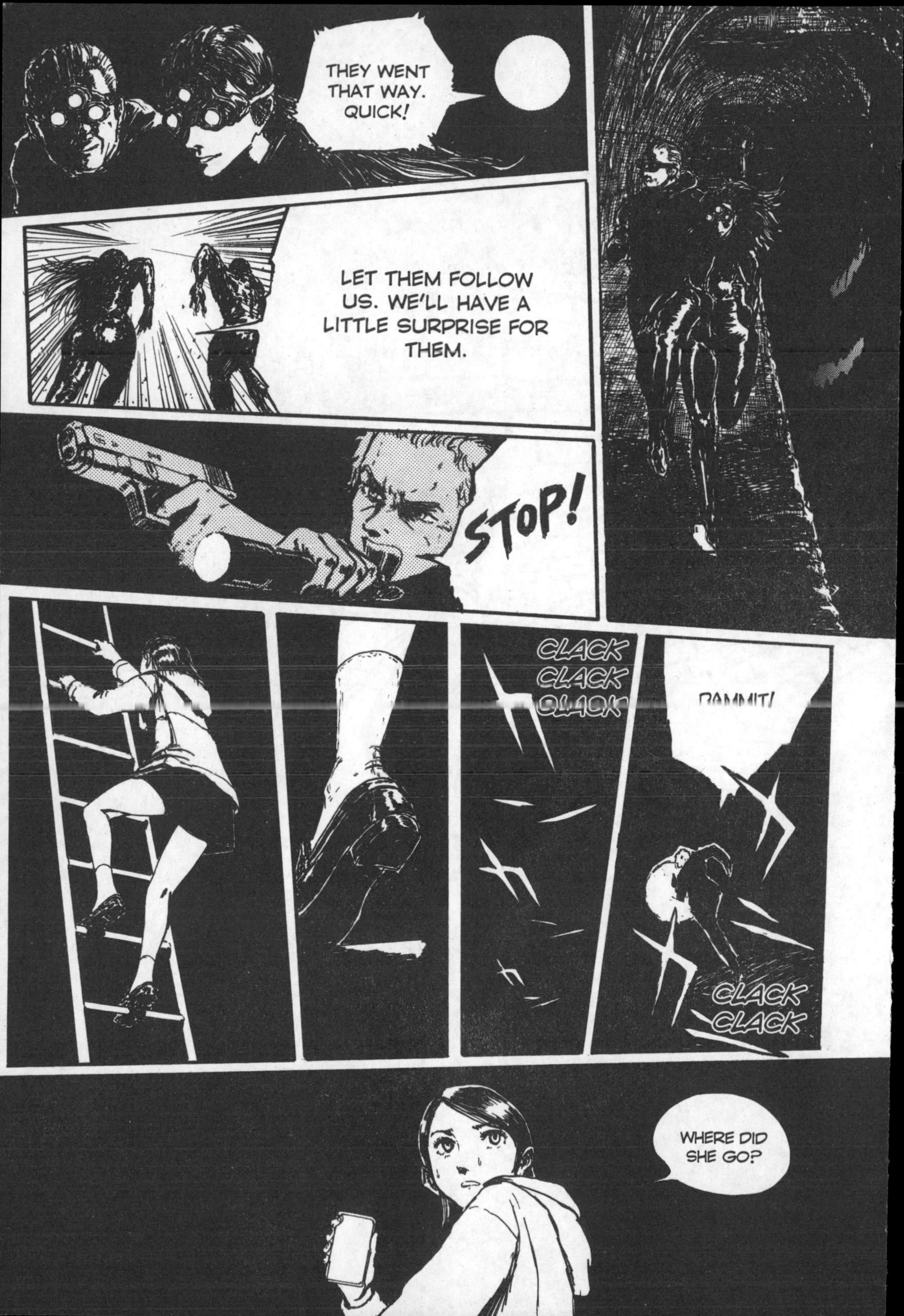
THEY WENT THAT WAY. QUICK!
LET THEM FOLLOW US. WE'LL HAVE A LITTLE SURPRISE FOR THEM.
STOP!
DAMMIT!
CLACK CLACK
CLACK CLACK CLACK
WHERE DID SHE GO?

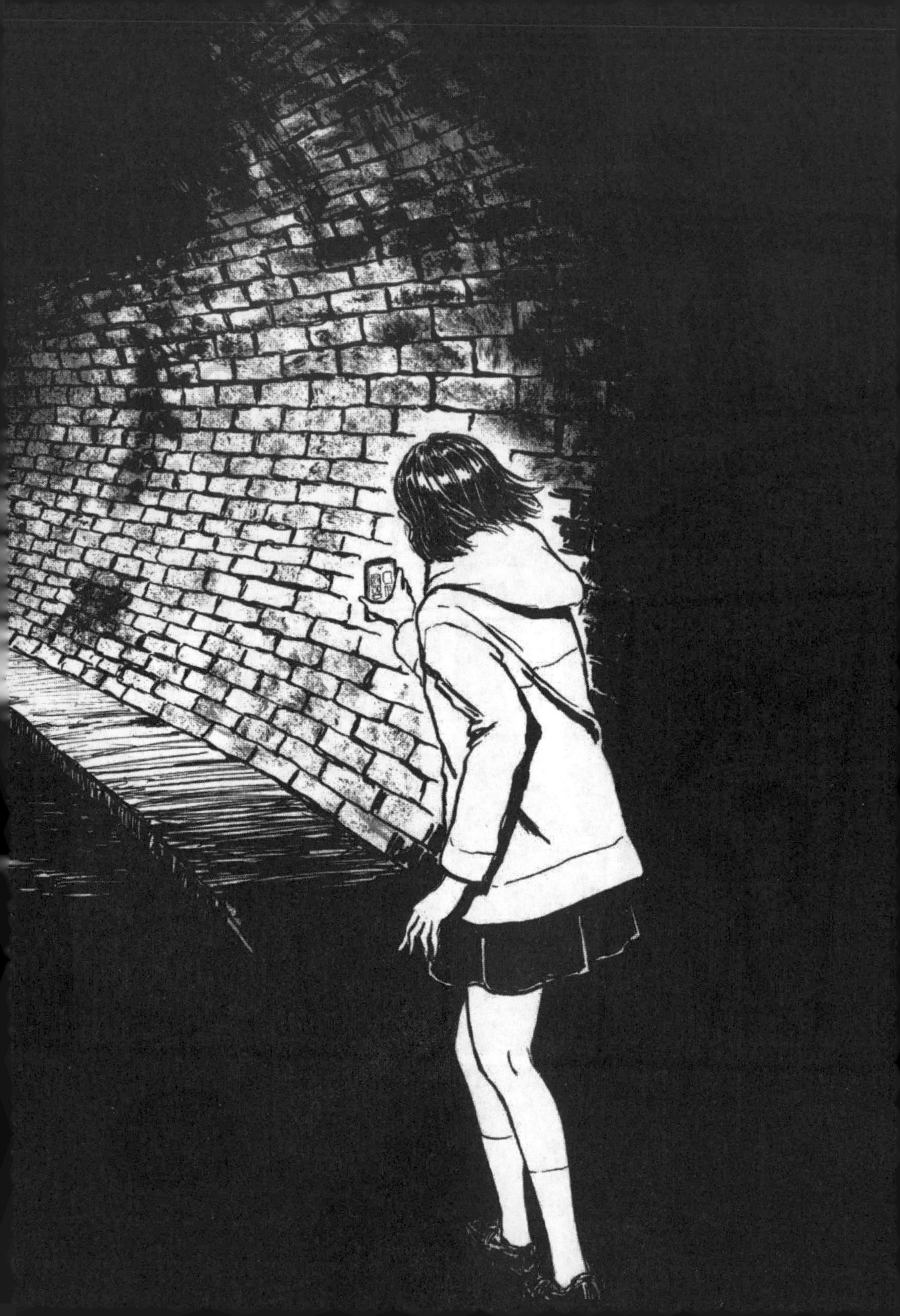

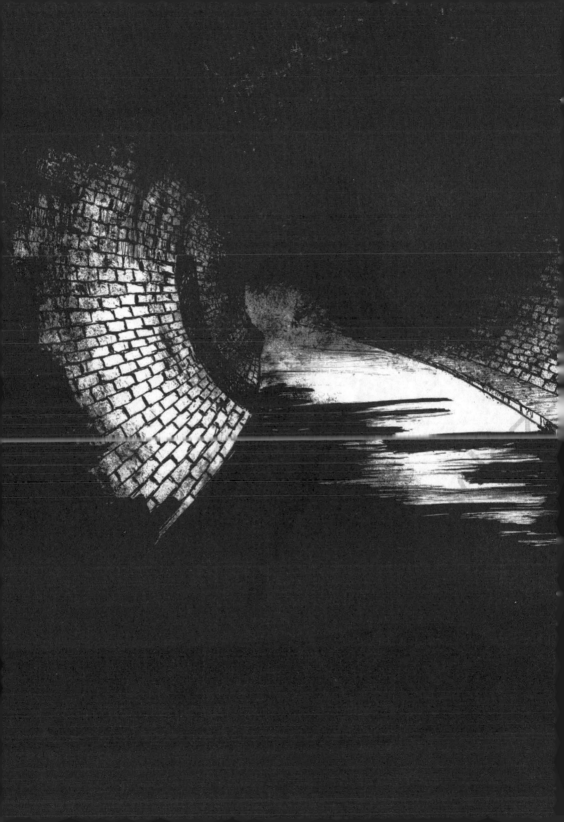

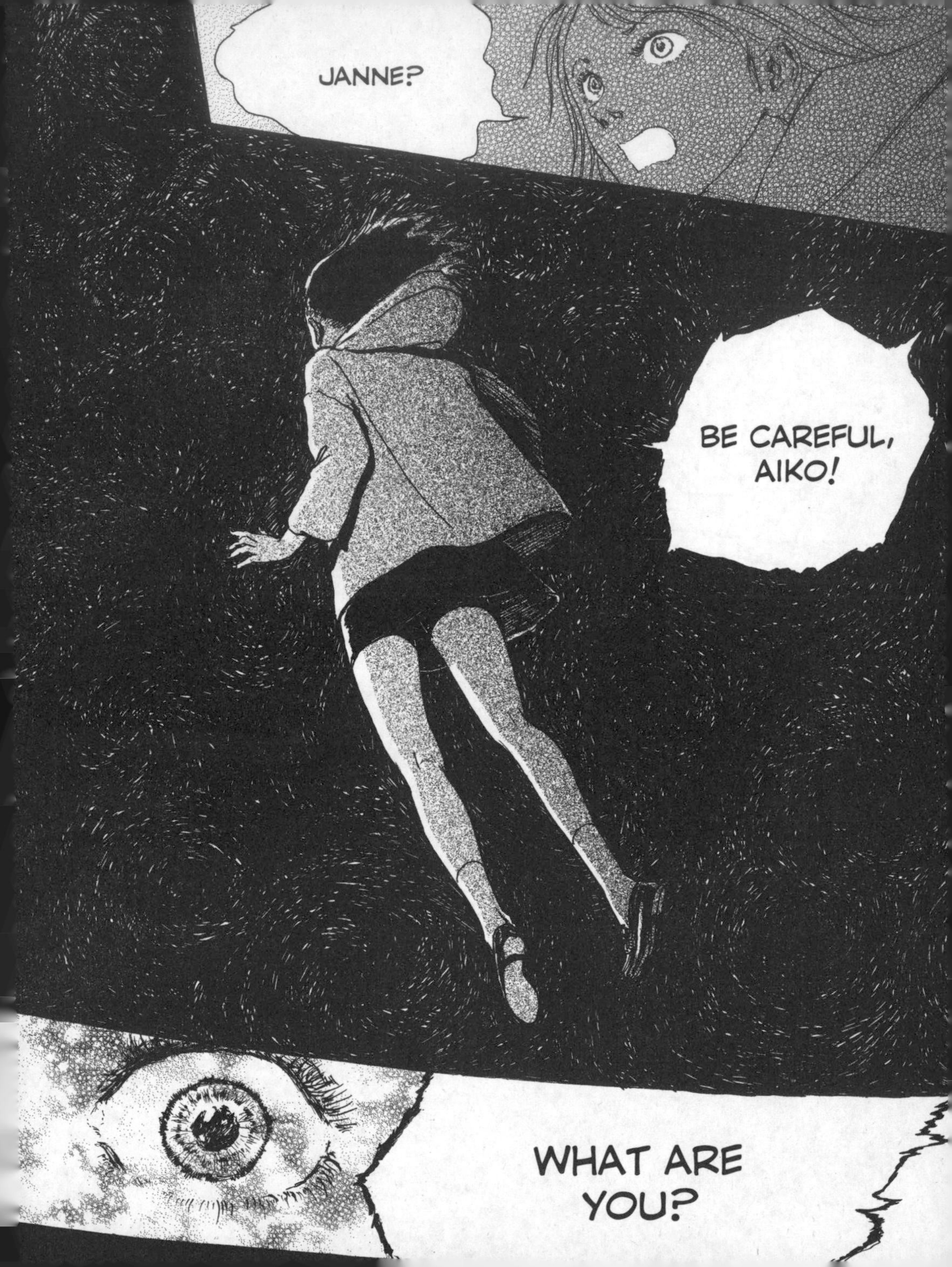
JANNE?
BE CAREFUL, AIKO!
WHAT ARE YOU?

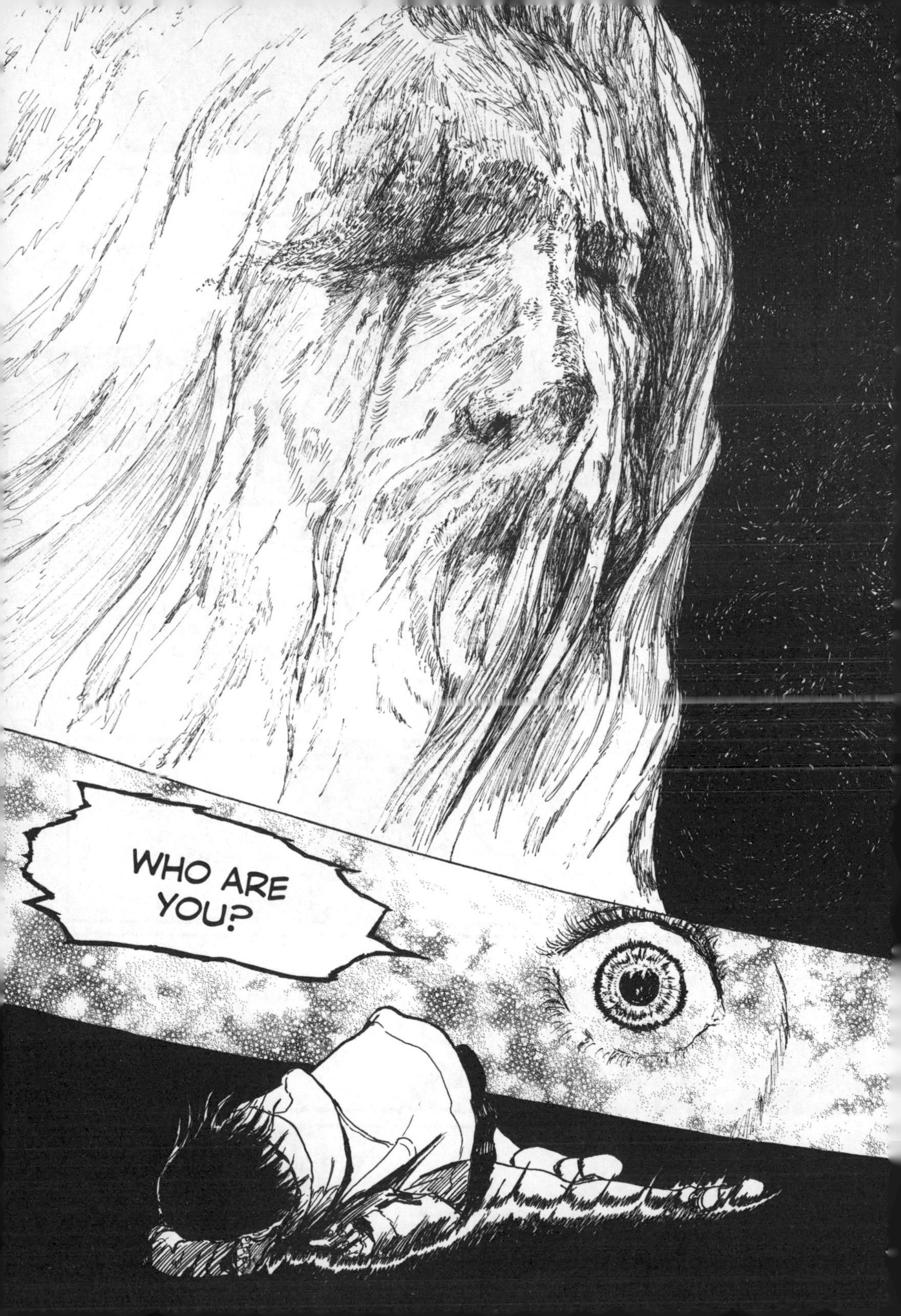
WHO ARE YOU?

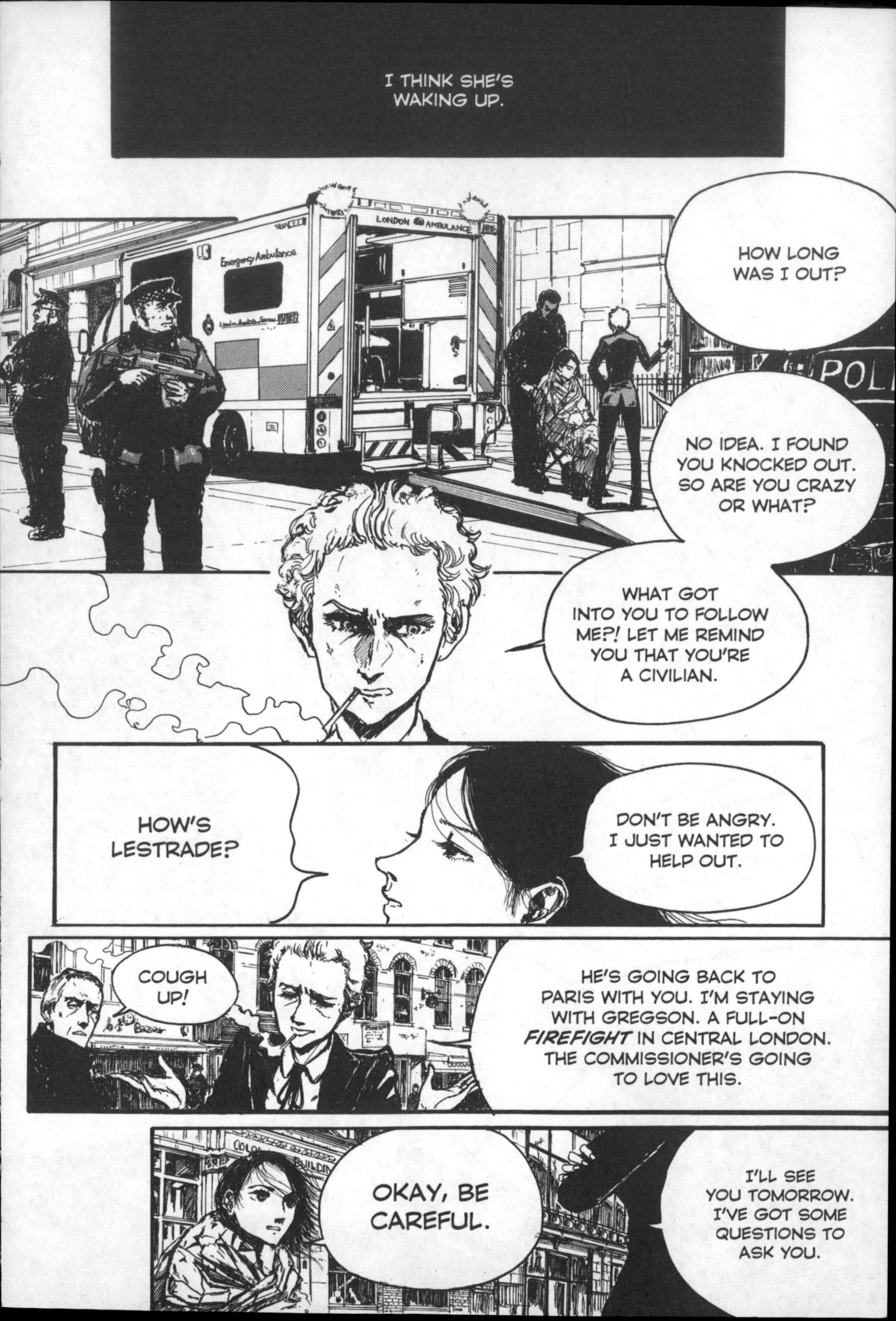
I THINK SHE'S WAKING UP.
HOW LONG WAS I OUT?
NO IDEA. I FOUND YOU KNOCKED OUT. SO ARE YOU CRAZY OR WHAT?
WHAT GOT INTO YOU TO FOLLOW ME?! LET ME REMIND YOU THAT YOU'RE A CIVILIAN.
DON'T BE ANGRY. I JUST WANTED TO HELP OUT.
HOW'S LESTRADE?
HE'S GOING BACK TO PARIS WITH YOU. I'M STAYING WITH GREGSON. A FULL-ON *FIREFIGHT* IN CENTRAL LONDON. THE COMMISSIONER'S GOING TO LOVE THIS.
COUGH UP!
I'LL SEE YOU TOMORROW. I'VE GOT SOME QUESTIONS TO ASK YOU.
OKAY, BE CAREFUL.

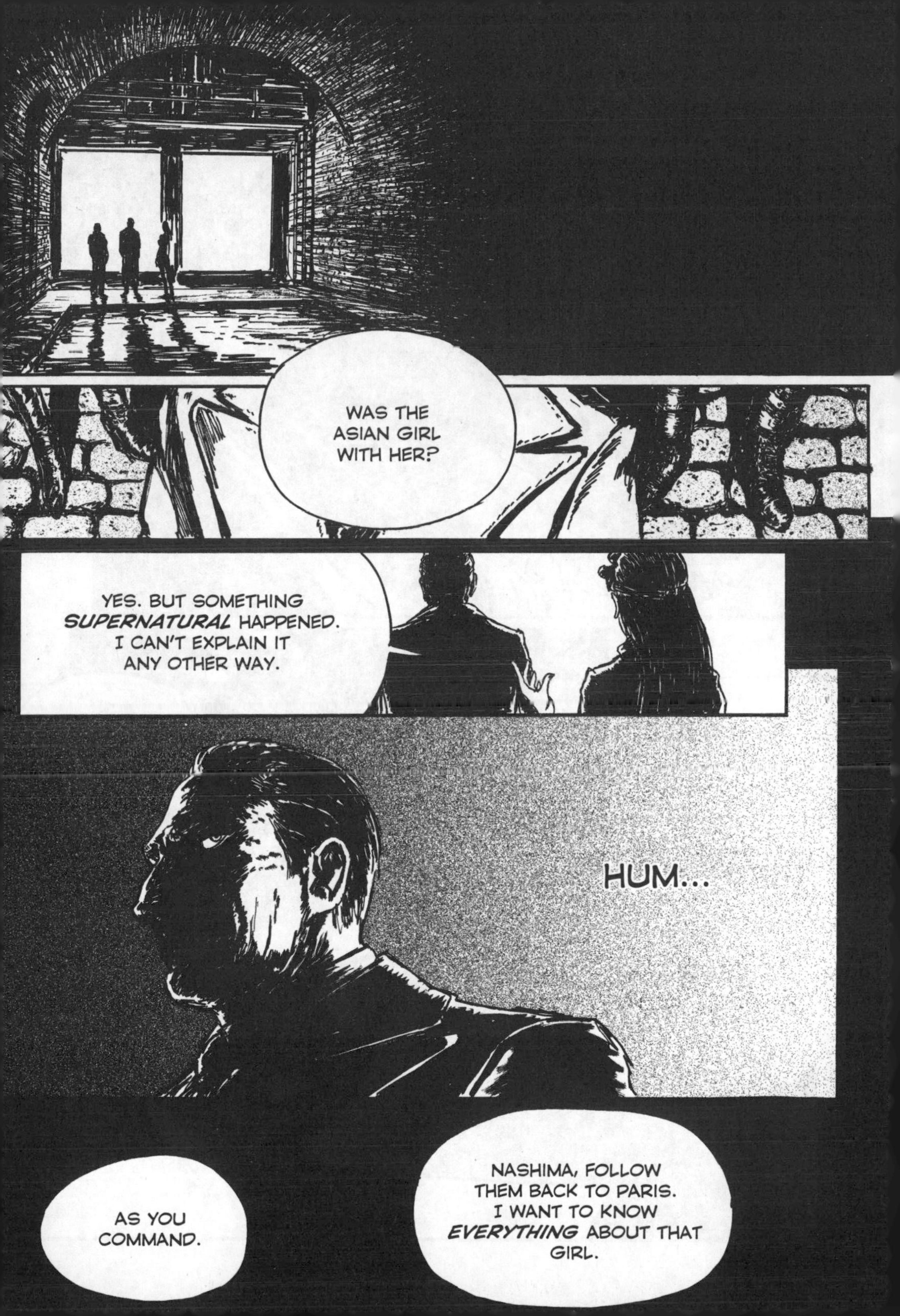
WAS THE ASIAN GIRL WITH HER?
YES. BUT SOMETHING *SUPERNATURAL* HAPPENED. I CAN'T EXPLAIN IT ANY OTHER WAY.
HUM...
NASHIMA, FOLLOW THEM BACK TO PARIS. I WANT TO KNOW *EVERYTHING* ABOUT THAT GIRL.
AS YOU COMMAND.

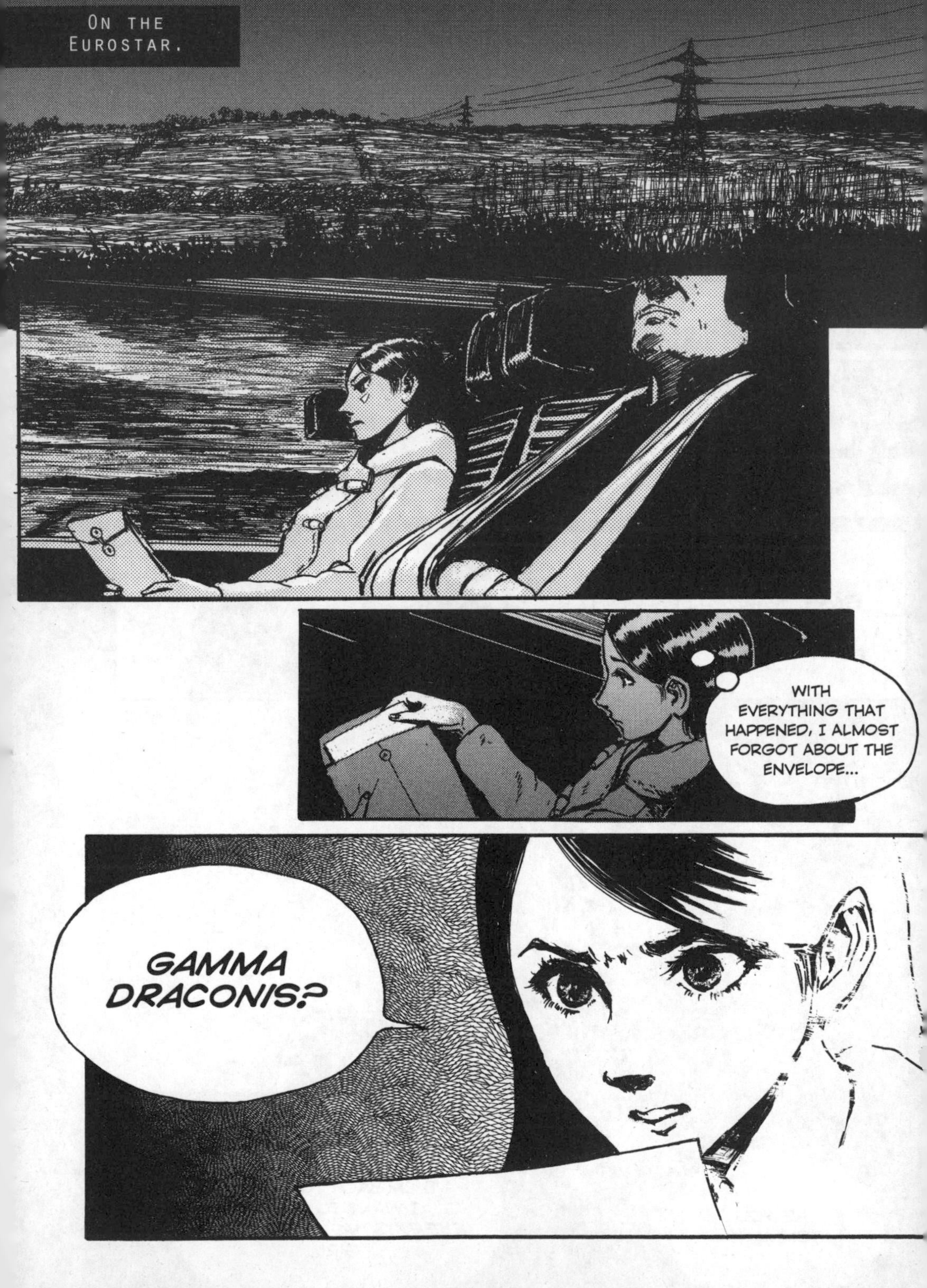
On the Eurostar.
With everything that happened, I almost forgot about the envelope...
Gamma Draconis?

CHAPTER 6

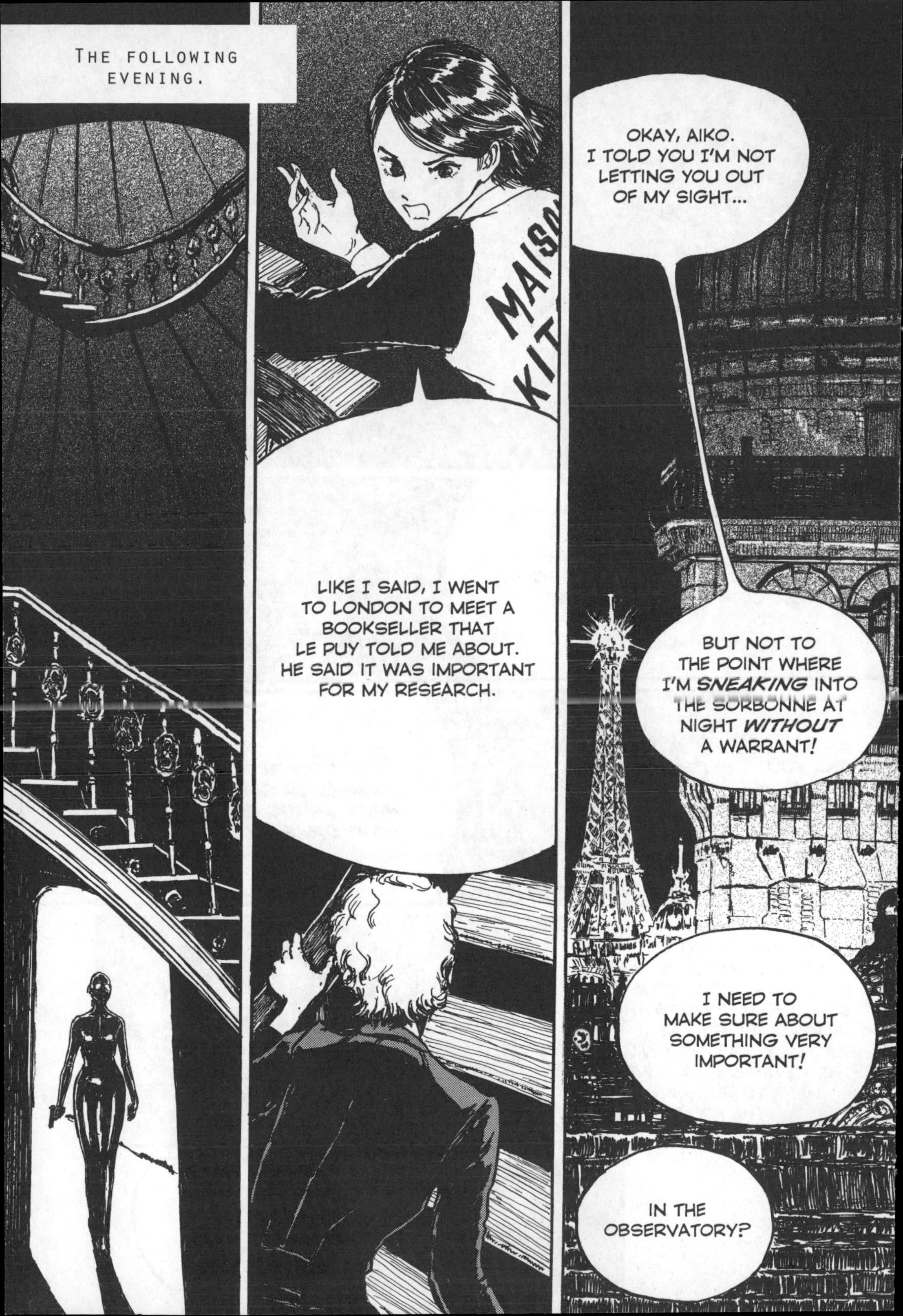
OKAY, AIKO. I TOLD YOU I'M NOT LETTING YOU OUT OF MY SIGHT...
BUT NOT TO THE POINT WHERE I'M *SNEAKING* INTO THE SORBONNE AT NIGHT *WITHOUT* A WARRANT!
I NEED TO MAKE SURE ABOUT SOMETHING VERY IMPORTANT!
IN THE OBSERVATORY?
MAISON KIT
LIKE I SAID, I WENT TO LONDON TO MEET A BOOKSELLER THAT LE PUY TOLD ME ABOUT. HE SAID IT WAS IMPORTANT FOR MY RESEARCH.
THE FOLLOWING EVENING.

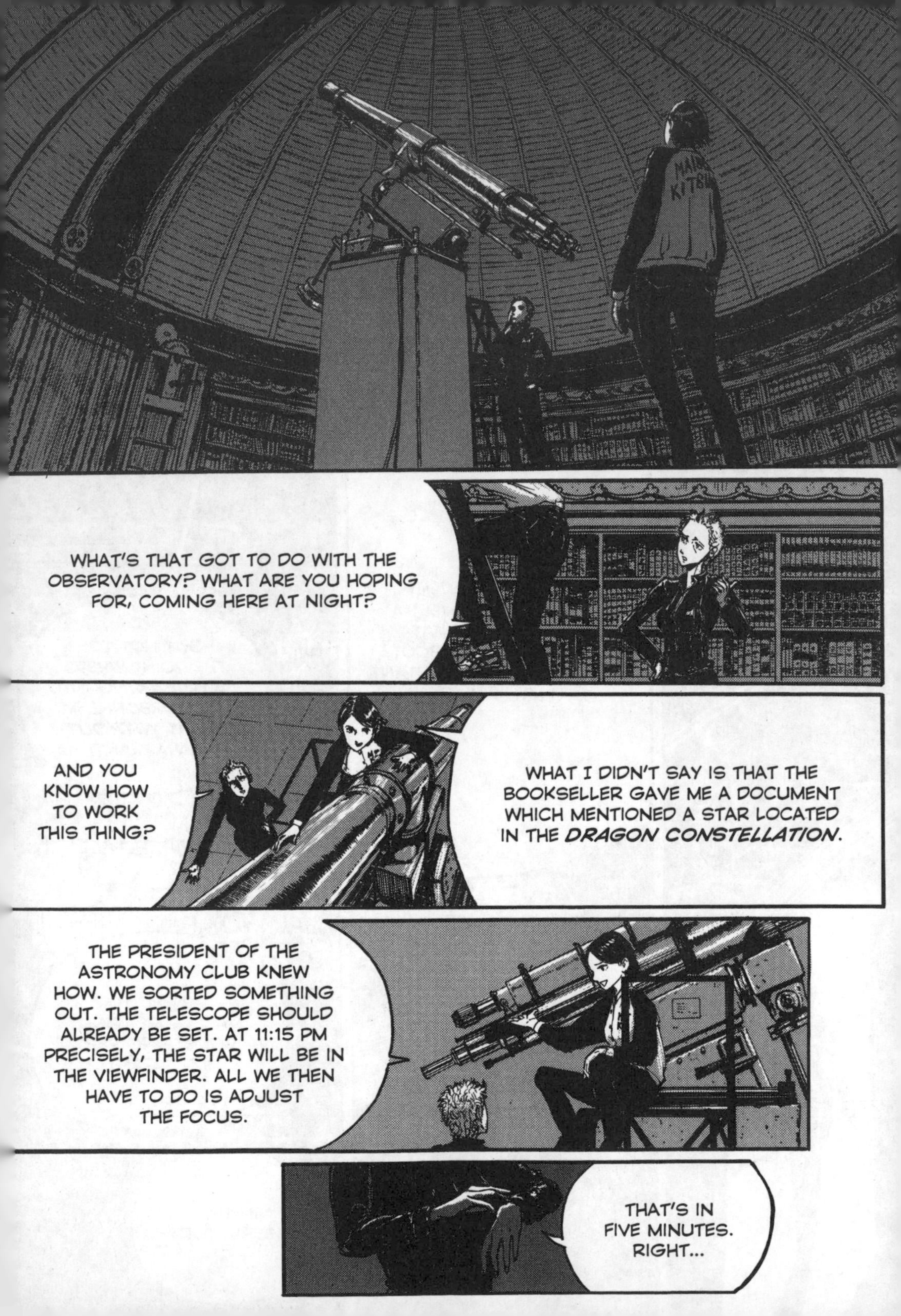
WHAT'S THAT GOT TO DO WITH THE OBSERVATORY? WHAT ARE YOU HOPING FOR, COMING HERE AT NIGHT?
WHAT I DIDN'T SAY IS THAT THE BOOKSELLER GAVE ME A DOCUMENT WHICH MENTIONED A STAR LOCATED IN THE *DRAGON CONSTELLATION*.
AND YOU KNOW HOW TO WORK THIS THING?
THE PRESIDENT OF THE ASTRONOMY CLUB KNEW HOW. WE SORTED SOMETHING OUT. THE TELESCOPE SHOULD ALREADY BE SET. AT 11:15 PM PRECISELY, THE STAR WILL BE IN THE VIEWFINDER. ALL WE THEN HAVE TO DO IS ADJUST THE FOCUS.
THAT'S IN FIVE MINUTES. RIGHT...

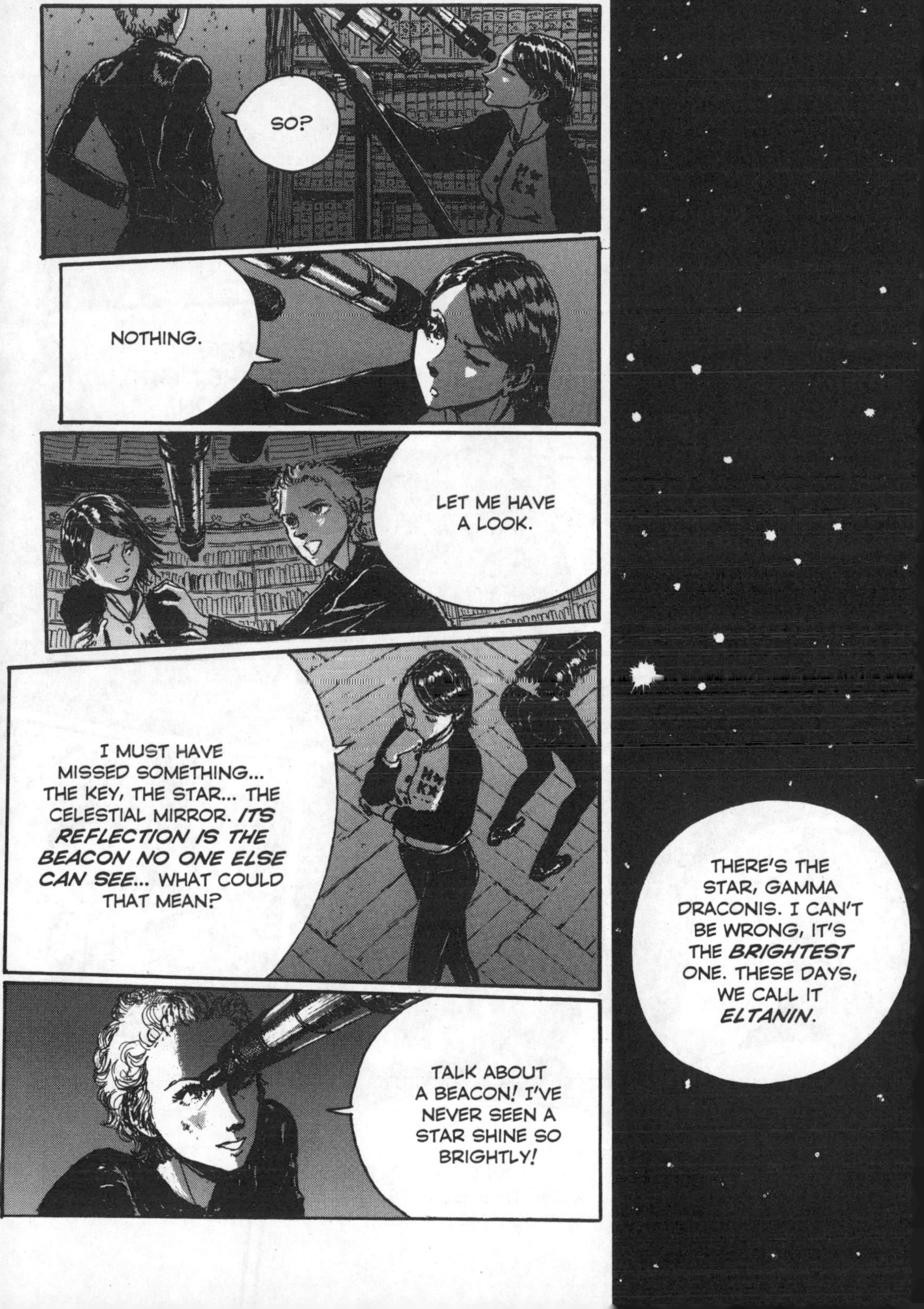
THERE'S THE STAR, GAMMA DRACONIS. I CAN'T BE WRONG, IT'S THE *BRIGHTEST* ONE. THESE DAYS, WE CALL IT *ELTANIN*.
SO?
NOTHING.
LET ME HAVE A LOOK.
I MUST HAVE MISSED SOMETHING... THE KEY, THE STAR... THE CELESTIAL MIRROR. *ITS REFLECTION IS THE BEACON NO ONE ELSE CAN SEE...* WHAT COULD THAT MEAN?
TALK ABOUT A BEACON! I'VE NEVER SEEN A STAR SHINE SO BRIGHTLY!

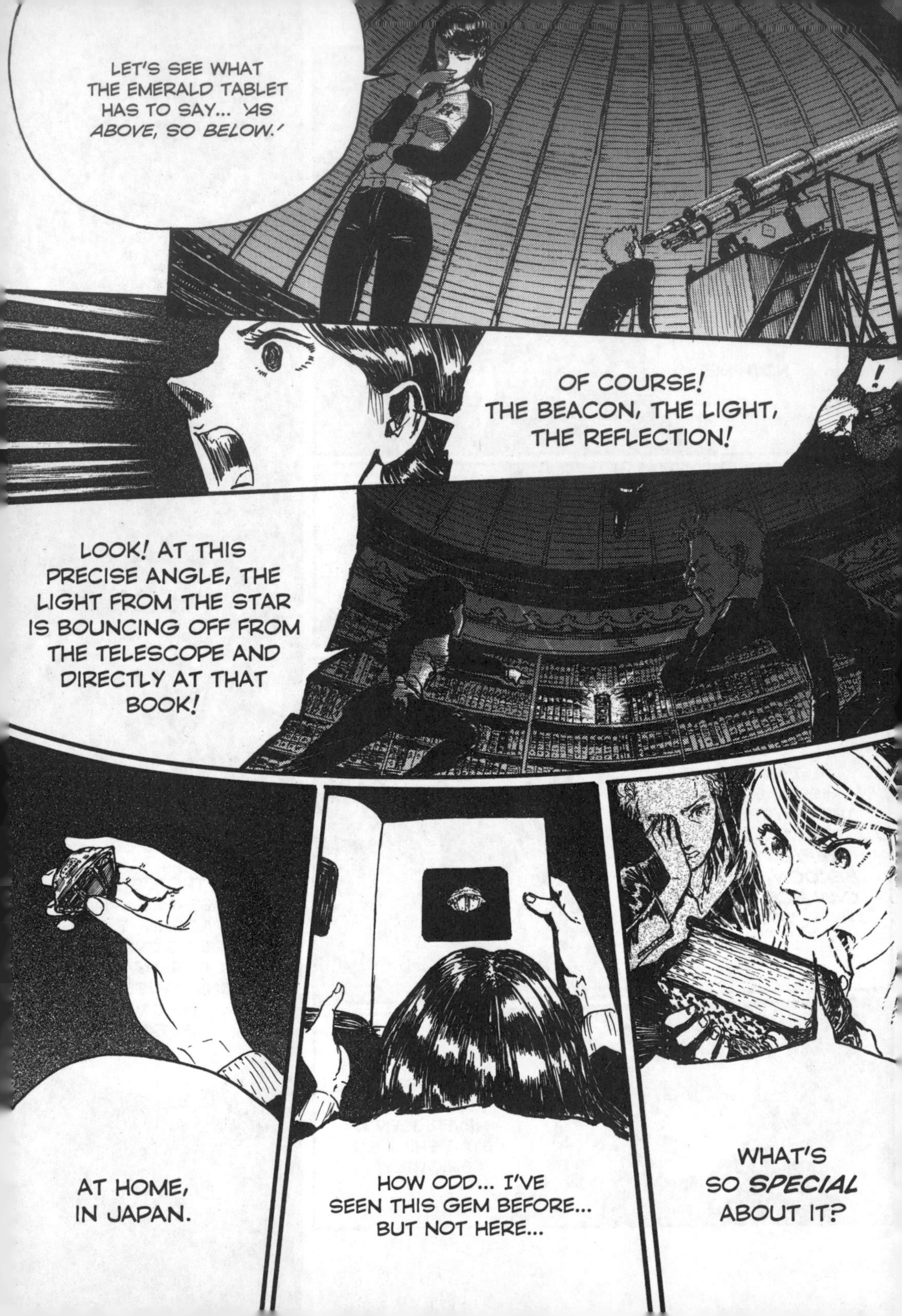
LET'S SEE WHAT THE EMERALD TABLET HAS TO SAY... 'AS *ABOVE*, SO *BELOW*.'
!
OF COURSE! THE BEACON, THE LIGHT, THE REFLECTION!
LOOK! AT THIS PRECISE ANGLE, THE LIGHT FROM THE STAR IS BOUNCING OFF FROM THE TELESCOPE AND DIRECTLY AT THAT BOOK!
WHAT'S SO *SPECIAL* ABOUT IT?
HOW ODD... I'VE SEEN THIS GEM BEFORE... BUT NOT HERE...
AT HOME, IN JAPAN.

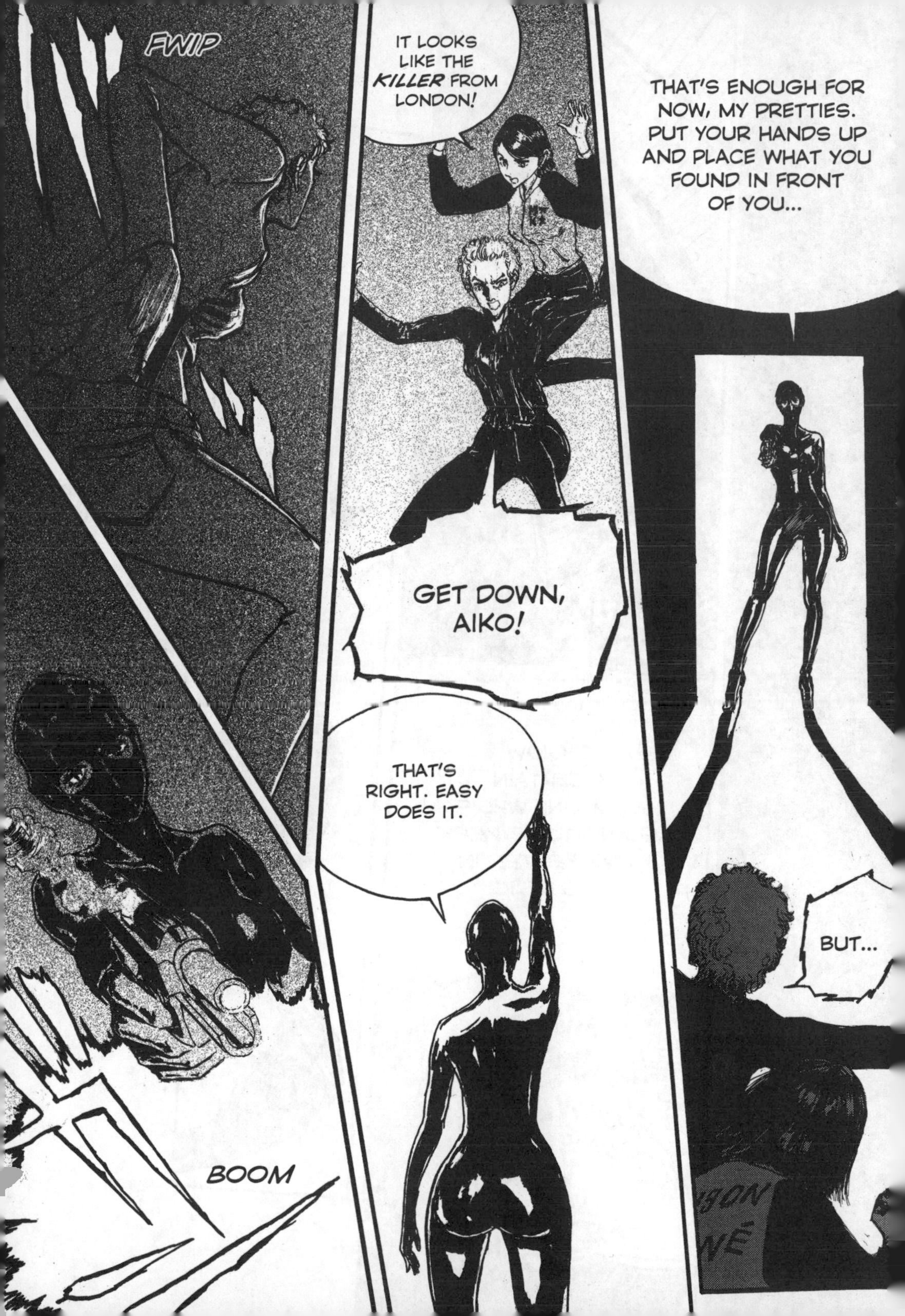
THAT'S ENOUGH FOR NOW, MY PRETTIES. PUT YOUR HANDS UP AND PLACE WHAT YOU FOUND IN FRONT OF YOU...
BUT...
IT LOOKS LIKE THE *KILLER* FROM LONDON!
GET DOWN, AIKO!
THAT'S RIGHT. EASY DOES IT.
FWIP
BOOM

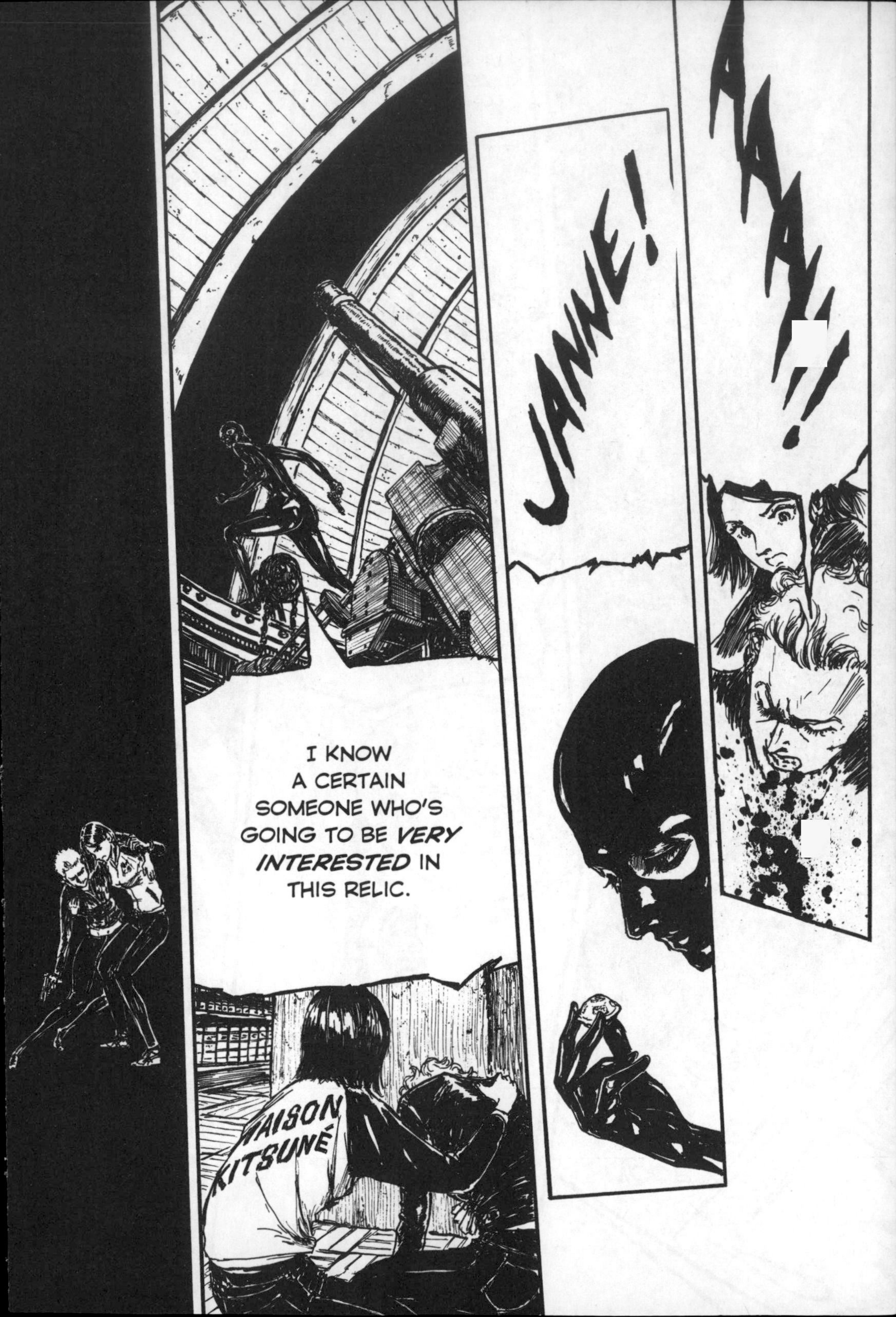
AAAA!!
JANNE!
I KNOW A CERTAIN SOMEONE WHO'S GOING TO BE ***VERY INTERESTED*** IN THIS RELIC.
MAISON KITSUNÉ

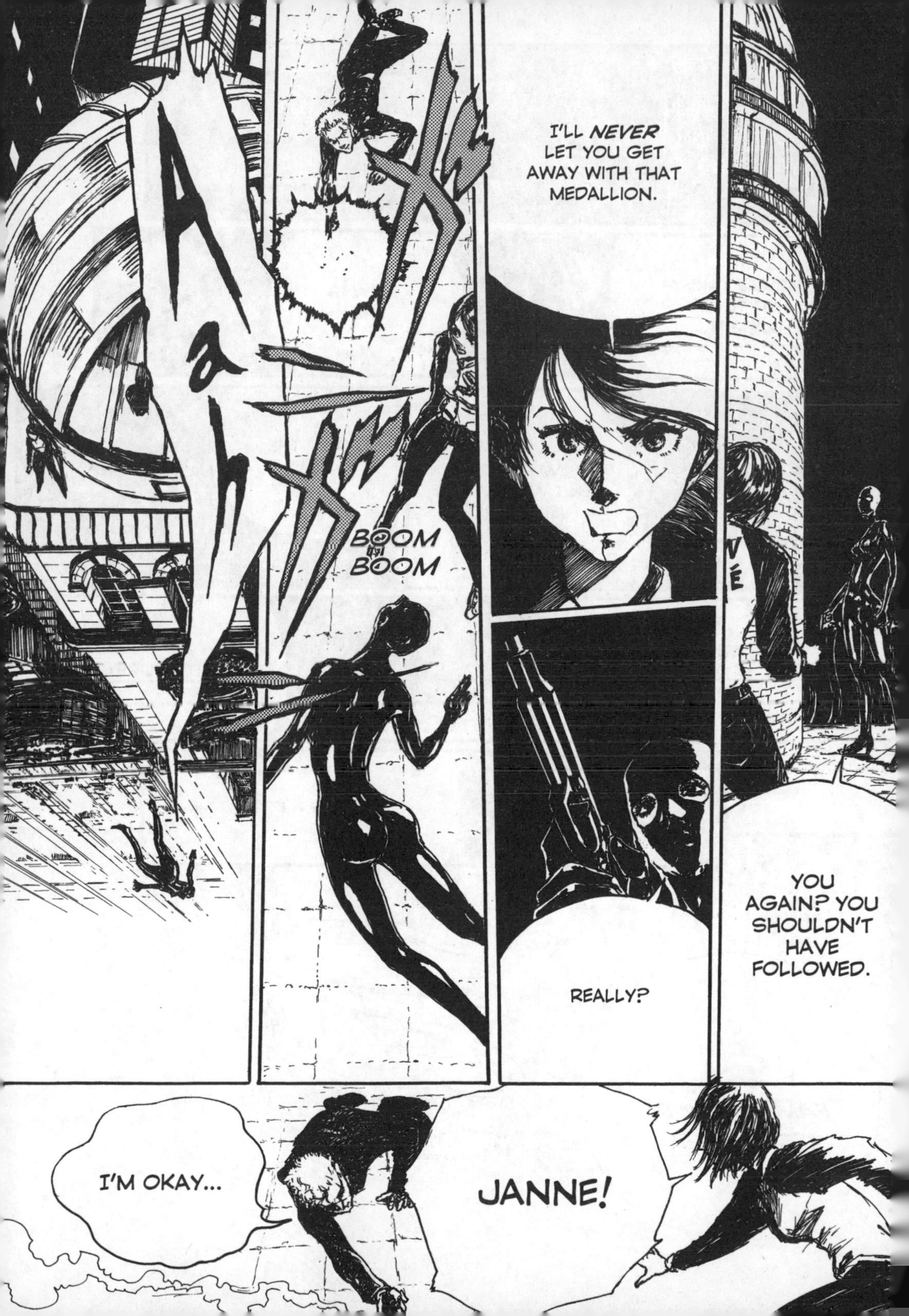
YOU AGAIN? YOU SHOULDN'T HAVE FOLLOWED.
I'LL NEVER LET YOU GET AWAY WITH THAT MEDALLION.
REALLY?
BOOM BOOM
Aah
JANNE!
I'M OKAY...

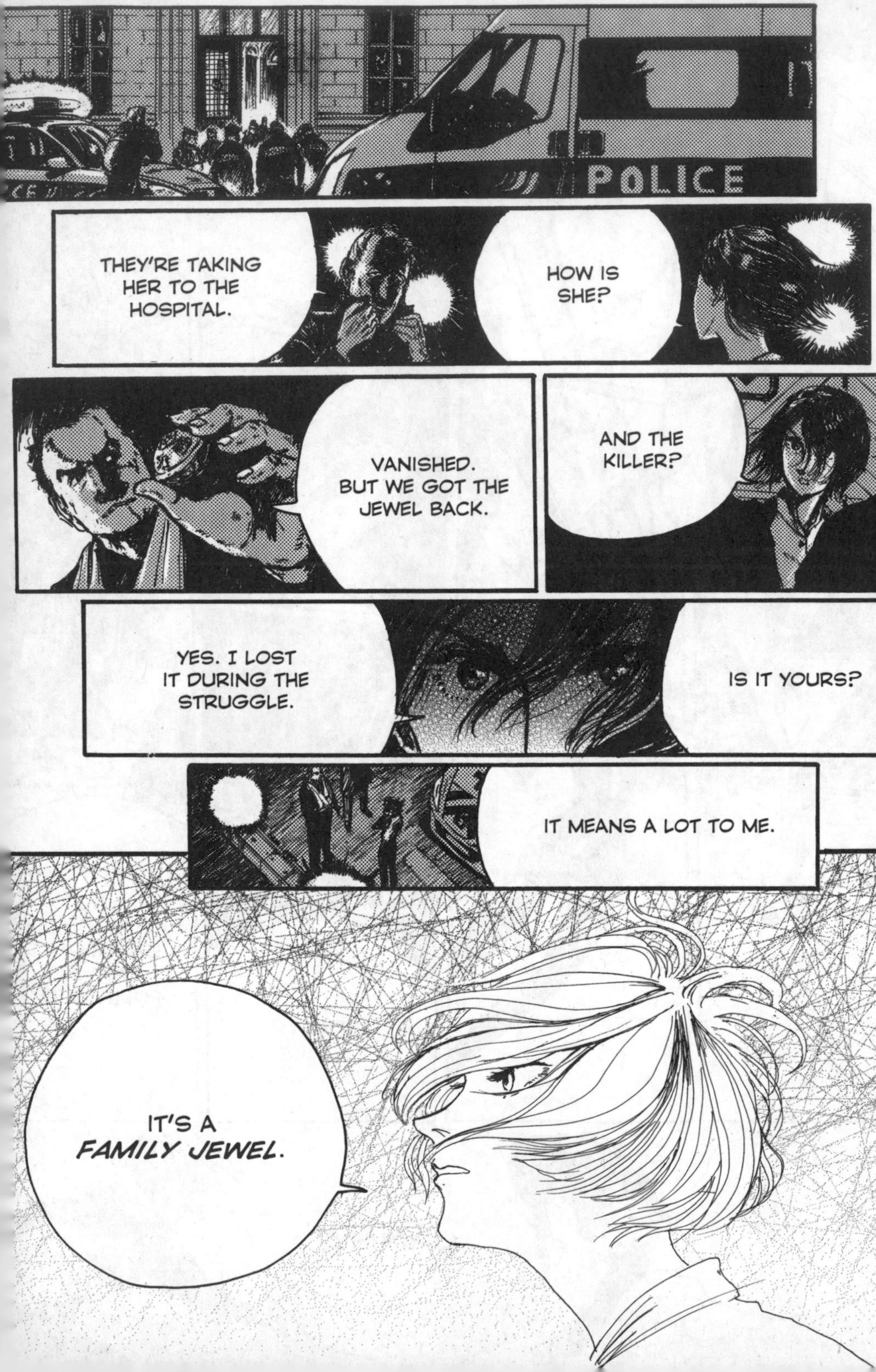
POLICE
HOW IS SHE?
THEY'RE TAKING HER TO THE HOSPITAL.
AND THE KILLER?
VANISHED. BUT WE GOT THE JEWEL BACK.
IS IT YOURS?
YES. I LOST IT DURING THE STRUGGLE.
IT MEANS A LOT TO ME.
IT'S A *FAMILY JEWEL*.

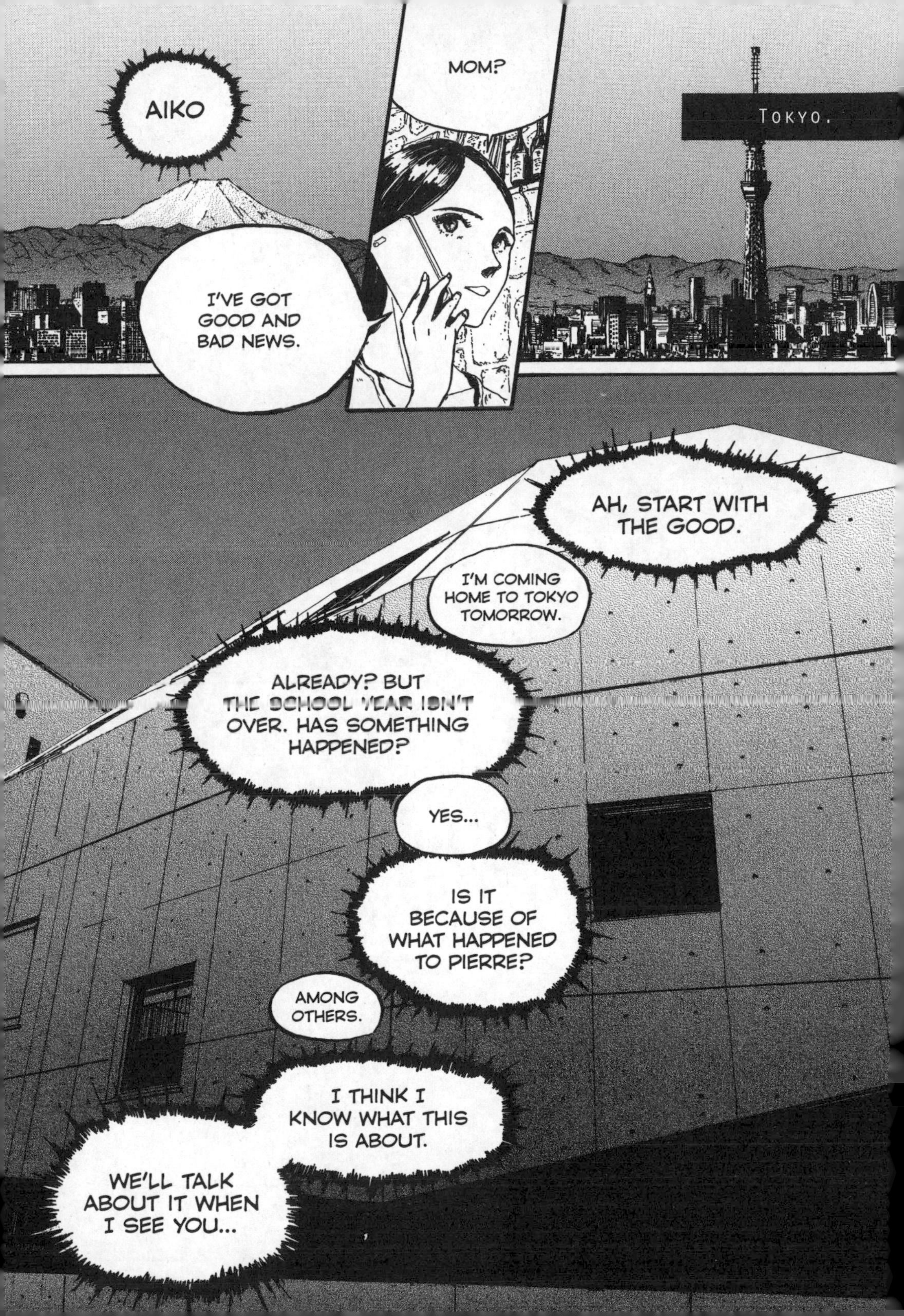
TOKYO.
MOM?
AIKO
I'VE GOT GOOD AND BAD NEWS.
AH, START WITH THE GOOD.
I'M COMING HOME TO TOKYO TOMORROW.
ALREADY? BUT THE SCHOOL YEAR ISN'T OVER. HAS SOMETHING HAPPENED?
YES...
IS IT BECAUSE OF WHAT HAPPENED TO PIERRE?
AMONG OTHERS.
I THINK I KNOW WHAT THIS IS ABOUT.
WE'LL TALK ABOUT IT WHEN I SEE YOU...

Act II

Prologue

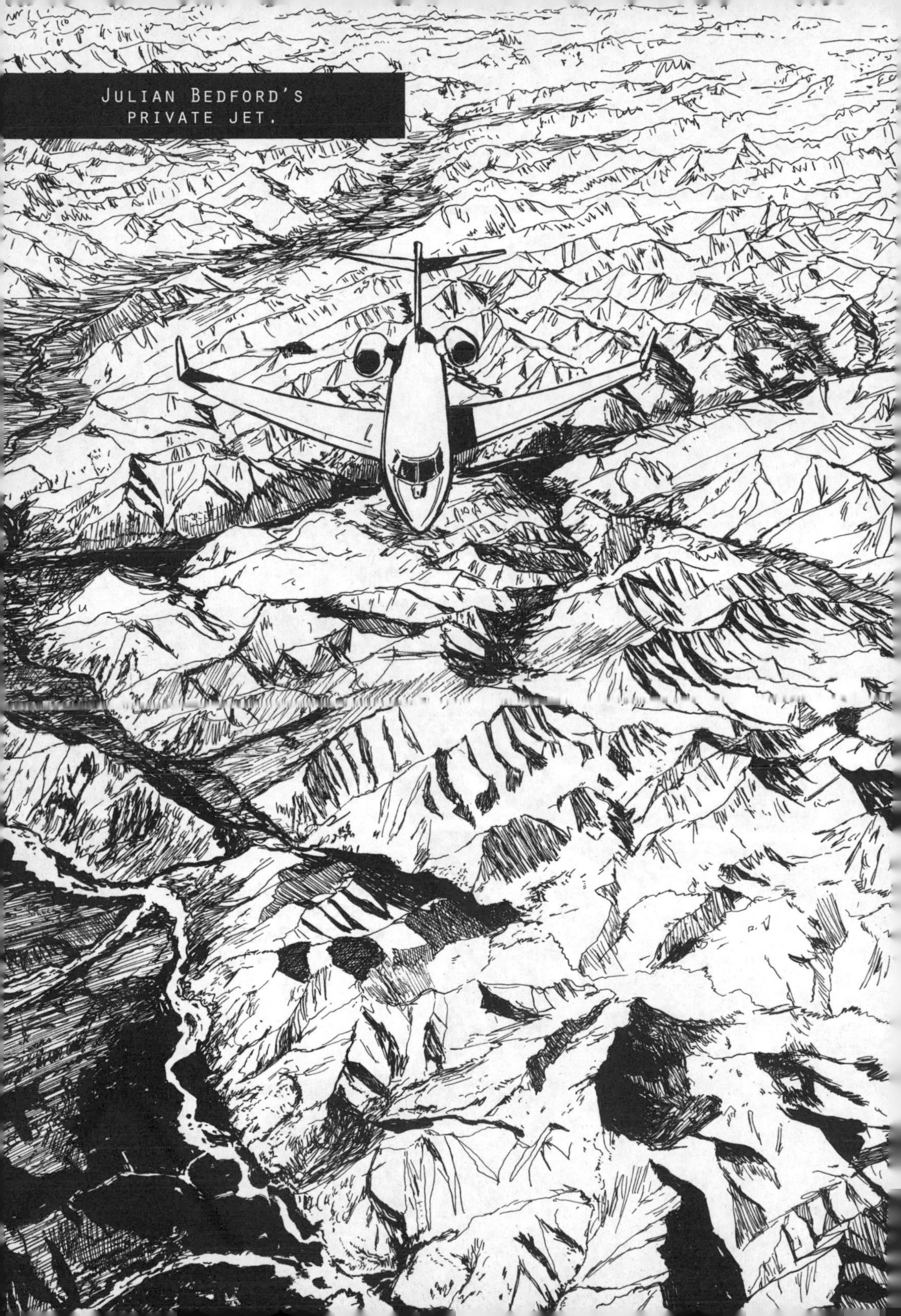
JULIAN BEDFORD'S
PRIVATE JET.

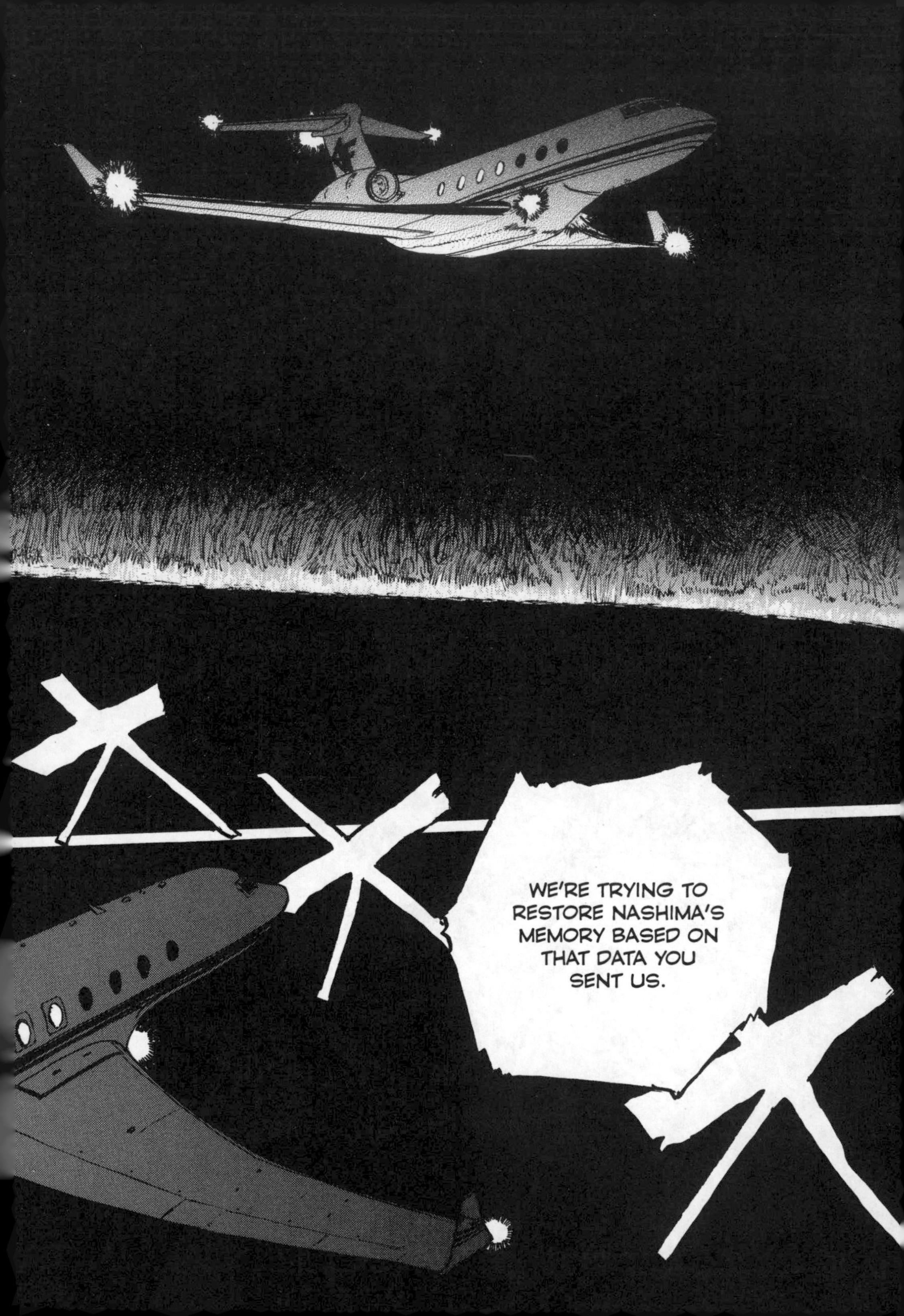
WE'RE TRYING TO RESTORE NASHIMA'S MEMORY BASED ON THAT DATA YOU SENT US.

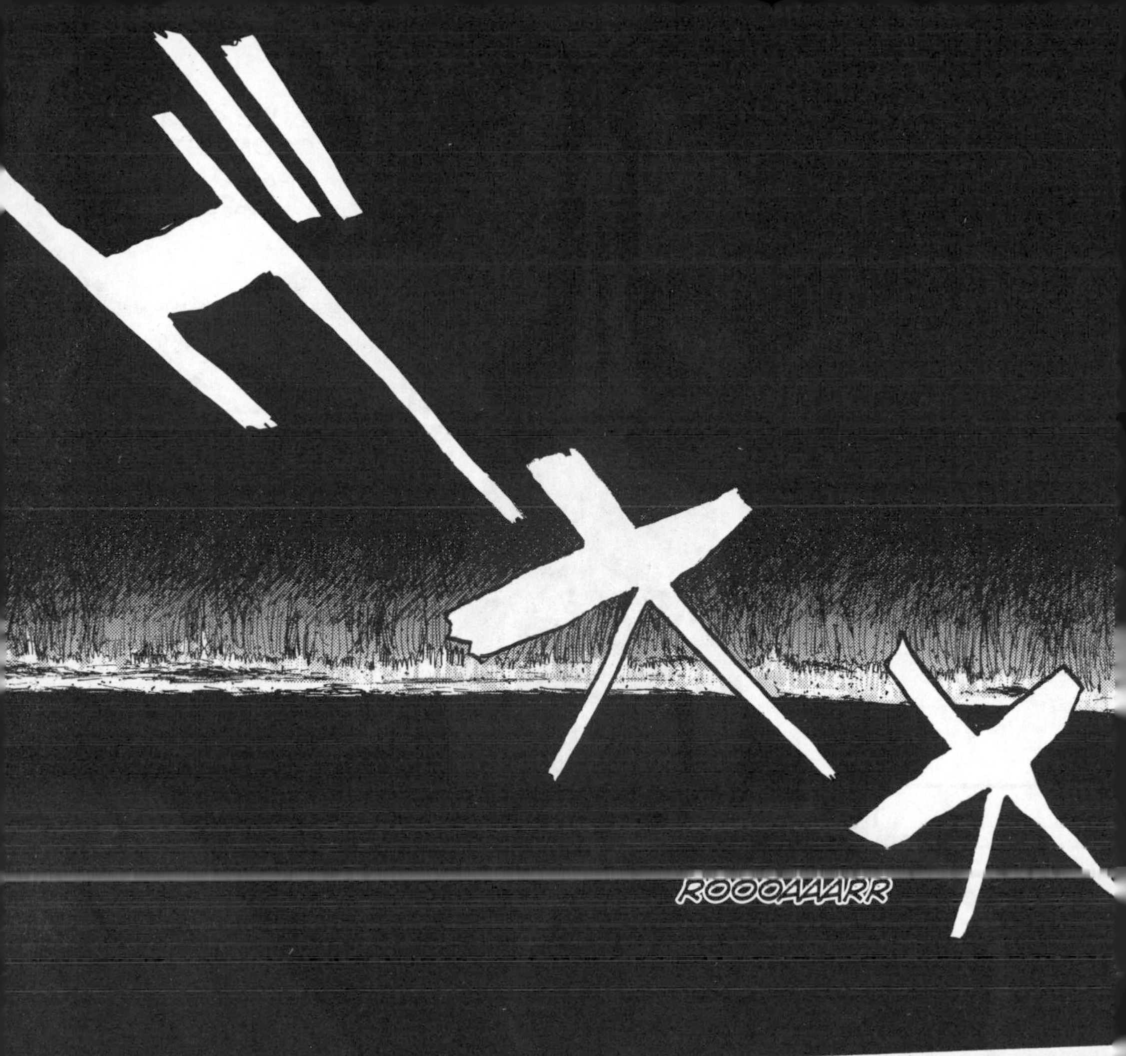
ROOOAAARR

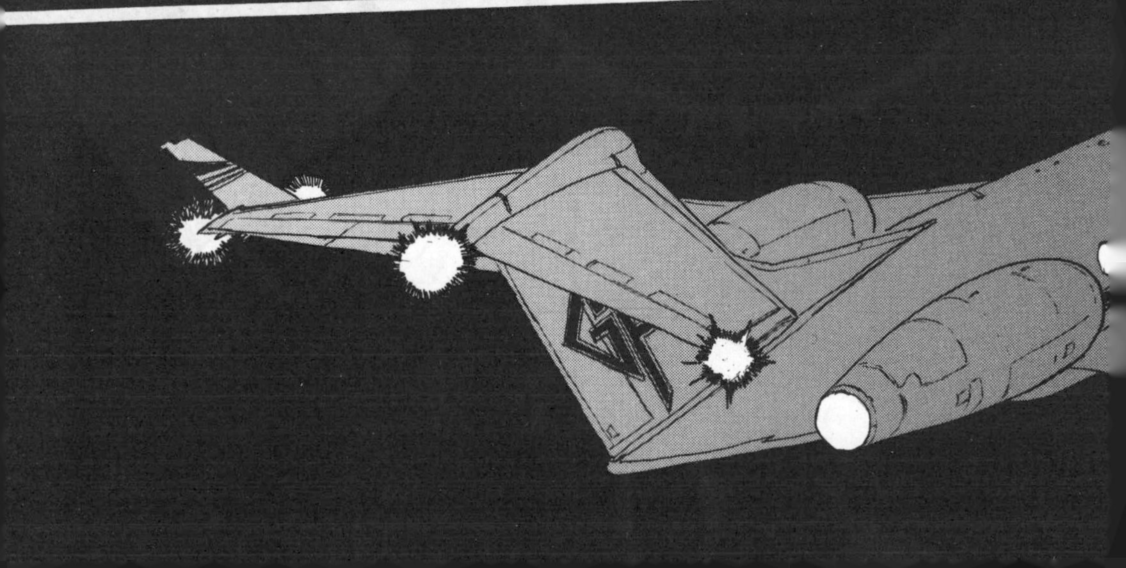

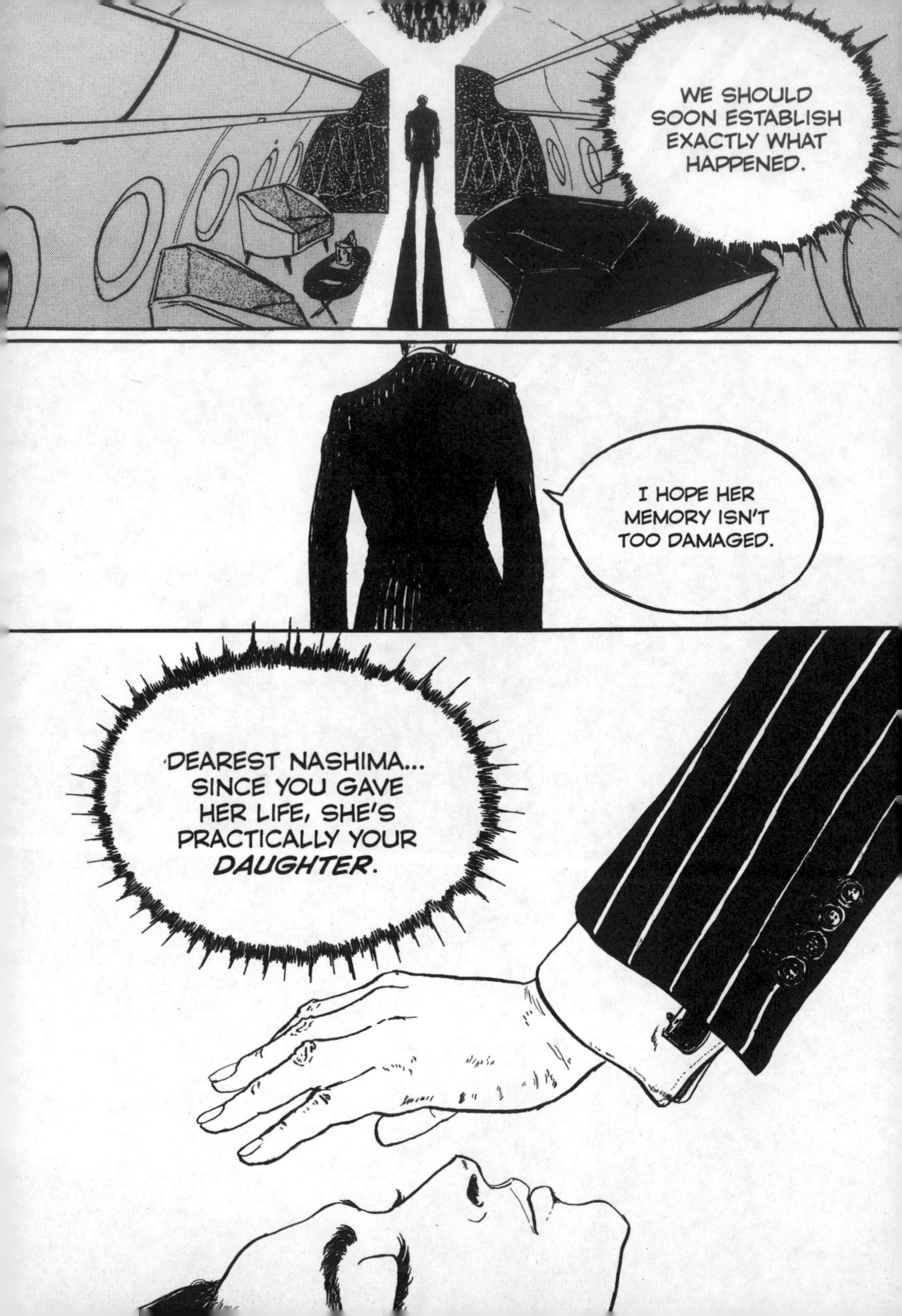
WE SHOULD SOON ESTABLISH EXACTLY WHAT HAPPENED.
I HOPE HER MEMORY ISN'T TOO DAMAGED.
DEAREST NASHIMA... SINCE YOU GAVE HER LIFE, SHE'S PRACTICALLY YOUR *DAUGHTER*.

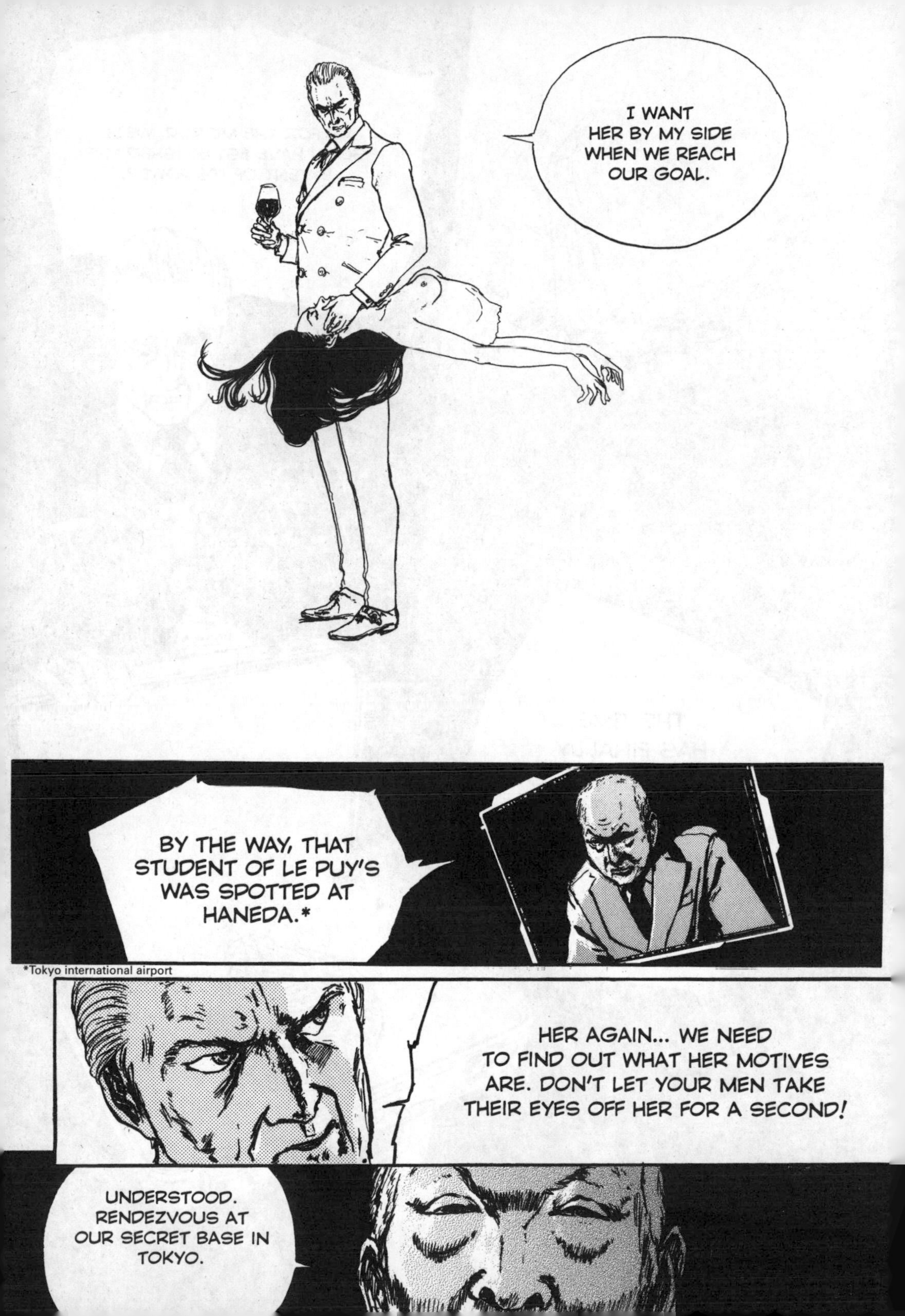
I WANT HER BY MY SIDE WHEN WE REACH OUR GOAL.
BY THE WAY, THAT STUDENT OF LE PUY'S WAS SPOTTED AT HANEDA.*
HER AGAIN... WE NEED TO FIND OUT WHAT HER MOTIVES ARE. DON'T LET YOUR MEN TAKE THEIR EYES OFF HER FOR A SECOND!
UNDERSTOOD. RENDEZVOUS AT OUR SECRET BASE IN TOKYO.
*Tokyo international airport

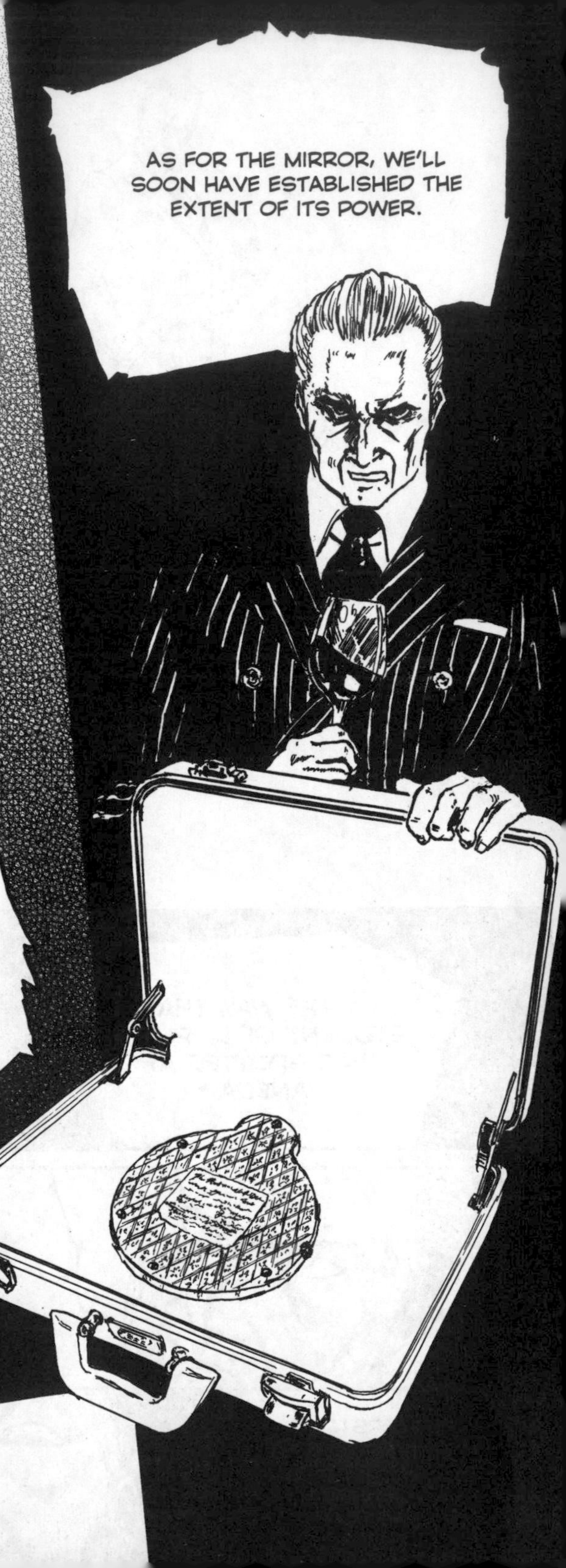
AS FOR THE MIRROR, WE'LL SOON HAVE ESTABLISHED THE EXTENT OF ITS POWER.

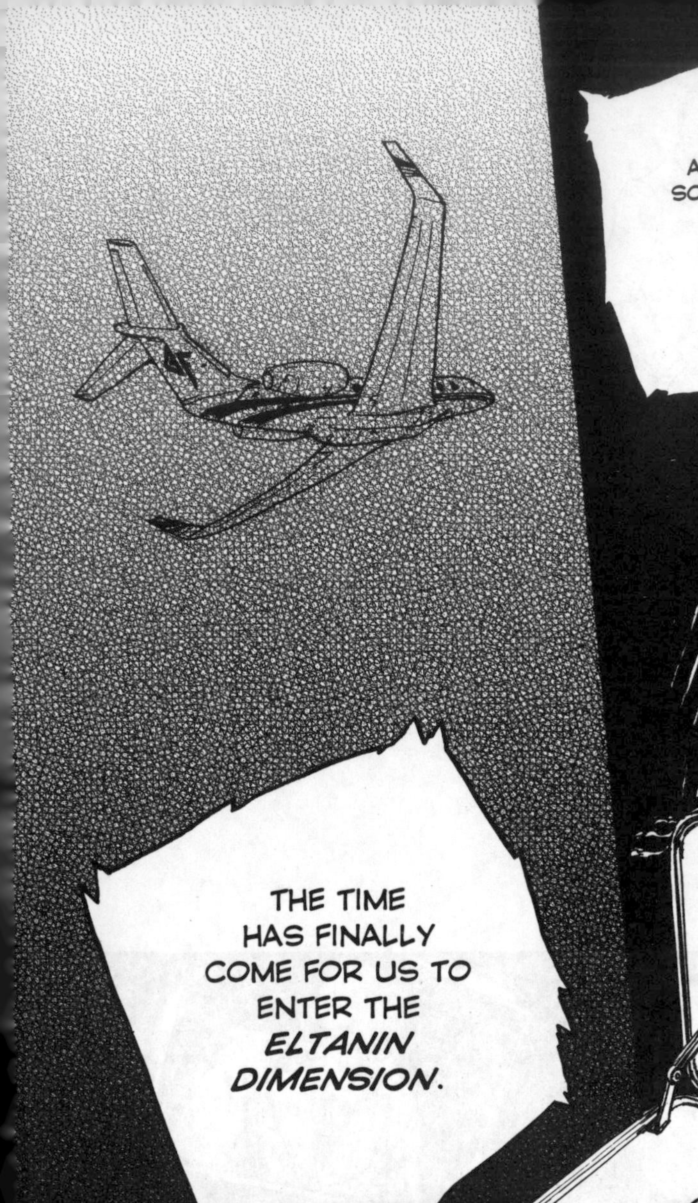
THE TIME HAS FINALLY COME FOR US TO ENTER THE *ELTANIN DIMENSION*.

CHAPTER 1

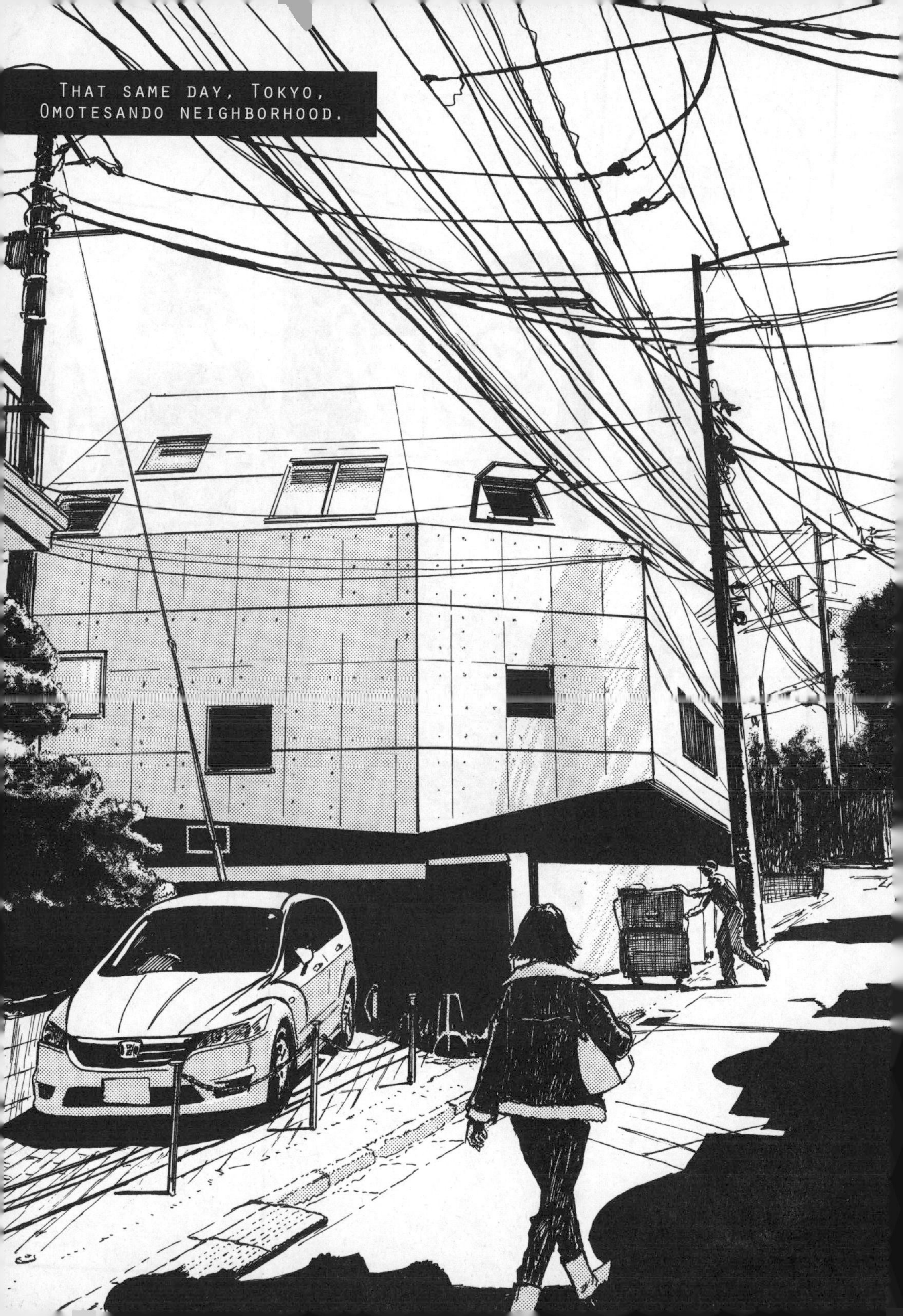
That same day, Tokyo,
Omotesando neighborhood.

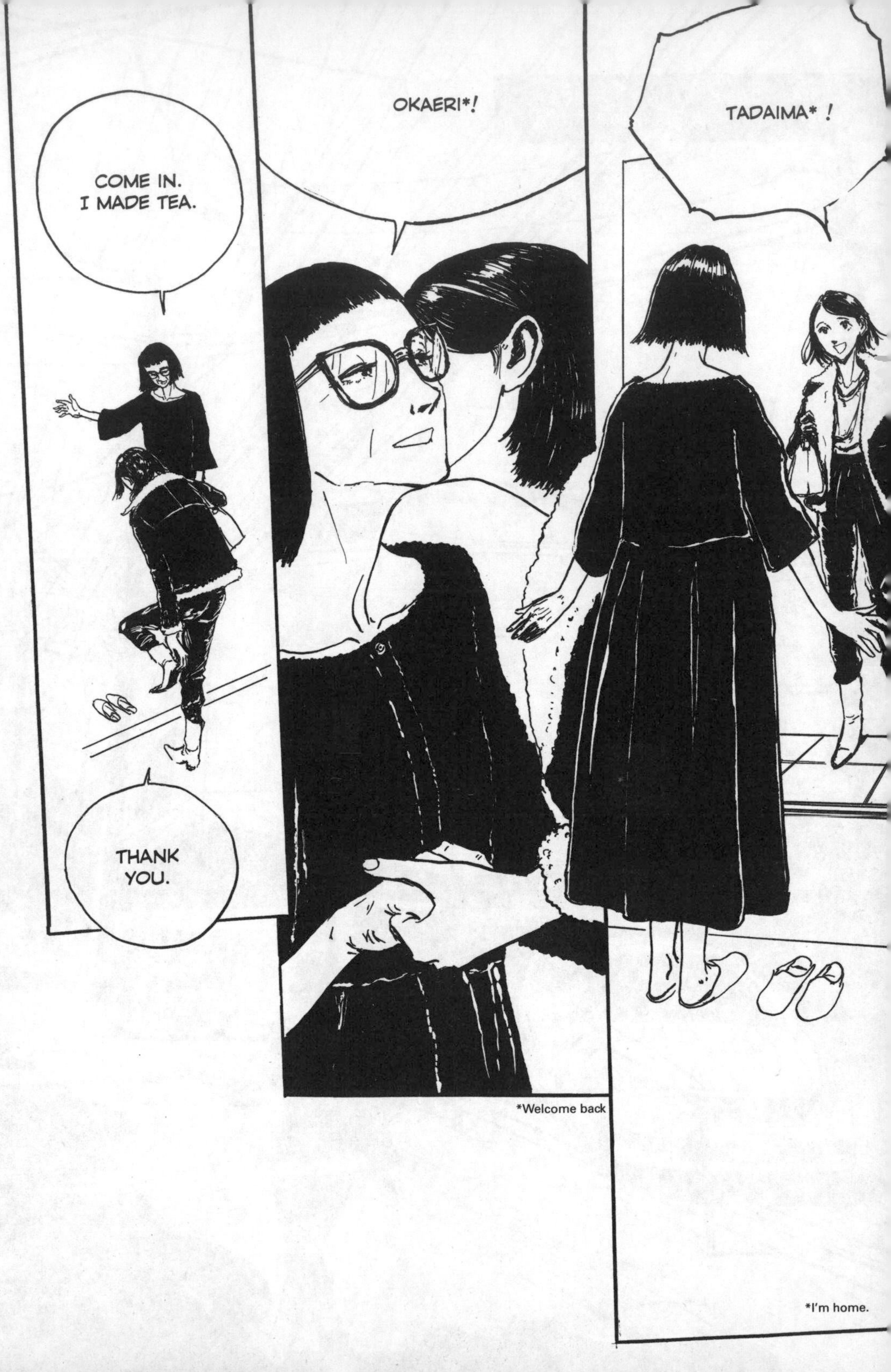
TADAIMA* !
*I'm home.
OKAERI*!
*Welcome back
COME IN. I MADE TEA.
THANK YOU.

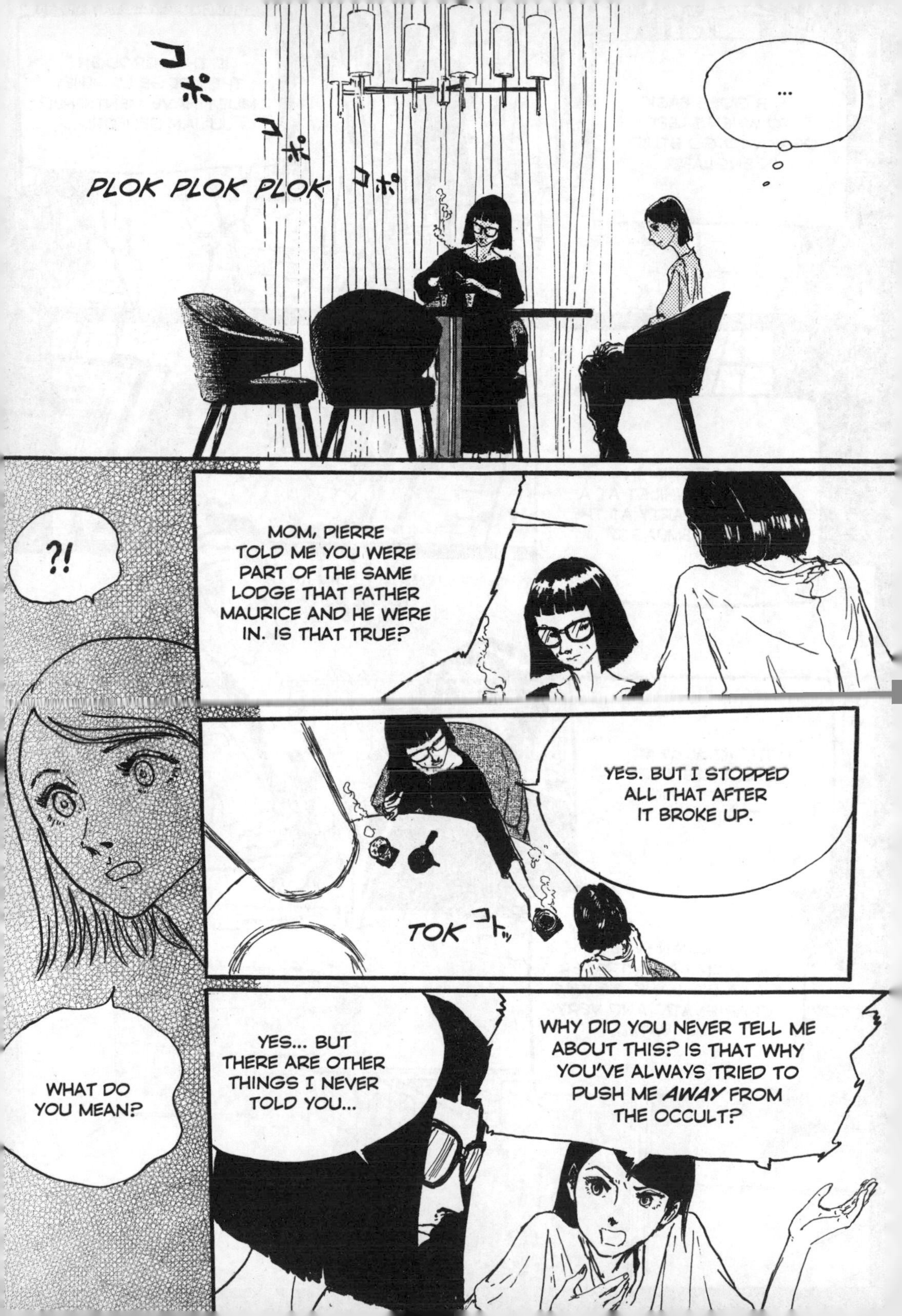
...
コポ
コポ
コポ
PLOK PLOK PLOK
MOM, PIERRE TOLD ME YOU WERE PART OF THE SAME LODGE THAT FATHER MAURICE AND HE WERE IN. IS THAT TRUE?
YES. BUT I STOPPED ALL THAT AFTER IT BROKE UP.
TOK コトッ
WHY DID YOU NEVER TELL ME ABOUT THIS? IS THAT WHY YOU'VE ALWAYS TRIED TO PUSH ME *AWAY* FROM THE OCCULT?
YES... BUT THERE ARE OTHER THINGS I NEVER TOLD YOU...
?!
WHAT DO YOU MEAN?

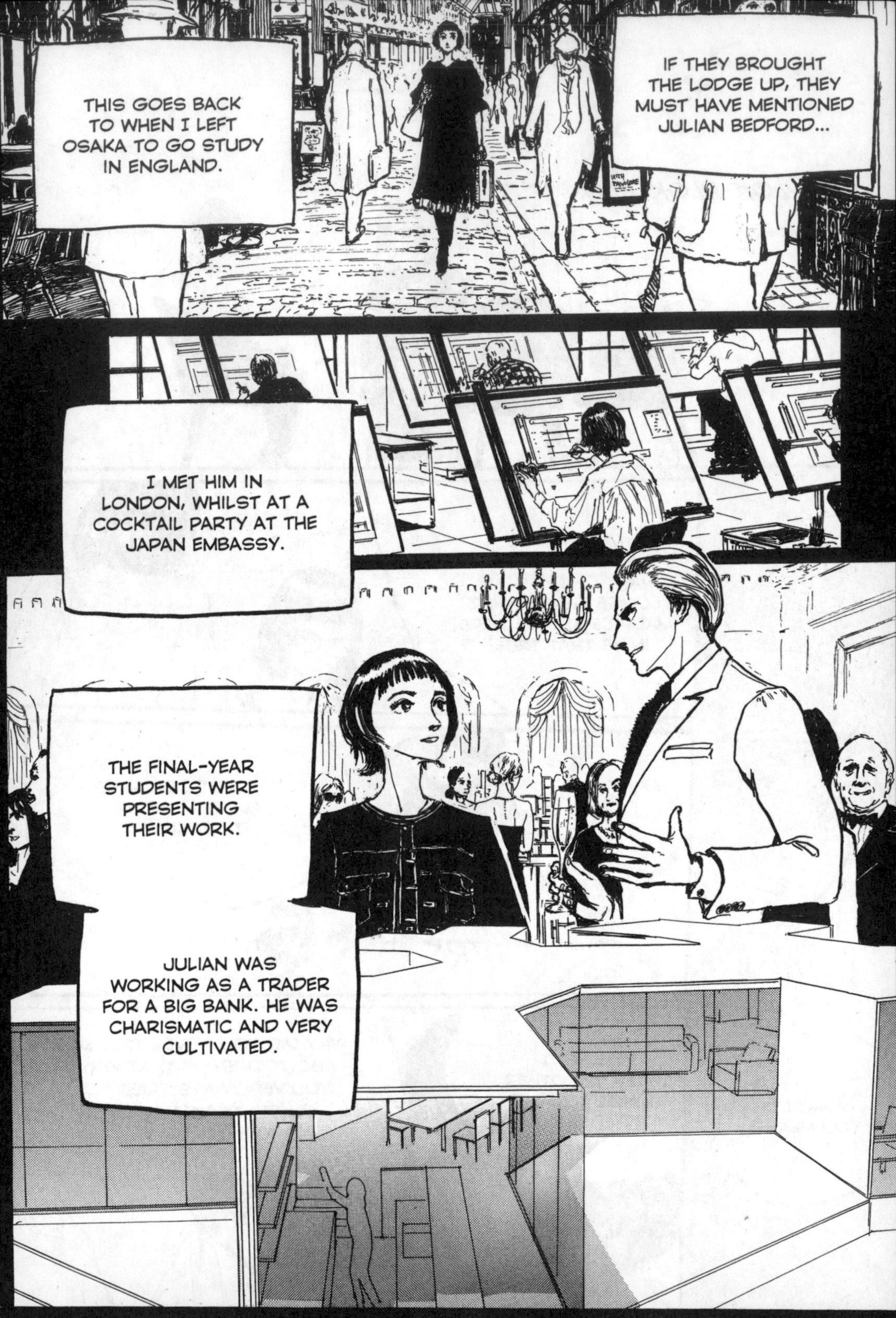
IF THEY BROUGHT THE LODGE UP, THEY MUST HAVE MENTIONED JULIAN BEDFORD...
THIS GOES BACK TO WHEN I LEFT OSAKA TO GO STUDY IN ENGLAND.
I MET HIM IN LONDON, WHILST AT A COCKTAIL PARTY AT THE JAPAN EMBASSY.
THE FINAL-YEAR STUDENTS WERE PRESENTING THEIR WORK.
JULIAN WAS WORKING AS A TRADER FOR A BIG BANK. HE WAS CHARISMATIC AND VERY CULTIVATED.

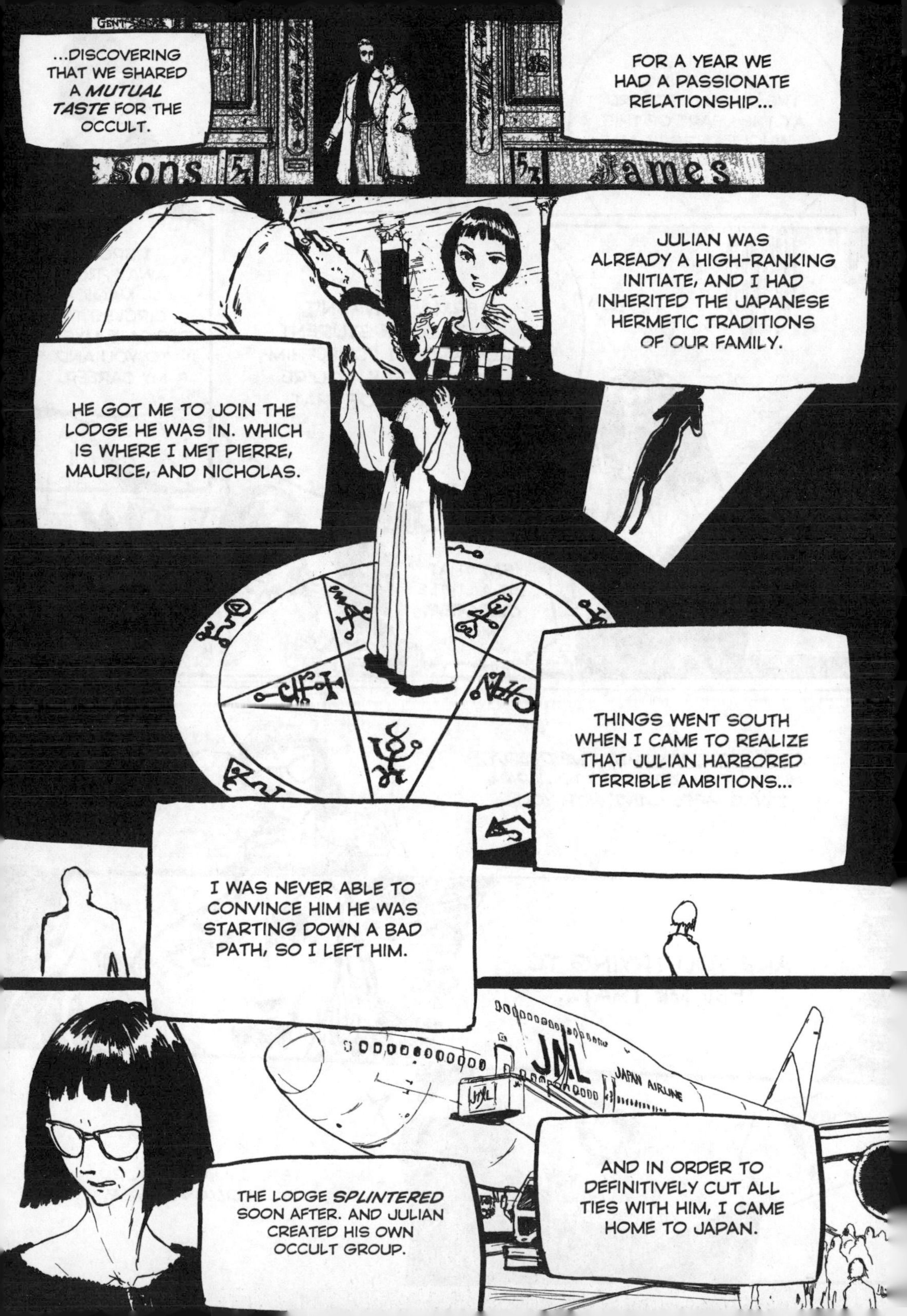

...DISCOVERING THAT WE SHARED A *MUTUAL TASTE* FOR THE OCCULT.
Sons
James
FOR A YEAR WE HAD A PASSIONATE RELATIONSHIP...
JULIAN WAS ALREADY A HIGH-RANKING INITIATE, AND I HAD INHERITED THE JAPANESE HERMETIC TRADITIONS OF OUR FAMILY.
HE GOT ME TO JOIN THE LODGE HE WAS IN. WHICH IS WHERE I MET PIERRE, MAURICE, AND NICHOLAS.
THINGS WENT SOUTH WHEN I CAME TO REALIZE THAT JULIAN HARBORED TERRIBLE AMBITIONS...
I WAS NEVER ABLE TO CONVINCE HIM HE WAS STARTING DOWN A BAD PATH, SO I LEFT HIM.
JAPAN AIRLINE
THE LODGE *SPLINTERED* SOON AFTER. AND JULIAN CREATED HIS OWN OCCULT GROUP.
AND IN ORDER TO DEFINITIVELY CUT ALL TIES WITH HIM, I CAME HOME TO JAPAN.

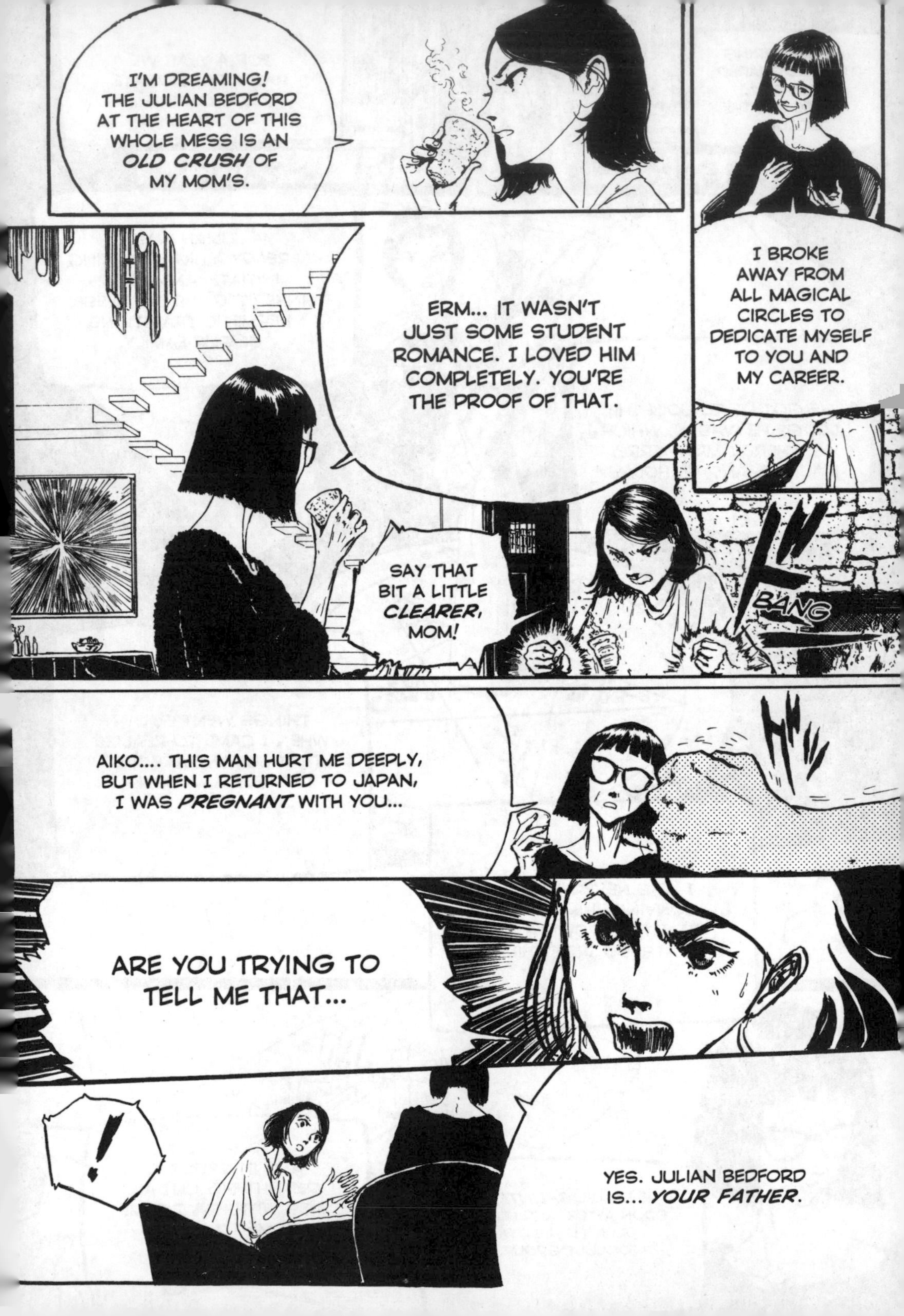

I BROKE AWAY FROM ALL MAGICAL CIRCLES TO DEDICATE MYSELF TO YOU AND MY CAREER.
I'M DREAMING! THE JULIAN BEDFORD AT THE HEART OF THIS WHOLE MESS IS AN OLD CRUSH OF MY MOM'S.
ERM... IT WASN'T JUST SOME STUDENT ROMANCE. I LOVED HIM COMPLETELY. YOU'RE THE PROOF OF THAT.
BANG
SAY THAT BIT A LITTLE CLEARER, MOM!
AIKO.... THIS MAN HURT ME DEEPLY, BUT WHEN I RETURNED TO JAPAN, I WAS PREGNANT WITH YOU...
ARE YOU TRYING TO TELL ME THAT...
YES. JULIAN BEDFORD IS... YOUR FATHER.
!

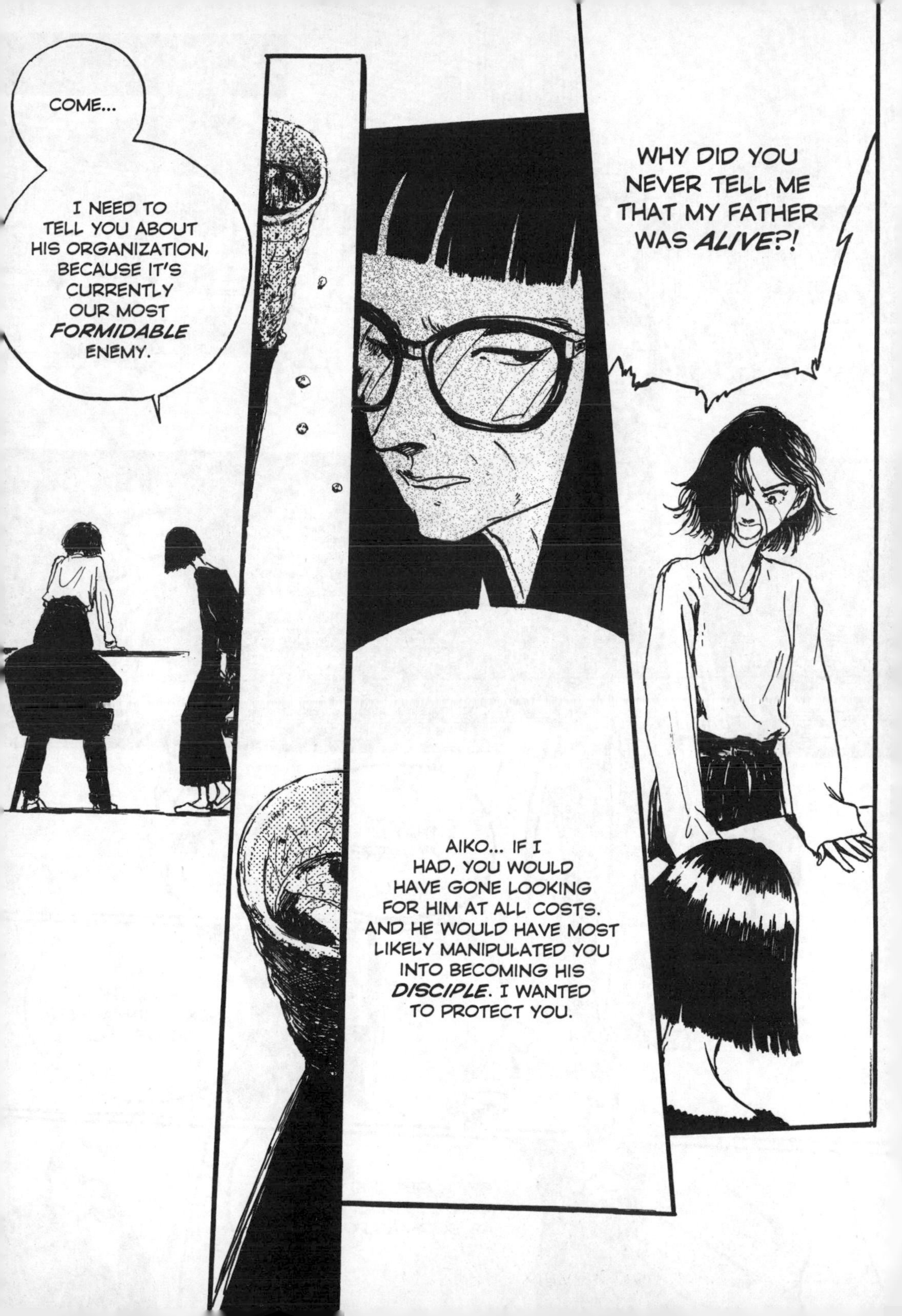
WHY DID YOU NEVER TELL ME THAT MY FATHER WAS *ALIVE*?!
AIKO... IF I HAD, YOU WOULD HAVE GONE LOOKING FOR HIM AT ALL COSTS. AND HE WOULD HAVE MOST LIKELY MANIPULATED YOU INTO BECOMING HIS *DISCIPLE*. I WANTED TO PROTECT YOU.
COME...
I NEED TO TELL YOU ABOUT HIS ORGANIZATION, BECAUSE IT'S CURRENTLY OUR MOST *FORMIDABLE* ENEMY.

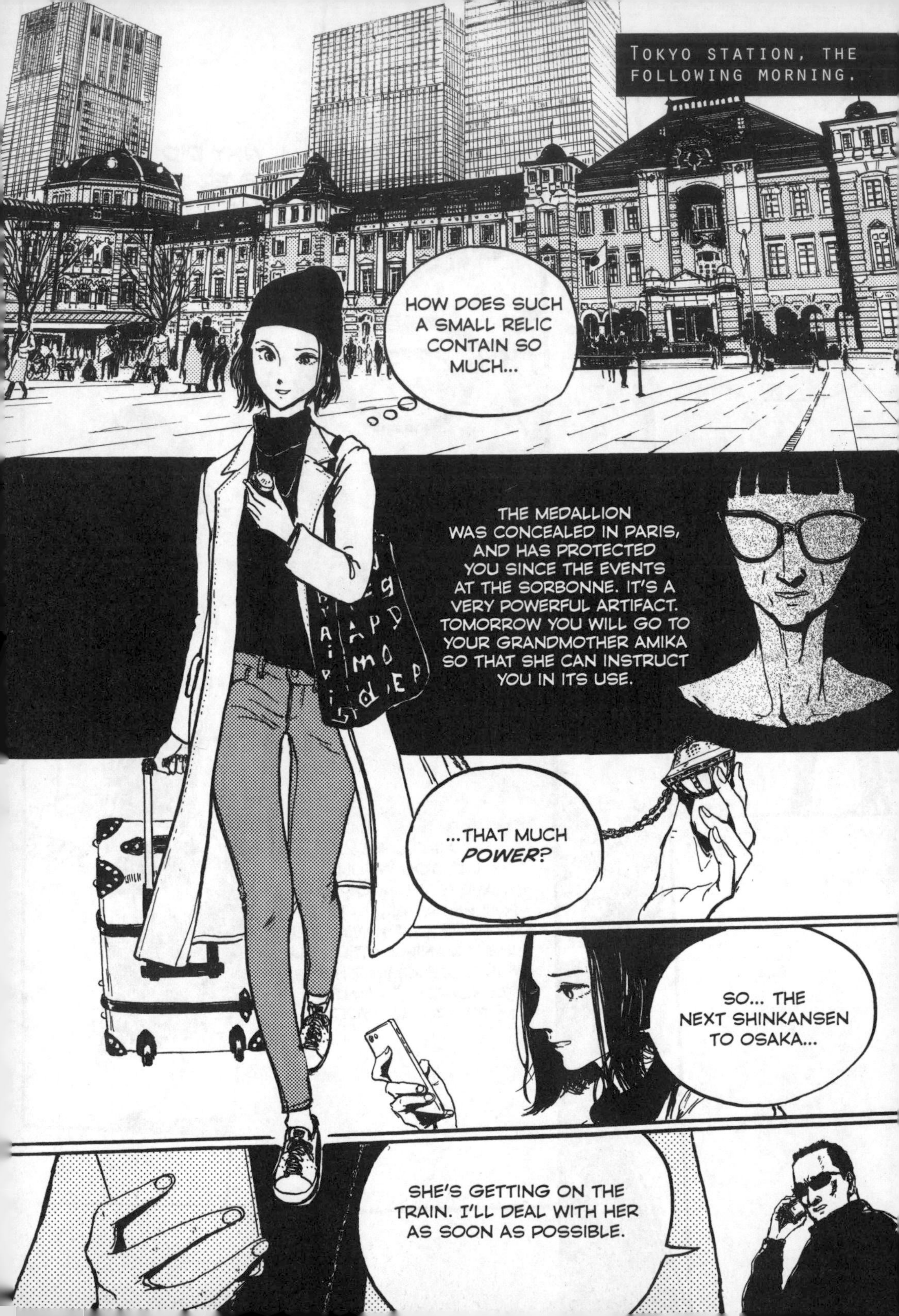
TOKYO STATION, THE FOLLOWING MORNING.
HOW DOES SUCH A SMALL RELIC CONTAIN SO MUCH...
THE MEDALLION WAS CONCEALED IN PARIS, AND HAS PROTECTED YOU SINCE THE EVENTS AT THE SORBONNE. IT'S A VERY POWERFUL ARTIFACT. TOMORROW YOU WILL GO TO YOUR GRANDMOTHER AMIKA SO THAT SHE CAN INSTRUCT YOU IN ITS USE.
...THAT MUCH *POWER*?
SO... THE NEXT SHINKANSEN TO OSAKA...
SHE'S GETTING ON THE TRAIN. I'LL DEAL WITH HER AS SOON AS POSSIBLE.

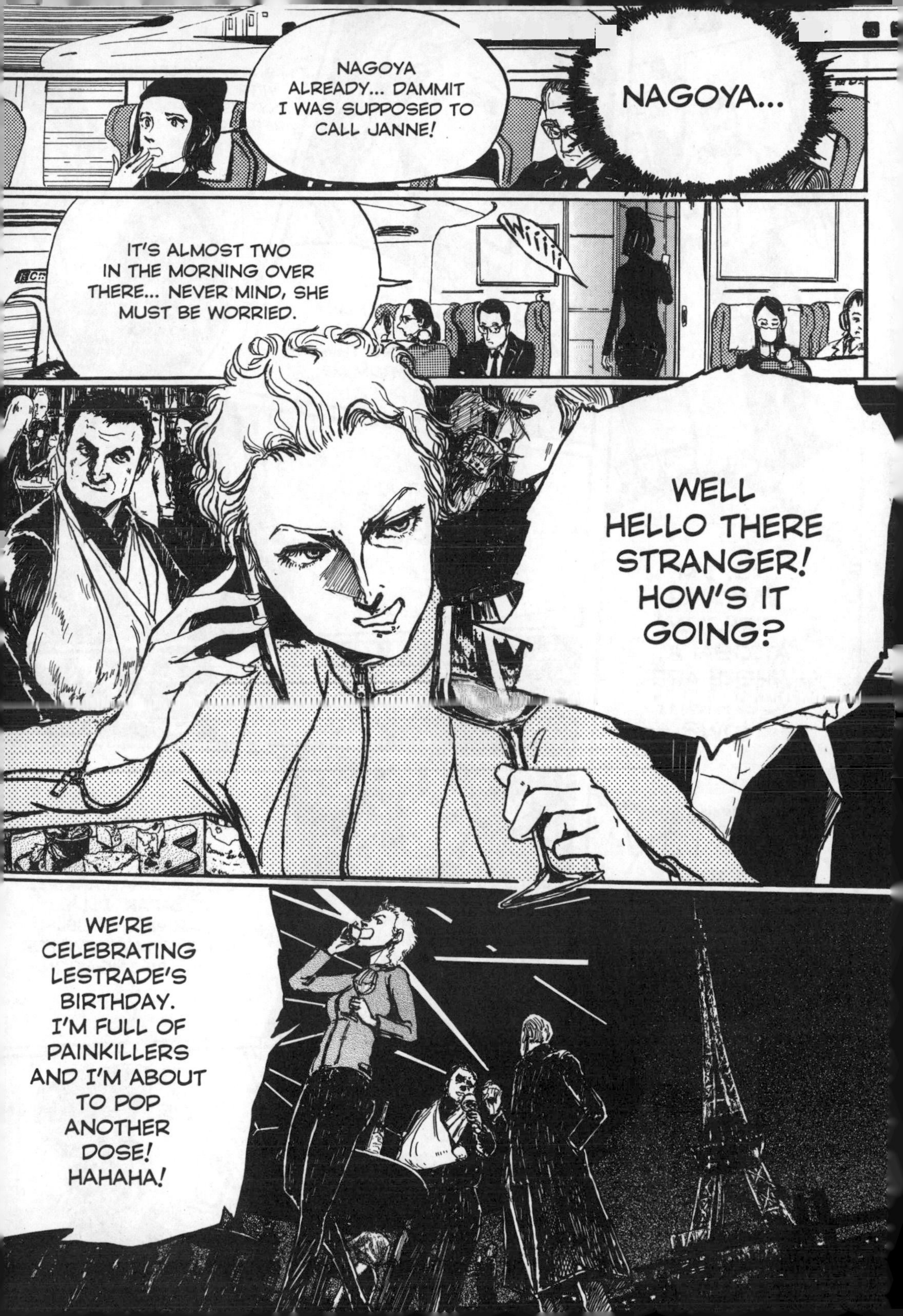
NAGOYA...
NAGOYA ALREADY... DAMMIT I WAS SUPPOSED TO CALL JANNE!
IT'S ALMOST TWO IN THE MORNING OVER THERE... NEVER MIND, SHE MUST BE WORRIED.
WELL HELLO THERE STRANGER! HOW'S IT GOING?
WE'RE CELEBRATING LESTRADE'S BIRTHDAY. I'M FULL OF PAINKILLERS AND I'M ABOUT TO POP ANOTHER DOSE! HAHAHA!

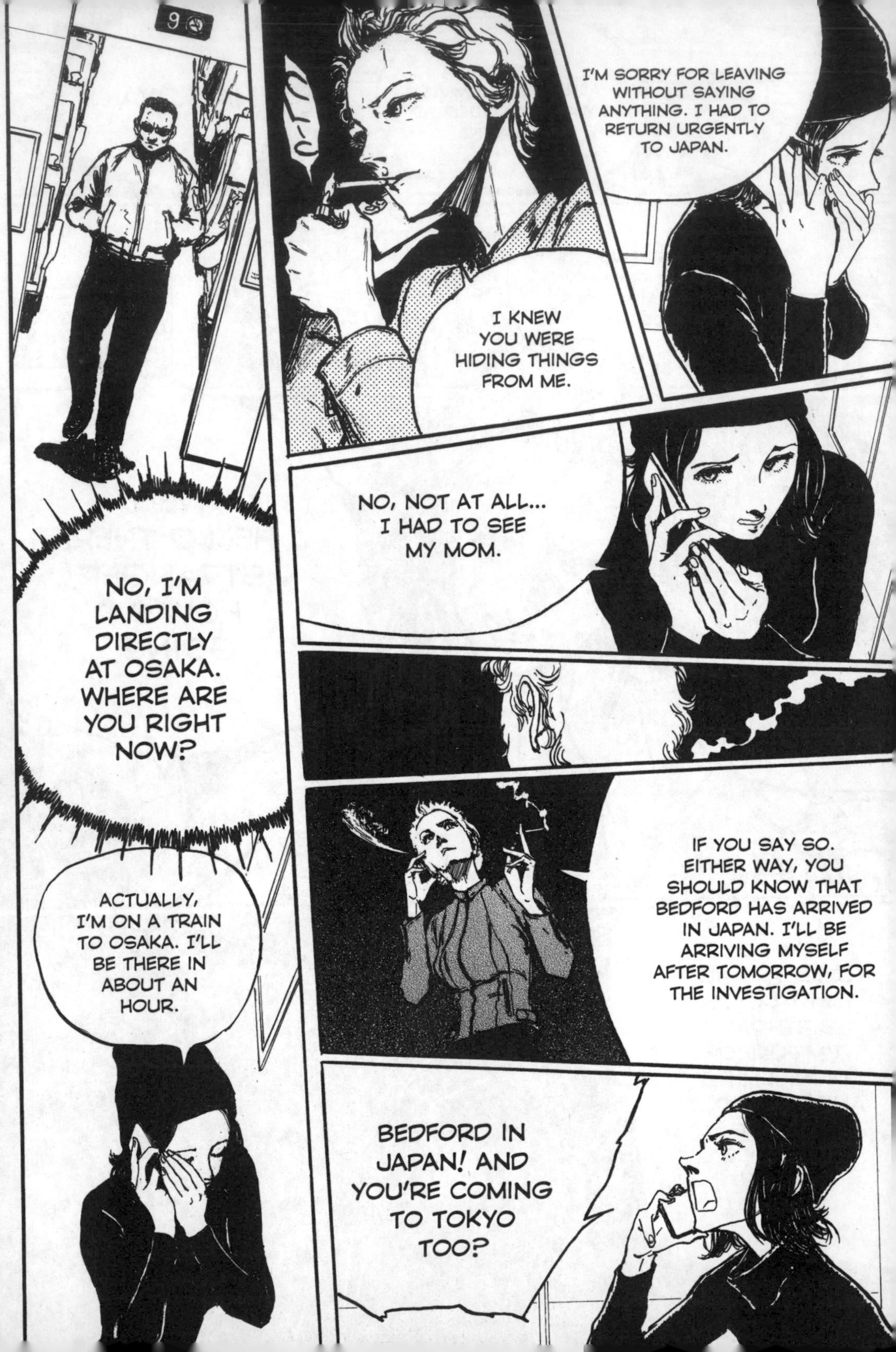
I'M SORRY FOR LEAVING WITHOUT SAYING ANYTHING. I HAD TO RETURN URGENTLY TO JAPAN.
I KNEW YOU WERE HIDING THINGS FROM ME.
NO, NOT AT ALL... I HAD TO SEE MY MOM.
IF YOU SAY SO. EITHER WAY, YOU SHOULD KNOW THAT BEDFORD HAS ARRIVED IN JAPAN. I'LL BE ARRIVING MYSELF AFTER TOMORROW, FOR THE INVESTIGATION.
BEDFORD IN JAPAN! AND YOU'RE COMING TO TOKYO TOO?
NO, I'M LANDING DIRECTLY AT OSAKA. WHERE ARE YOU RIGHT NOW?
ACTUALLY, I'M ON A TRAIN TO OSAKA. I'LL BE THERE IN ABOUT AN HOUR.

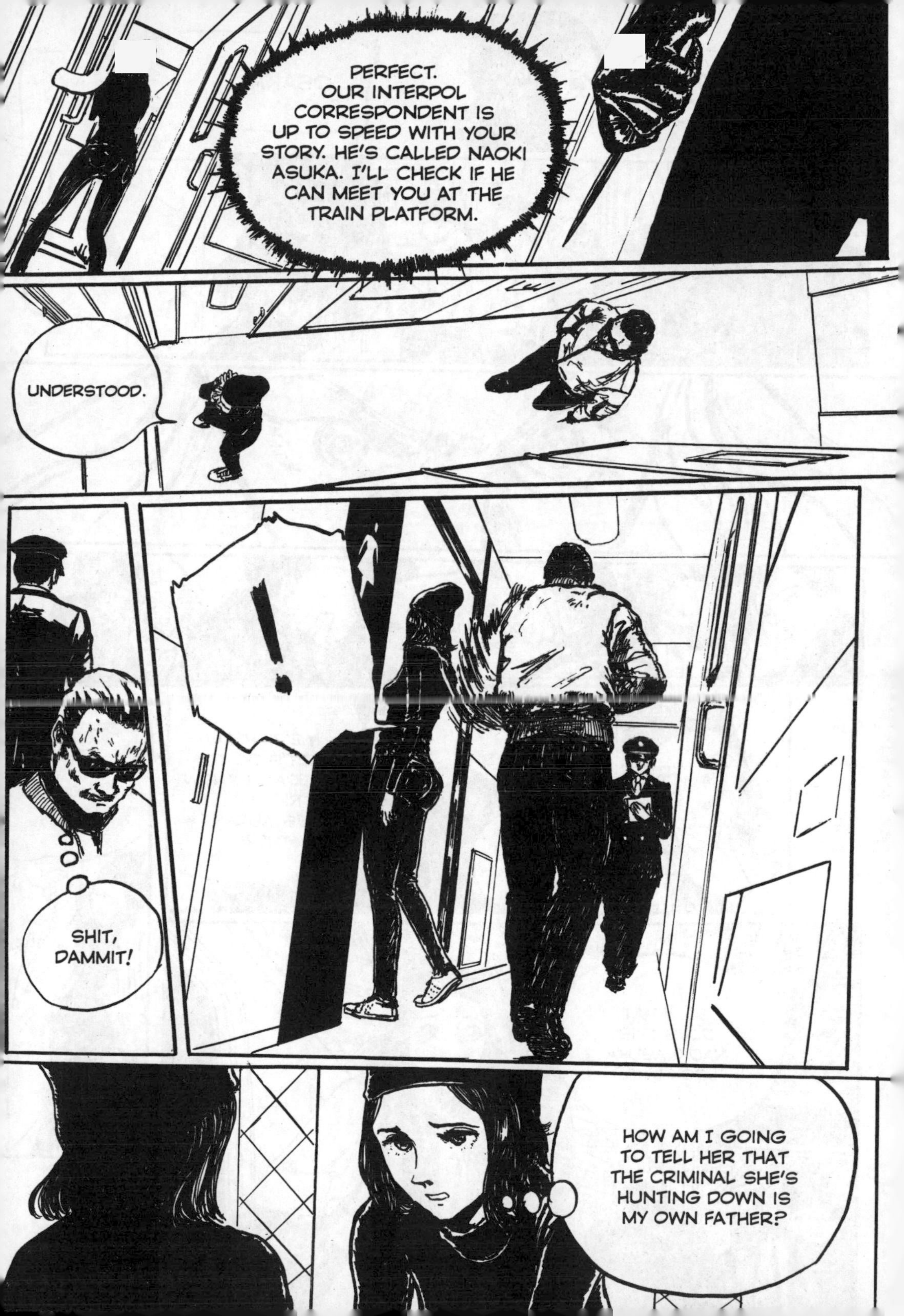
PERFECT. OUR INTERPOL CORRESPONDENT IS UP TO SPEED WITH YOUR STORY. HE'S CALLED NAOKI ASUKA. I'LL CHECK IF HE CAN MEET YOU AT THE TRAIN PLATFORM.
UNDERSTOOD.
!
SHIT, DAMMIT!
HOW AM I GOING TO TELL HER THAT THE CRIMINAL SHE'S HUNTING DOWN IS MY OWN FATHER?

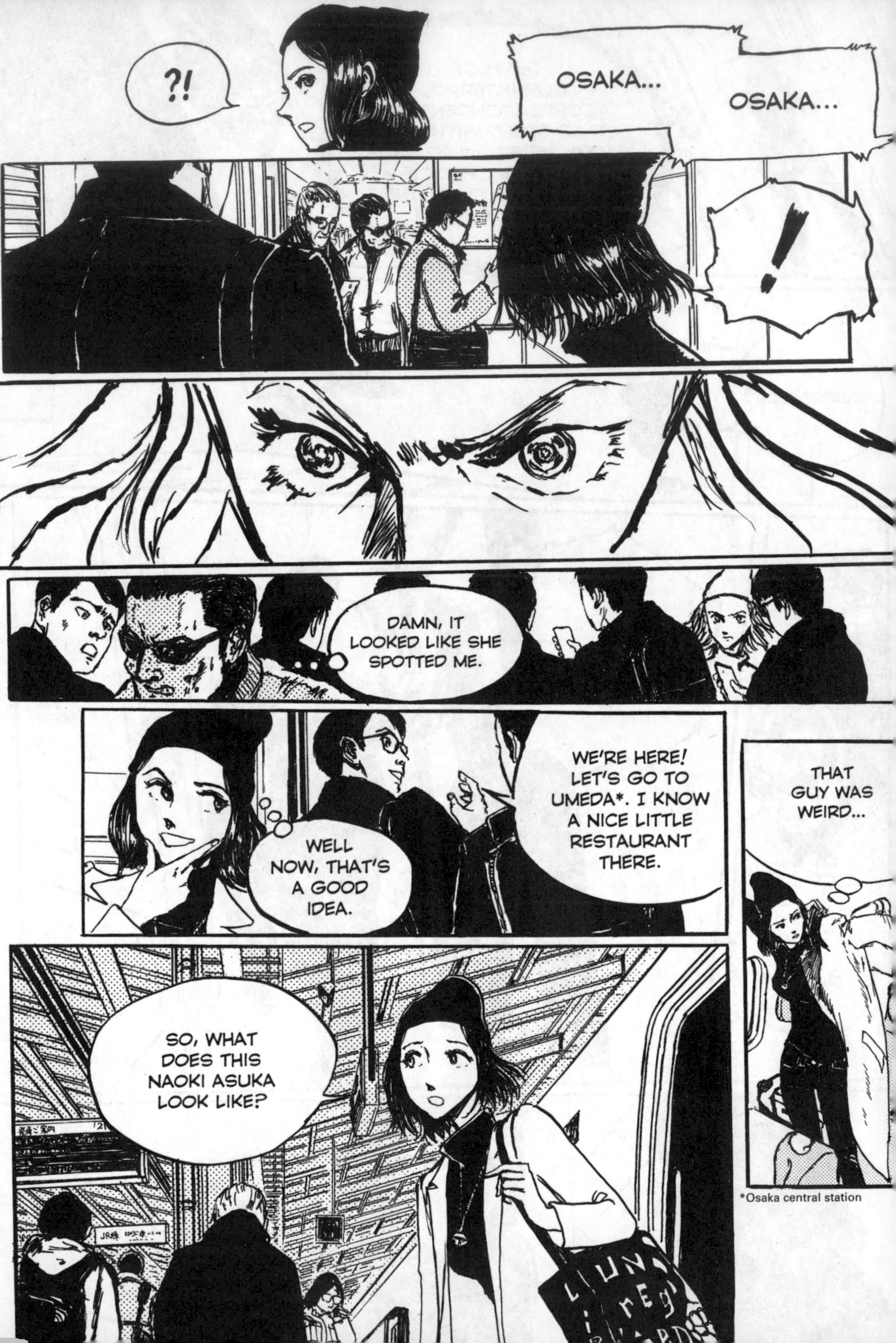
OSAKA... OSAKA...
?!
!
DAMN, IT LOOKED LIKE SHE SPOTTED ME.
THAT GUY WAS WEIRD...
WE'RE HERE! LET'S GO TO UMEDA*. I KNOW A NICE LITTLE RESTAURANT THERE.
WELL NOW, THAT'S A GOOD IDEA.
SO, WHAT DOES THIS NAOKI ASUKA LOOK LIKE?

*Osaka central station

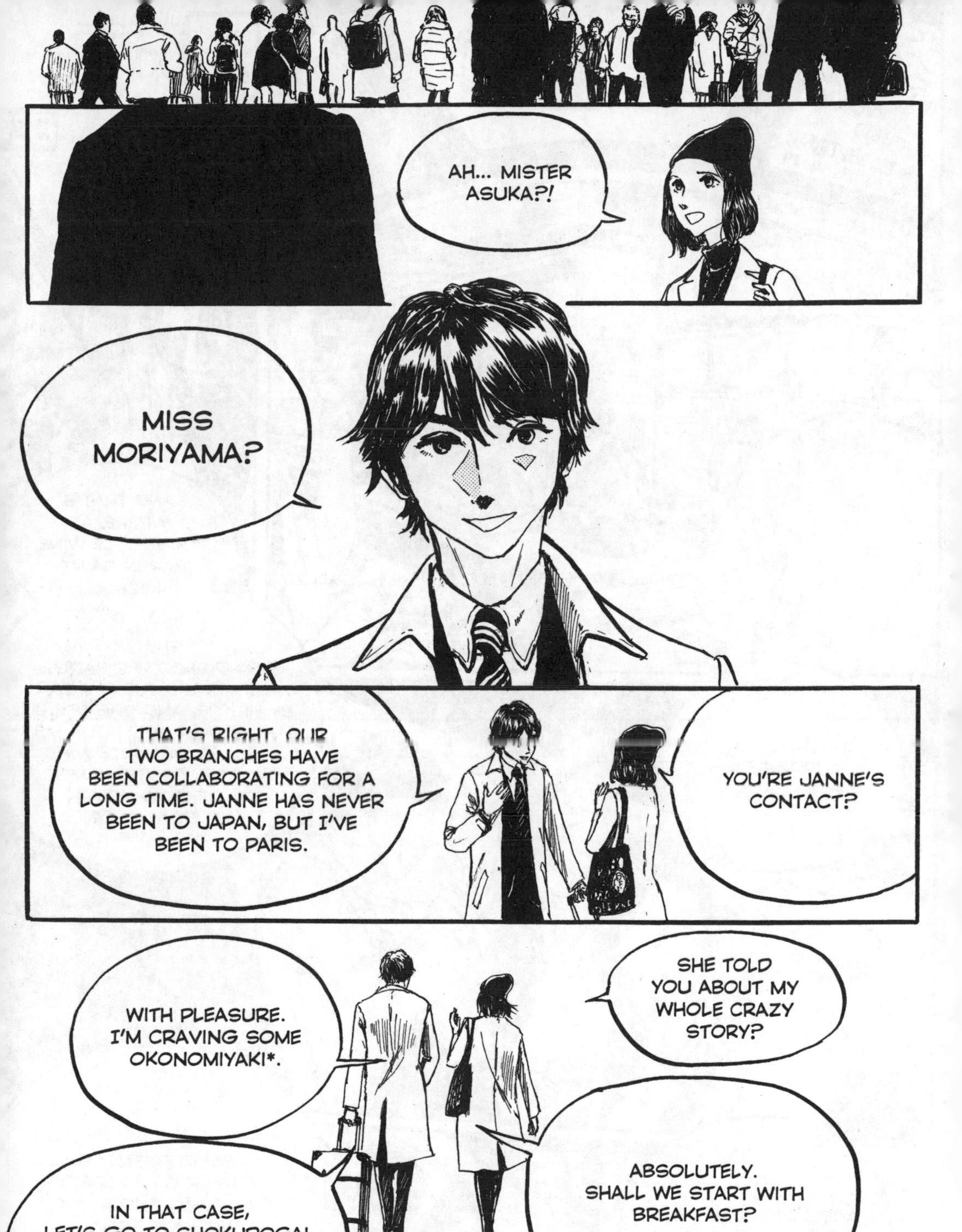
AH... MISTER ASUKA?!
MISS MORIYAMA?
YOU'RE JANNE'S CONTACT?
THAT'S RIGHT. OUR TWO BRANCHES HAVE BEEN COLLABORATING FOR A LONG TIME. JANNE HAS NEVER BEEN TO JAPAN, BUT I'VE BEEN TO PARIS.
SHE TOLD YOU ABOUT MY WHOLE CRAZY STORY?
ABSOLUTELY. SHALL WE START WITH BREAKFAST?
WITH PLEASURE. I'M CRAVING SOME OKONOMIYAKI*.
IN THAT CASE, LET'S GO TO SHOKUDOGAI. I'M GUESSING YOU'VE NOT STOPPED BY IN A WHILE.

*popular Osaka dish

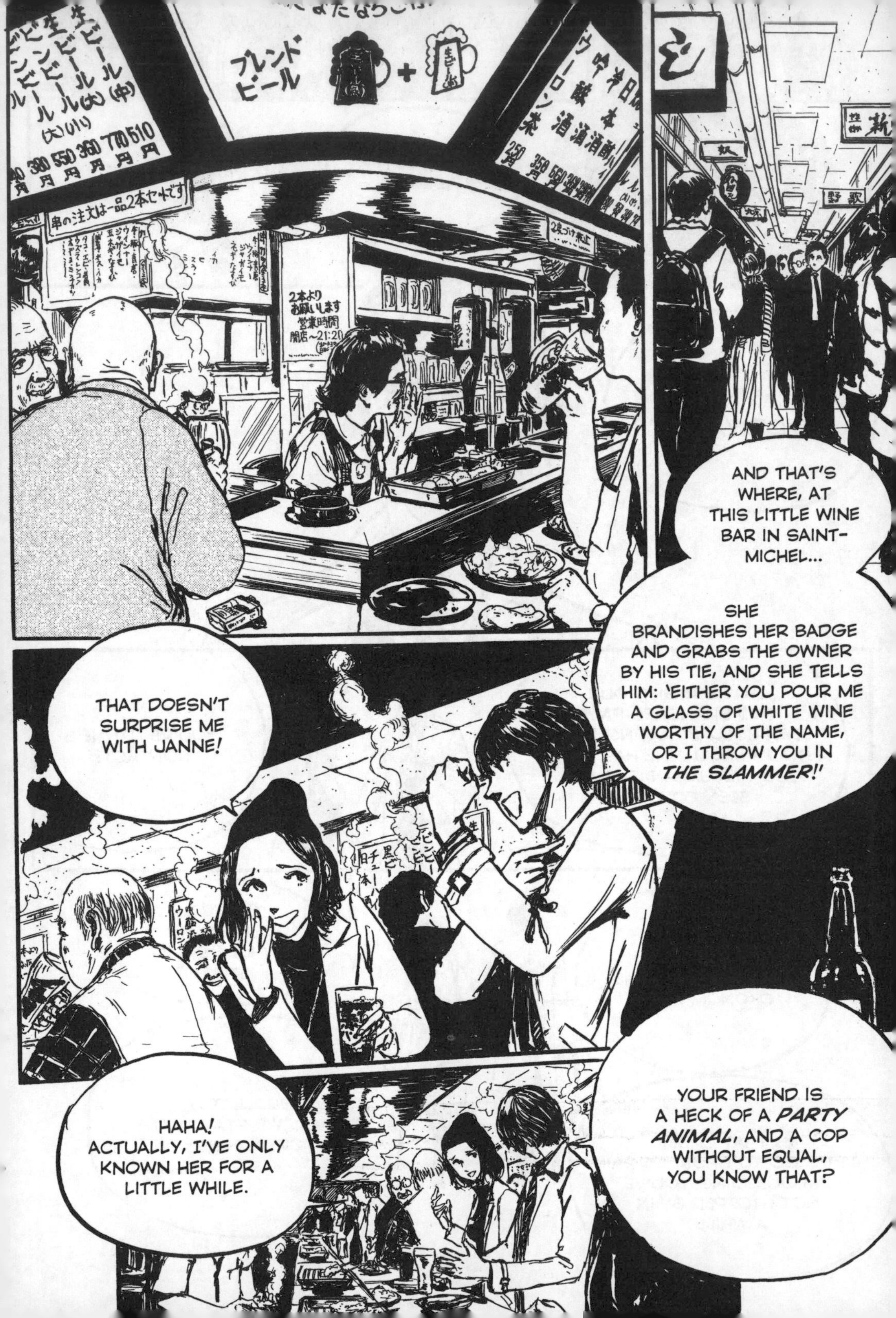
ブレンドビール
串の注文は一品2本セットです
2本よりお願いします
AND THAT'S WHERE, AT THIS LITTLE WINE BAR IN SAINT-MICHEL...
SHE BRANDISHES HER BADGE AND GRABS THE OWNER BY HIS TIE, AND SHE TELLS HIM: 'EITHER YOU POUR ME A GLASS OF WHITE WINE WORTHY OF THE NAME, OR I THROW YOU IN *THE SLAMMER!*'
THAT DOESN'T SURPRISE ME WITH JANNE!
YOUR FRIEND IS A HECK OF A *PARTY ANIMAL*, AND A COP WITHOUT EQUAL, YOU KNOW THAT?
HAHA! ACTUALLY, I'VE ONLY KNOWN HER FOR A LITTLE WHILE.

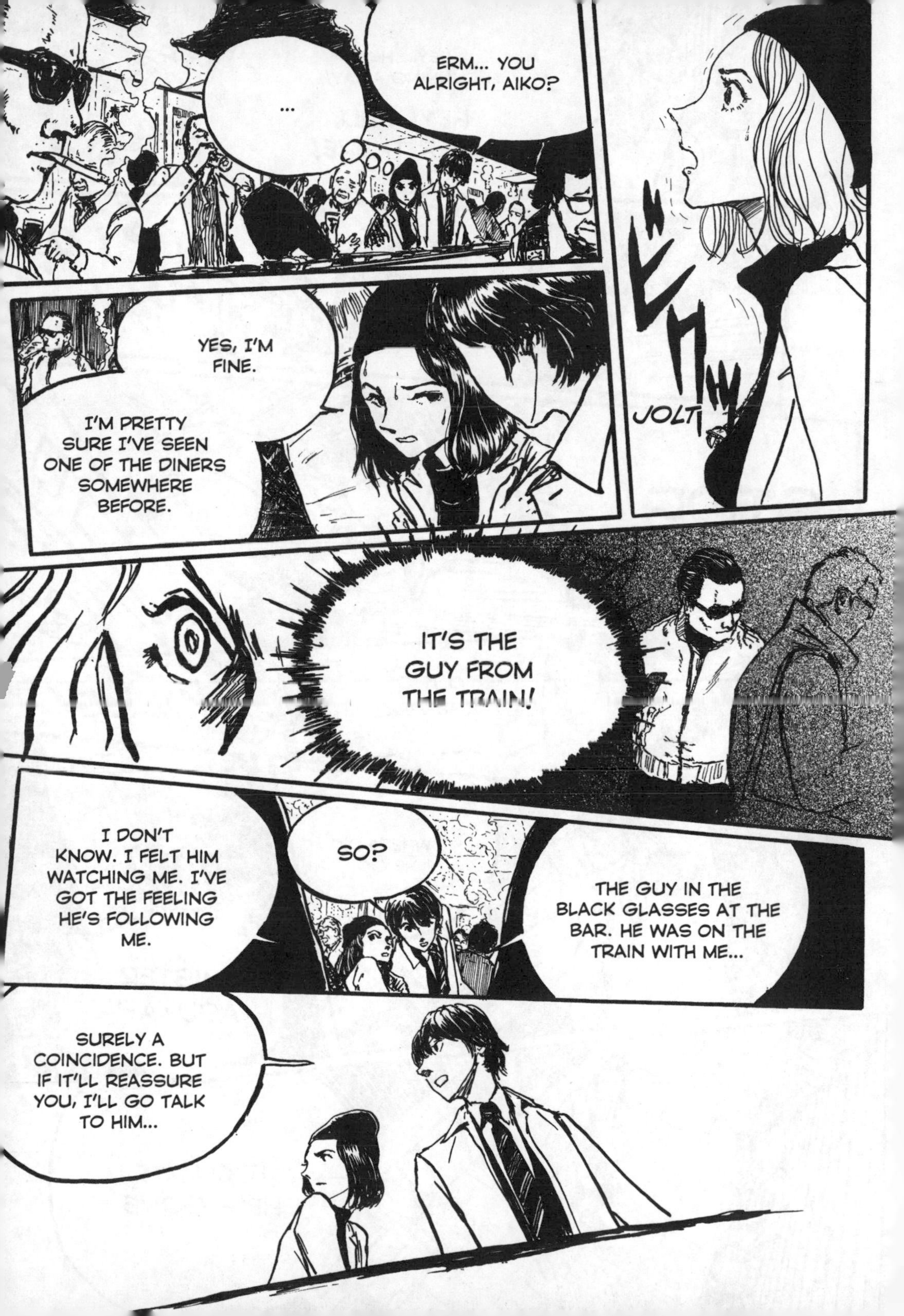
JOLT
ERM... YOU ALRIGHT, AIKO?
...
YES, I'M FINE.
I'M PRETTY SURE I'VE SEEN ONE OF THE DINERS SOMEWHERE BEFORE.
IT'S THE GUY FROM THE TRAIN!
THE GUY IN THE BLACK GLASSES AT THE BAR. HE WAS ON THE TRAIN WITH ME...
SO?
I DON'T KNOW. I FELT HIM WATCHING ME. I'VE GOT THE FEELING HE'S FOLLOWING ME.
SURELY A COINCIDENCE. BUT IF IT'LL REASSURE YOU, I'LL GO TALK TO HIM...

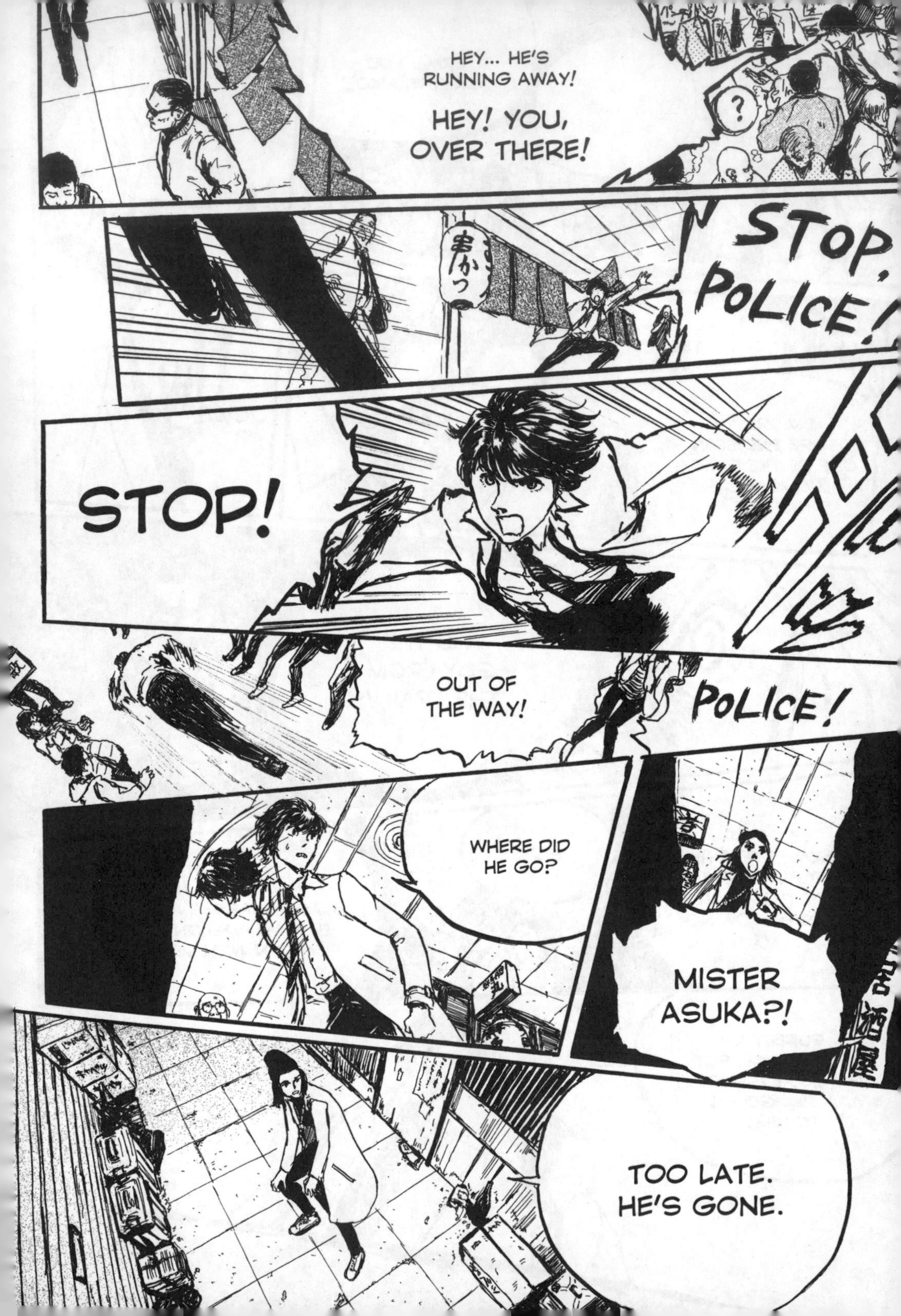
HEY... HE'S RUNNING AWAY!
HEY! YOU, OVER THERE!
STOP, POLICE!
STOP!
POLICE!
OUT OF THE WAY!
MISTER ASUKA?!
WHERE DID HE GO?
TOO LATE. HE'S GONE.

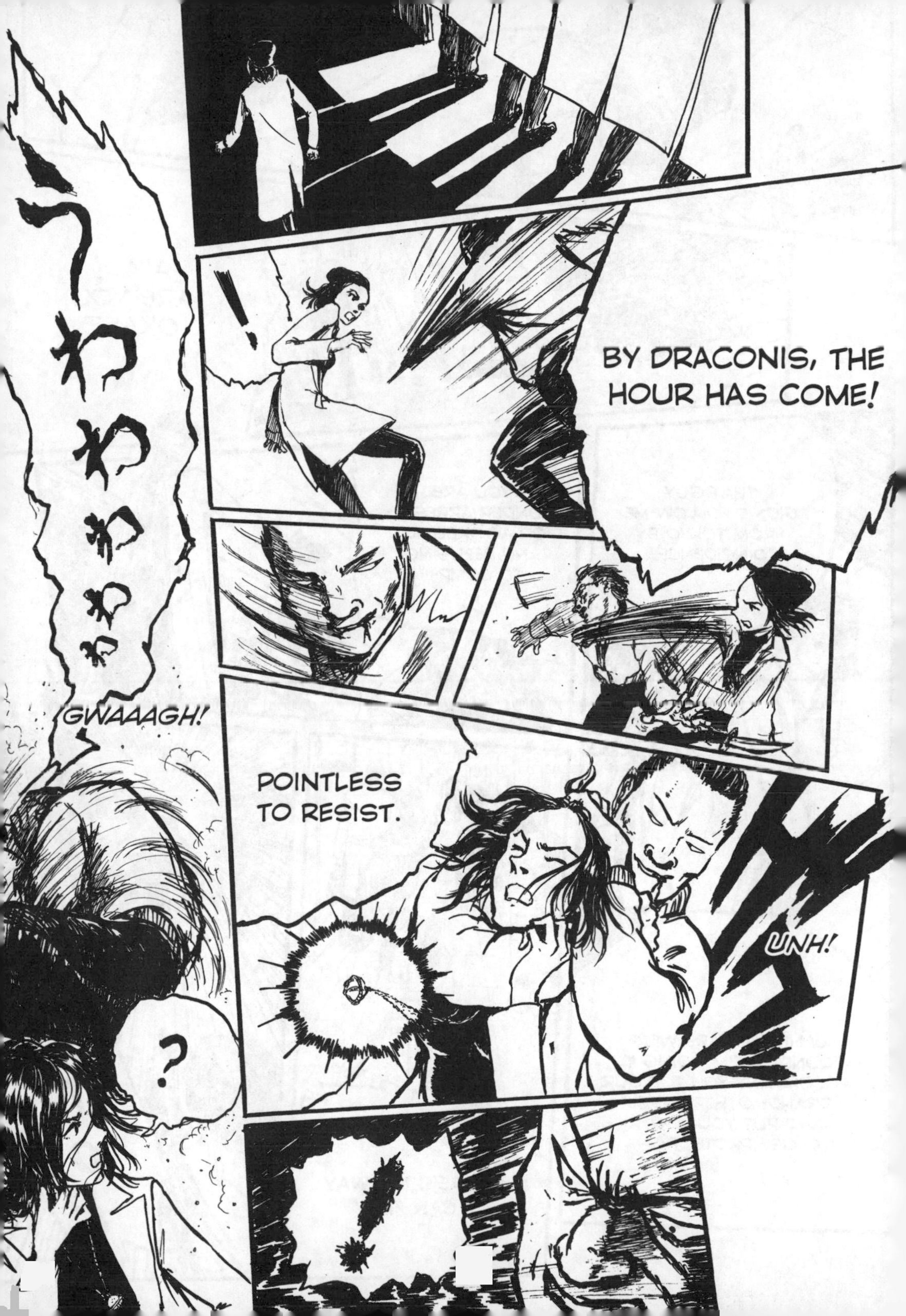
BY DRACONIS, THE HOUR HAS COME!
!
うわわわわわ
GWAAAGH!
POINTLESS TO RESIST.
UNH!
?
!

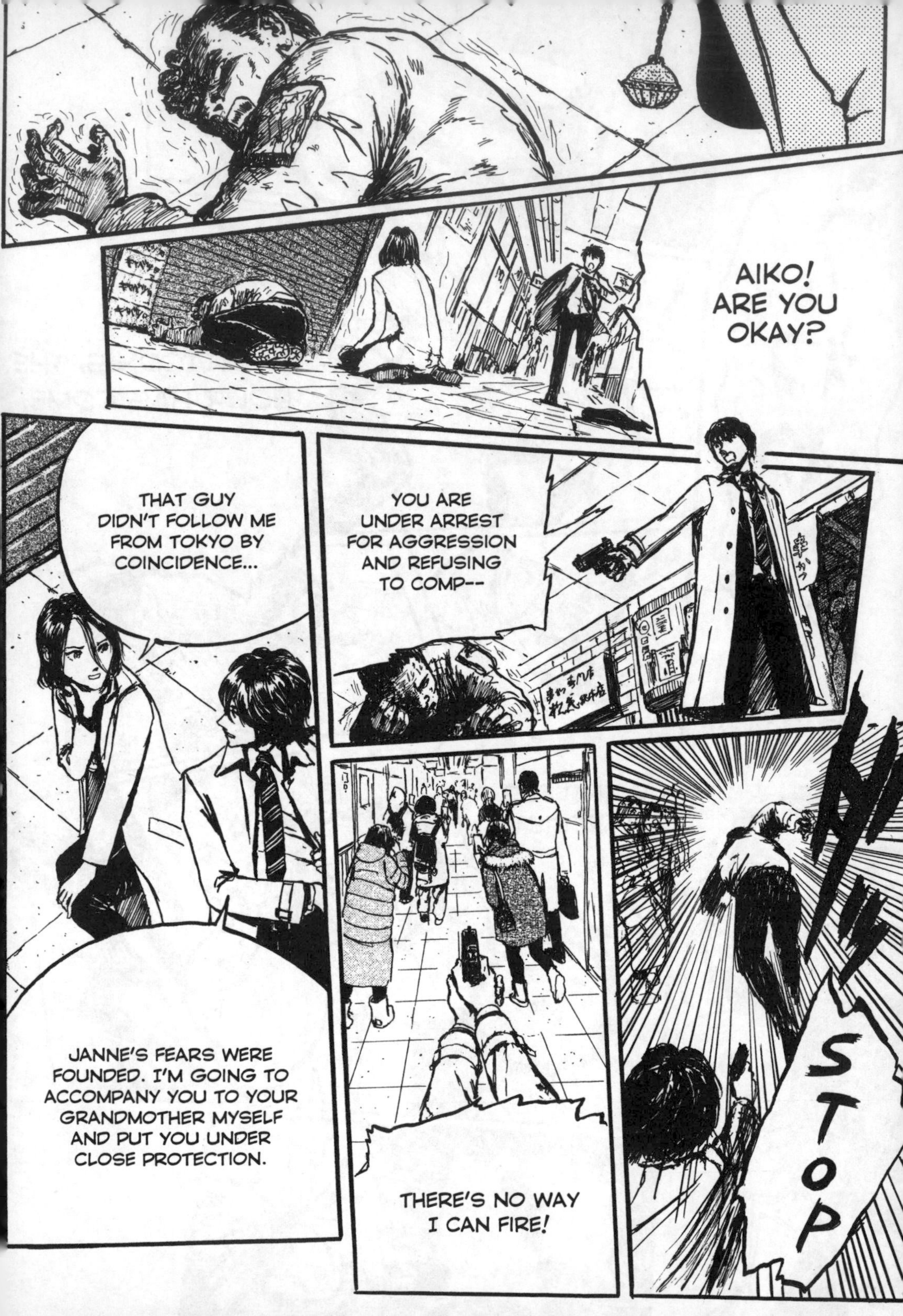
AIKO! ARE YOU OKAY?
YOU ARE UNDER ARREST FOR AGGRESSION AND REFUSING TO COMP--
STOP
THERE'S NO WAY I CAN FIRE!
THAT GUY DIDN'T FOLLOW ME FROM TOKYO BY COINCIDENCE...
JANNE'S FEARS WERE FOUNDED. I'M GOING TO ACCOMPANY YOU TO YOUR GRANDMOTHER MYSELF AND PUT YOU UNDER CLOSE PROTECTION.

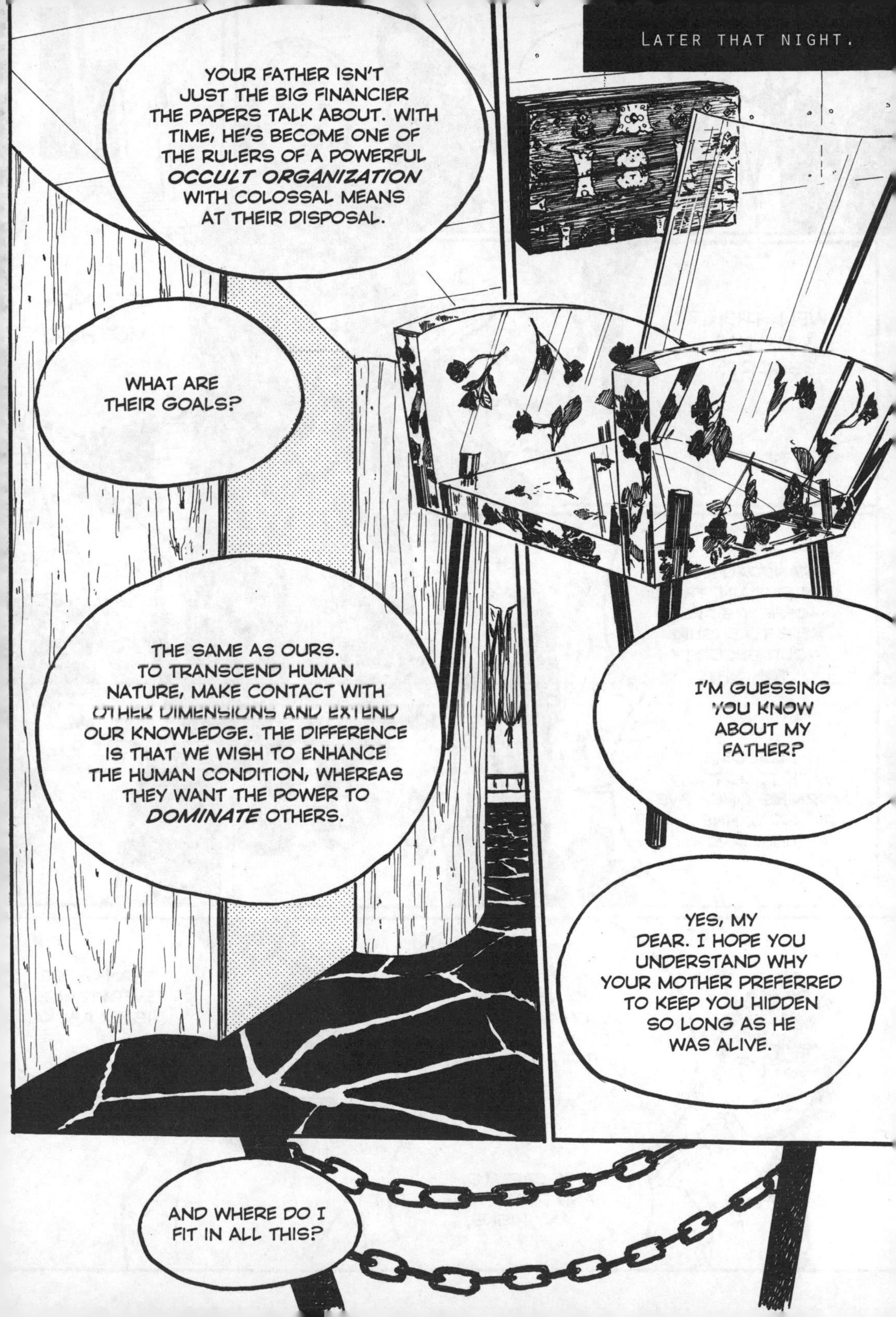
LATER THAT NIGHT.
I'M GUESSING YOU KNOW ABOUT MY FATHER?
YES, MY DEAR. I HOPE YOU UNDERSTAND WHY YOUR MOTHER PREFERRED TO KEEP YOU HIDDEN SO LONG AS HE WAS ALIVE.
YOUR FATHER ISN'T JUST THE BIG FINANCIER THE PAPERS TALK ABOUT. WITH TIME, HE'S BECOME ONE OF THE RULERS OF A POWERFUL *OCCULT ORGANIZATION* WITH COLOSSAL MEANS AT THEIR DISPOSAL.
WHAT ARE THEIR GOALS?
THE SAME AS OURS. TO TRANSCEND HUMAN NATURE, MAKE CONTACT WITH OTHER DIMENSIONS AND EXTEND OUR KNOWLEDGE. THE DIFFERENCE IS THAT WE WISH TO ENHANCE THE HUMAN CONDITION, WHEREAS THEY WANT THE POWER TO *DOMINATE* OTHERS.
AND WHERE DO I FIT IN ALL THIS?

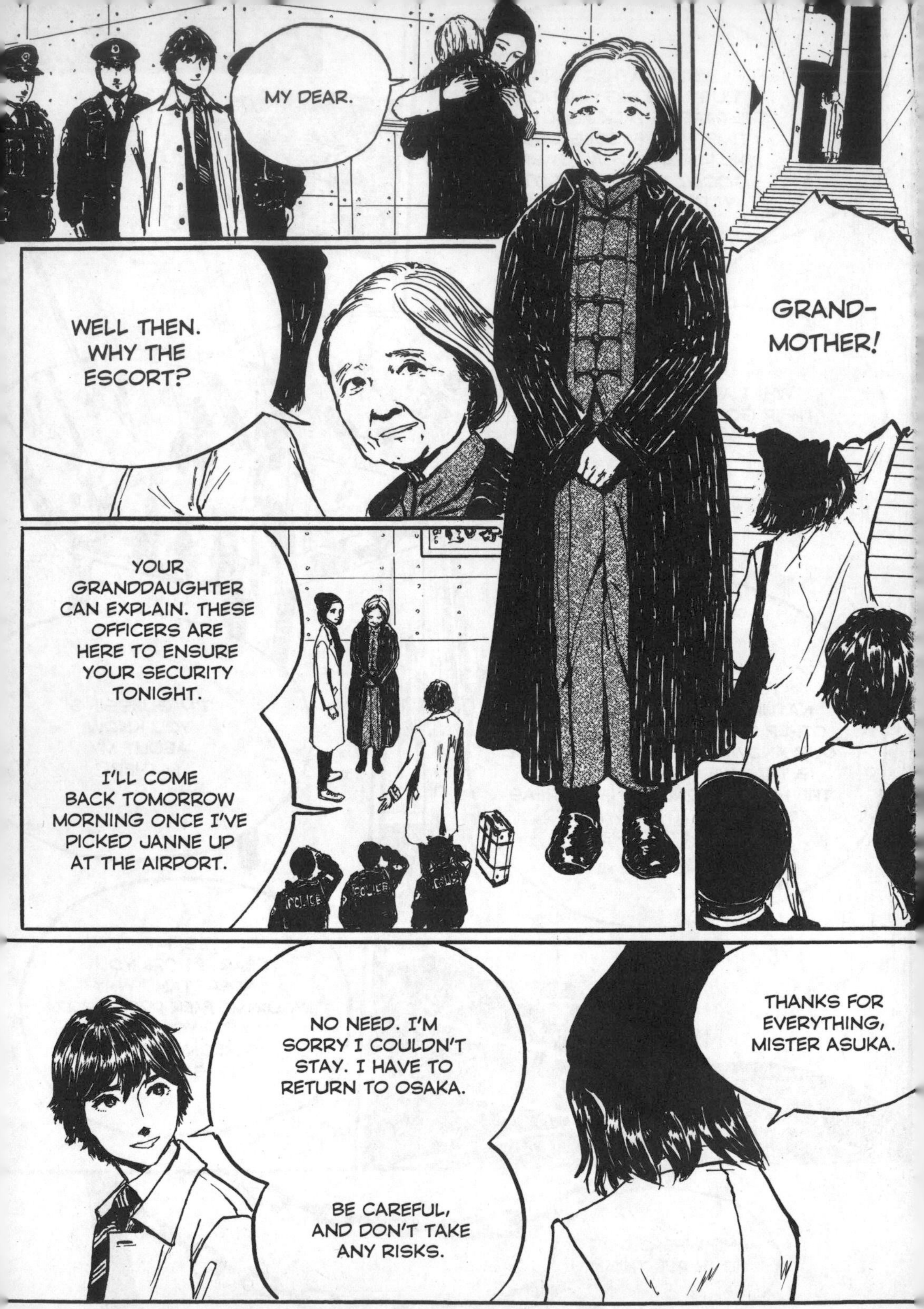
GRAND-MOTHER!
MY DEAR.
WELL THEN. WHY THE ESCORT?
YOUR GRANDDAUGHTER CAN EXPLAIN. THESE OFFICERS ARE HERE TO ENSURE YOUR SECURITY TONIGHT.
I'LL COME BACK TOMORROW MORNING ONCE I'VE PICKED JANNE UP AT THE AIRPORT.
THANKS FOR EVERYTHING, MISTER ASUKA.
NO NEED. I'M SORRY I COULDN'T STAY. I HAVE TO RETURN TO OSAKA.
BE CAREFUL, AND DON'T TAKE ANY RISKS.

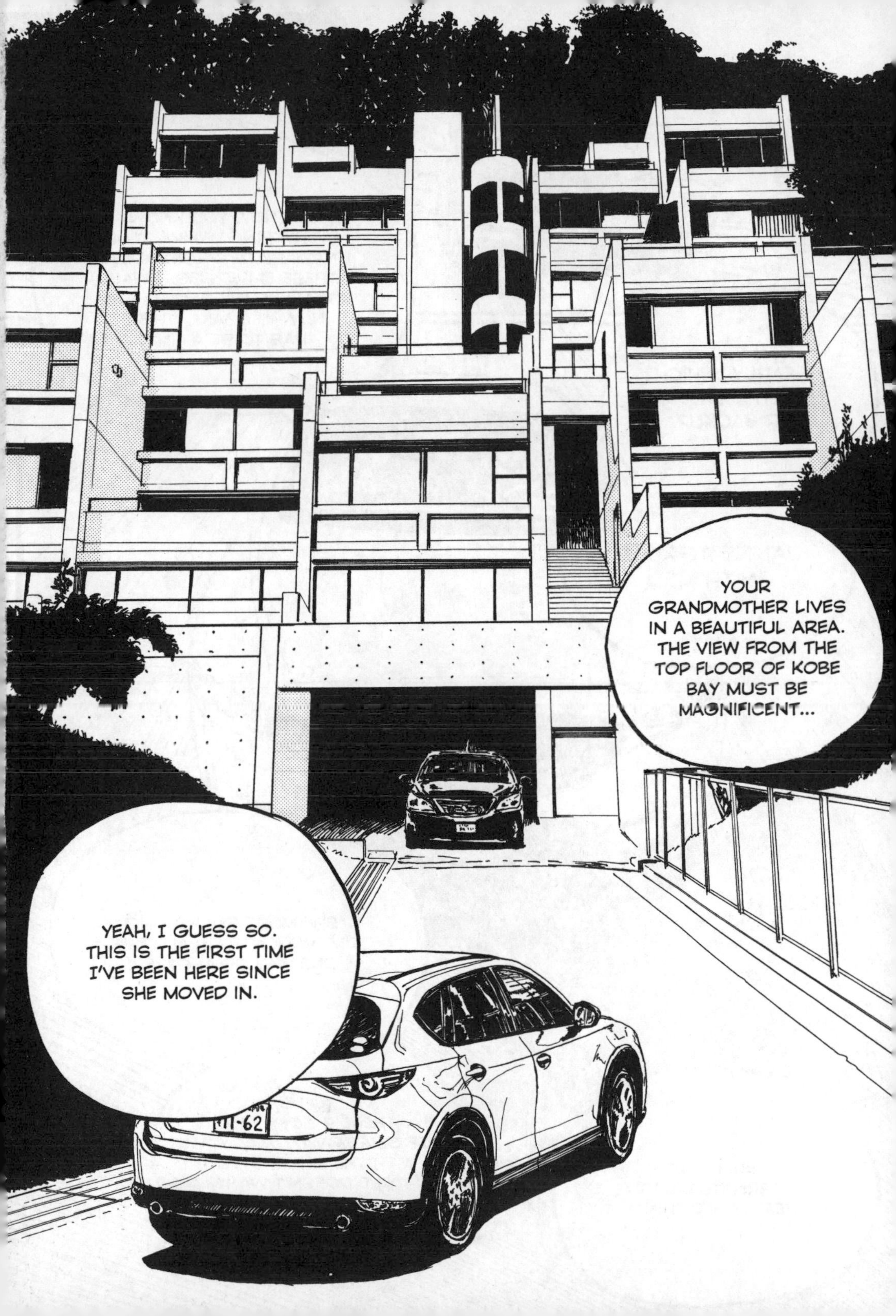
YOUR GRANDMOTHER LIVES IN A BEAUTIFUL AREA. THE VIEW FROM THE TOP FLOOR OF KOBE BAY MUST BE MAGNIFICENT...
YEAH, I GUESS SO. THIS IS THE FIRST TIME I'VE BEEN HERE SINCE SHE MOVED IN.

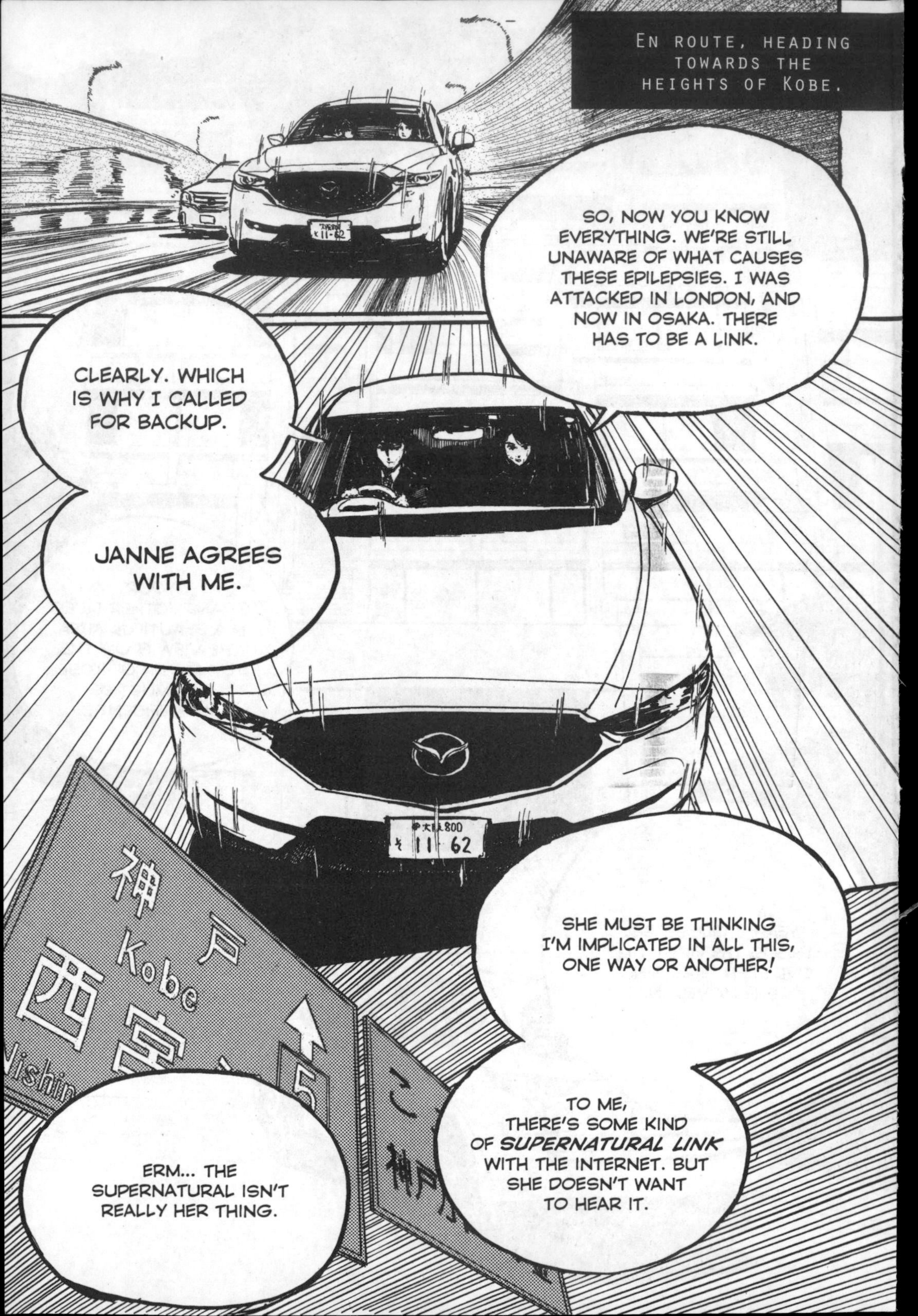
En route, heading towards the heights of Kobe.
SO, NOW YOU KNOW EVERYTHING. WE'RE STILL UNAWARE OF WHAT CAUSES THESE EPILEPSIES. I WAS ATTACKED IN LONDON, AND NOW IN OSAKA. THERE HAS TO BE A LINK.
CLEARLY. WHICH IS WHY I CALLED FOR BACKUP.
JANNE AGREES WITH ME.
SHE MUST BE THINKING I'M IMPLICATED IN ALL THIS, ONE WAY OR ANOTHER!
TO ME, THERE'S SOME KIND OF ***SUPERNATURAL LINK*** WITH THE INTERNET. BUT SHE DOESN'T WANT TO HEAR IT.
神戸
Kobe
ERM... THE SUPERNATURAL ISN'T REALLY HER THING.

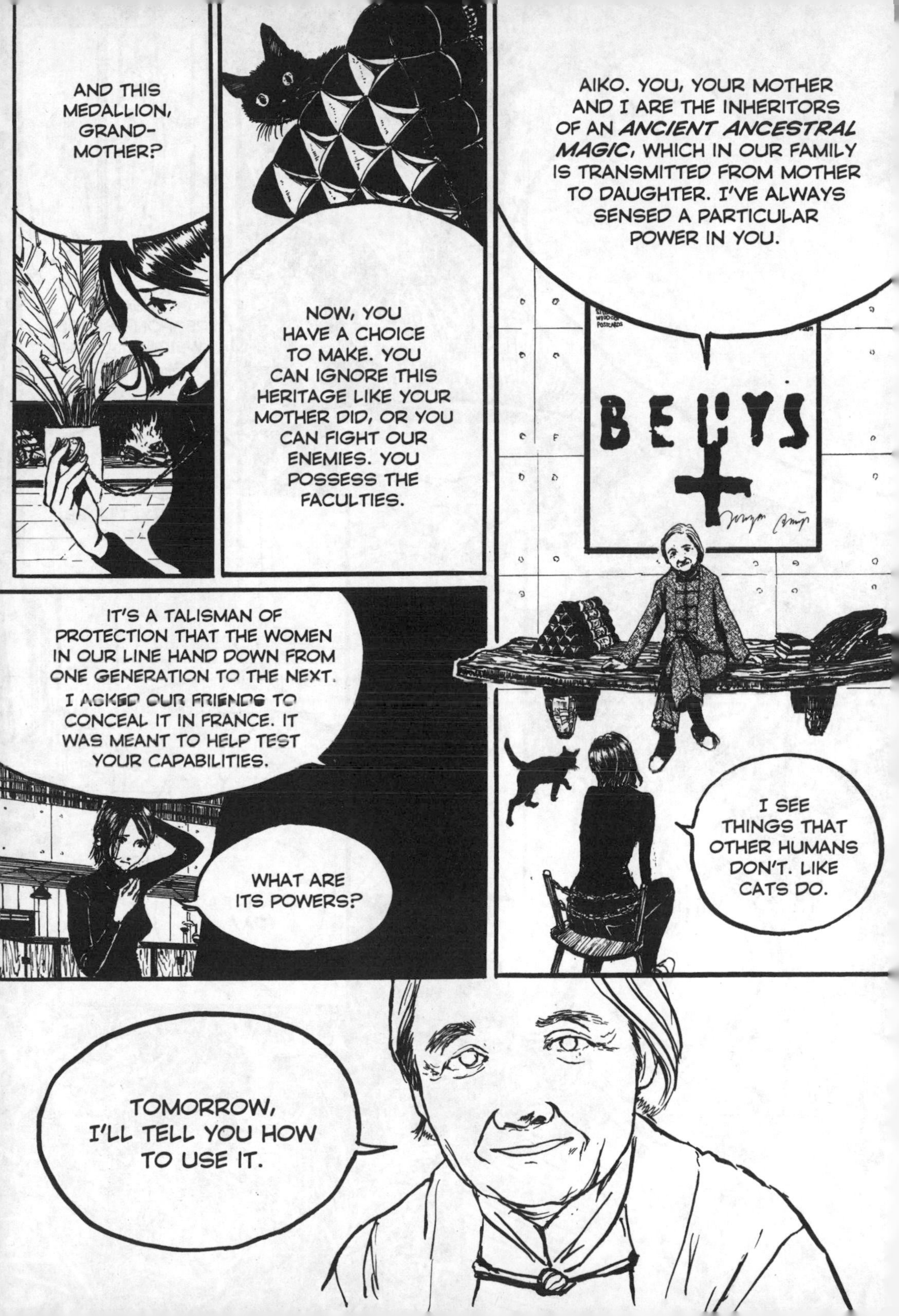
AIKO. YOU, YOUR MOTHER AND I ARE THE INHERITORS OF AN *ANCIENT ANCESTRAL MAGIC*, WHICH IN OUR FAMILY IS TRANSMITTED FROM MOTHER TO DAUGHTER. I'VE ALWAYS SENSED A PARTICULAR POWER IN YOU.
BEUYS
I SEE THINGS THAT OTHER HUMANS DON'T. LIKE CATS DO.
NOW, YOU HAVE A CHOICE TO MAKE. YOU CAN IGNORE THIS HERITAGE LIKE YOUR MOTHER DID, OR YOU CAN FIGHT OUR ENEMIES. YOU POSSESS THE FACULTIES.
AND THIS MEDALLION, GRAND-MOTHER?
IT'S A TALISMAN OF PROTECTION THAT THE WOMEN IN OUR LINE HAND DOWN FROM ONE GENERATION TO THE NEXT.
I ASKED OUR FRIENDS TO CONCEAL IT IN FRANCE. IT WAS MEANT TO HELP TEST YOUR CAPABILITIES.
WHAT ARE ITS POWERS?
TOMORROW, I'LL TELL YOU HOW TO USE IT.

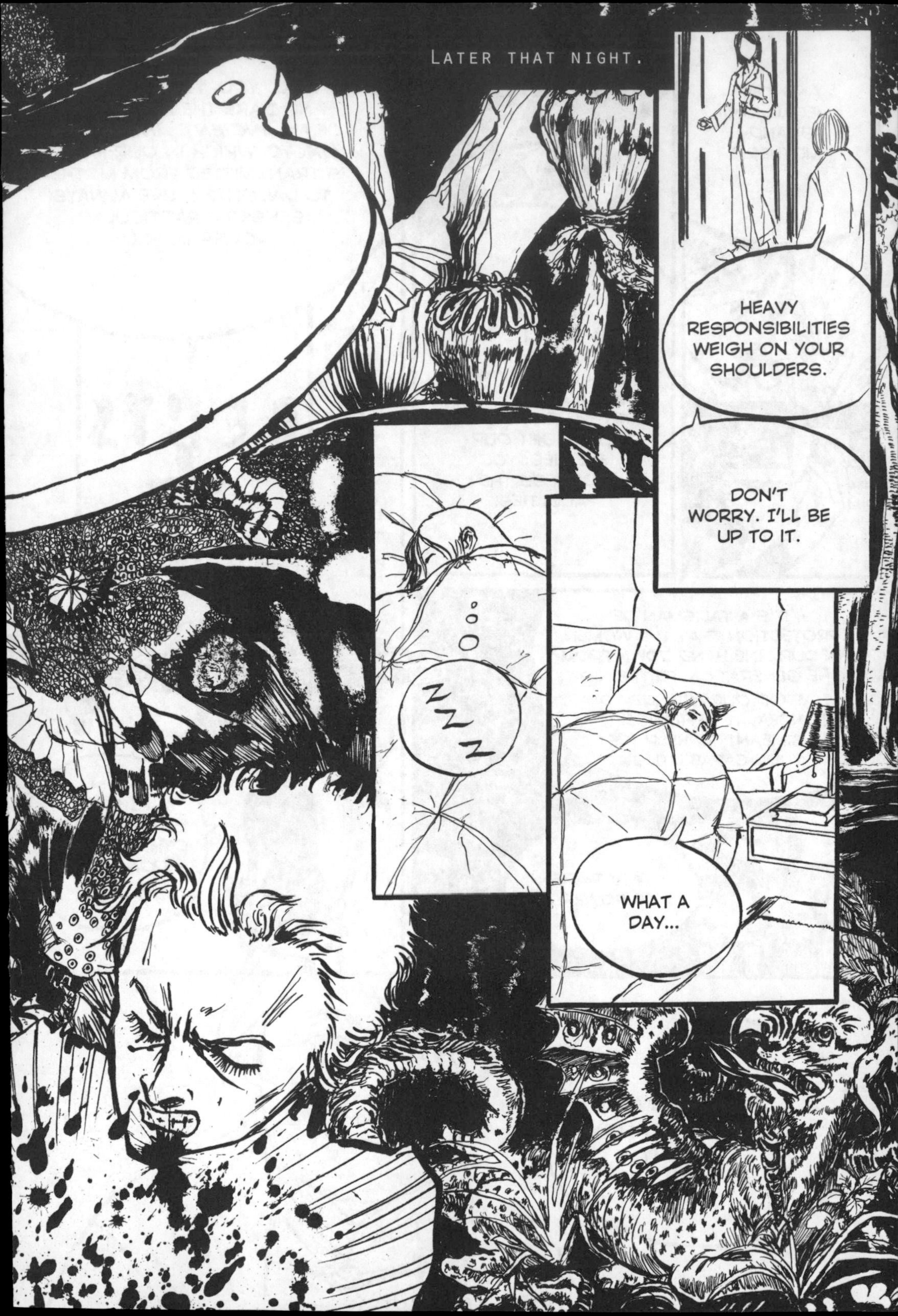
LATER THAT NIGHT.
HEAVY RESPONSIBILITIES WEIGH ON YOUR SHOULDERS.
DON'T WORRY. I'LL BE UP TO IT.
WHAT A DAY...
ZZZ

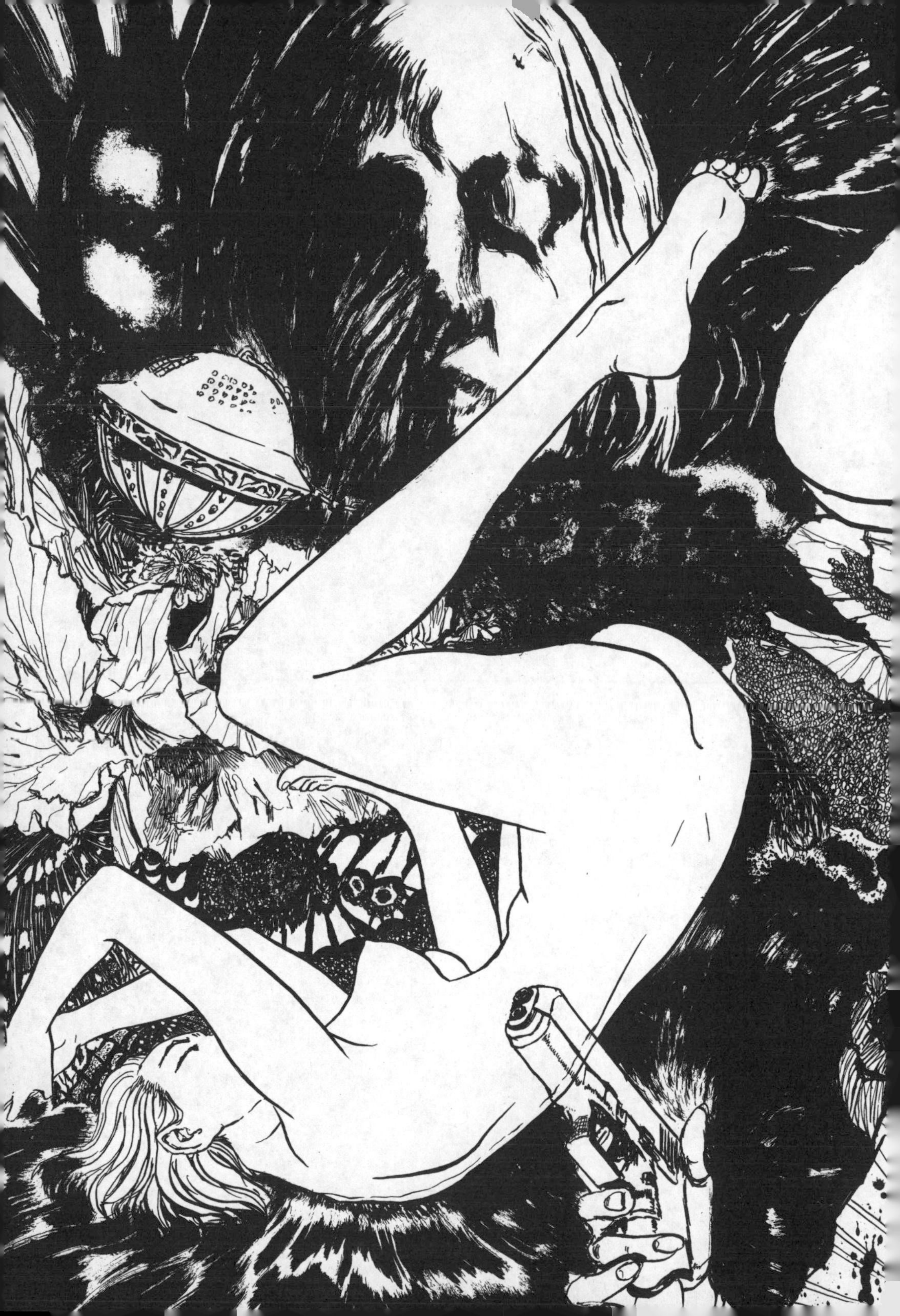

CHAPTER 2

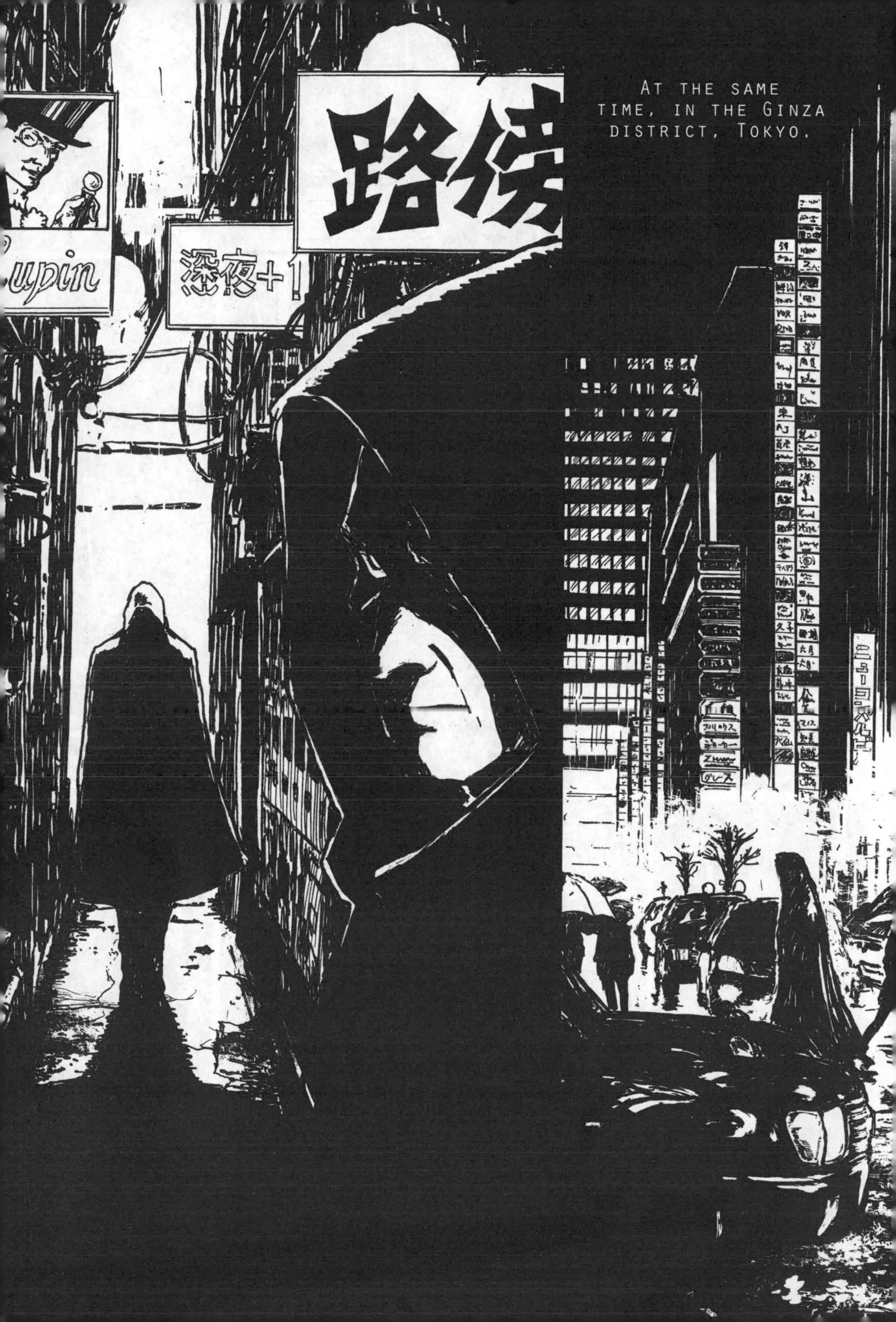
At the same time, in the Ginza district, Tokyo.
upin
深夜+1

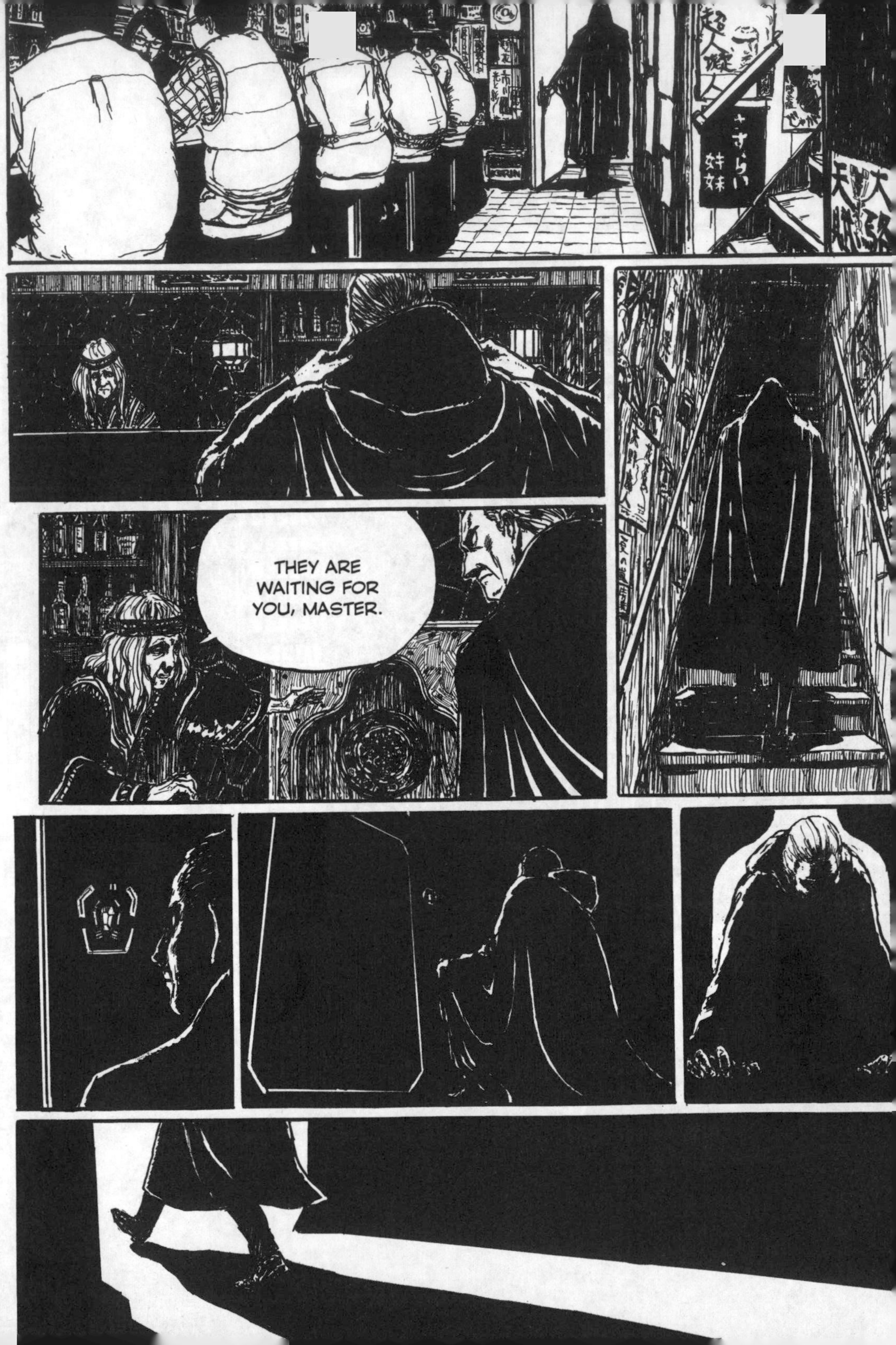
THEY ARE WAITING FOR YOU, MASTER.

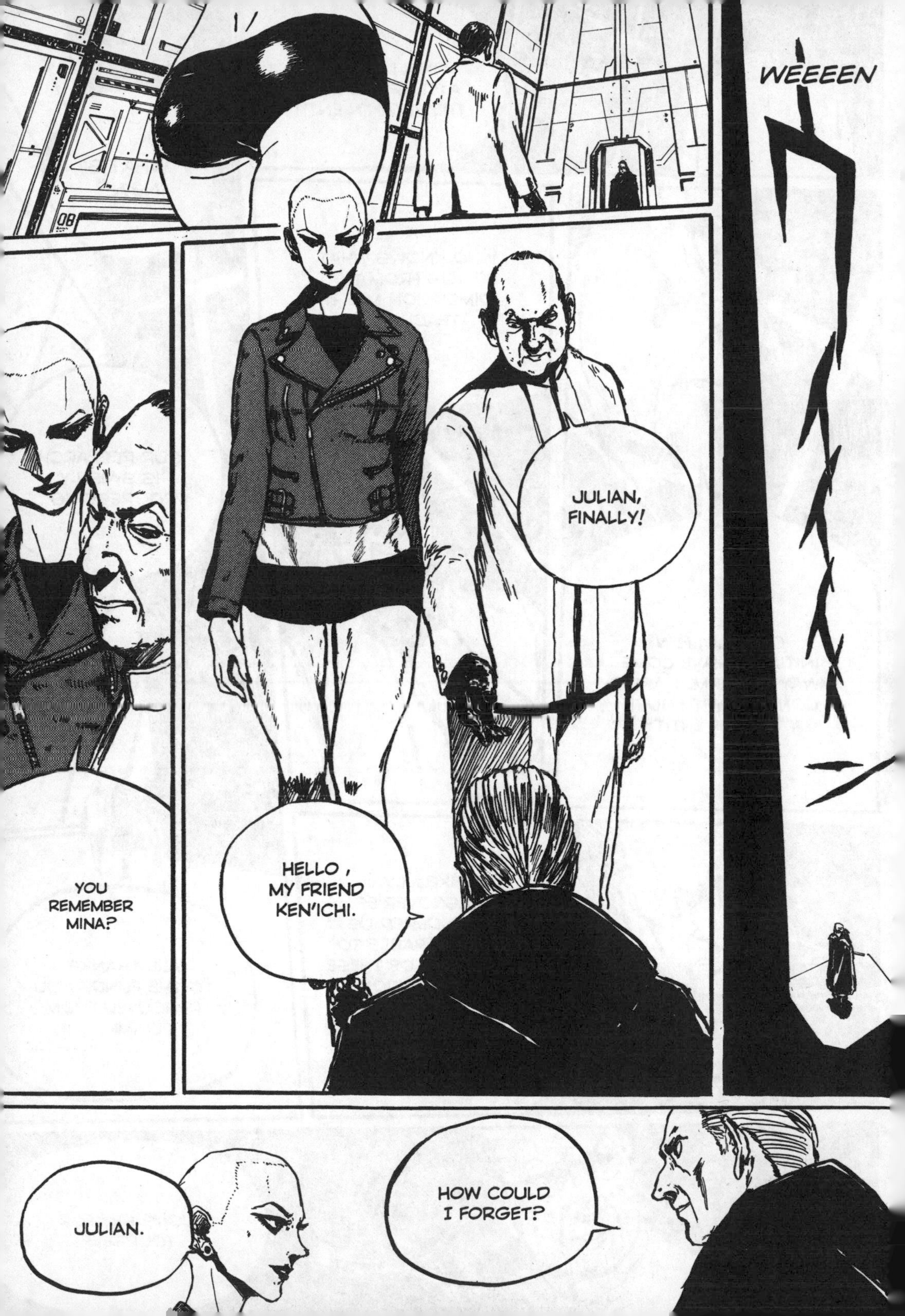
WEEEEN
JULIAN, FINALLY!
HELLO, MY FRIEND KEN'ICHI.
YOU REMEMBER MINA?
HOW COULD I FORGET?
JULIAN.

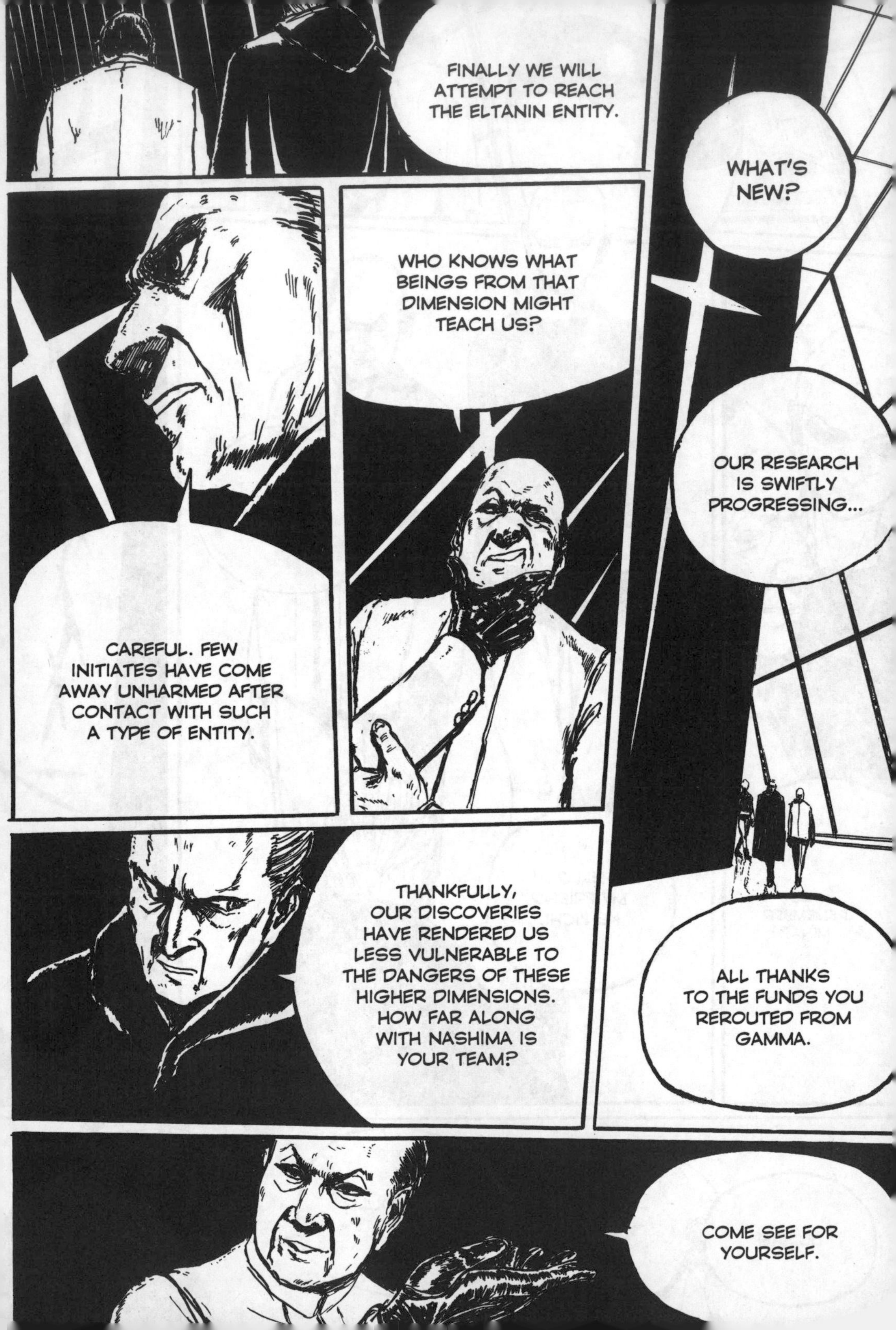
WHAT'S NEW?
OUR RESEARCH IS SWIFTLY PROGRESSING...
ALL THANKS TO THE FUNDS YOU REROUTED FROM GAMMA.
FINALLY WE WILL ATTEMPT TO REACH THE ELTANIN ENTITY.
WHO KNOWS WHAT BEINGS FROM THAT DIMENSION MIGHT TEACH US?
CAREFUL. FEW INITIATES HAVE COME AWAY UNHARMED AFTER CONTACT WITH SUCH A TYPE OF ENTITY.
THANKFULLY, OUR DISCOVERIES HAVE RENDERED US LESS VULNERABLE TO THE DANGERS OF THESE HIGHER DIMENSIONS. HOW FAR ALONG WITH NASHIMA IS YOUR TEAM?
COME SEE FOR YOURSELF.

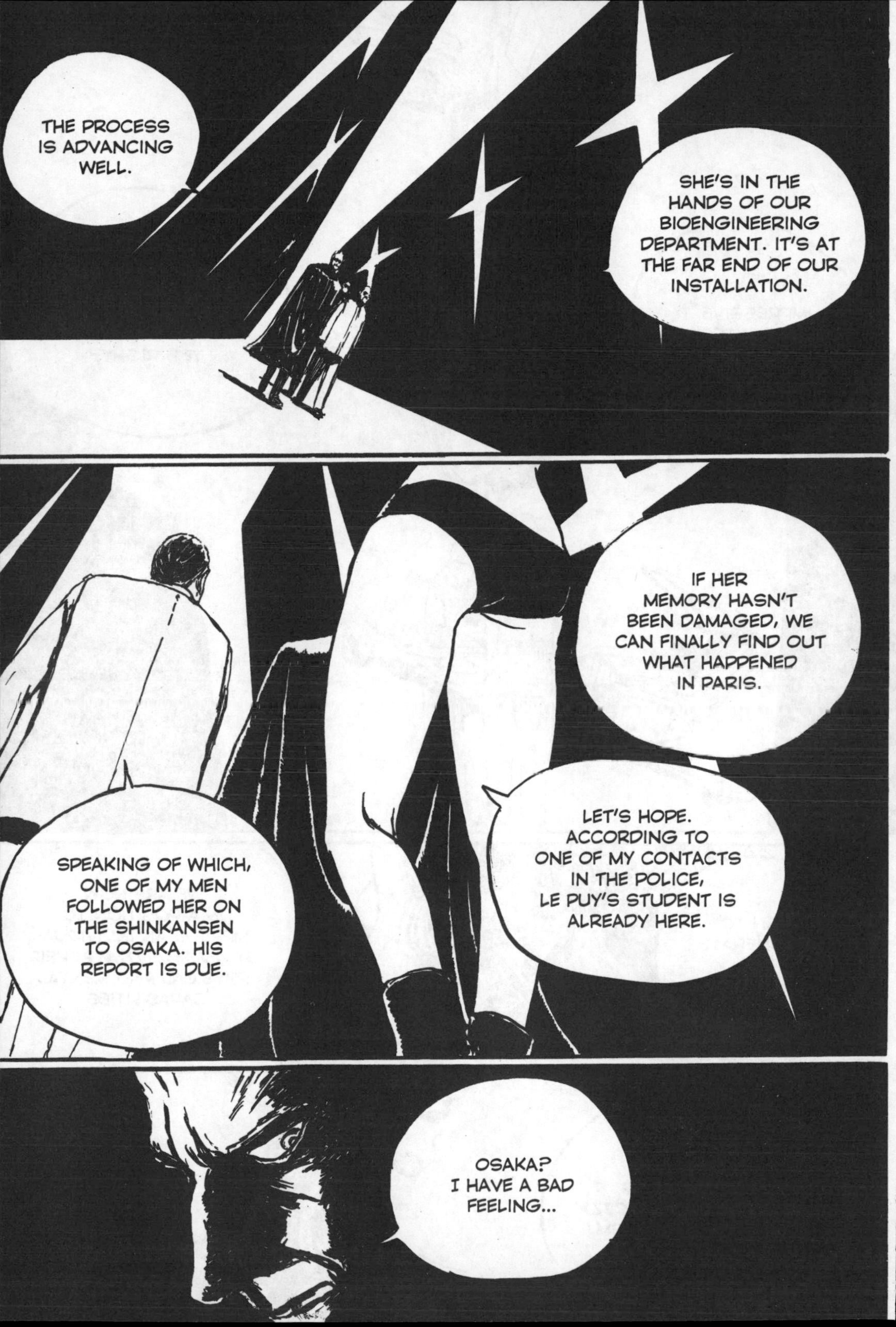
THE PROCESS IS ADVANCING WELL.
SHE'S IN THE HANDS OF OUR BIOENGINEERING DEPARTMENT. IT'S AT THE FAR END OF OUR INSTALLATION.
IF HER MEMORY HASN'T BEEN DAMAGED, WE CAN FINALLY FIND OUT WHAT HAPPENED IN PARIS.
LET'S HOPE. ACCORDING TO ONE OF MY CONTACTS IN THE POLICE, LE PUY'S STUDENT IS ALREADY HERE.
SPEAKING OF WHICH, ONE OF MY MEN FOLLOWED HER ON THE SHINKANSEN TO OSAKA. HIS REPORT IS DUE.
OSAKA? I HAVE A BAD FEELING...

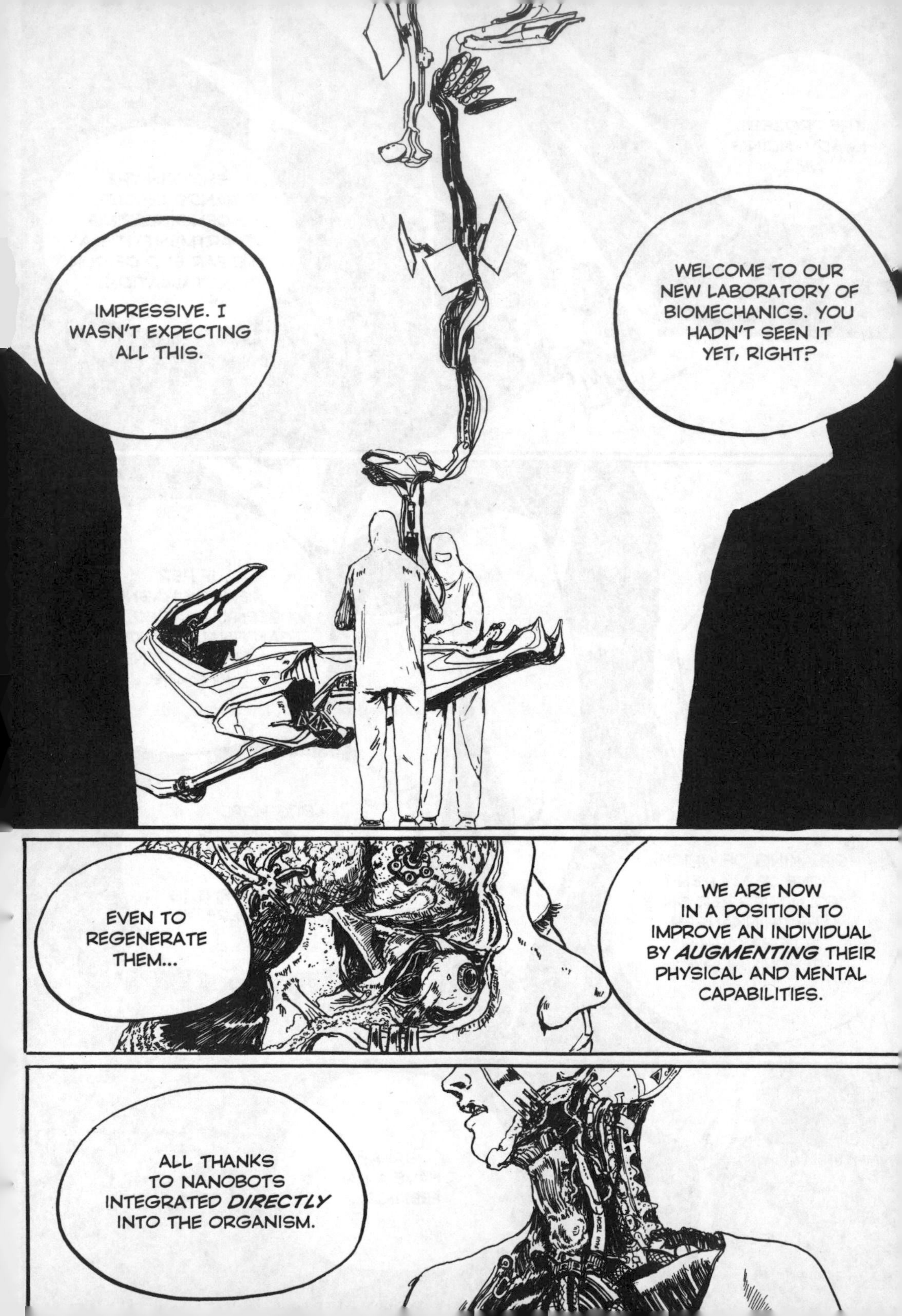
WELCOME TO OUR NEW LABORATORY OF BIOMECHANICS. YOU HADN'T SEEN IT YET, RIGHT?
IMPRESSIVE. I WASN'T EXPECTING ALL THIS.
WE ARE NOW IN A POSITION TO IMPROVE AN INDIVIDUAL BY *AUGMENTING* THEIR PHYSICAL AND MENTAL CAPABILITIES.
EVEN TO REGENERATE THEM...
ALL THANKS TO NANOBOTS INTEGRATED *DIRECTLY* INTO THE ORGANISM.

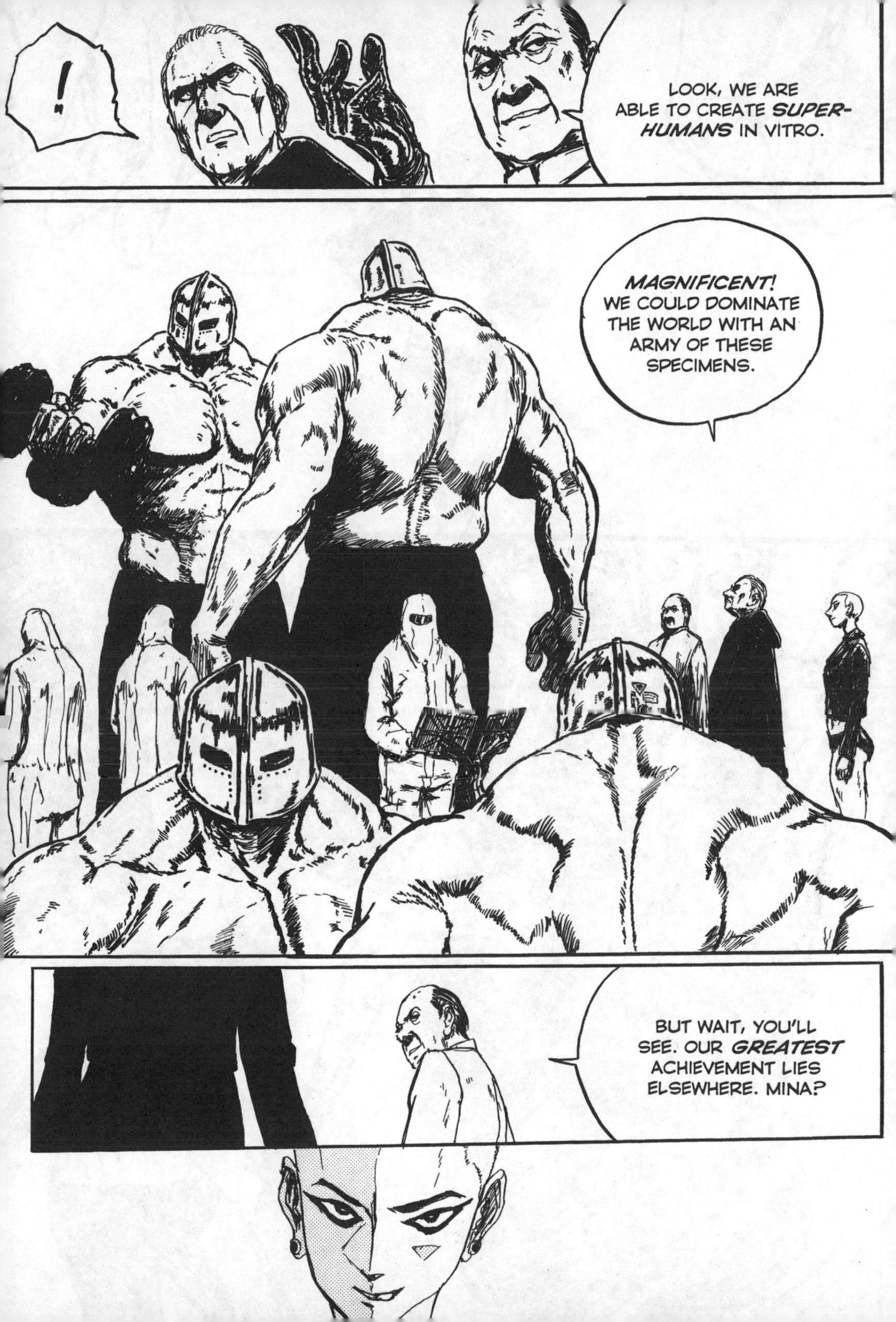
LOOK, WE ARE ABLE TO CREATE *SUPER-HUMANS* IN VITRO.
!
MAGNIFICENT! WE COULD DOMINATE THE WORLD WITH AN ARMY OF THESE SPECIMENS.
BUT WAIT, YOU'LL SEE. OUR *GREATEST* ACHIEVEMENT LIES ELSEWHERE. MINA?

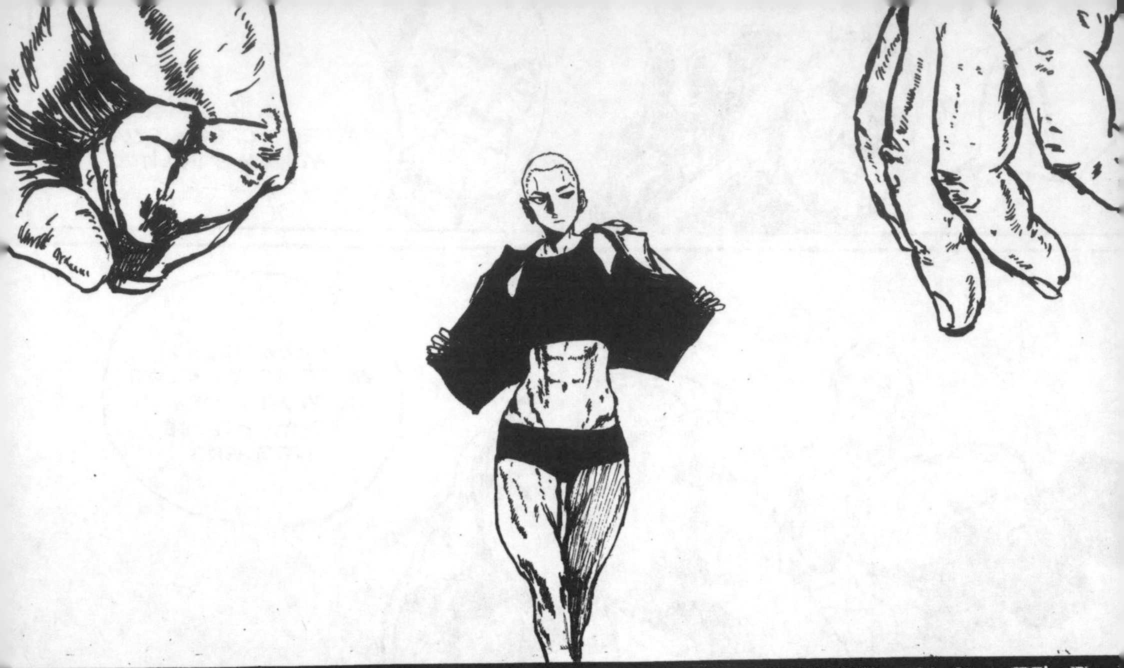

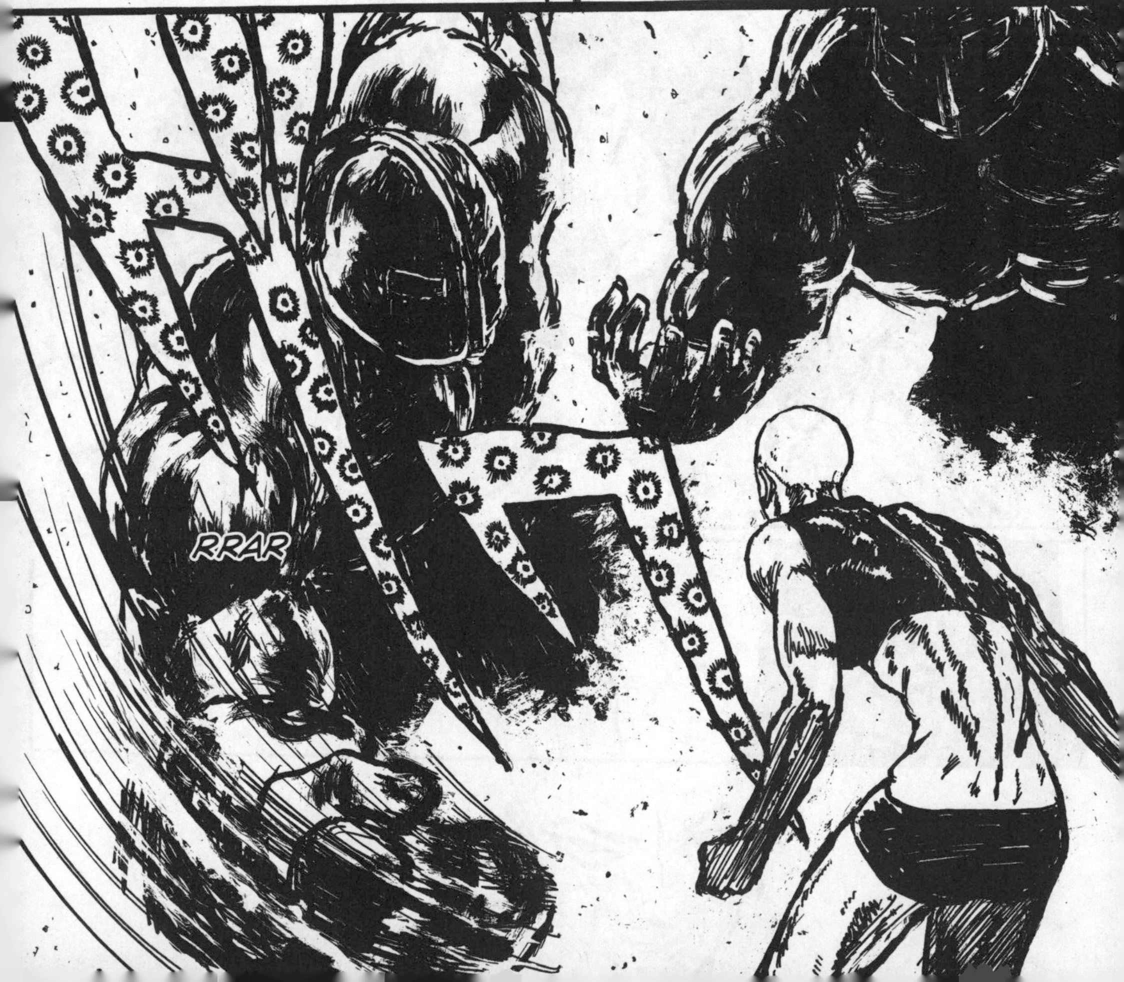
RRAR

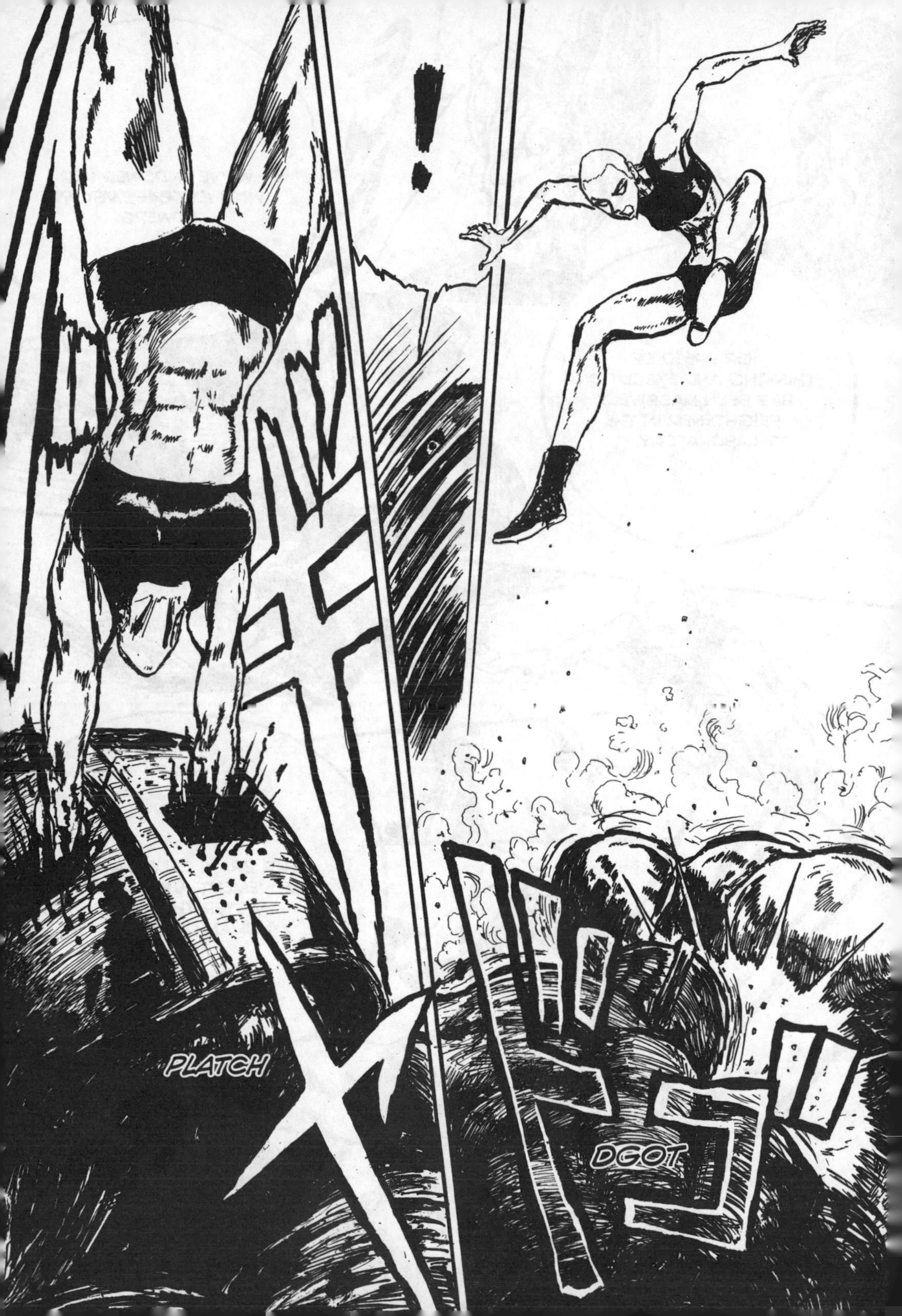
!
DGOT
PLATCH

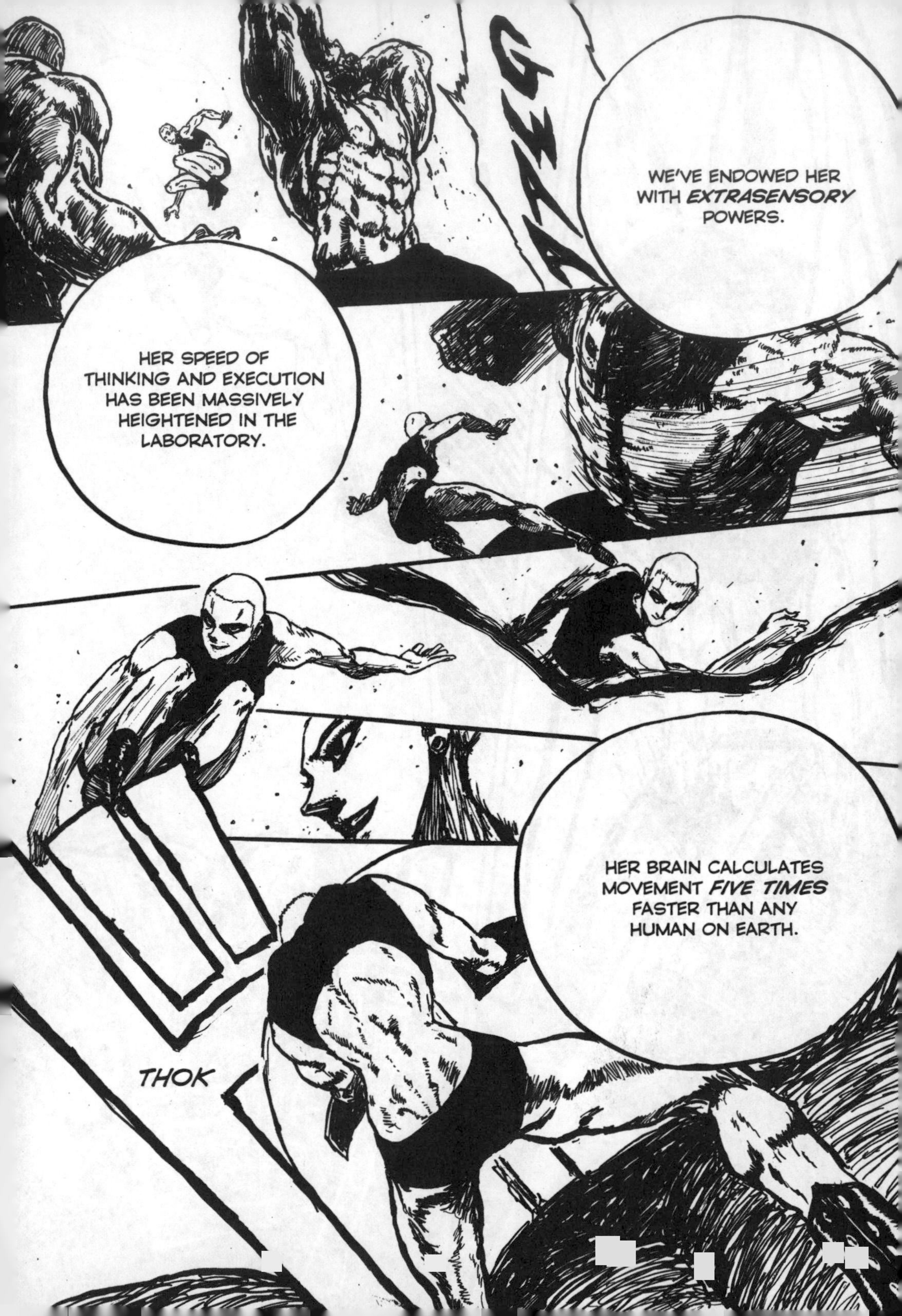

WE'VE ENDOWED HER WITH *EXTRASENSORY* POWERS.
GWAA
HER SPEED OF THINKING AND EXECUTION HAS BEEN MASSIVELY HEIGHTENED IN THE LABORATORY.
HER BRAIN CALCULATES MOVEMENT *FIVE TIMES* FASTER THAN ANY HUMAN ON EARTH.
THOK

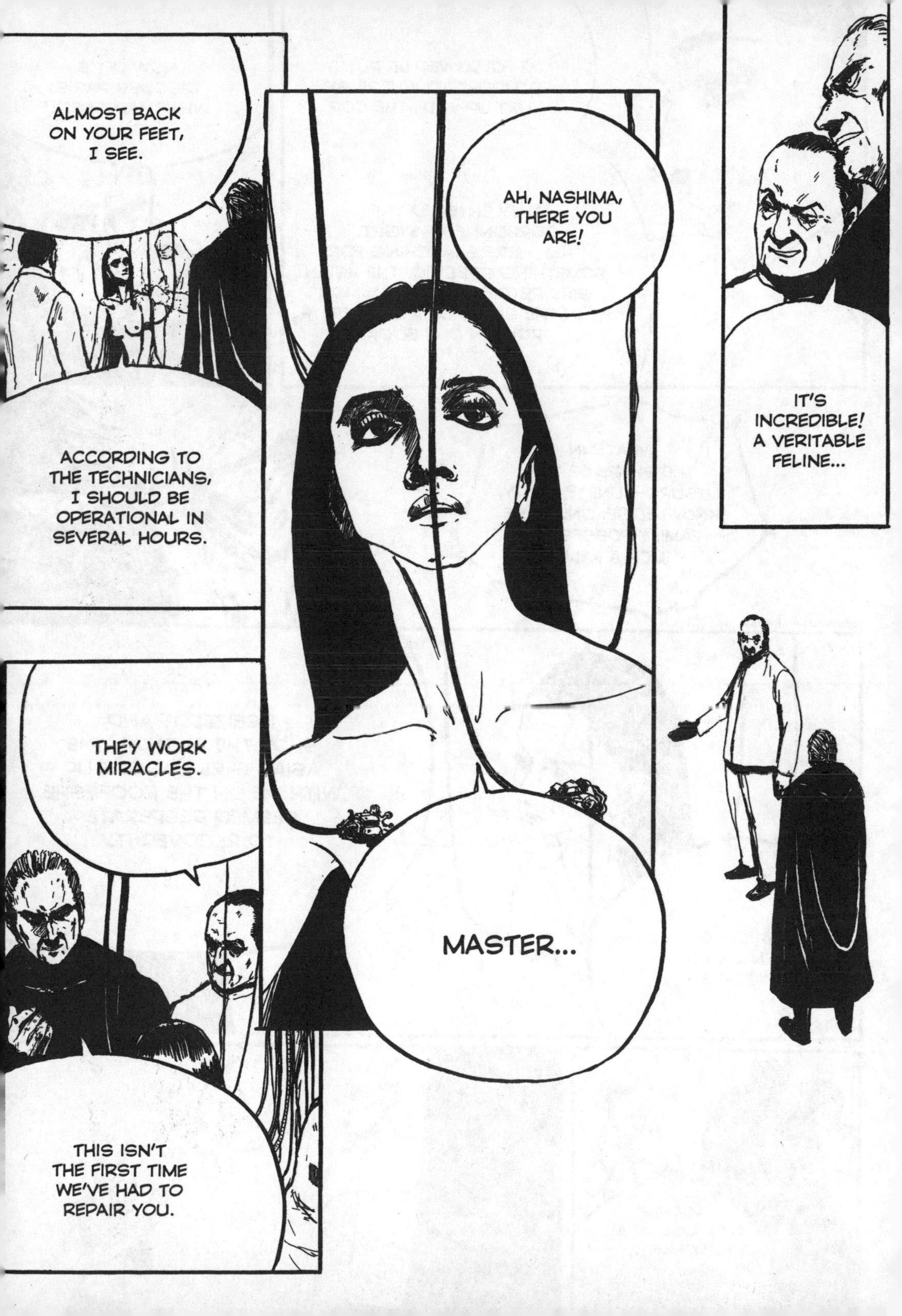
IT'S INCREDIBLE! A VERITABLE FELINE...
AH, NASHIMA, THERE YOU ARE!
MASTER...
ALMOST BACK ON YOUR FEET, I SEE.
ACCORDING TO THE TECHNICIANS, I SHOULD BE OPERATIONAL IN SEVERAL HOURS.
THEY WORK MIRACLES.
THIS ISN'T THE FIRST TIME WE'VE HAD TO REPAIR YOU.

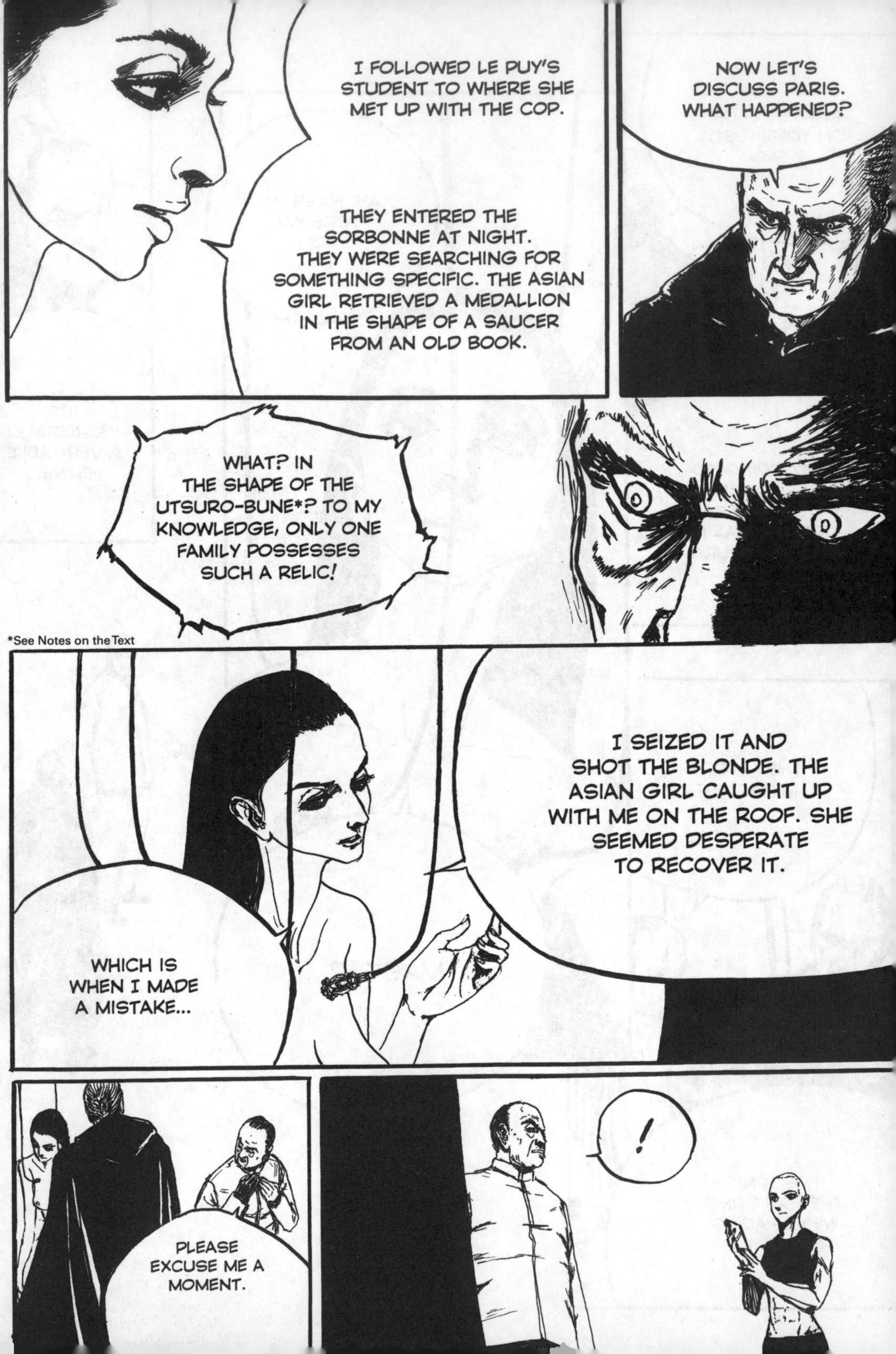
NOW LET'S DISCUSS PARIS. WHAT HAPPENED?
I FOLLOWED LE PUY'S STUDENT TO WHERE SHE MET UP WITH THE COP.
THEY ENTERED THE SORBONNE AT NIGHT. THEY WERE SEARCHING FOR SOMETHING SPECIFIC. THE ASIAN GIRL RETRIEVED A MEDALLION IN THE SHAPE OF A SAUCER FROM AN OLD BOOK.
WHAT? IN THE SHAPE OF THE UTSURO-BUNE*? TO MY KNOWLEDGE, ONLY ONE FAMILY POSSESSES SUCH A RELIC!
I SEIZED IT AND SHOT THE BLONDE. THE ASIAN GIRL CAUGHT UP WITH ME ON THE ROOF. SHE SEEMED DESPERATE TO RECOVER IT.
WHICH IS WHEN I MADE A MISTAKE...
!
PLEASE EXCUSE ME A MOMENT.

*See Notes on the Text

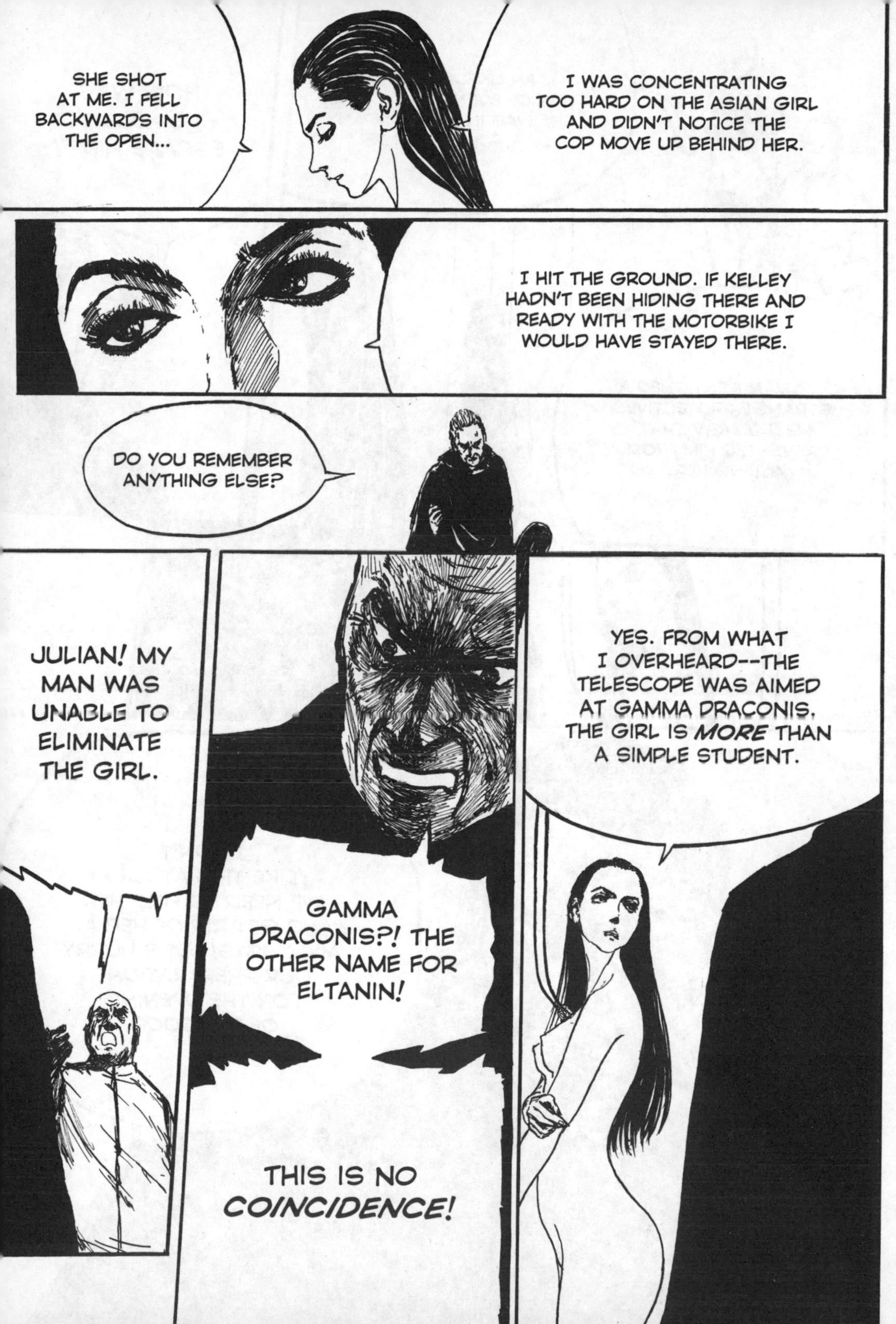
I WAS CONCENTRATING TOO HARD ON THE ASIAN GIRL AND DIDN'T NOTICE THE COP MOVE UP BEHIND HER.
SHE SHOT AT ME. I FELL BACKWARDS INTO THE OPEN...
I HIT THE GROUND. IF KELLEY HADN'T BEEN HIDING THERE AND READY WITH THE MOTORBIKE I WOULD HAVE STAYED THERE.
DO YOU REMEMBER ANYTHING ELSE?
YES. FROM WHAT I OVERHEARD--THE TELESCOPE WAS AIMED AT GAMMA DRACONIS. THE GIRL IS *MORE* THAN A SIMPLE STUDENT.
GAMMA DRACONIS?! THE OTHER NAME FOR ELTANIN!
THIS IS NO *COINCIDENCE!*
JULIAN! MY MAN WAS UNABLE TO ELIMINATE THE GIRL.

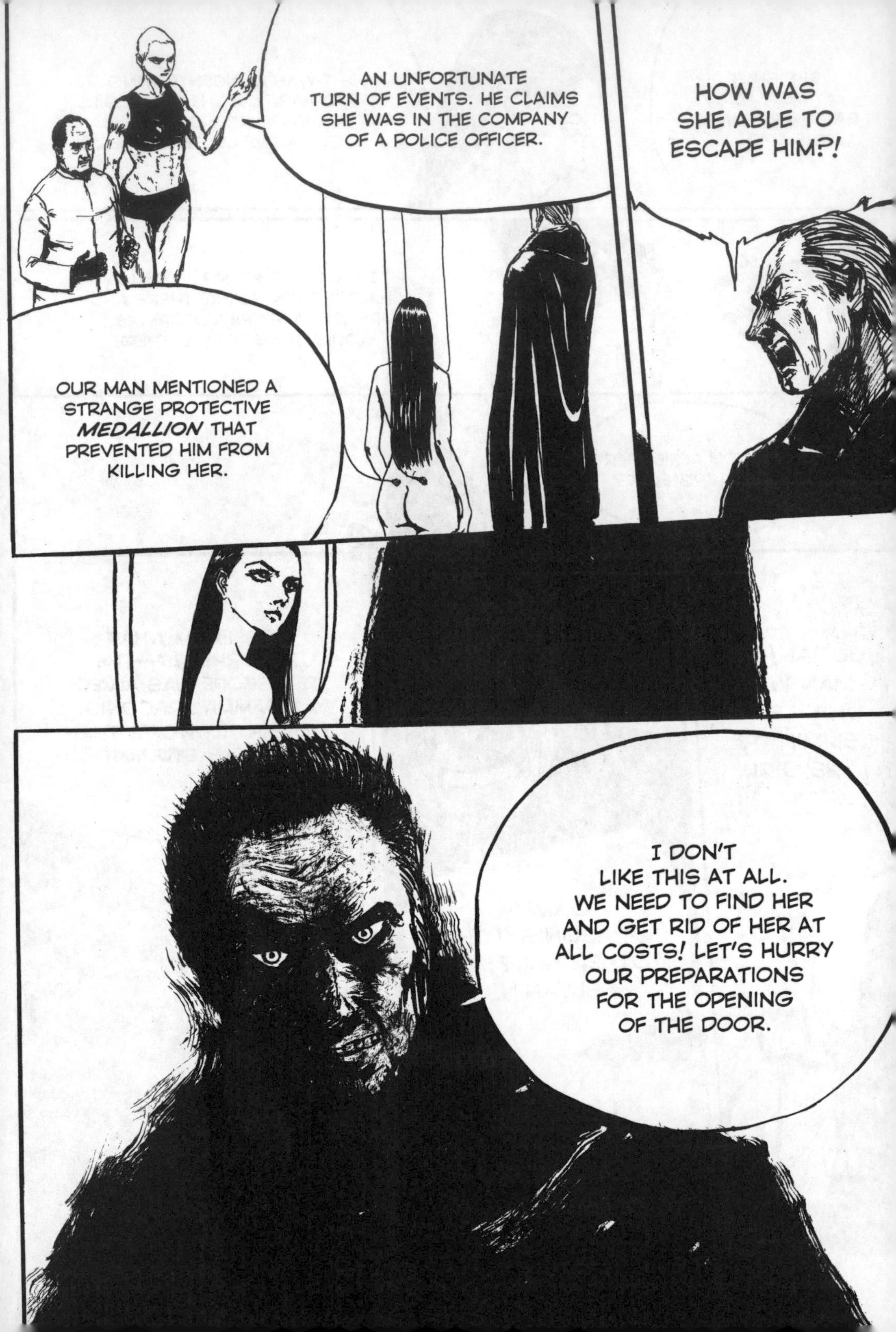
HOW WAS SHE ABLE TO ESCAPE HIM?!
AN UNFORTUNATE TURN OF EVENTS. HE CLAIMS SHE WAS IN THE COMPANY OF A POLICE OFFICER.
OUR MAN MENTIONED A STRANGE PROTECTIVE *MEDALLION* THAT PREVENTED HIM FROM KILLING HER.
I DON'T LIKE THIS AT ALL. WE NEED TO FIND HER AND GET RID OF HER AT ALL COSTS! LET'S HURRY OUR PREPARATIONS FOR THE OPENING OF THE DOOR.

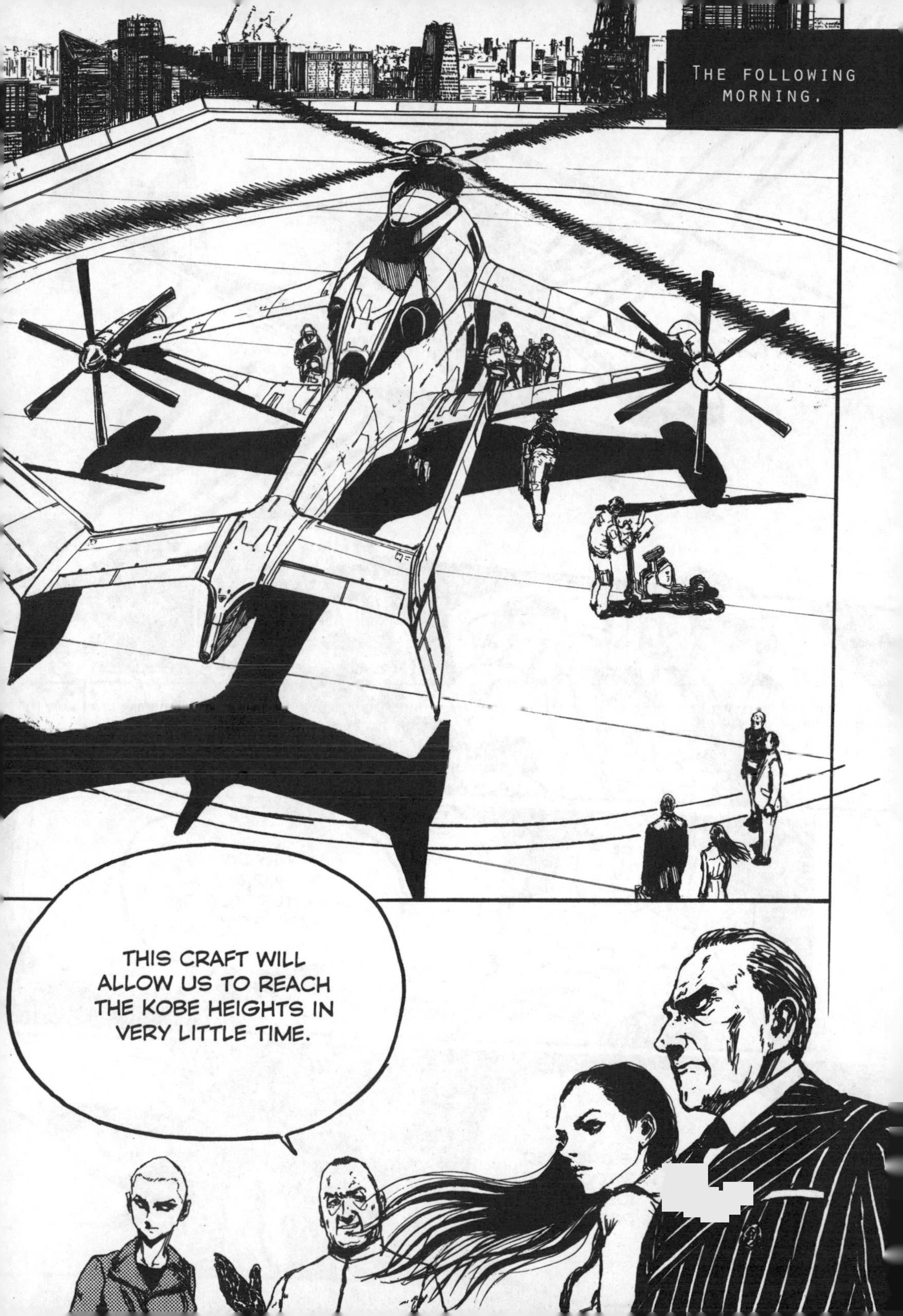
THE FOLLOWING MORNING.
THIS CRAFT WILL ALLOW US TO REACH THE KOBE HEIGHTS IN VERY LITTLE TIME.

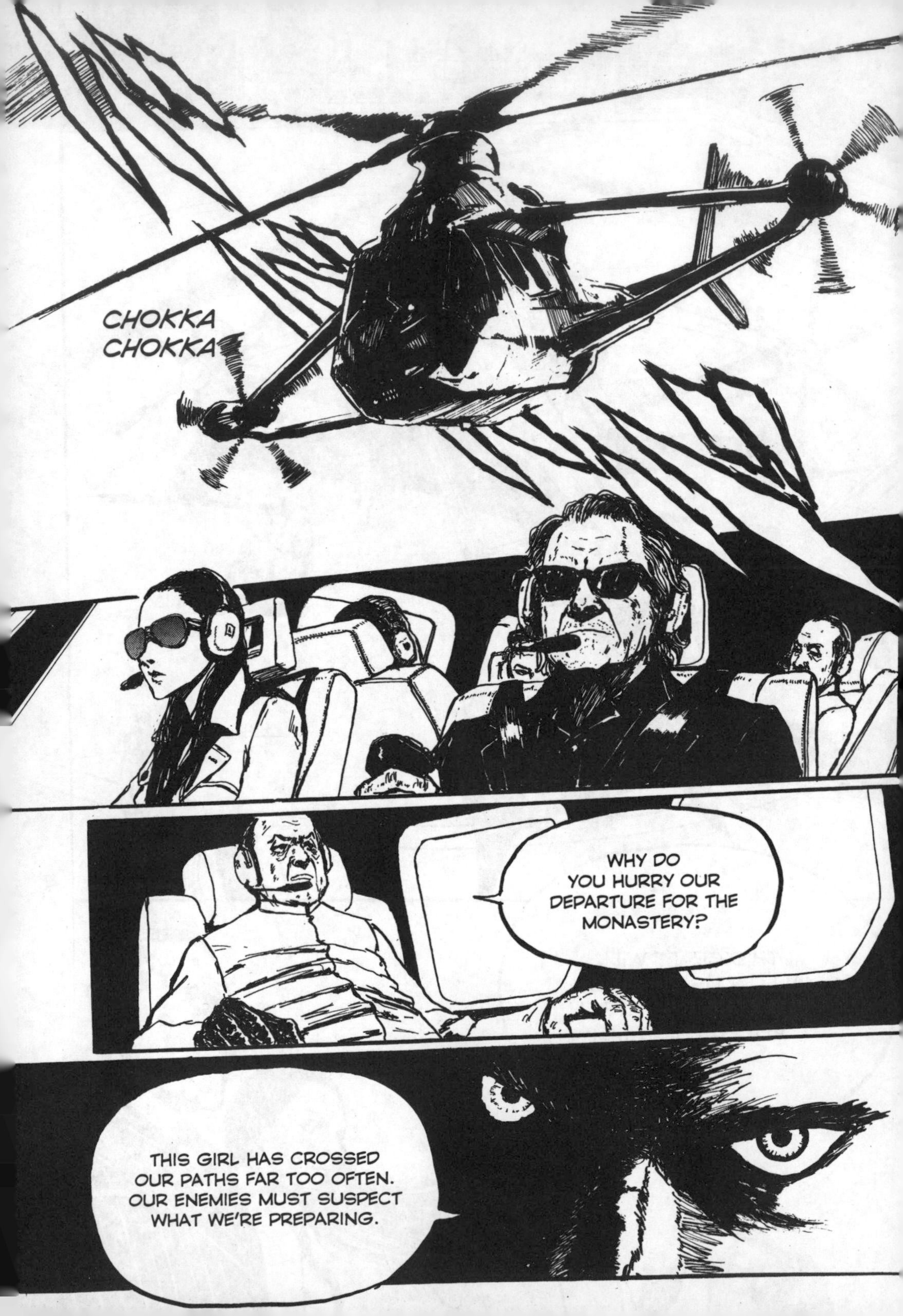
CHOKKA CHOKKA
WHY DO YOU HURRY OUR DEPARTURE FOR THE MONASTERY?
THIS GIRL HAS CROSSED OUR PATHS FAR TOO OFTEN. OUR ENEMIES MUST SUSPECT WHAT WE'RE PREPARING.

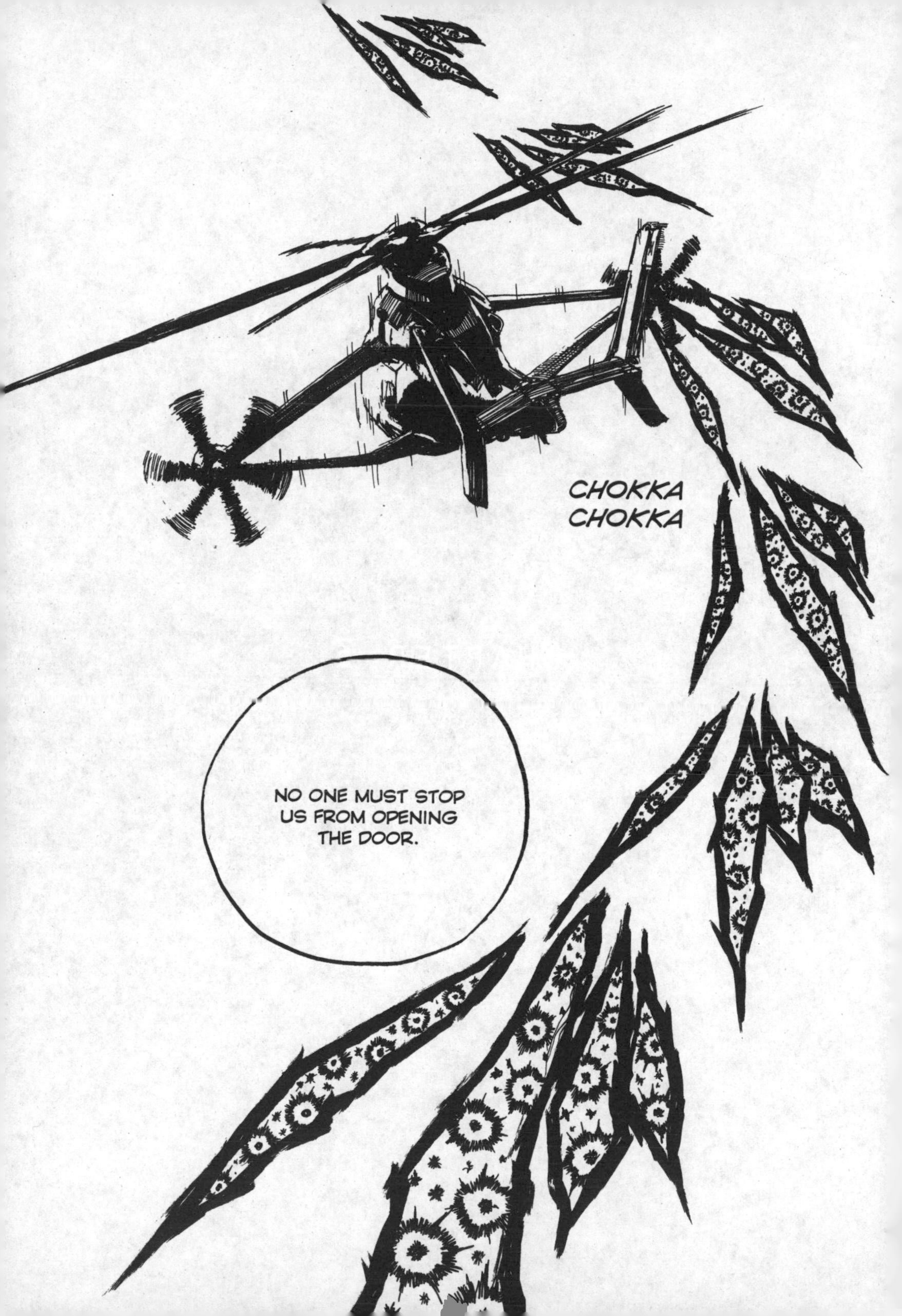
CHOKKA
CHOKKA
NO ONE MUST STOP US FROM OPENING THE DOOR.

CHAPTER 3

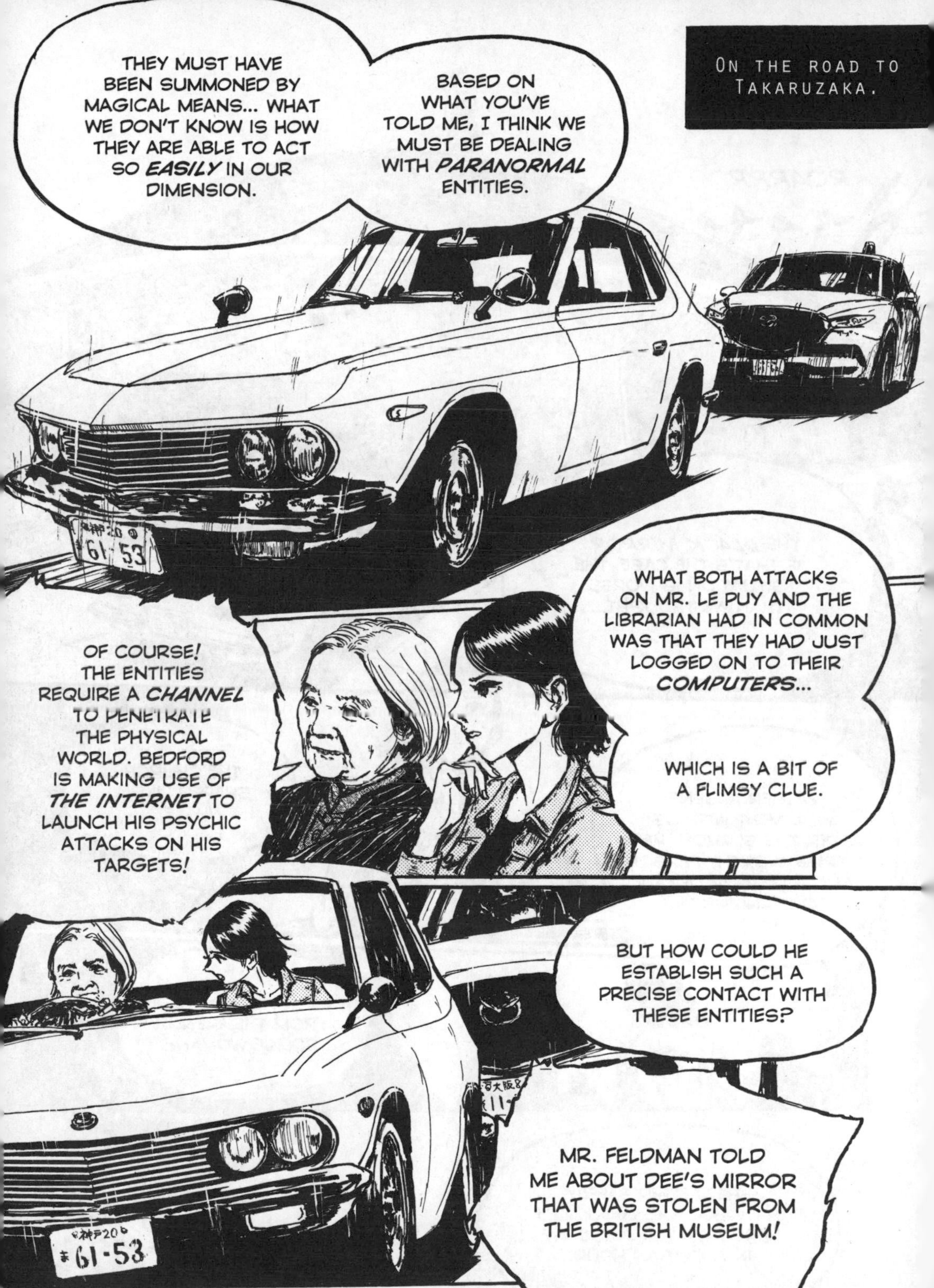
On the road to Takaruzaka.
BASED ON WHAT YOU'VE TOLD ME, I THINK WE MUST BE DEALING WITH *PARANORMAL* ENTITIES.
THEY MUST HAVE BEEN SUMMONED BY MAGICAL MEANS... WHAT WE DON'T KNOW IS HOW THEY ARE ABLE TO ACT SO *EASILY* IN OUR DIMENSION.
WHAT BOTH ATTACKS ON MR. LE PUY AND THE LIBRARIAN HAD IN COMMON WAS THAT THEY HAD JUST LOGGED ON TO THEIR *COMPUTERS*...
WHICH IS A BIT OF A FLIMSY CLUE.
OF COURSE! THE ENTITIES REQUIRE A *CHANNEL* TO PENETRATE THE PHYSICAL WORLD. BEDFORD IS MAKING USE OF *THE INTERNET* TO LAUNCH HIS PSYCHIC ATTACKS ON HIS TARGETS!
BUT HOW COULD HE ESTABLISH SUCH A PRECISE CONTACT WITH THESE ENTITIES?
MR. FELDMAN TOLD ME ABOUT DEE'S MIRROR THAT WAS STOLEN FROM THE BRITISH MUSEUM!

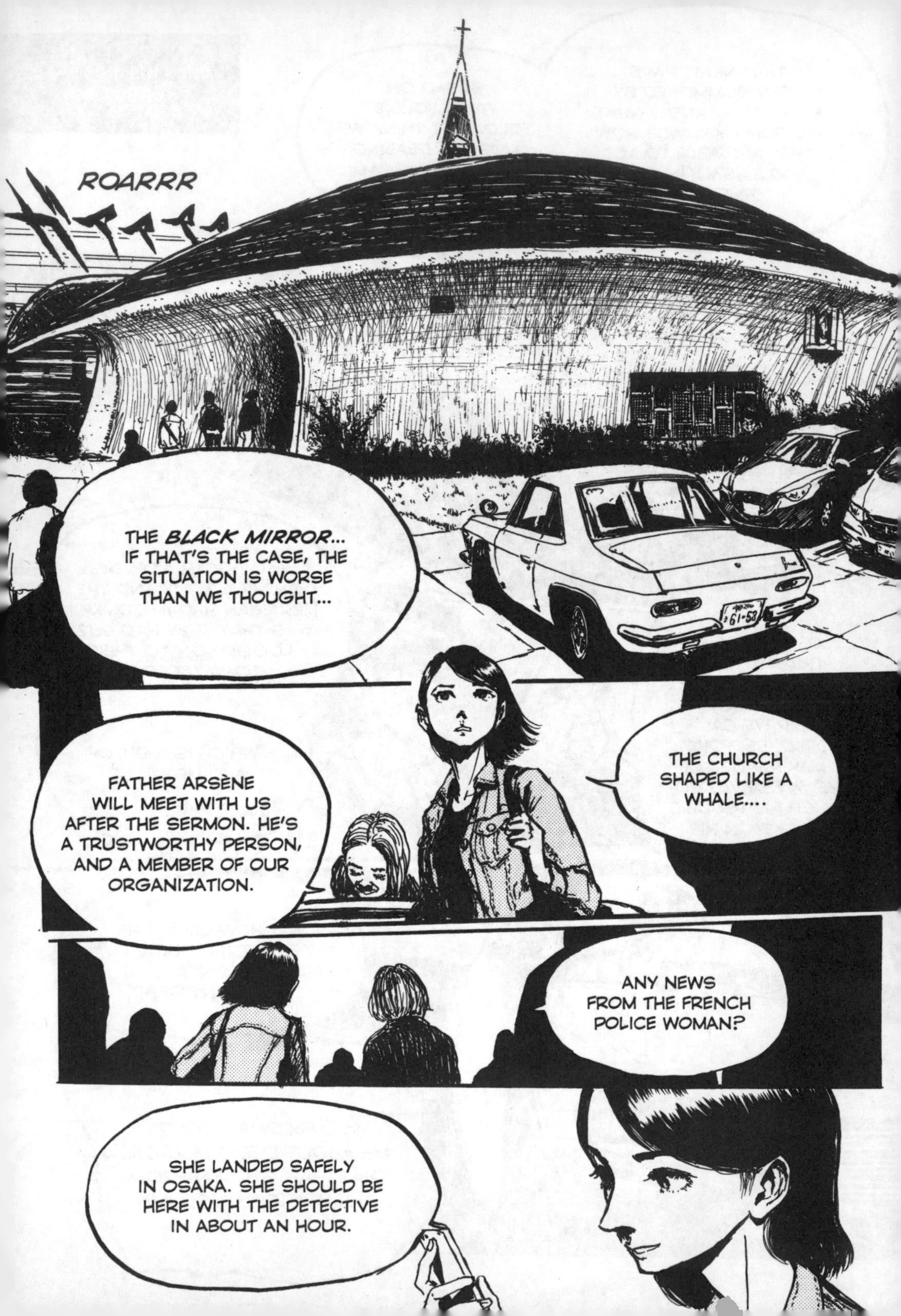
ROARRR
THE BLACK MIRROR... IF THAT'S THE CASE, THE SITUATION IS WORSE THAN WE THOUGHT...
THE CHURCH SHAPED LIKE A WHALE....
FATHER ARSÈNE WILL MEET WITH US AFTER THE SERMON. HE'S A TRUSTWORTHY PERSON, AND A MEMBER OF OUR ORGANIZATION.
ANY NEWS FROM THE FRENCH POLICE WOMAN?
SHE LANDED SAFELY IN OSAKA. SHE SHOULD BE HERE WITH THE DETECTIVE IN ABOUT AN HOUR.

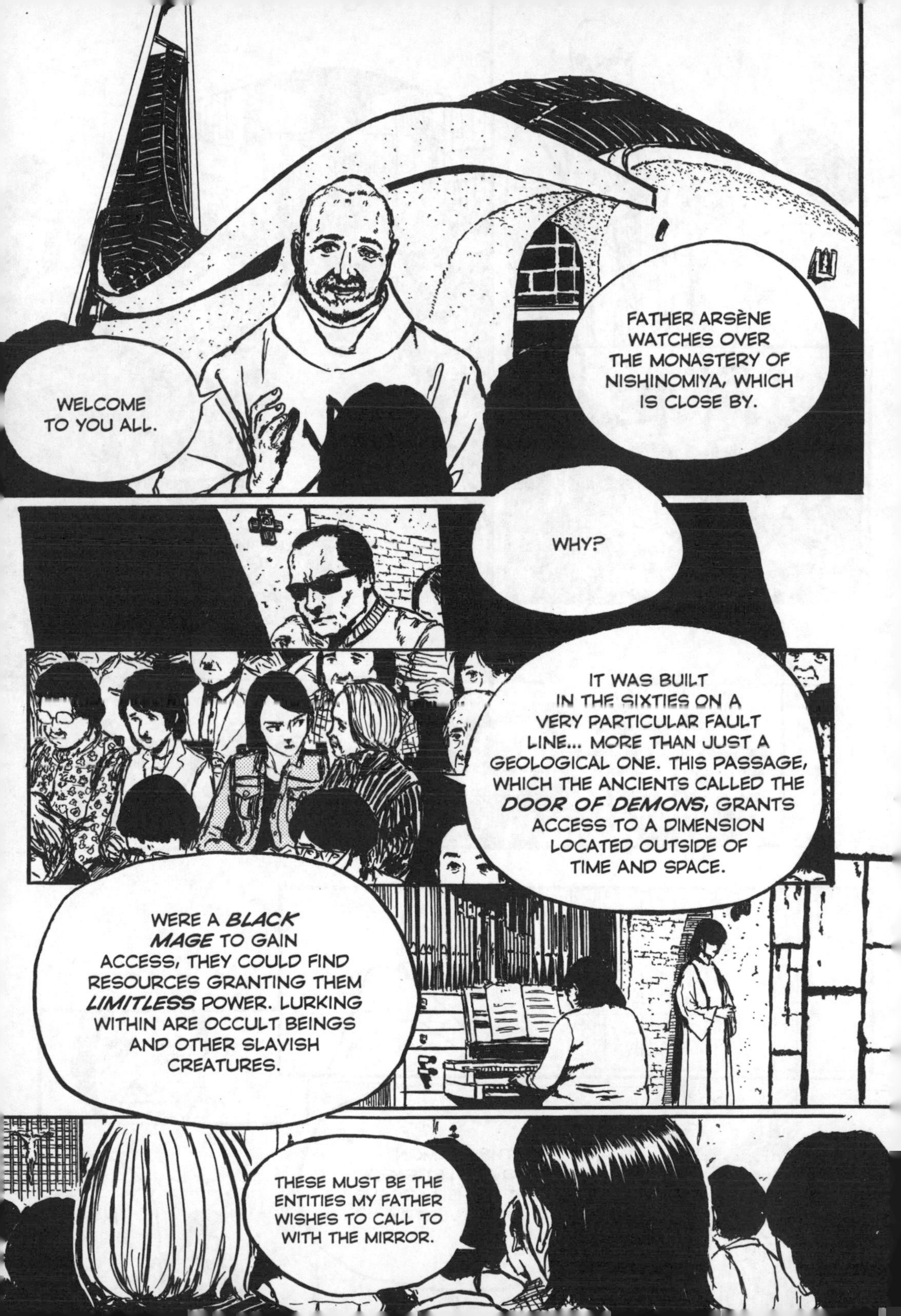
FATHER ARSÈNE WATCHES OVER THE MONASTERY OF NISHINOMIYA, WHICH IS CLOSE BY.
WELCOME TO YOU ALL.
WHY?
IT WAS BUILT IN THE SIXTIES ON A VERY PARTICULAR FAULT LINE... MORE THAN JUST A GEOLOGICAL ONE. THIS PASSAGE, WHICH THE ANCIENTS CALLED THE *DOOR OF DEMONS,* GRANTS ACCESS TO A DIMENSION LOCATED OUTSIDE OF TIME AND SPACE.
WERE A *BLACK MAGE* TO GAIN ACCESS, THEY COULD FIND RESOURCES GRANTING THEM *LIMITLESS* POWER. LURKING WITHIN ARE OCCULT BEINGS AND OTHER SLAVISH CREATURES.
THESE MUST BE THE ENTITIES MY FATHER WISHES TO CALL TO WITH THE MIRROR.

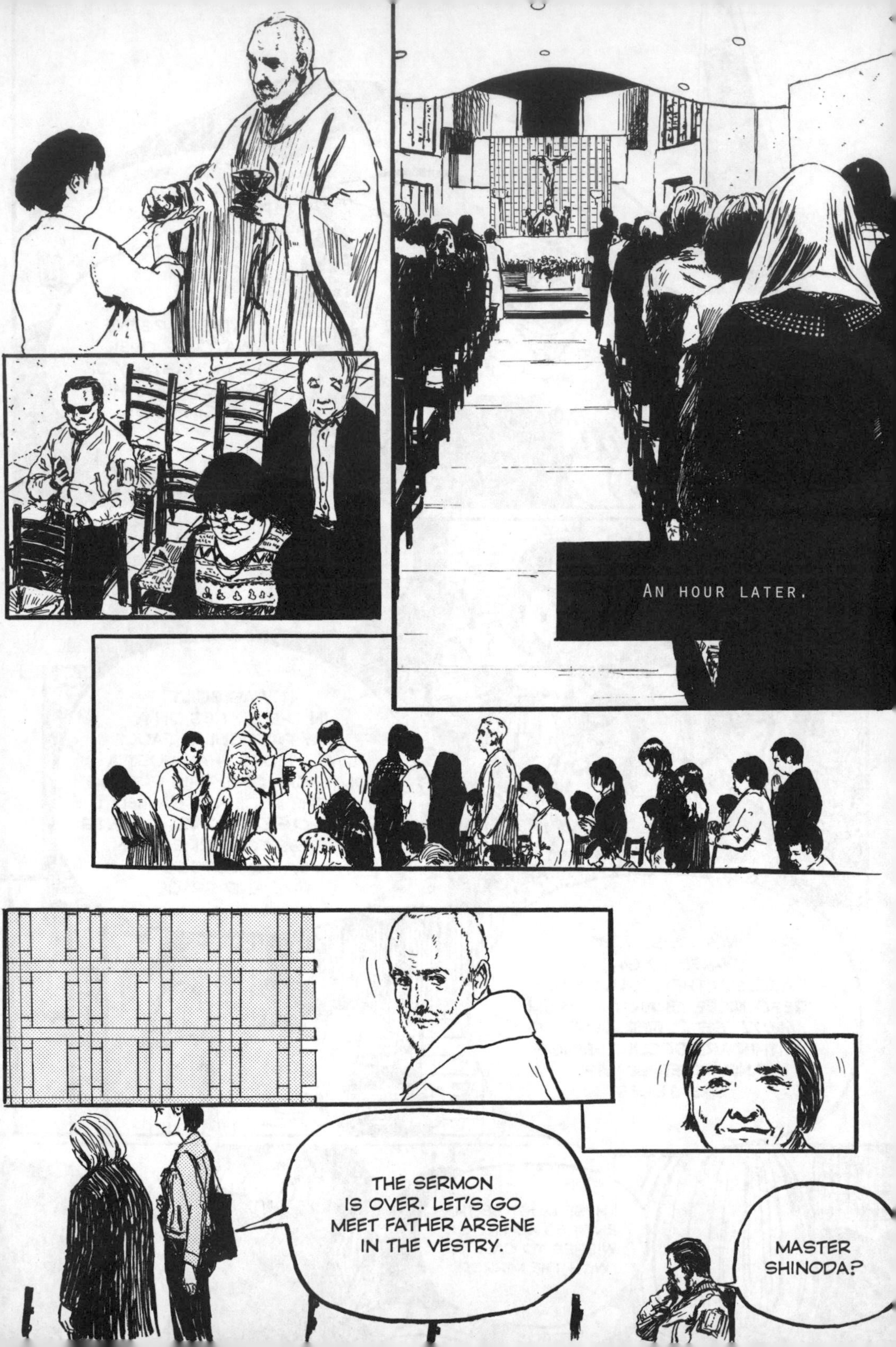
AN HOUR LATER.
MASTER SHINODA?
THE SERMON IS OVER. LET'S GO MEET FATHER ARSÈNE IN THE VESTRY.

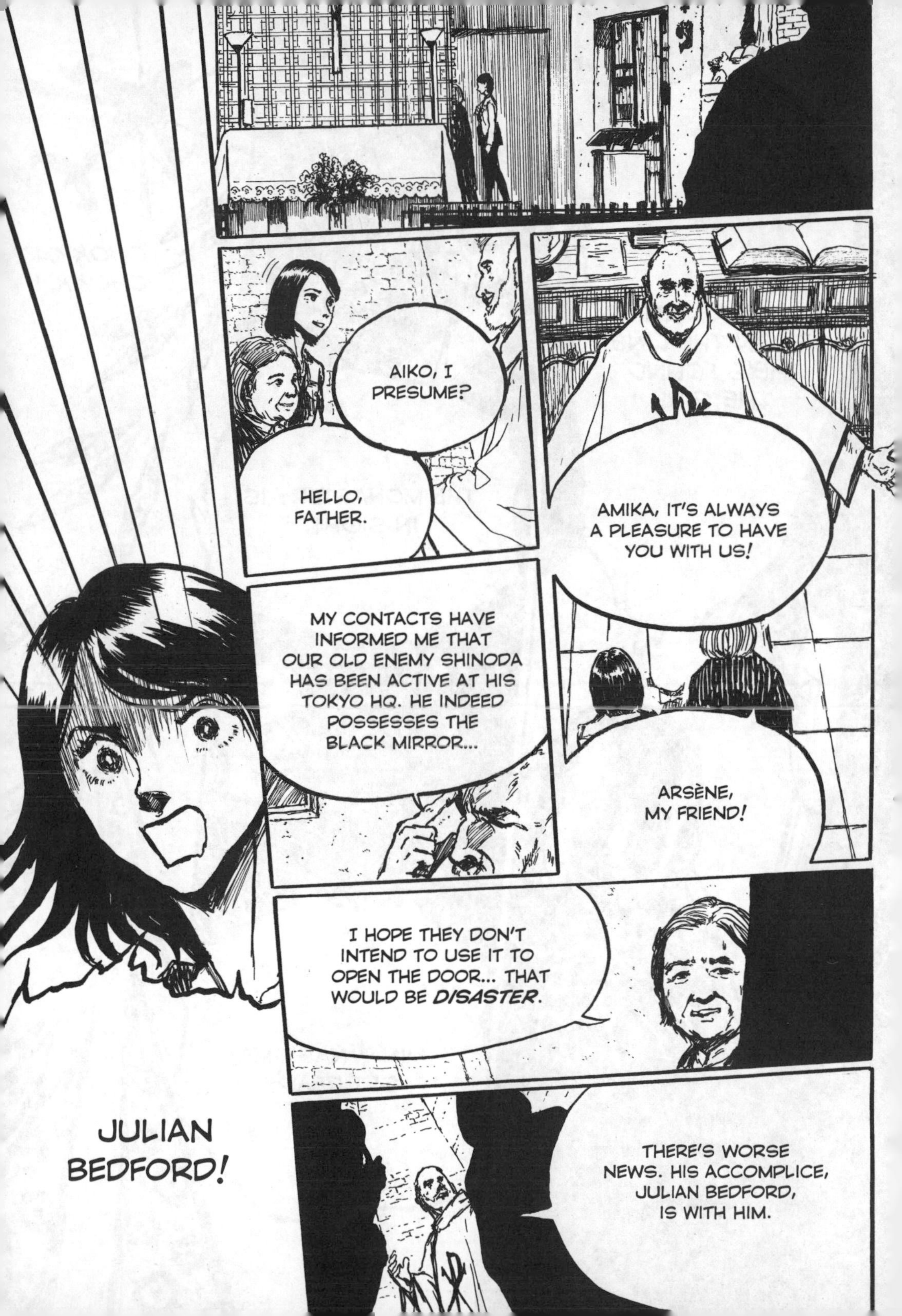
AMIKA, IT'S ALWAYS A PLEASURE TO HAVE YOU WITH US!
AIKO, I PRESUME?
HELLO, FATHER.
ARSÈNE, MY FRIEND!
MY CONTACTS HAVE INFORMED ME THAT OUR OLD ENEMY SHINODA HAS BEEN ACTIVE AT HIS TOKYO HQ. HE INDEED POSSESSES THE BLACK MIRROR...
I HOPE THEY DON'T INTEND TO USE IT TO OPEN THE DOOR... THAT WOULD BE *DISASTER*.
THERE'S WORSE NEWS. HIS ACCOMPLICE, JULIAN BEDFORD, IS WITH HIM.
JULIAN BEDFORD!

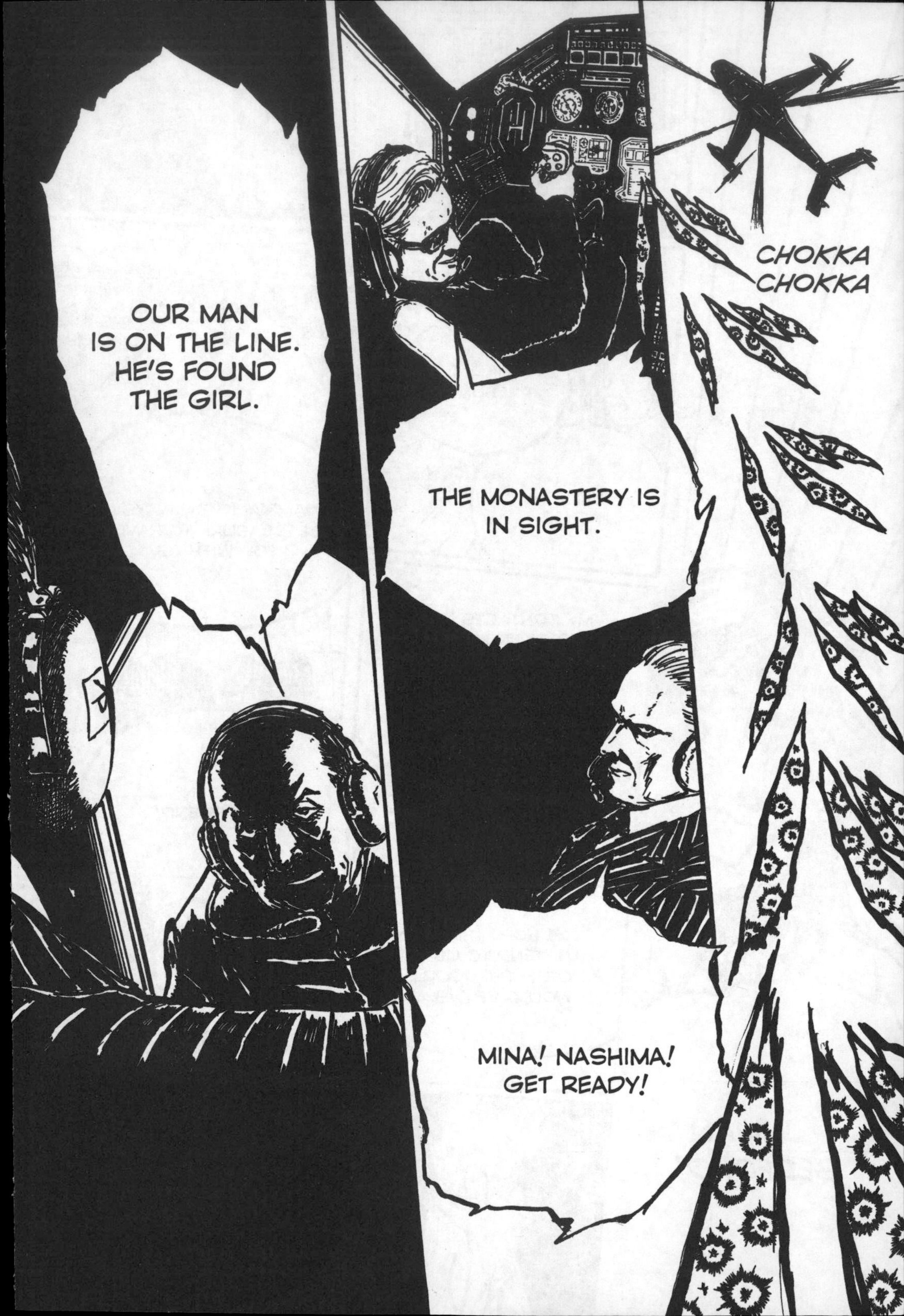
CHOKKA
CHOKKA
THE MONASTERY IS IN SIGHT.
MINA! NASHIMA! GET READY!
OUR MAN IS ON THE LINE. HE'S FOUND THE GIRL.

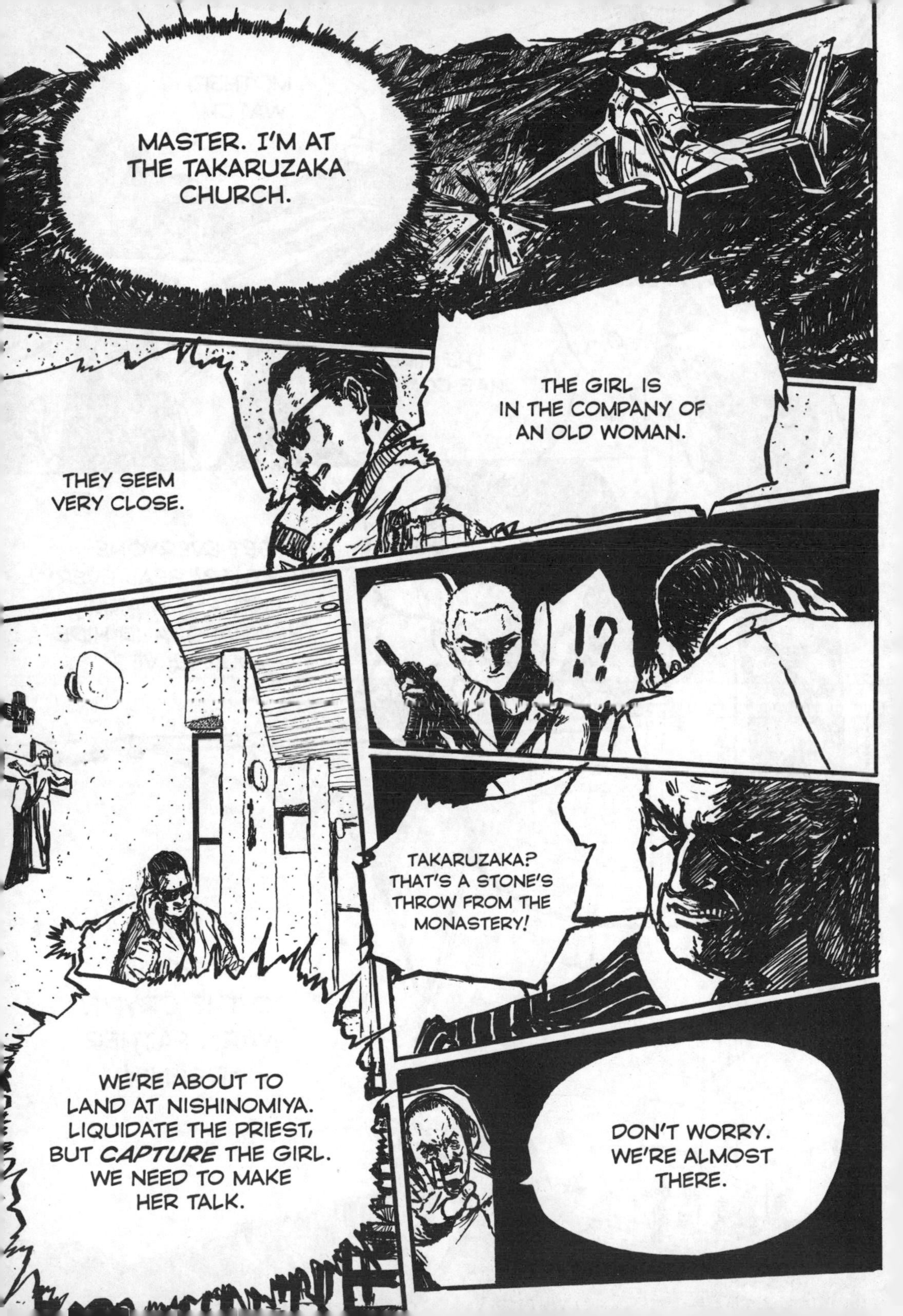
MASTER. I'M AT THE TAKARUZAKA CHURCH.
THE GIRL IS IN THE COMPANY OF AN OLD WOMAN.
THEY SEEM VERY CLOSE.
!?
TAKARUZAKA? THAT'S A STONE'S THROW FROM THE MONASTERY!
DON'T WORRY. WE'RE ALMOST THERE.
WE'RE ABOUT TO LAND AT NISHINOMIYA. LIQUIDATE THE PRIEST, BUT *CAPTURE* THE GIRL. WE NEED TO MAKE HER TALK.

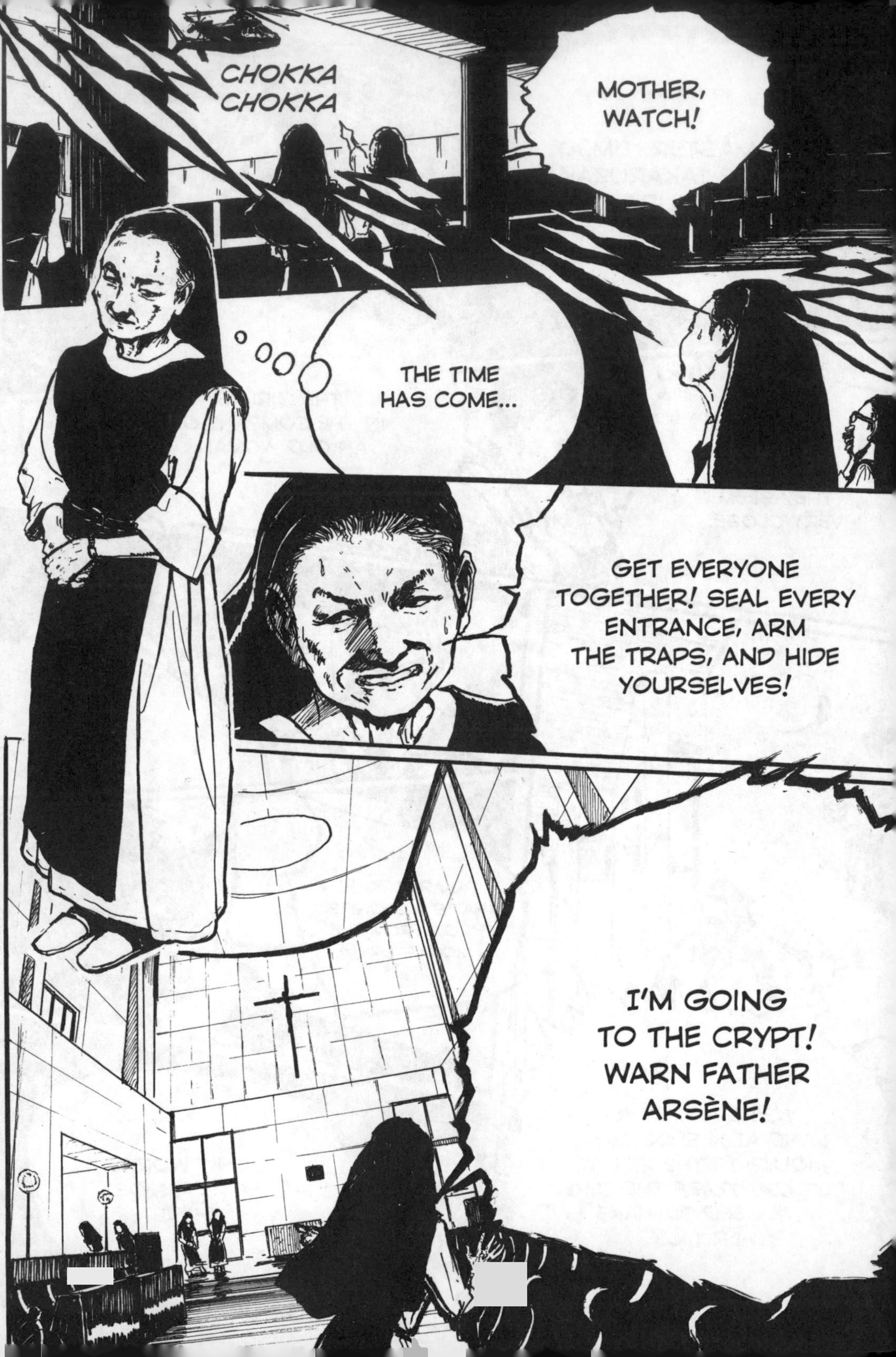
MOTHER, WATCH!
CHOKKA CHOKKA
THE TIME HAS COME...
GET EVERYONE TOGETHER! SEAL EVERY ENTRANCE, ARM THE TRAPS, AND HIDE YOURSELVES!
I'M GOING TO THE CRYPT! WARN FATHER ARSÈNE!

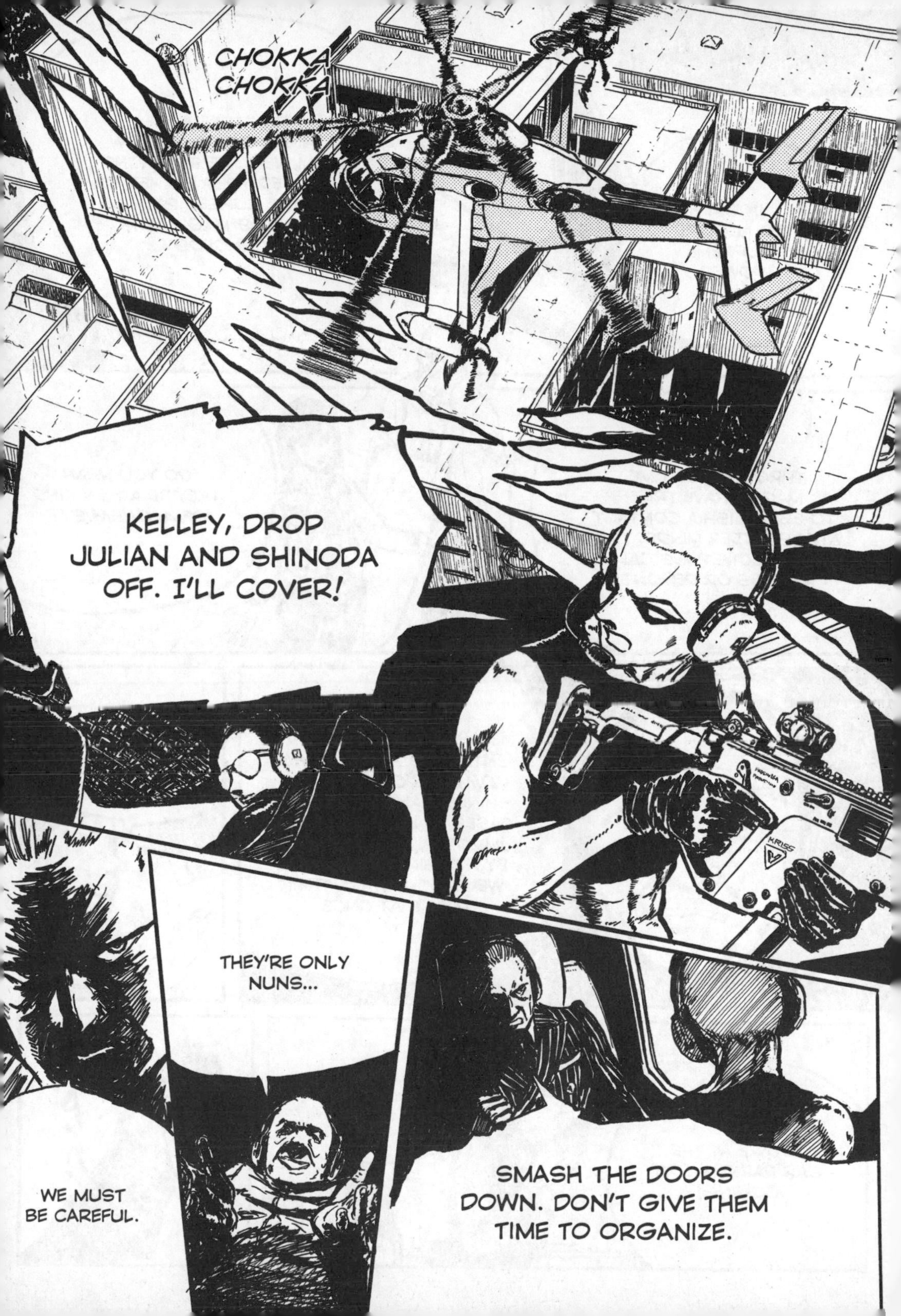
CHOKKA
CHOKKA
KELLEY, DROP JULIAN AND SHINODA OFF. I'LL COVER!
SMASH THE DOORS DOWN. DON'T GIVE THEM TIME TO ORGANIZE.
THEY'RE ONLY NUNS...
WE MUST BE CAREFUL.

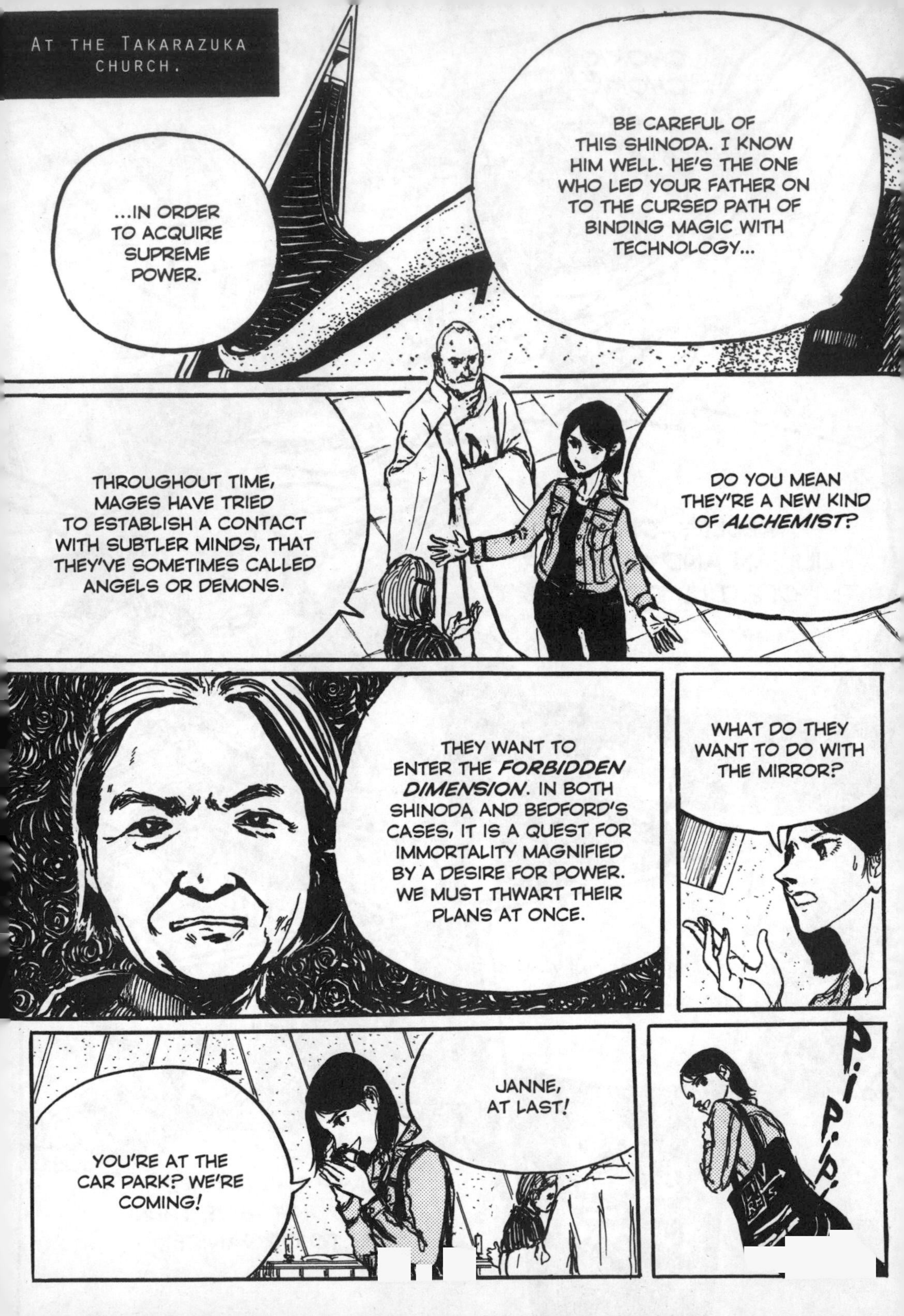
At the Takarazuka church.
BE CAREFUL OF THIS SHINODA. I KNOW HIM WELL. HE'S THE ONE WHO LED YOUR FATHER ON TO THE CURSED PATH OF BINDING MAGIC WITH TECHNOLOGY...
...IN ORDER TO ACQUIRE SUPREME POWER.
DO YOU MEAN THEY'RE A NEW KIND OF *ALCHEMIST*?
THROUGHOUT TIME, MAGES HAVE TRIED TO ESTABLISH A CONTACT WITH SUBTLER MINDS, THAT THEY'VE SOMETIMES CALLED ANGELS OR DEMONS.
WHAT DO THEY WANT TO DO WITH THE MIRROR?
THEY WANT TO ENTER THE *FORBIDDEN DIMENSION*. IN BOTH SHINODA AND BEDFORD'S CASES, IT IS A QUEST FOR IMMORTALITY MAGNIFIED BY A DESIRE FOR POWER. WE MUST THWART THEIR PLANS AT ONCE.
PI PI PI
JANNE, AT LAST!
YOU'RE AT THE CAR PARK? WE'RE COMING!

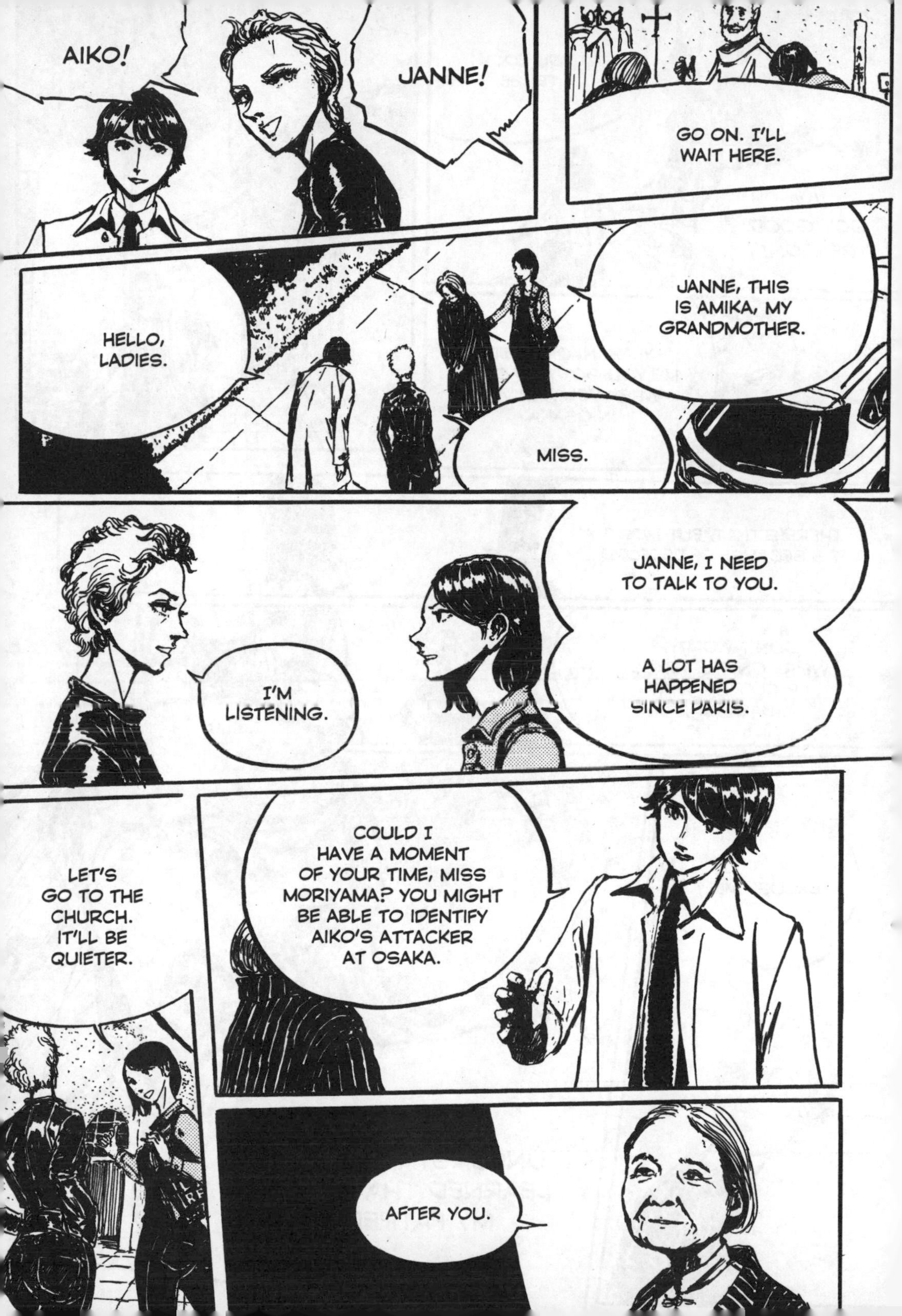
GO ON. I'LL WAIT HERE.
AIKO!
JANNE!
JANNE, THIS IS AMIKA, MY GRANDMOTHER.
MISS.
HELLO, LADIES.
JANNE, I NEED TO TALK TO YOU.
A LOT HAS HAPPENED SINCE PARIS.
I'M LISTENING.
COULD I HAVE A MOMENT OF YOUR TIME, MISS MORIYAMA? YOU MIGHT BE ABLE TO IDENTIFY AIKO'S ATTACKER AT OSAKA.
AFTER YOU.
LET'S GO TO THE CHURCH. IT'LL BE QUIETER.

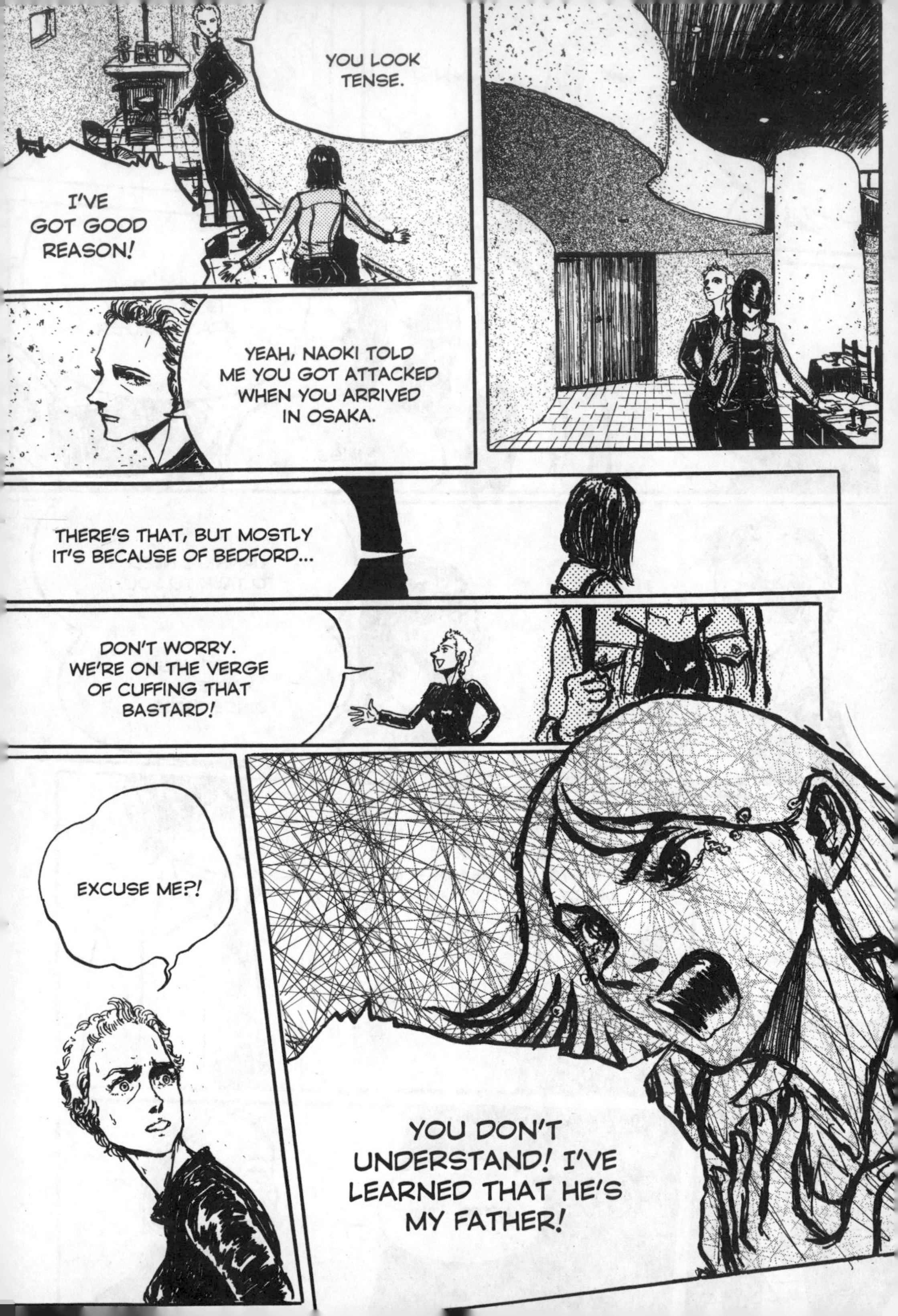
YOU LOOK TENSE.
I'VE GOT GOOD REASON!
YEAH, NAOKI TOLD ME YOU GOT ATTACKED WHEN YOU ARRIVED IN OSAKA.
THERE'S THAT, BUT MOSTLY IT'S BECAUSE OF BEDFORD...
DON'T WORRY. WE'RE ON THE VERGE OF CUFFING THAT BASTARD!
YOU DON'T UNDERSTAND! I'VE LEARNED THAT HE'S MY FATHER!
EXCUSE ME?!

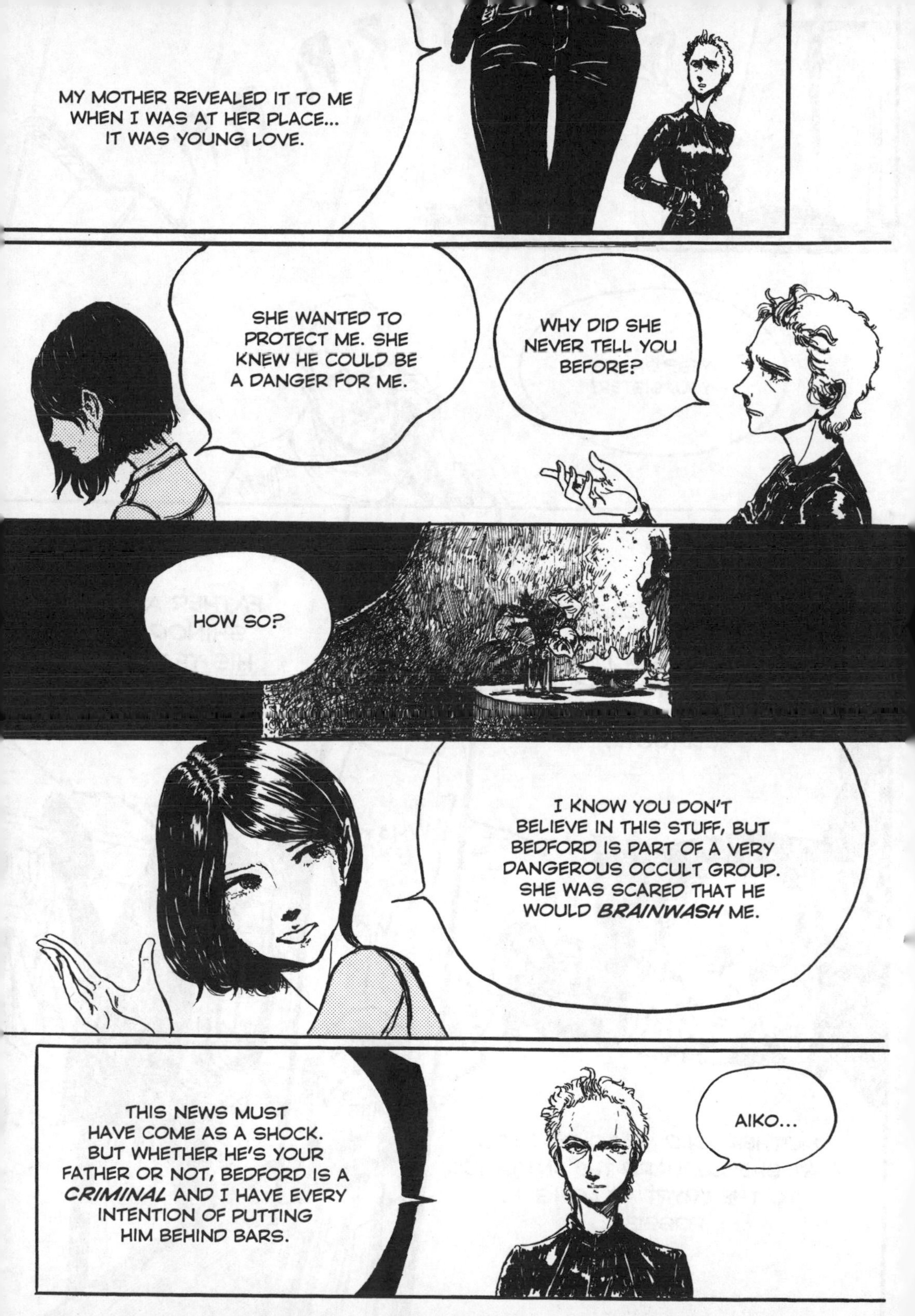
MY MOTHER REVEALED IT TO ME WHEN I WAS AT HER PLACE... IT WAS YOUNG LOVE.
WHY DID SHE NEVER TELL YOU BEFORE?
SHE WANTED TO PROTECT ME. SHE KNEW HE COULD BE A DANGER FOR ME.
HOW SO?
I KNOW YOU DON'T BELIEVE IN THIS STUFF, BUT BEDFORD IS PART OF A VERY DANGEROUS OCCULT GROUP. SHE WAS SCARED THAT HE WOULD *BRAINWASH* ME.
AIKO...
THIS NEWS MUST HAVE COME AS A SHOCK. BUT WHETHER HE'S YOUR FATHER OR NOT, BEDFORD IS A *CRIMINAL* AND I HAVE EVERY INTENTION OF PUTTING HIM BEHIND BARS.

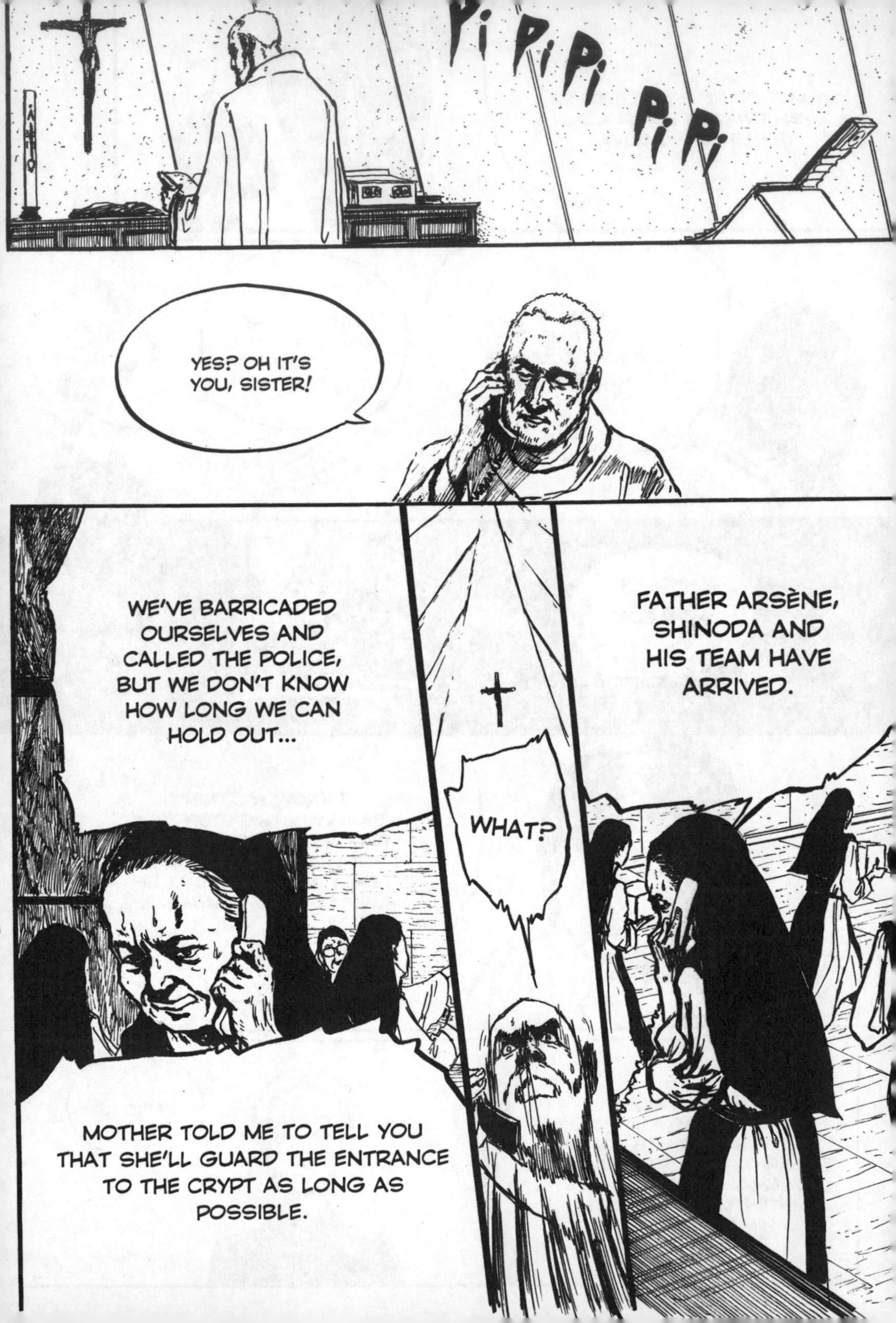
PiPiPi PiPiPi
YES? OH IT'S YOU, SISTER!
FATHER ARSÈNE, SHINODA AND HIS TEAM HAVE ARRIVED.
WHAT?
WE'VE BARRICADED OURSELVES AND CALLED THE POLICE, BUT WE DON'T KNOW HOW LONG WE CAN HOLD OUT...
MOTHER TOLD ME TO TELL YOU THAT SHE'LL GUARD THE ENTRANCE TO THE CRYPT AS LONG AS POSSIBLE.

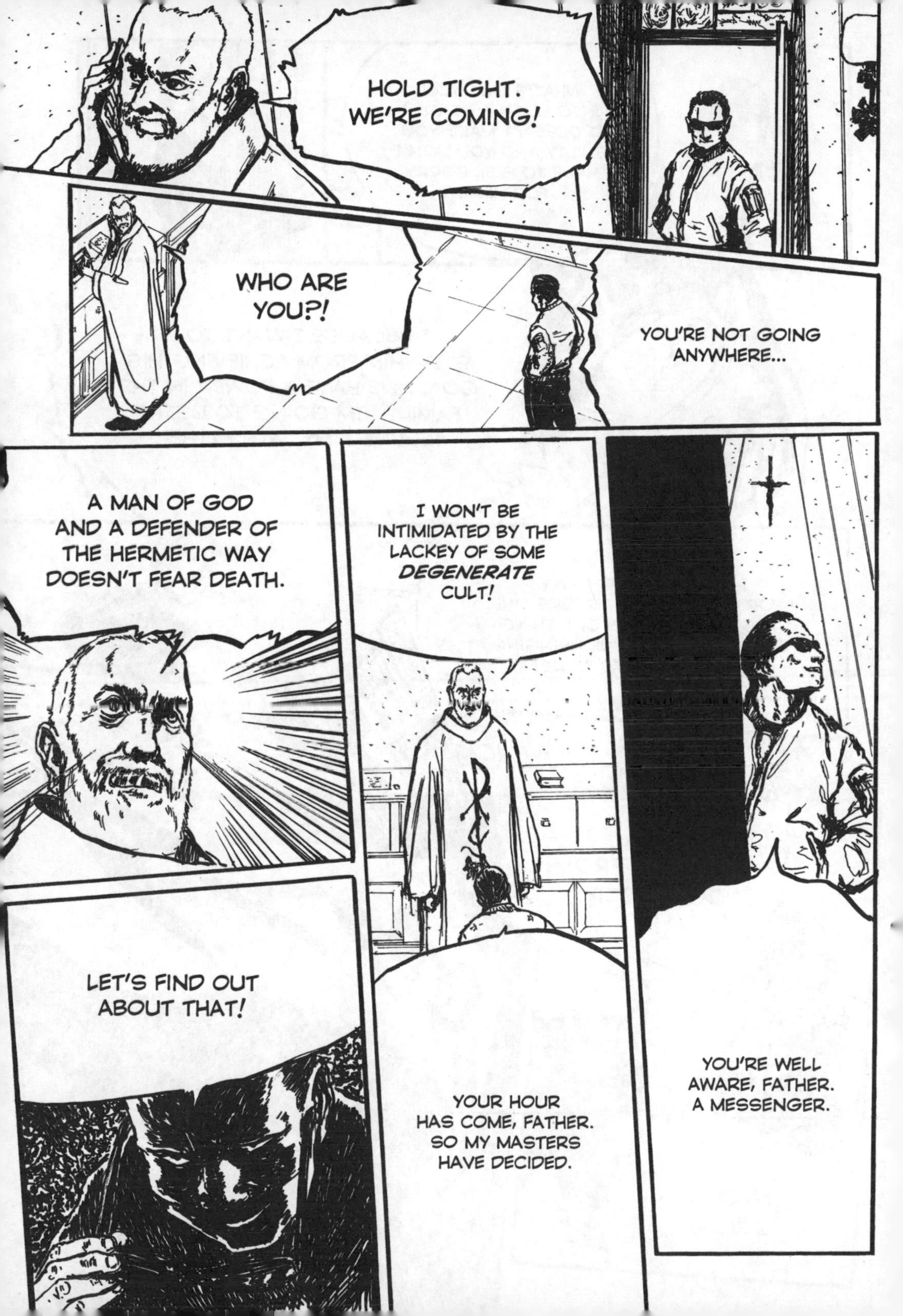
HOLD TIGHT. WE'RE COMING!
YOU'RE NOT GOING ANYWHERE...
WHO ARE YOU?!
YOU'RE WELL AWARE, FATHER. A MESSENGER.
I WON'T BE INTIMIDATED BY THE LACKEY OF SOME *DEGENERATE* CULT!
YOUR HOUR HAS COME, FATHER. SO MY MASTERS HAVE DECIDED.
A MAN OF GOD AND A DEFENDER OF THE HERMETIC WAY DOESN'T FEAR DEATH.
LET'S FIND OUT ABOUT THAT!

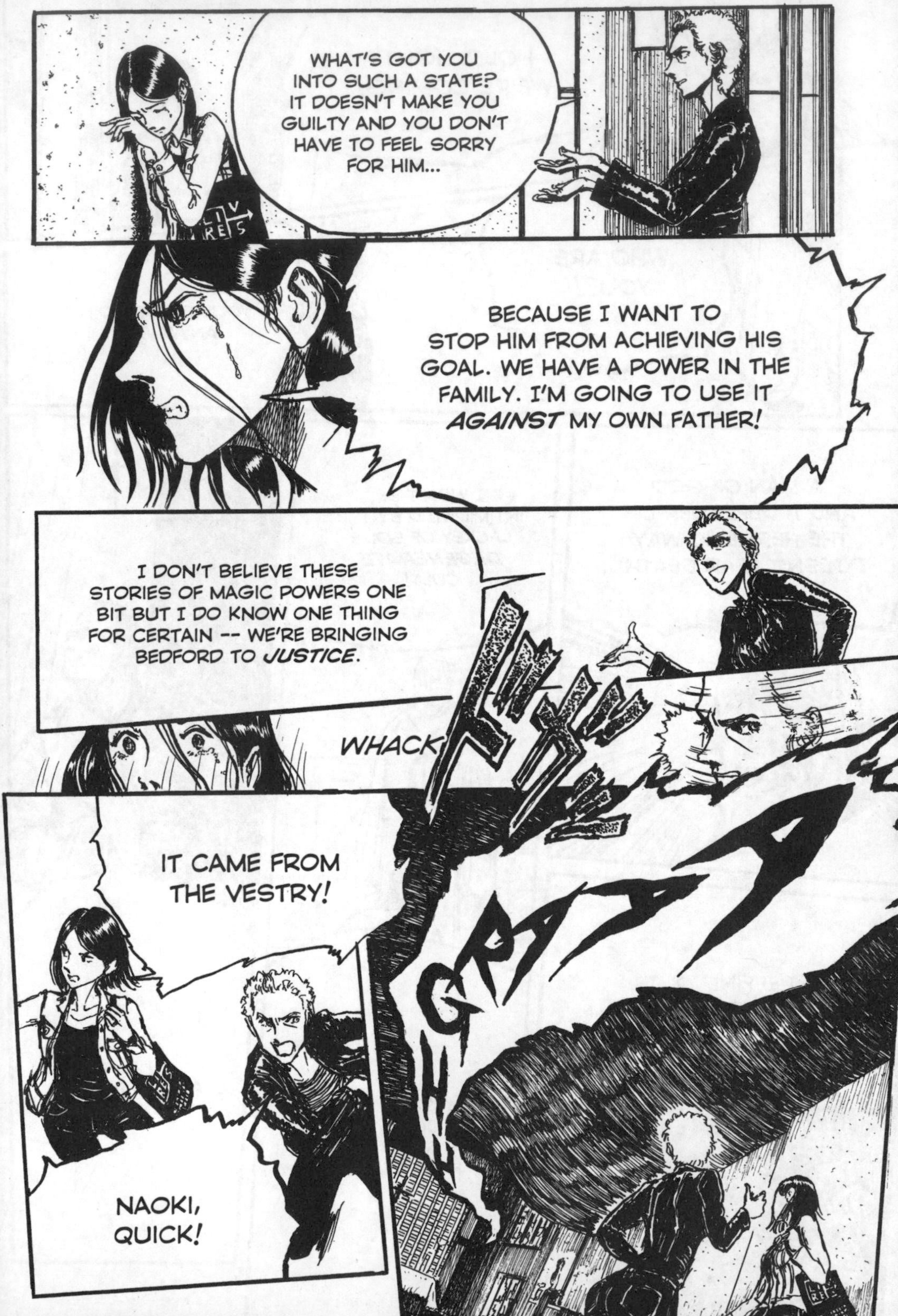
WHAT'S GOT YOU INTO SUCH A STATE? IT DOESN'T MAKE YOU GUILTY AND YOU DON'T HAVE TO FEEL SORRY FOR HIM...
BECAUSE I WANT TO STOP HIM FROM ACHIEVING HIS GOAL. WE HAVE A POWER IN THE FAMILY. I'M GOING TO USE IT *AGAINST* MY OWN FATHER!
I DON'T BELIEVE THESE STORIES OF MAGIC POWERS ONE BIT BUT I DO KNOW ONE THING FOR CERTAIN -- WE'RE BRINGING BEDFORD TO *JUSTICE*.
WHACK
GRAAAAH
IT CAME FROM THE VESTRY!
NAOKI, QUICK!

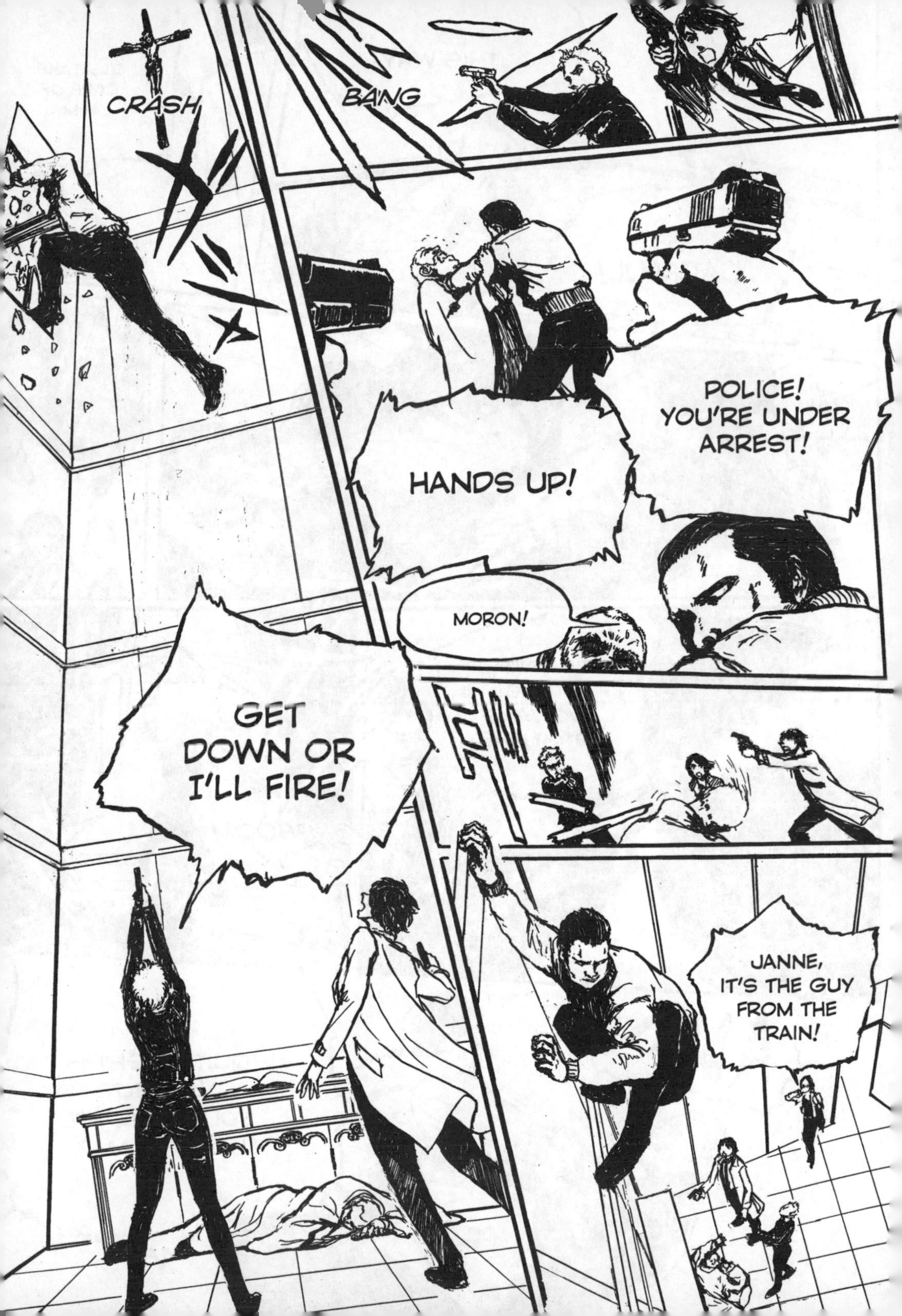
BANG
CRASH
POLICE! YOU'RE UNDER ARREST!
HANDS UP!
MORON!
GET DOWN OR I'LL FIRE!
JANNE, IT'S THE GUY FROM THE TRAIN!

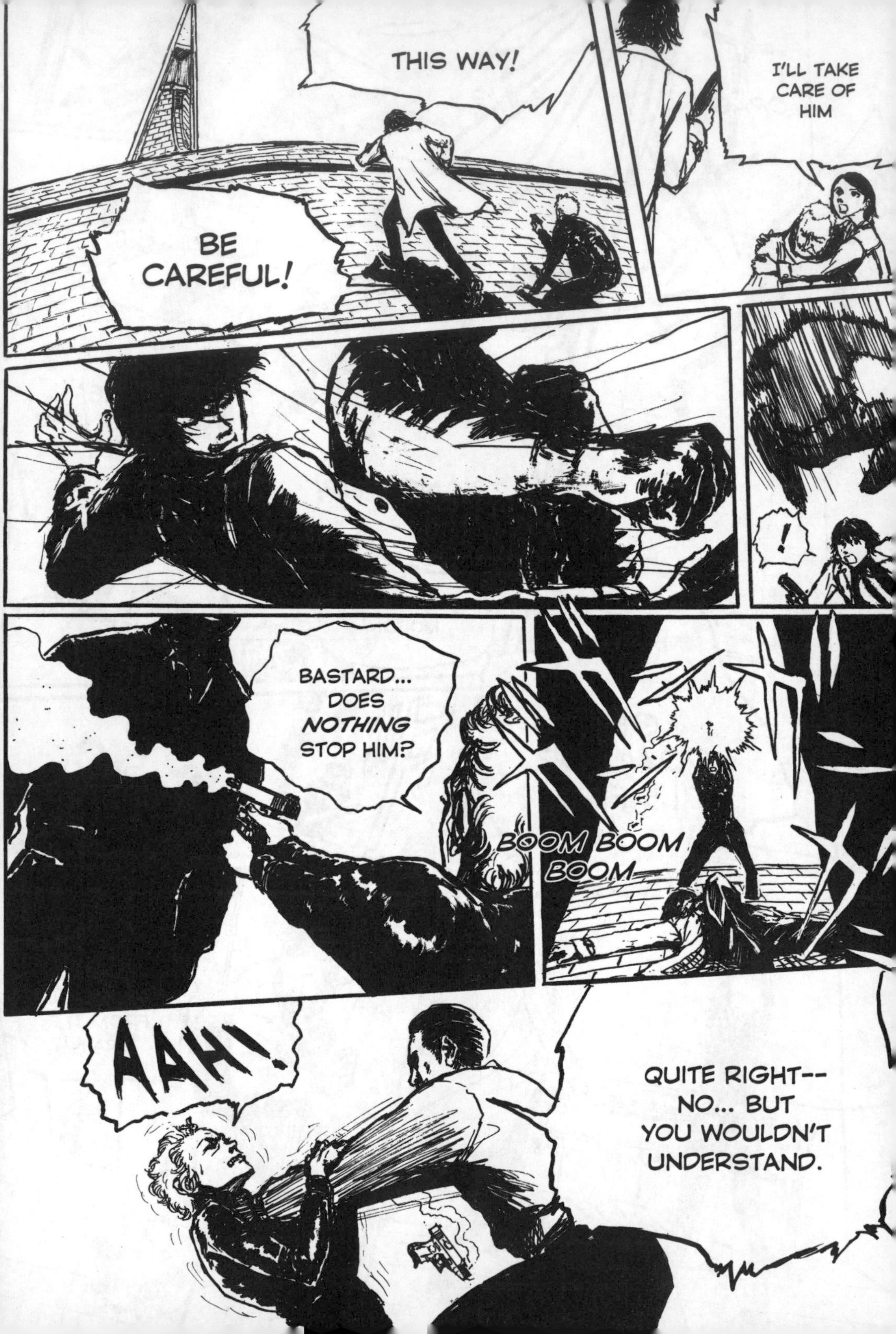
I'LL TAKE CARE OF HIM
THIS WAY!
BE CAREFUL!
!
BOOM BOOM BOOM
BASTARD... DOES *NOTHING* STOP HIM?
QUITE RIGHT-- NO... BUT YOU WOULDN'T UNDERSTAND.
AAH!

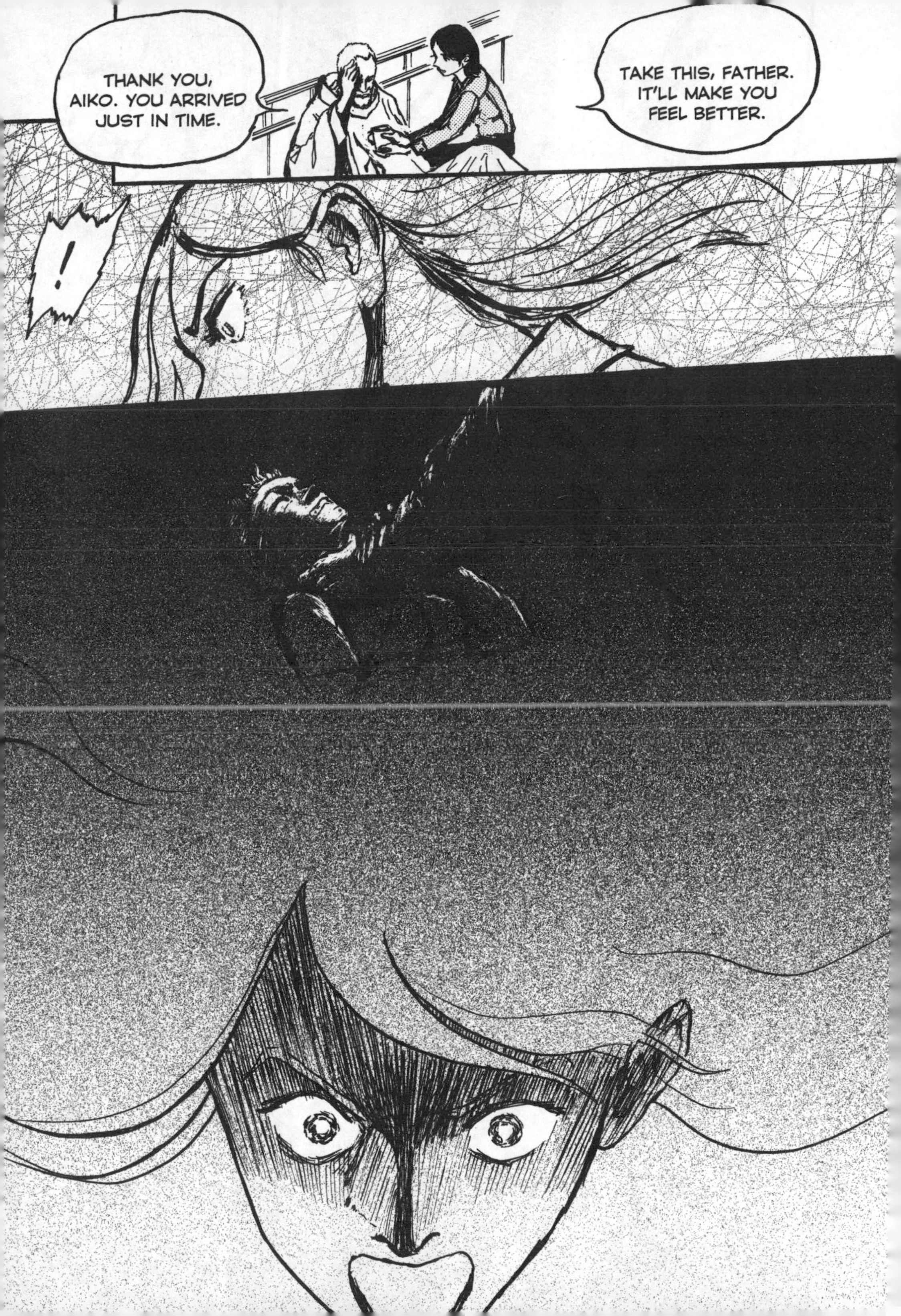
TAKE THIS, FATHER. IT'LL MAKE YOU FEEL BETTER.
THANK YOU, AIKO. YOU ARRIVED JUST IN TIME.
!

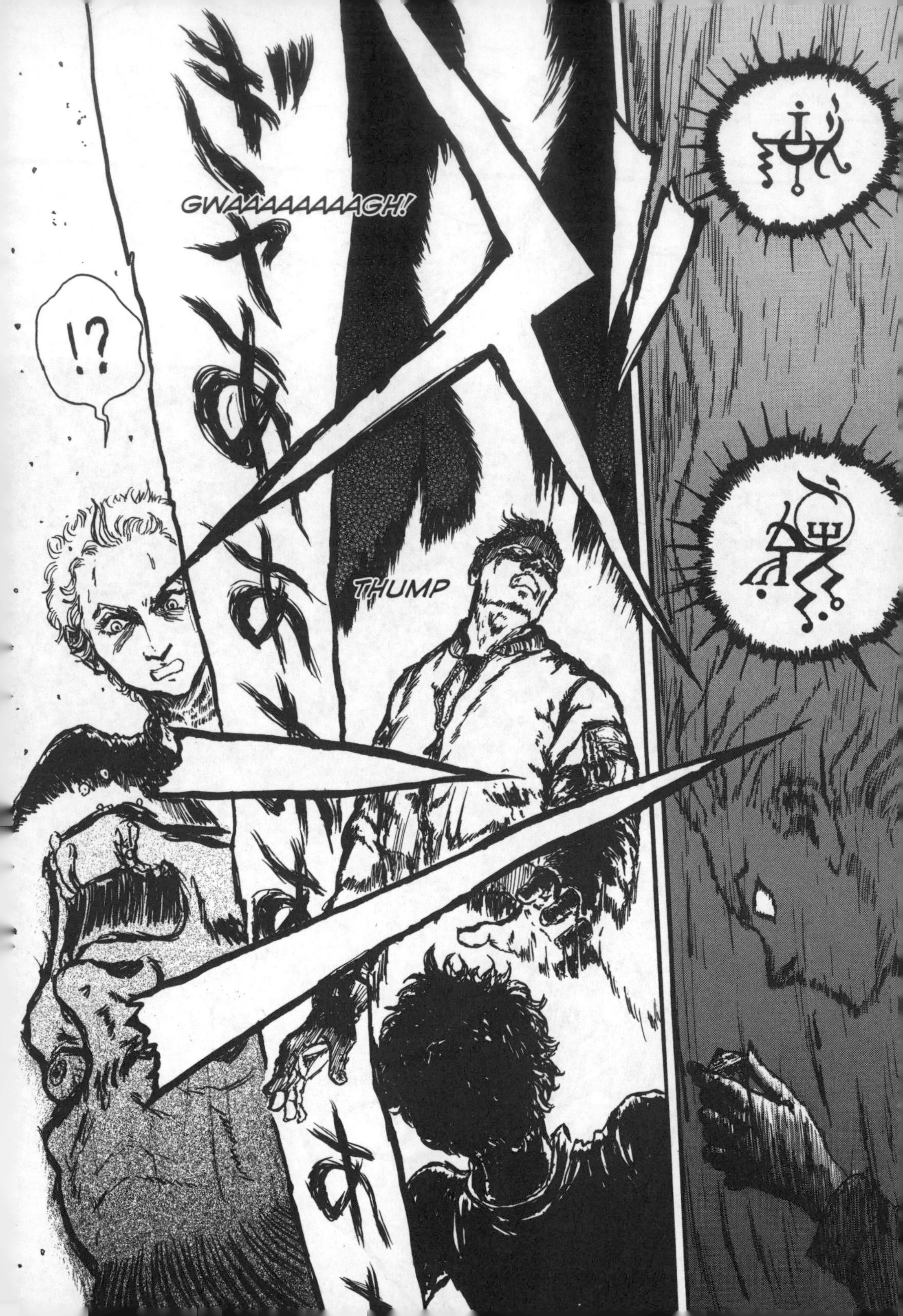
GWAAAAAAAAGH!
!?
THUMP

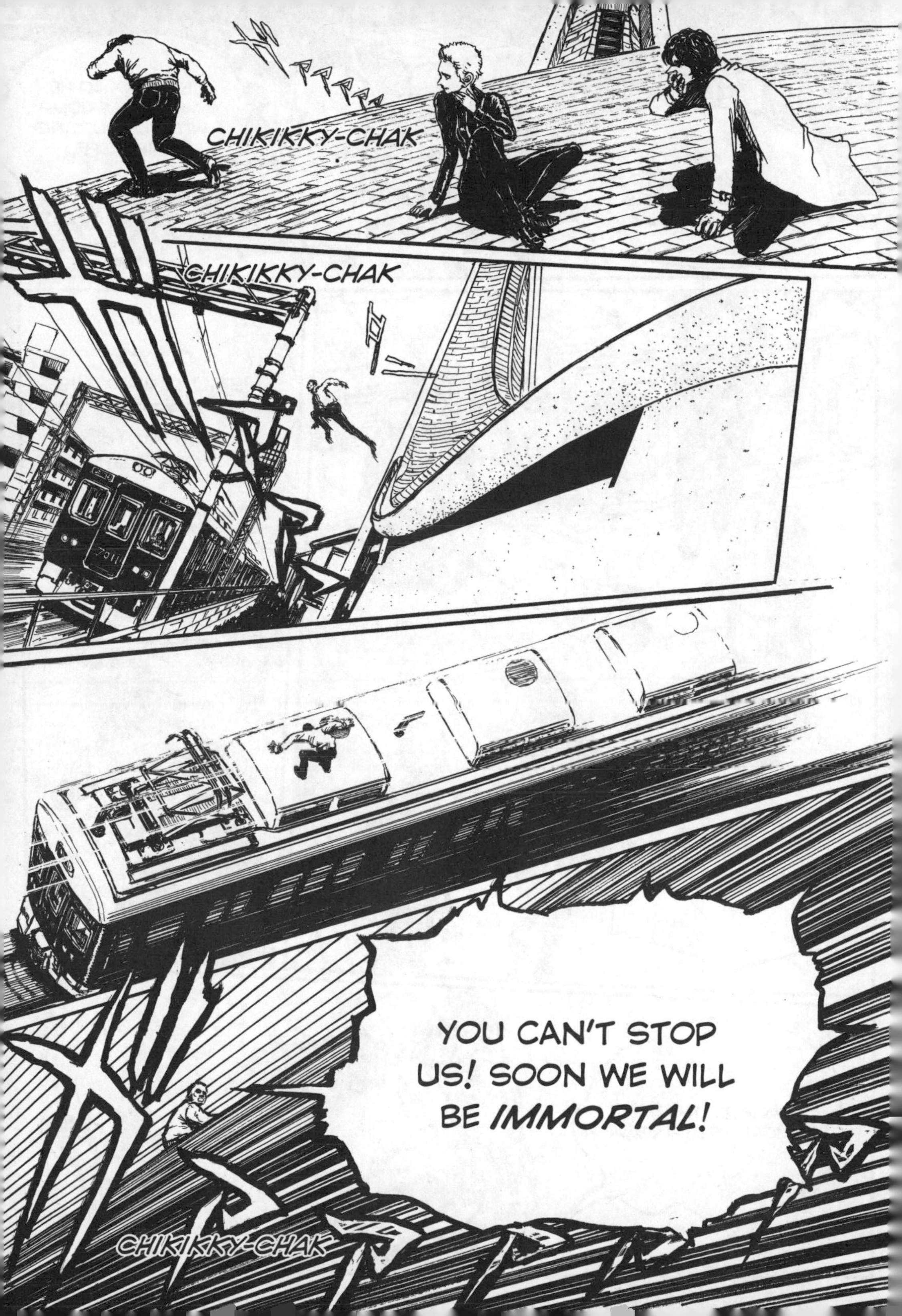
CHIKIKKY-CHAK
CHIKIKKY-CHAK
YOU CAN'T STOP US! SOON WE WILL BE IMMORTAL!
CHIKIKKY-CHAK

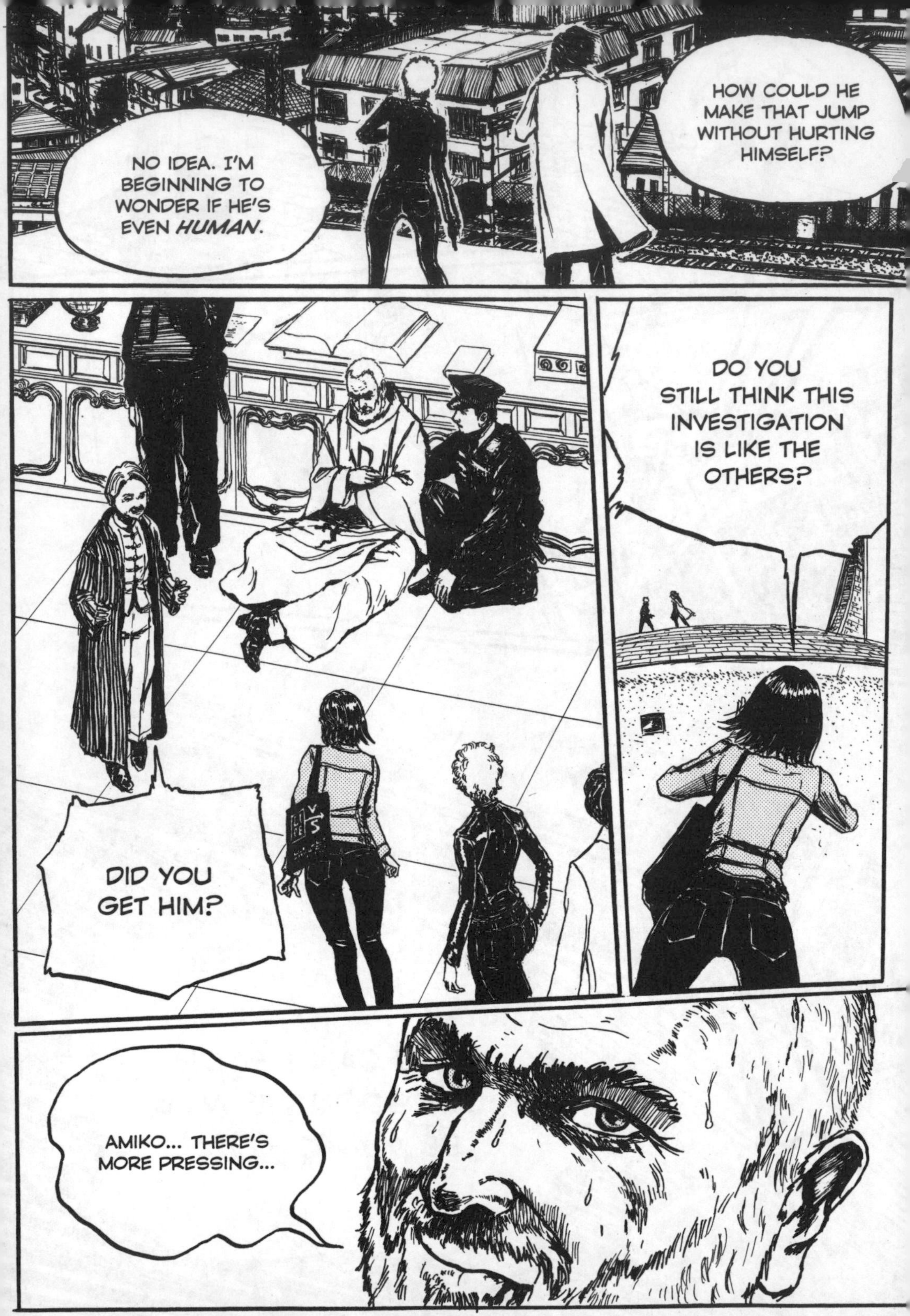
HOW COULD HE MAKE THAT JUMP WITHOUT HURTING HIMSELF?
NO IDEA. I'M BEGINNING TO WONDER IF HE'S EVEN *HUMAN*.
DO YOU STILL THINK THIS INVESTIGATION IS LIKE THE OTHERS?
DID YOU GET HIM?
AMIKO... THERE'S MORE PRESSING...

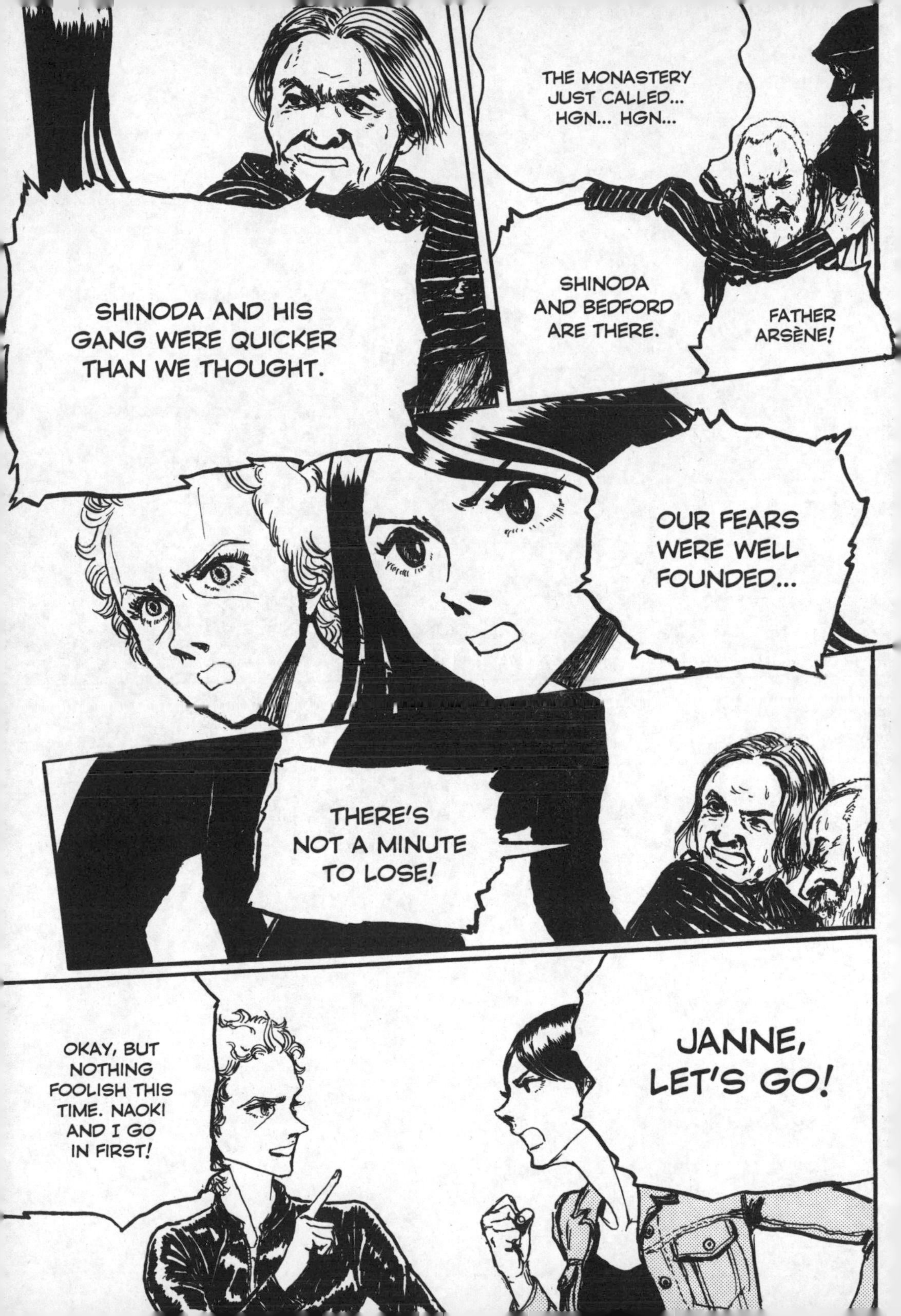

THE MONASTERY JUST CALLED... HGN... HGN...
FATHER ARSÈNE!
SHINODA AND BEDFORD ARE THERE.
SHINODA AND HIS GANG WERE QUICKER THAN WE THOUGHT.
OUR FEARS WERE WELL FOUNDED...
THERE'S NOT A MINUTE TO LOSE!
JANNE, LET'S GO!
OKAY, BUT NOTHING FOOLISH THIS TIME. NAOKI AND I GO IN FIRST!

CHAPTER 4

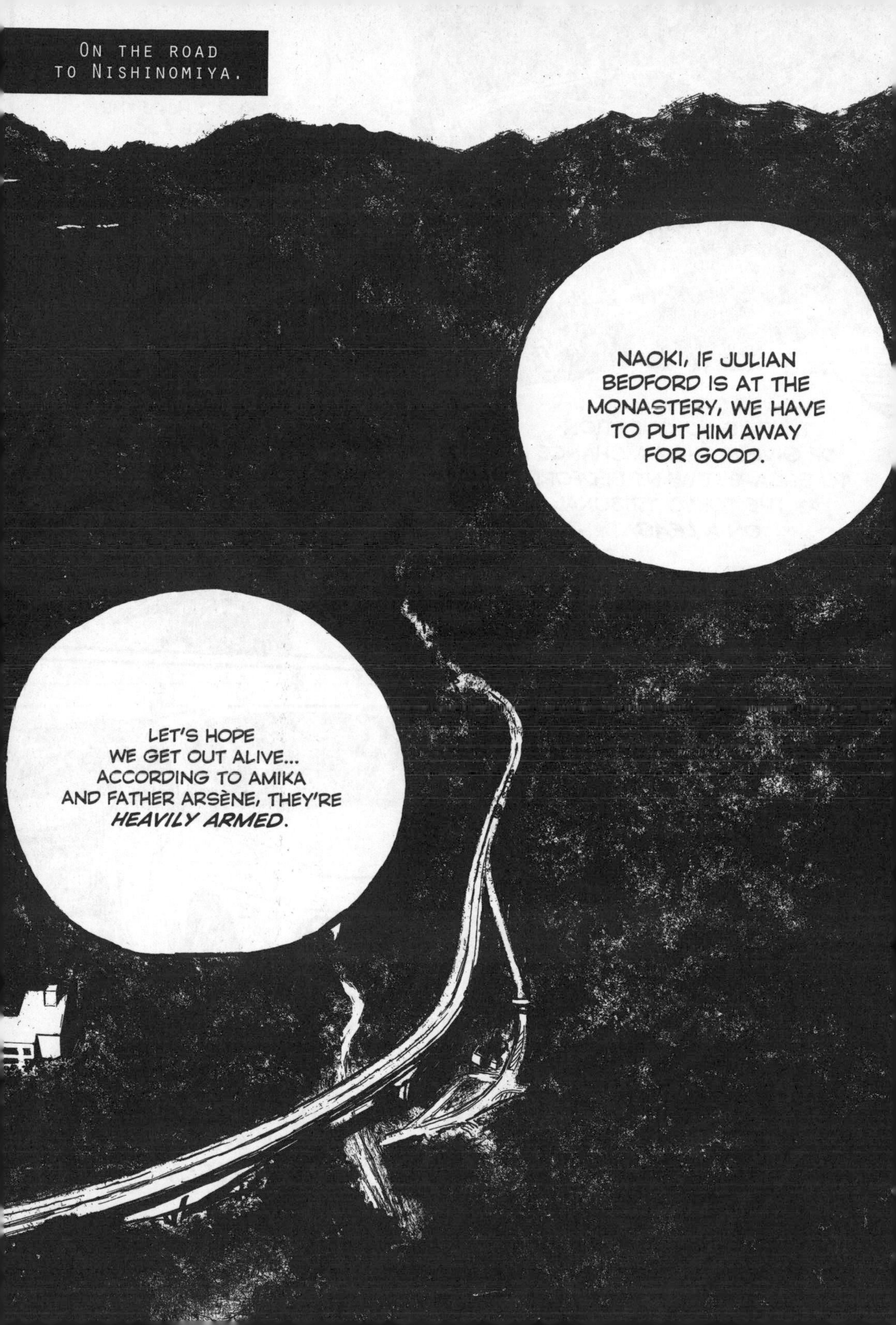
On the road to Nishinomiya.
NAOKI, IF JULIAN BEDFORD IS AT THE MONASTERY, WE HAVE TO PUT HIM AWAY FOR GOOD.
LET'S HOPE WE GET OUT ALIVE... ACCORDING TO AMIKA AND FATHER ARSÈNE, THEY'RE *HEAVILY ARMED*.

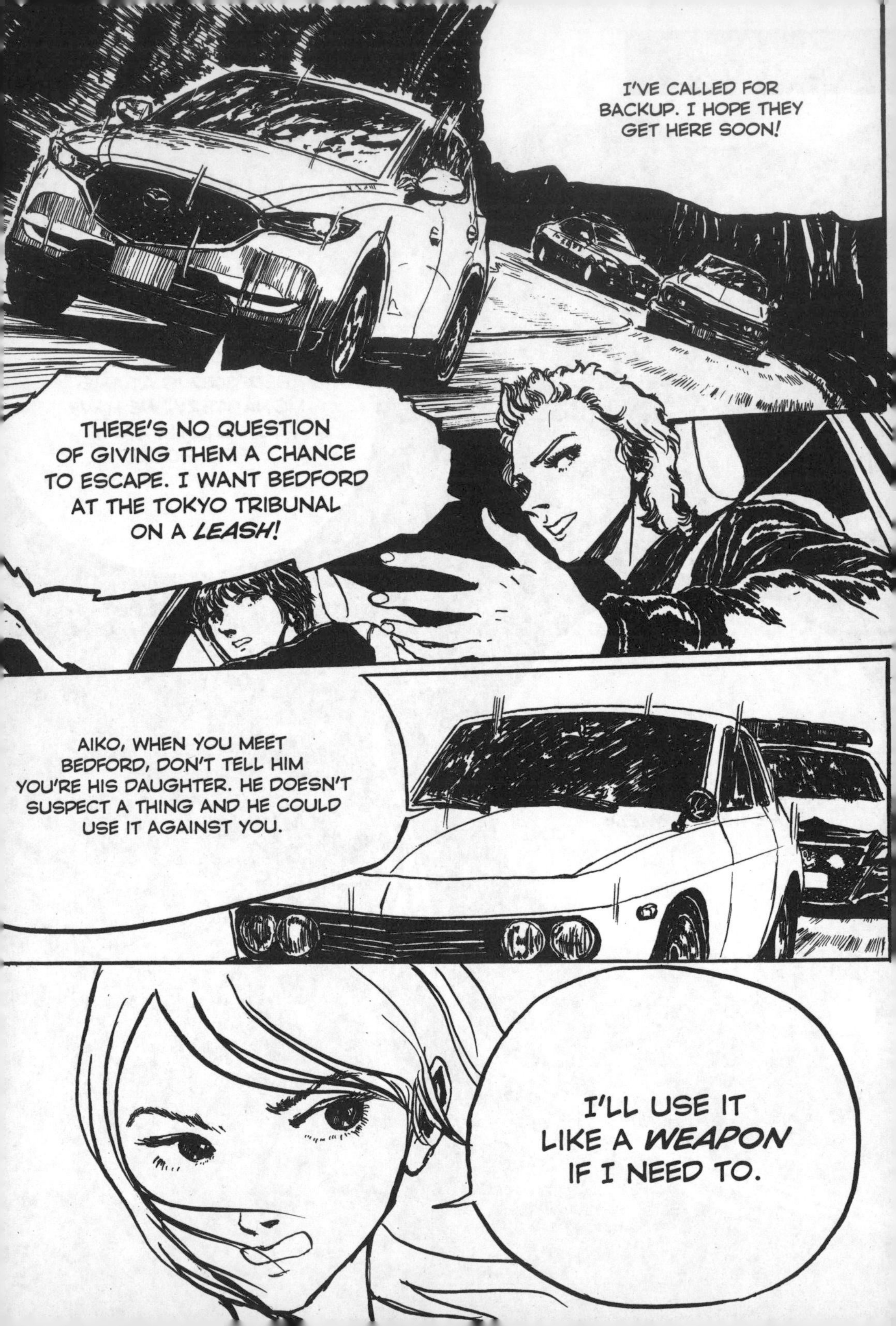
I'VE CALLED FOR BACKUP. I HOPE THEY GET HERE SOON!
THERE'S NO QUESTION OF GIVING THEM A CHANCE TO ESCAPE. I WANT BEDFORD AT THE TOKYO TRIBUNAL ON A *LEASH*!
AIKO, WHEN YOU MEET BEDFORD, DON'T TELL HIM YOU'RE HIS DAUGHTER. HE DOESN'T SUSPECT A THING AND HE COULD USE IT AGAINST YOU.
I'LL USE IT LIKE A *WEAPON* IF I NEED TO.

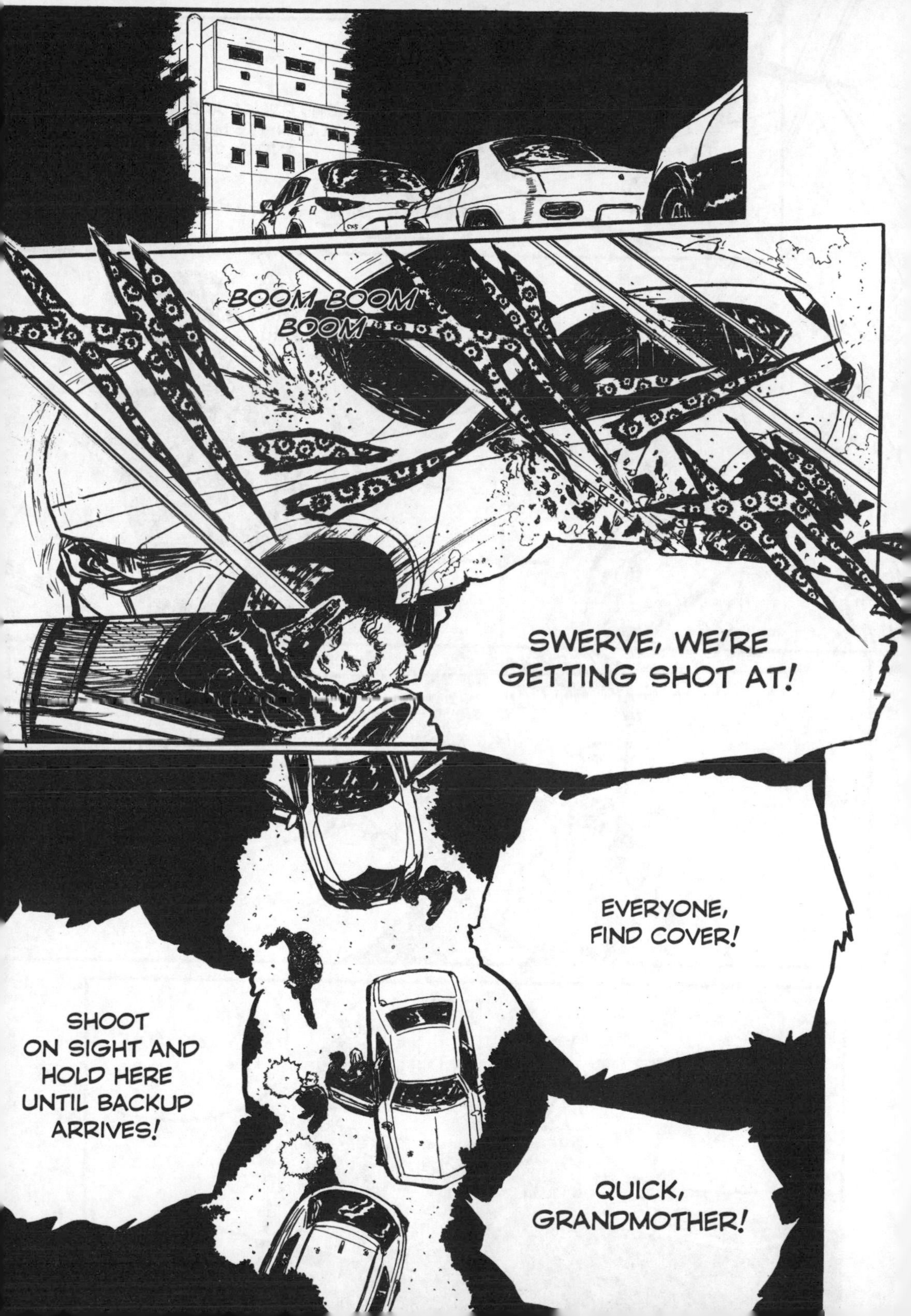
BOOM BOOM BOOM
SWERVE, WE'RE GETTING SHOT AT!
EVERYONE, FIND COVER!
SHOOT ON SIGHT AND HOLD HERE UNTIL BACKUP ARRIVES!
QUICK, GRANDMOTHER!

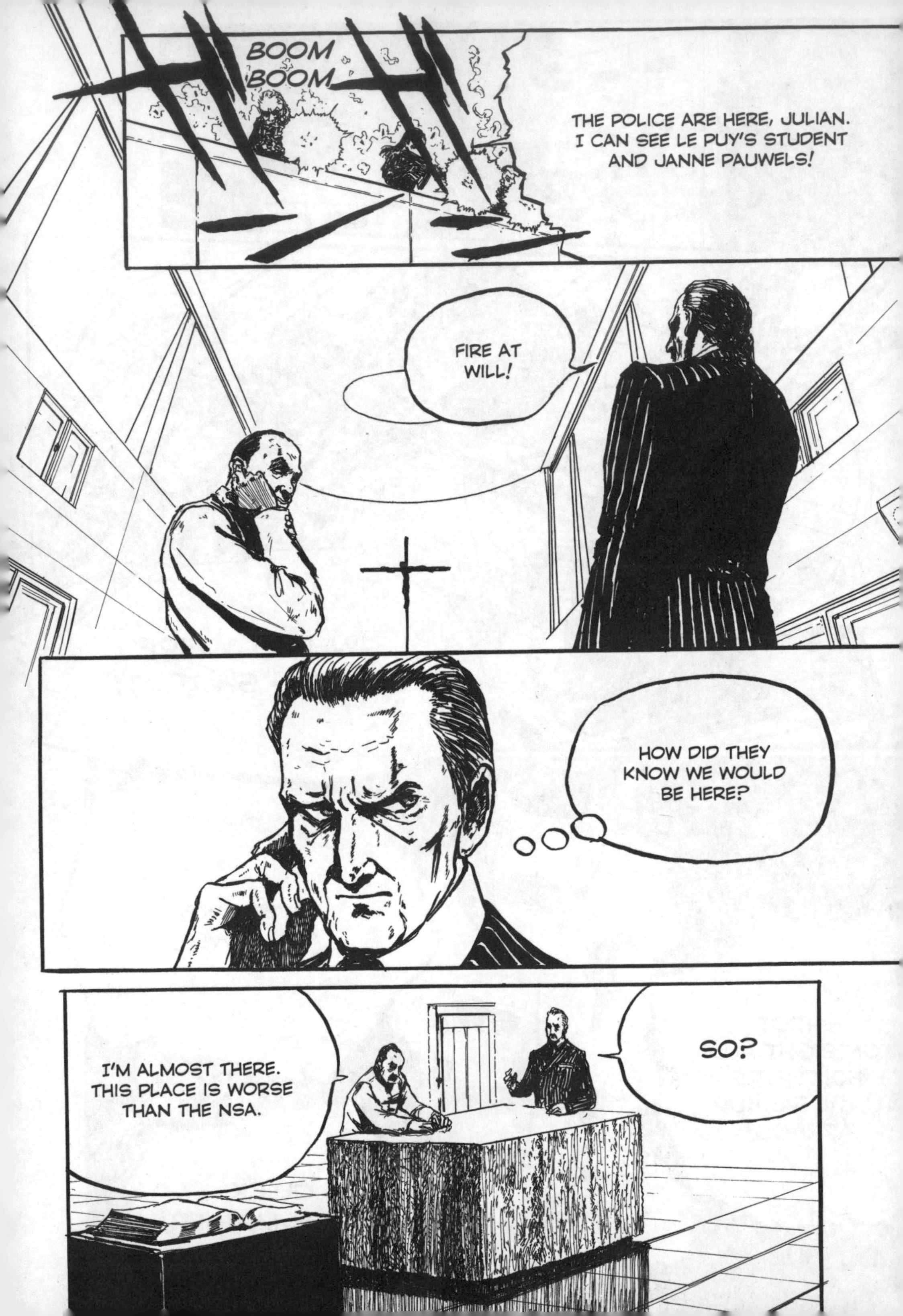
BOOM
BOOM
THE POLICE ARE HERE, JULIAN. I CAN SEE LE PUY'S STUDENT AND JANNE PAUWELS!
FIRE AT WILL!
HOW DID THEY KNOW WE WOULD BE HERE?
SO?
I'M ALMOST THERE. THIS PLACE IS WORSE THAN THE NSA.

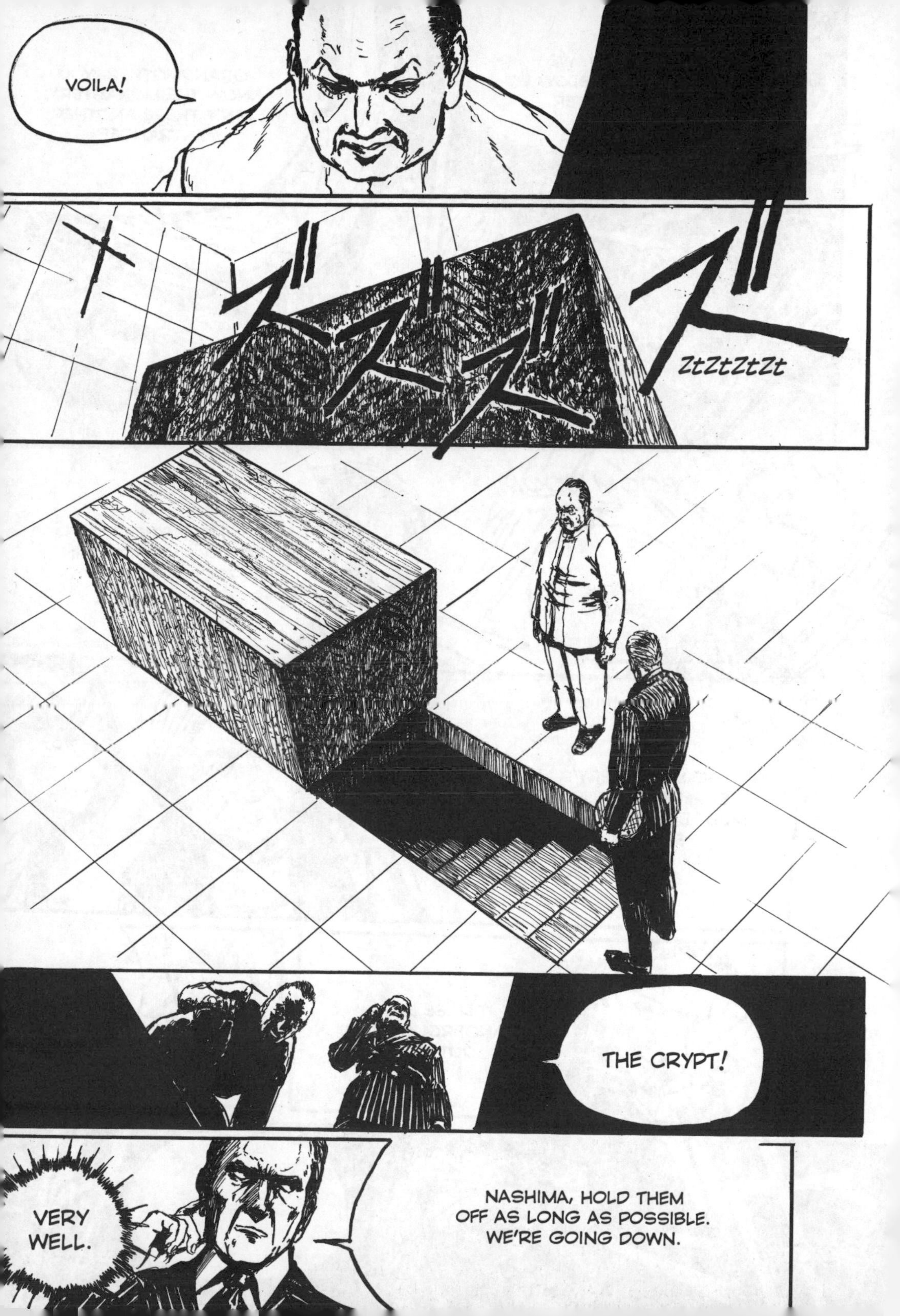
VOILA!
ズズズズ
ZtZtZtZt
THE CRYPT!
NASHIMA, HOLD THEM OFF AS LONG AS POSSIBLE. WE'RE GOING DOWN.
VERY WELL.

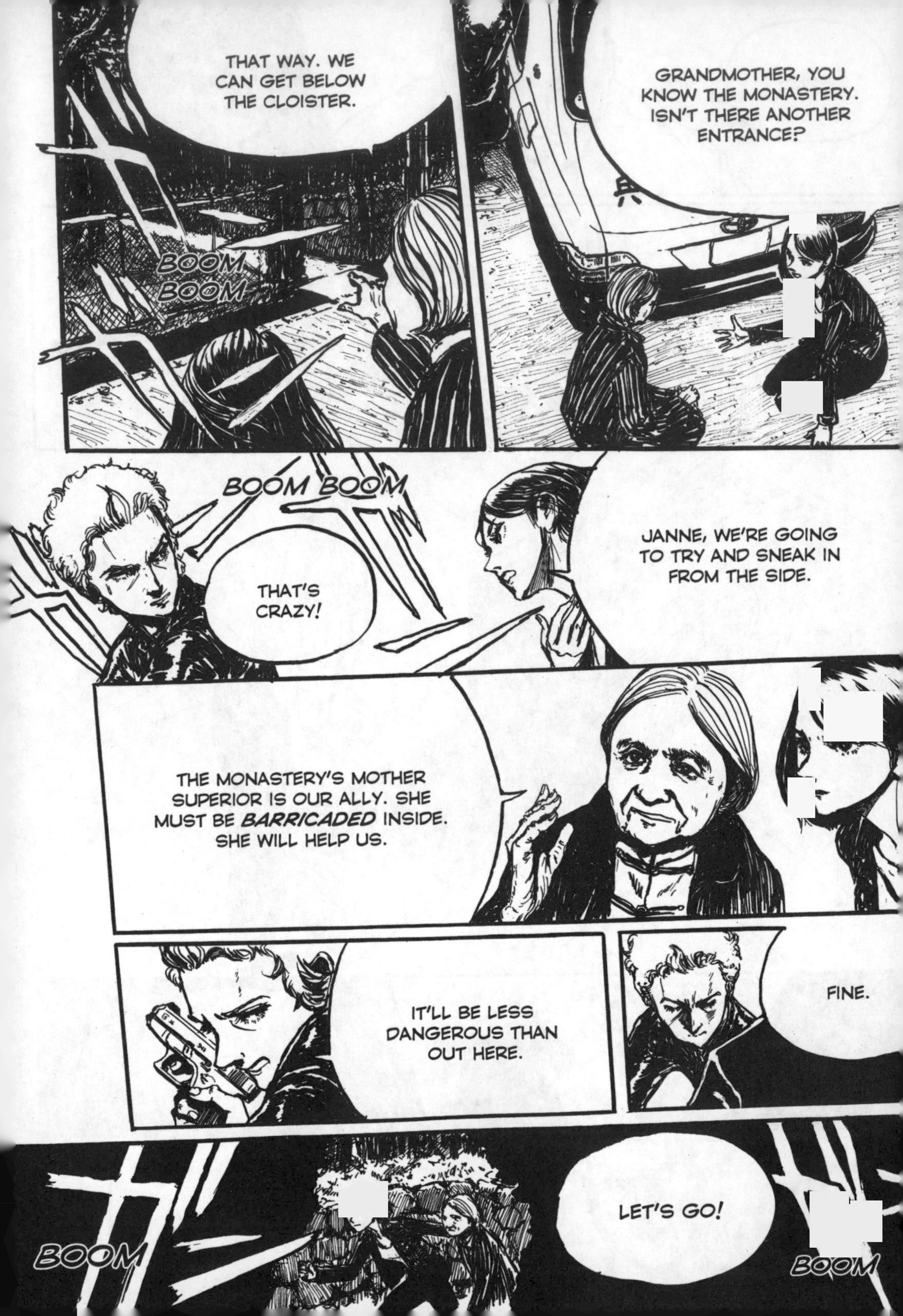
GRANDMOTHER, YOU KNOW THE MONASTERY. ISN'T THERE ANOTHER ENTRANCE?
THAT WAY. WE CAN GET BELOW THE CLOISTER.
BOOM BOOM
BOOM BOOM
JANNE, WE'RE GOING TO TRY AND SNEAK IN FROM THE SIDE.
THAT'S CRAZY!
THE MONASTERY'S MOTHER SUPERIOR IS OUR ALLY. SHE MUST BE *BARRICADED* INSIDE. SHE WILL HELP US.
FINE.
IT'LL BE LESS DANGEROUS THAN OUT HERE.
BOOM
LET'S GO!
BOOM

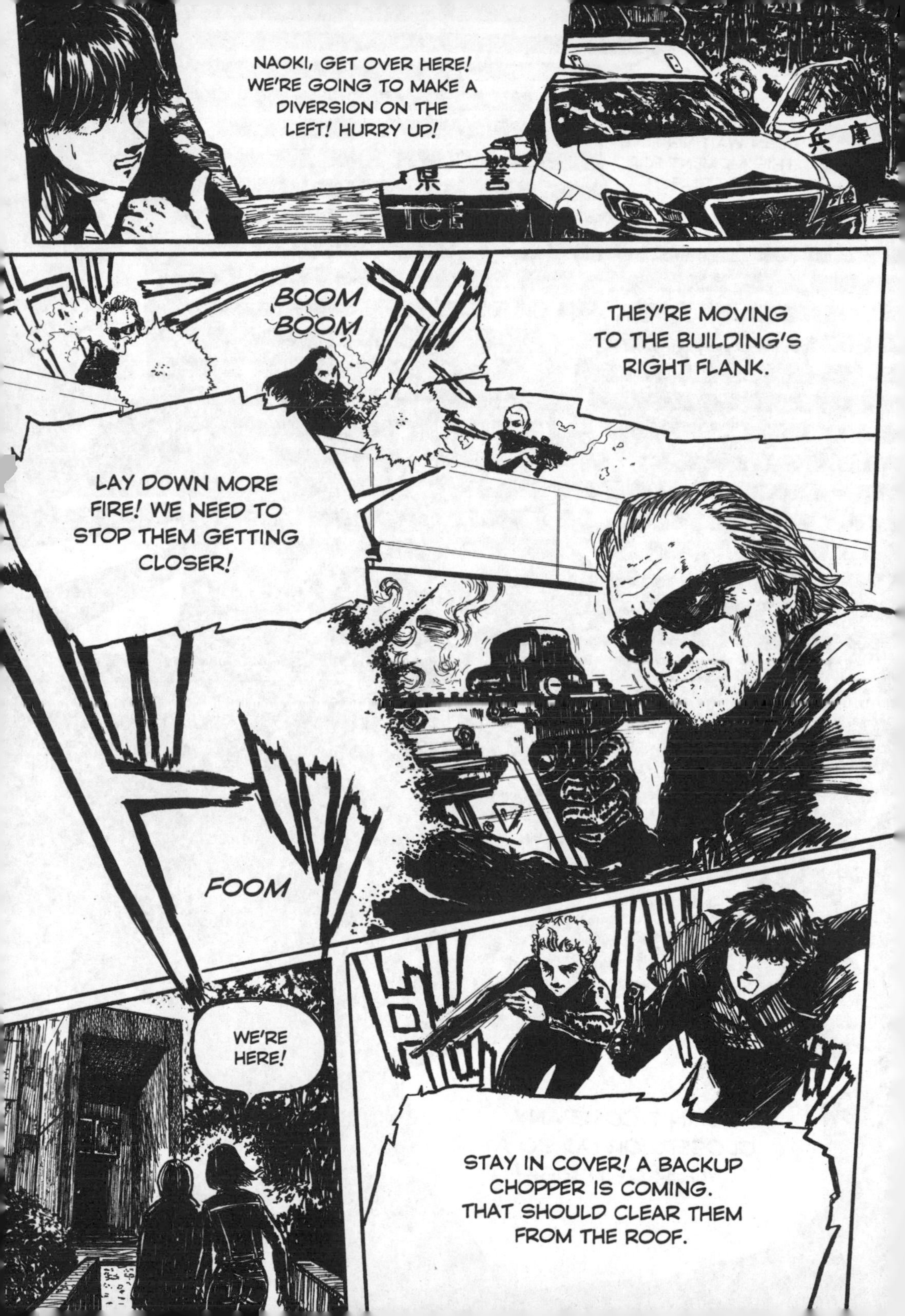
NAOKI, GET OVER HERE! WE'RE GOING TO MAKE A DIVERSION ON THE LEFT! HURRY UP!
兵庫
県警
THEY'RE MOVING TO THE BUILDING'S RIGHT FLANK.
BOOM BOOM
LAY DOWN MORE FIRE! WE NEED TO STOP THEM GETTING CLOSER!
FOOM
STAY IN COVER! A BACKUP CHOPPER IS COMING. THAT SHOULD CLEAR THEM FROM THE ROOF.
WE'RE HERE!

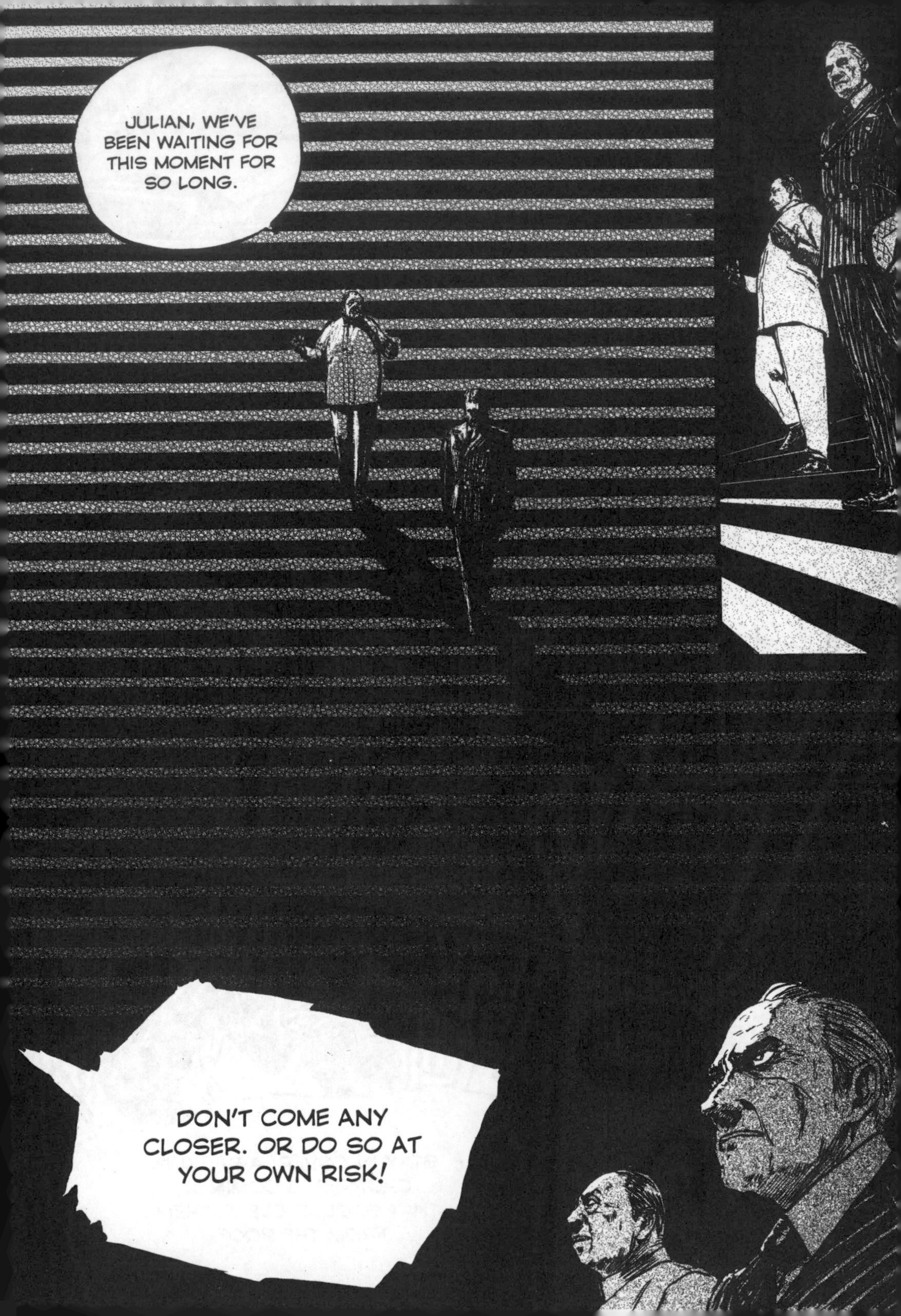
JULIAN, WE'VE BEEN WAITING FOR THIS MOMENT FOR SO LONG.
DON'T COME ANY CLOSER. OR DO SO AT YOUR OWN RISK!

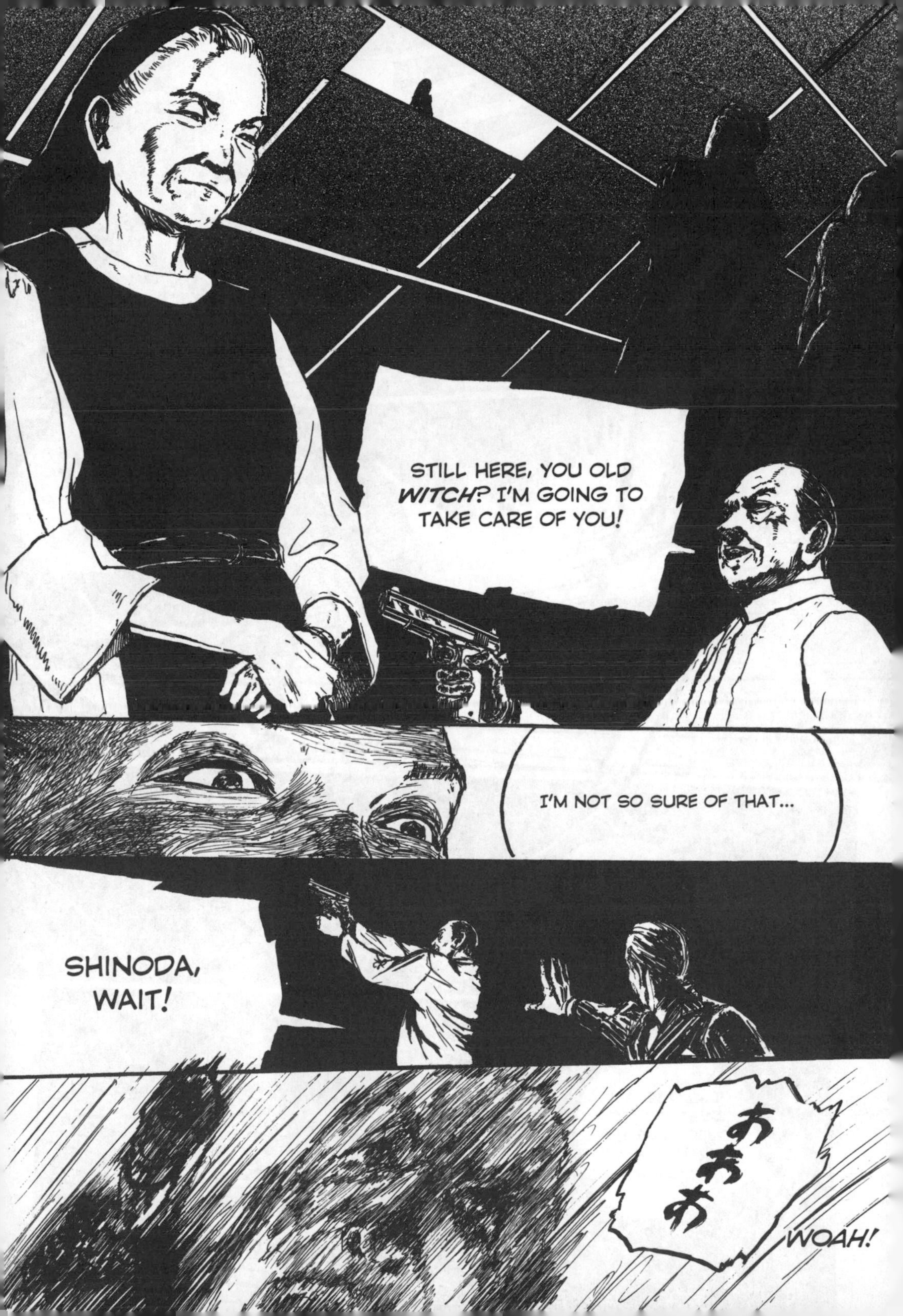
STILL HERE, YOU OLD *WITCH*? I'M GOING TO TAKE CARE OF YOU!
I'M NOT SO SURE OF THAT...
SHINODA, WAIT!
おおお
WOAH!

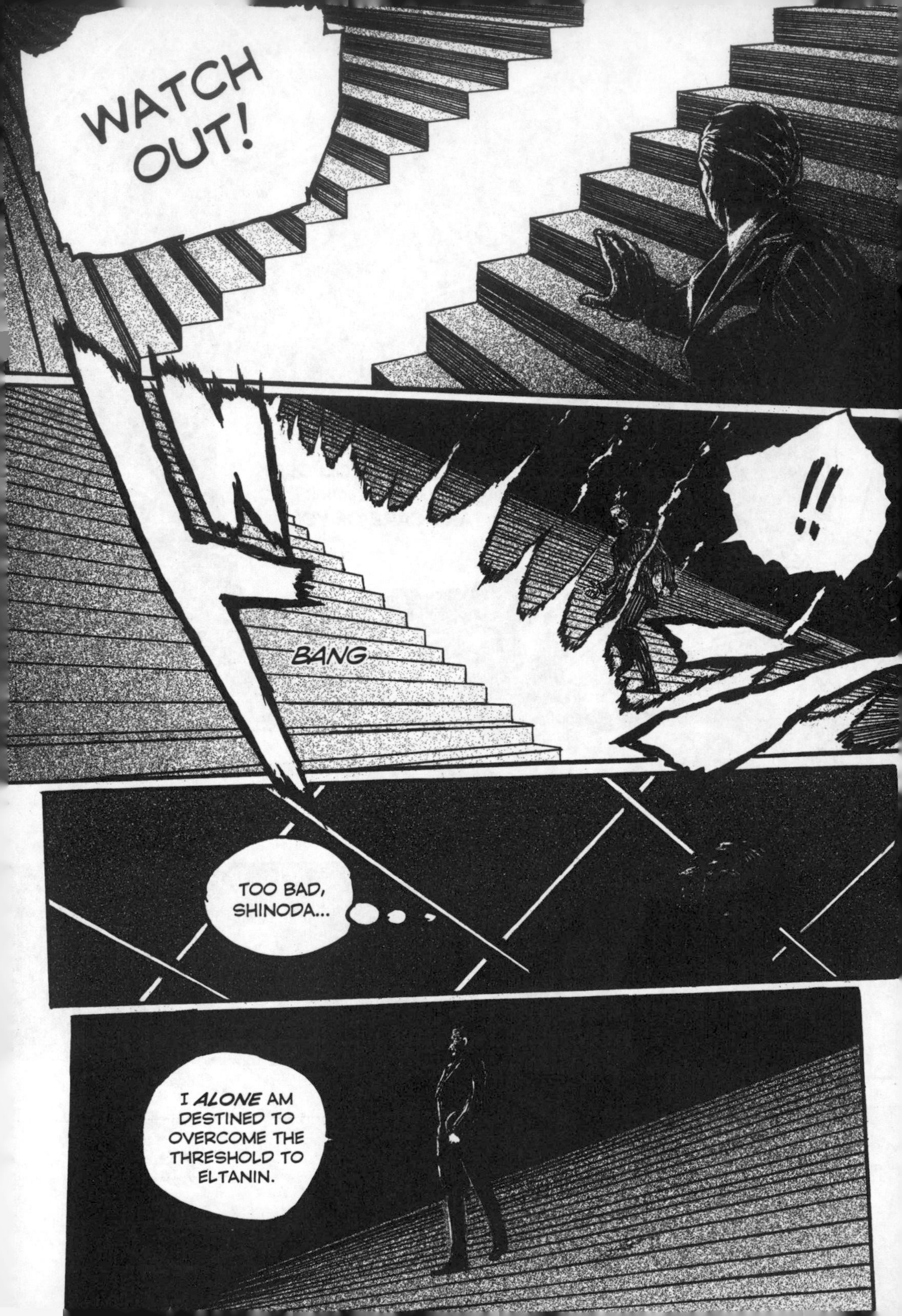
WATCH OUT!
!!
BANG
TOO BAD, SHINODA...
I *ALONE* AM DESTINED TO OVERCOME THE THRESHOLD TO ELTANIN.

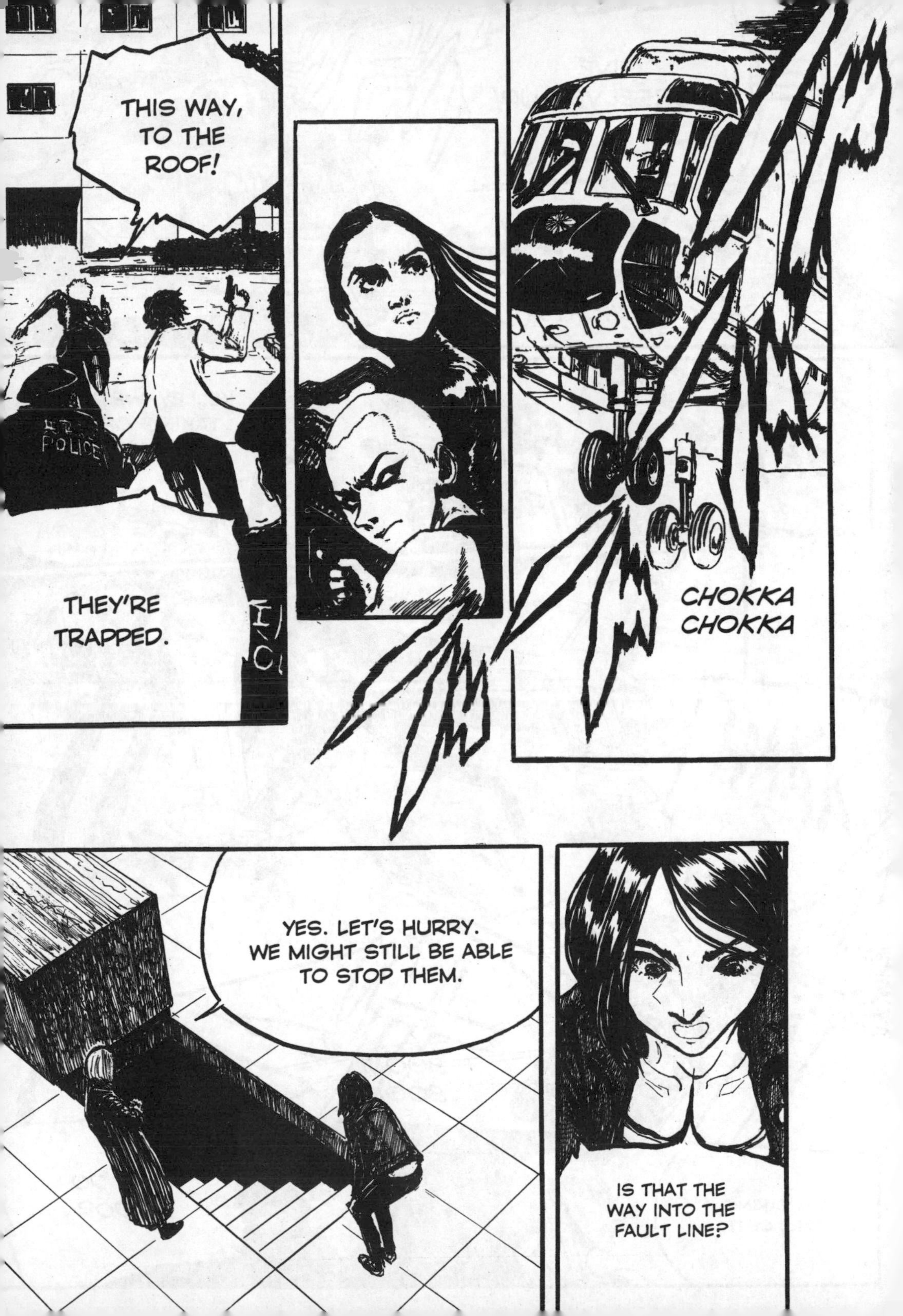
CHOKKA
CHOKKA
THIS WAY, TO THE ROOF!
POLICE
THEY'RE TRAPPED.
IS THAT THE WAY INTO THE FAULT LINE?
YES. LET'S HURRY. WE MIGHT STILL BE ABLE TO STOP THEM.

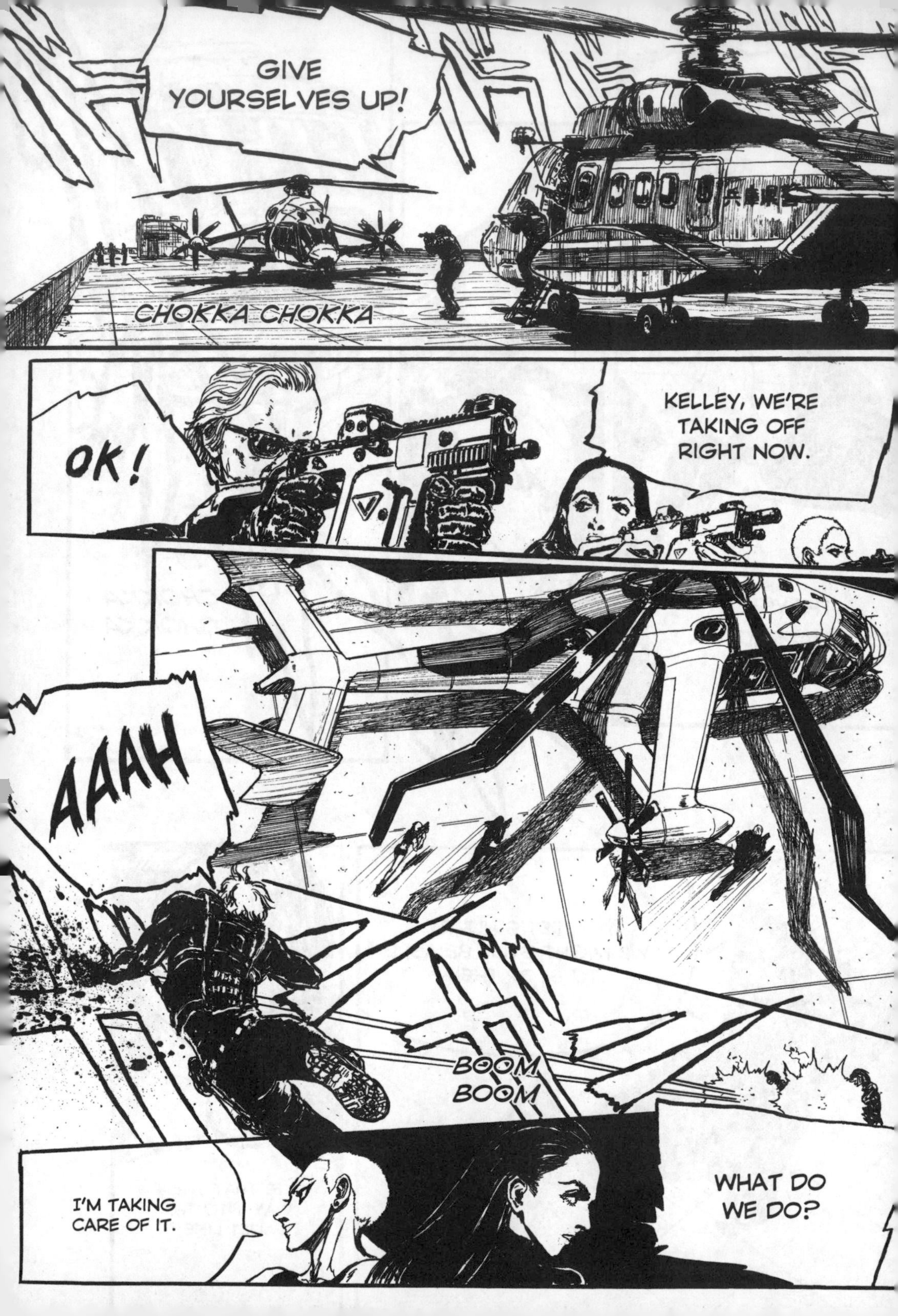
GIVE YOURSELVES UP!
CHOKKA CHOKKA
KELLEY, WE'RE TAKING OFF RIGHT NOW.
OK!
AAAH
BOOM BOOM
WHAT DO WE DO?
I'M TAKING CARE OF IT.

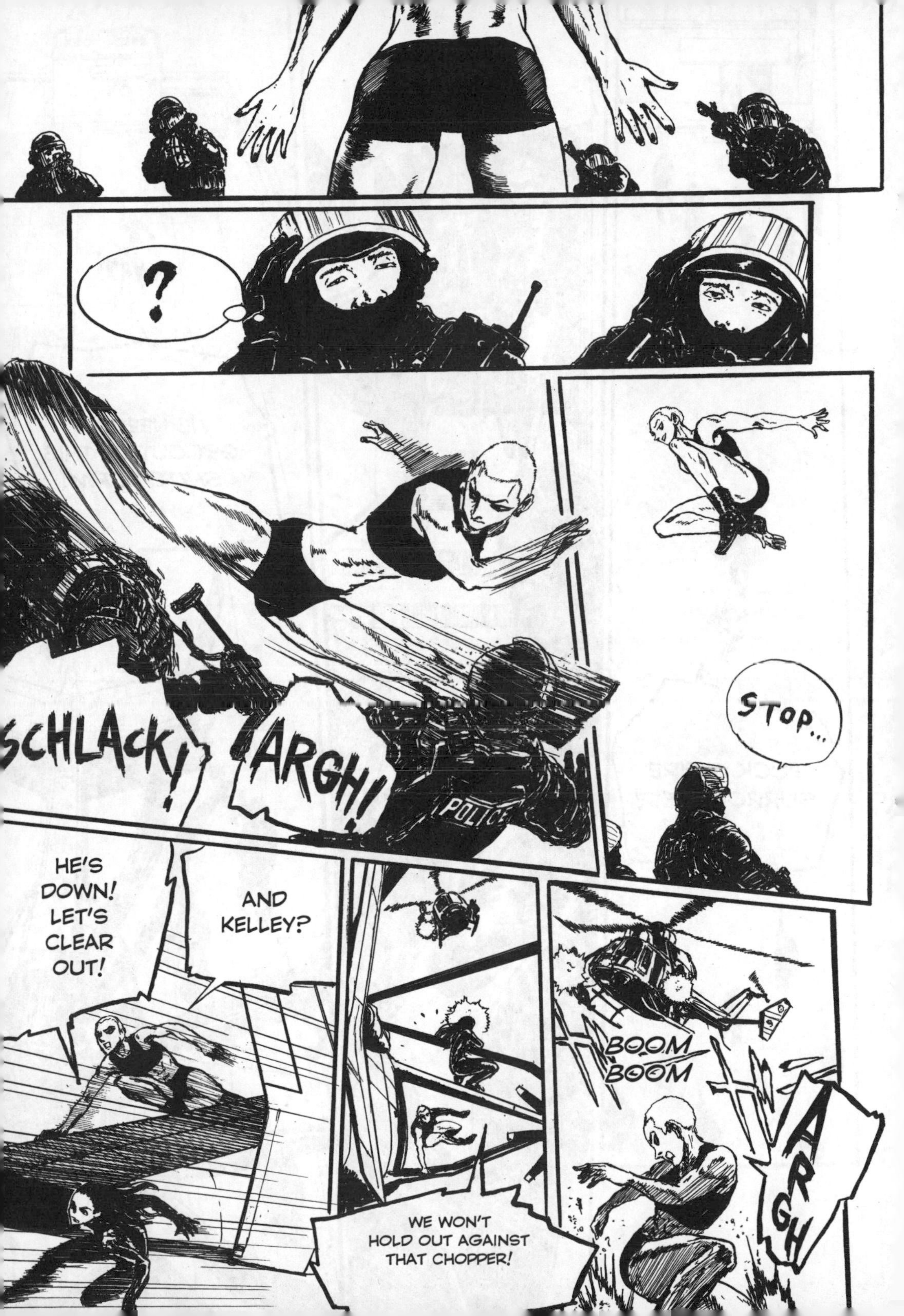
?
STOP...
SCHLACK!
ARGH!
BOOM BOOM
ARGH
WE WON'T HOLD OUT AGAINST THAT CHOPPER!
HE'S DOWN! LET'S CLEAR OUT!
AND KELLEY?

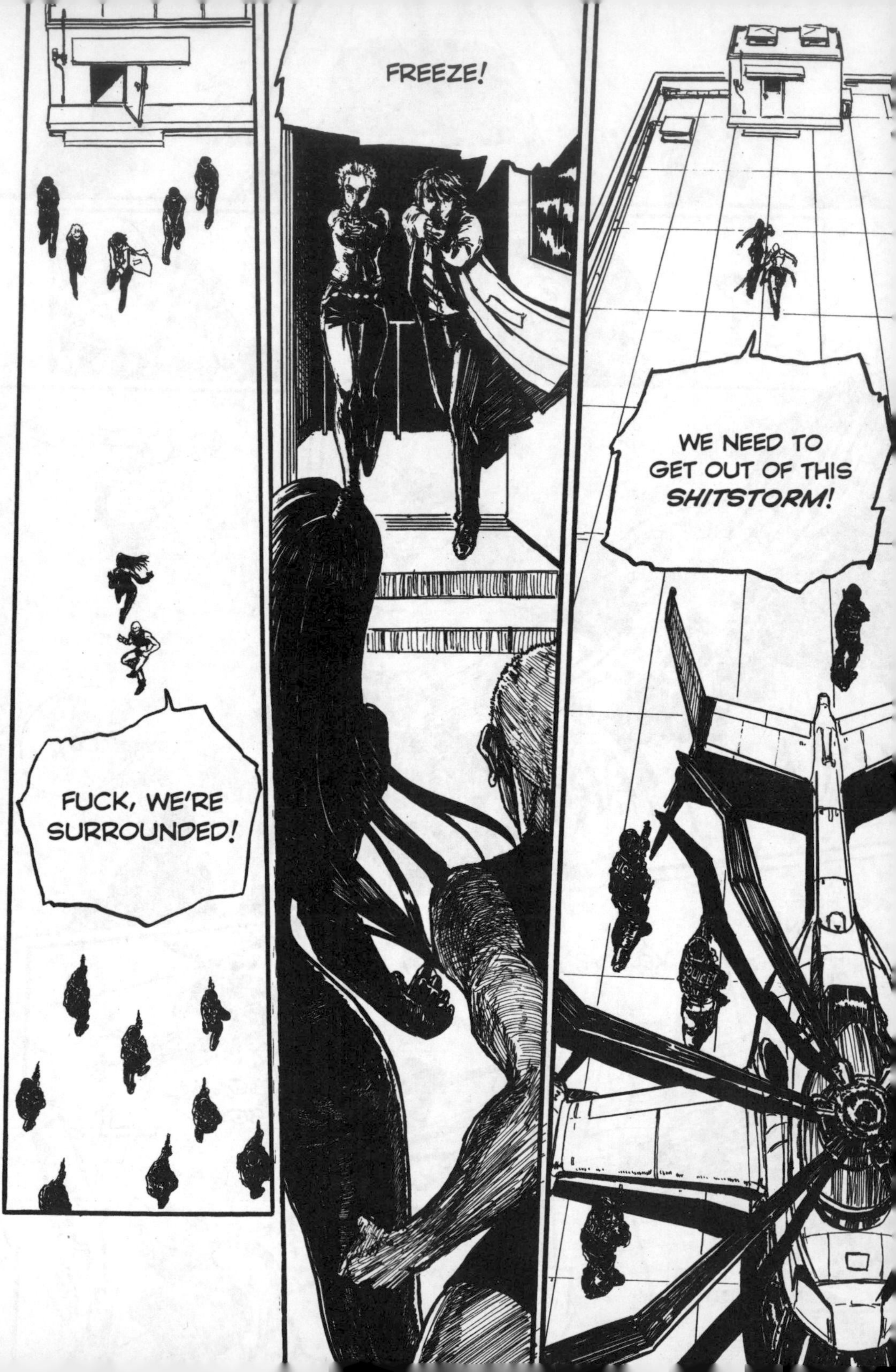
WE NEED TO GET OUT OF THIS *SHITSTORM!*
FREEZE!
FUCK, WE'RE SURROUNDED!

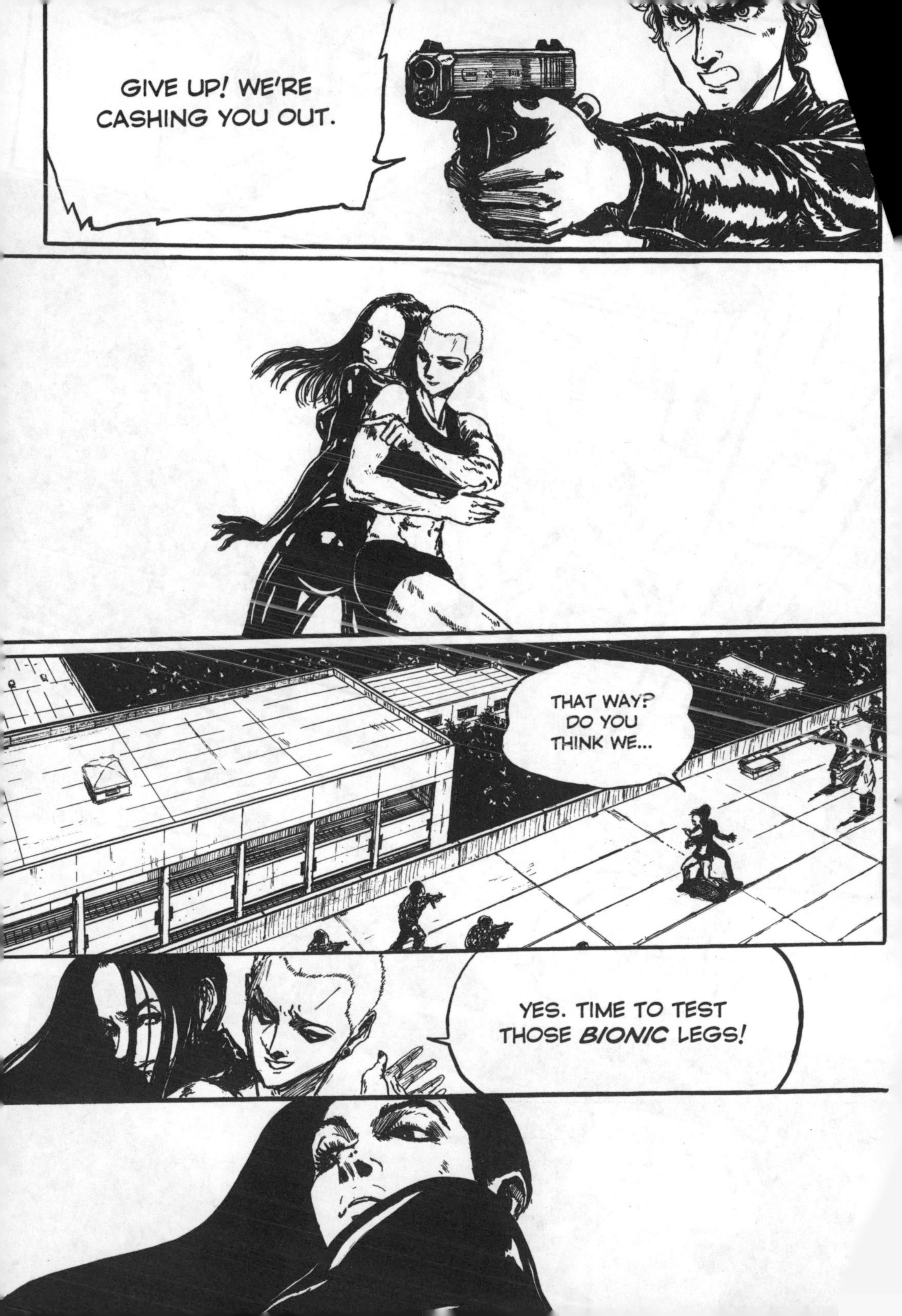
GIVE UP! WE'RE CASHING YOU OUT.
THAT WAY? DO YOU THINK WE...
YES. TIME TO TEST THOSE *BIONIC* LEGS!

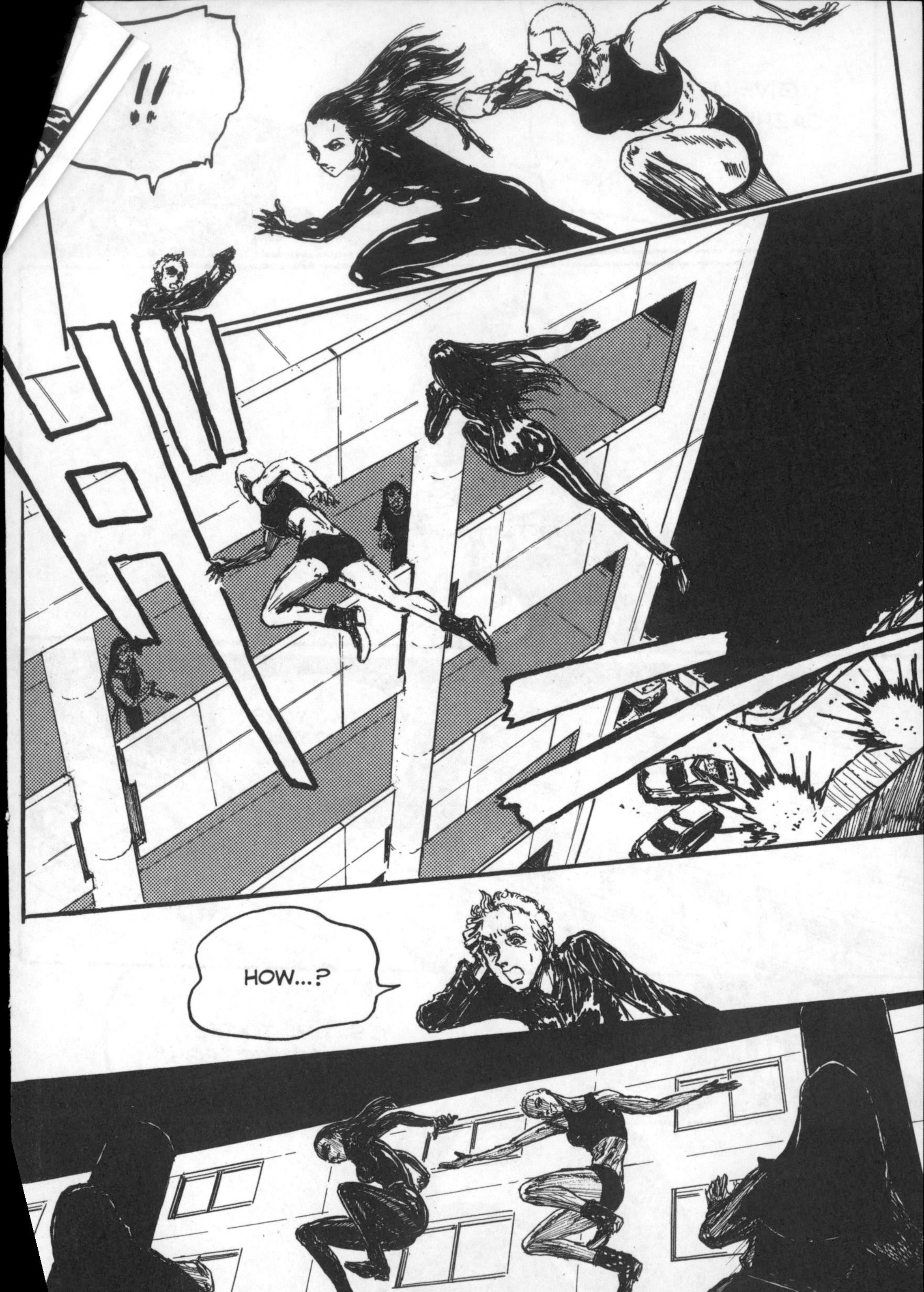
!!
HOW...?

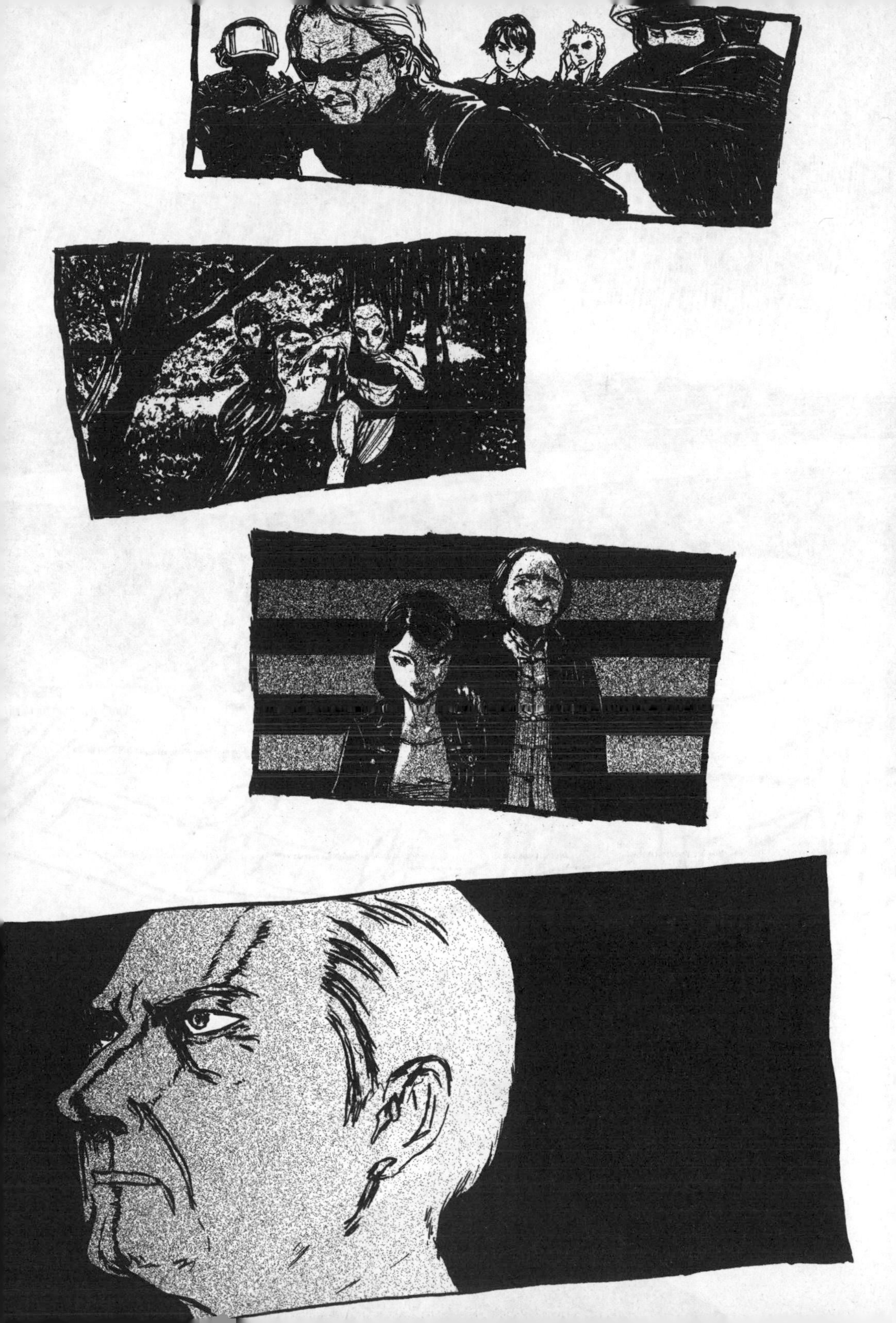

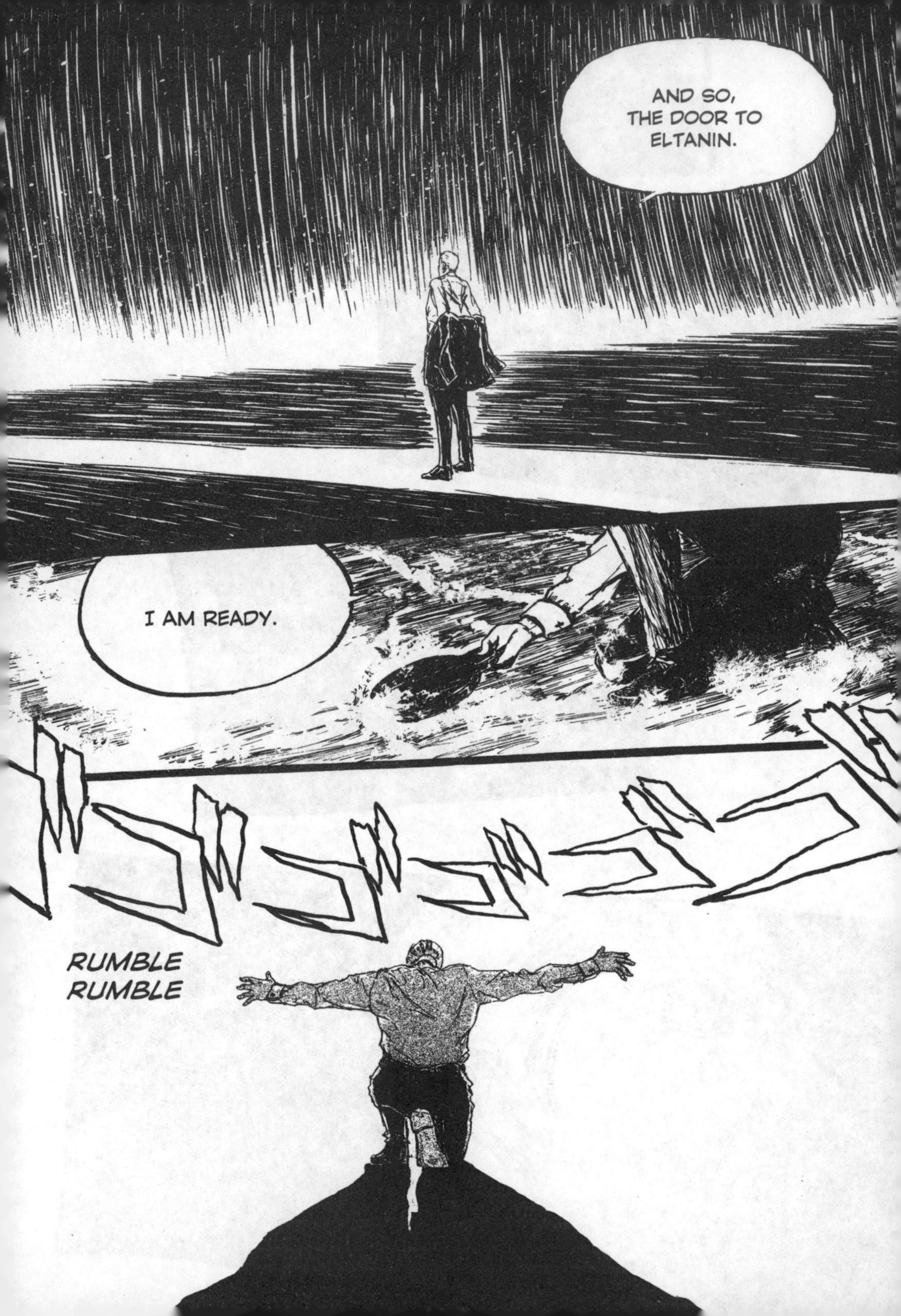
AND SO, THE DOOR TO ELTANIN.
I AM READY.
RUMBLE RUMBLE

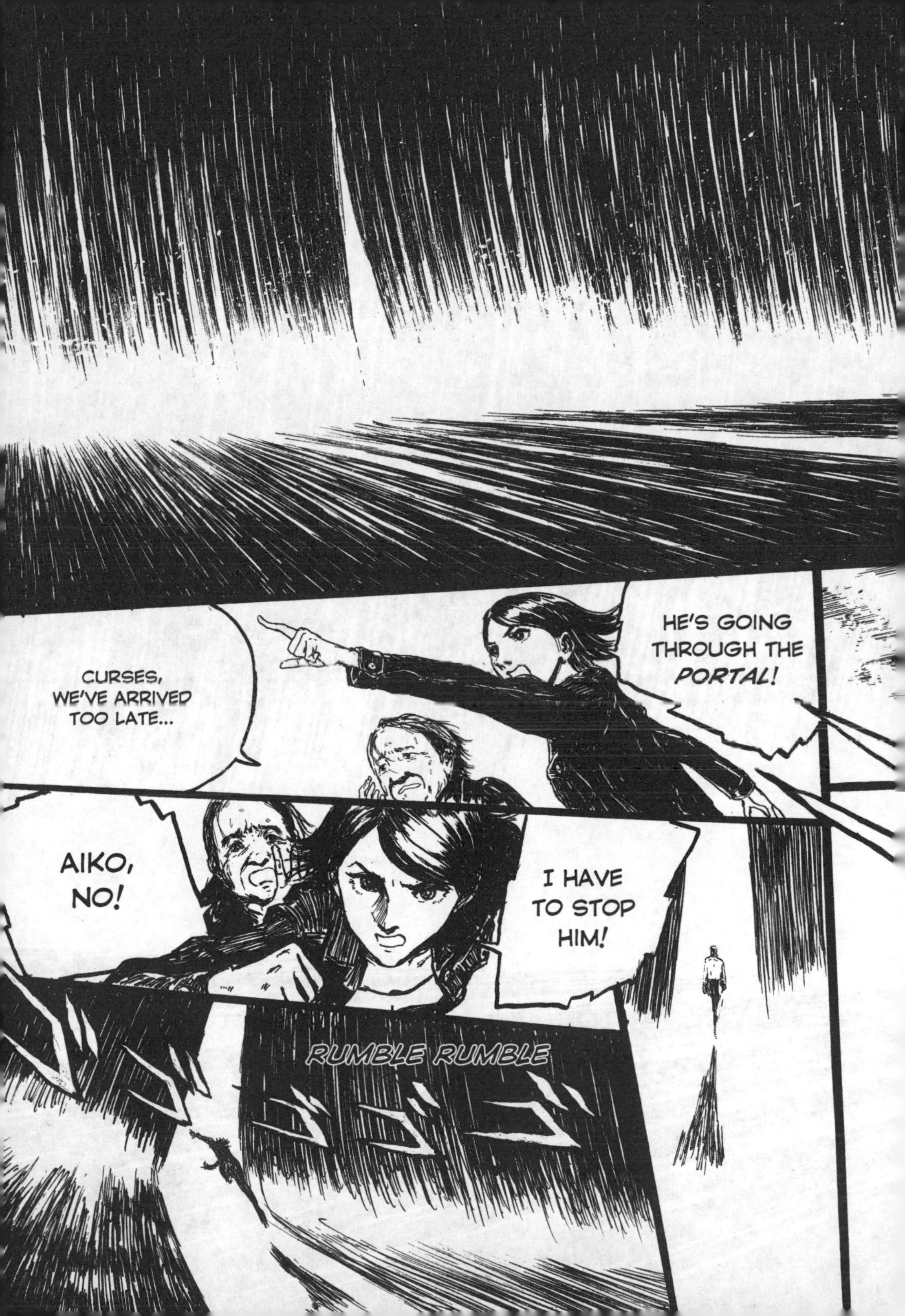
HE'S GOING THROUGH THE *PORTAL*!
CURSES, WE'VE ARRIVED TOO LATE...
I HAVE TO STOP HIM!
AIKO, NO!
RUMBLE RUMBLE

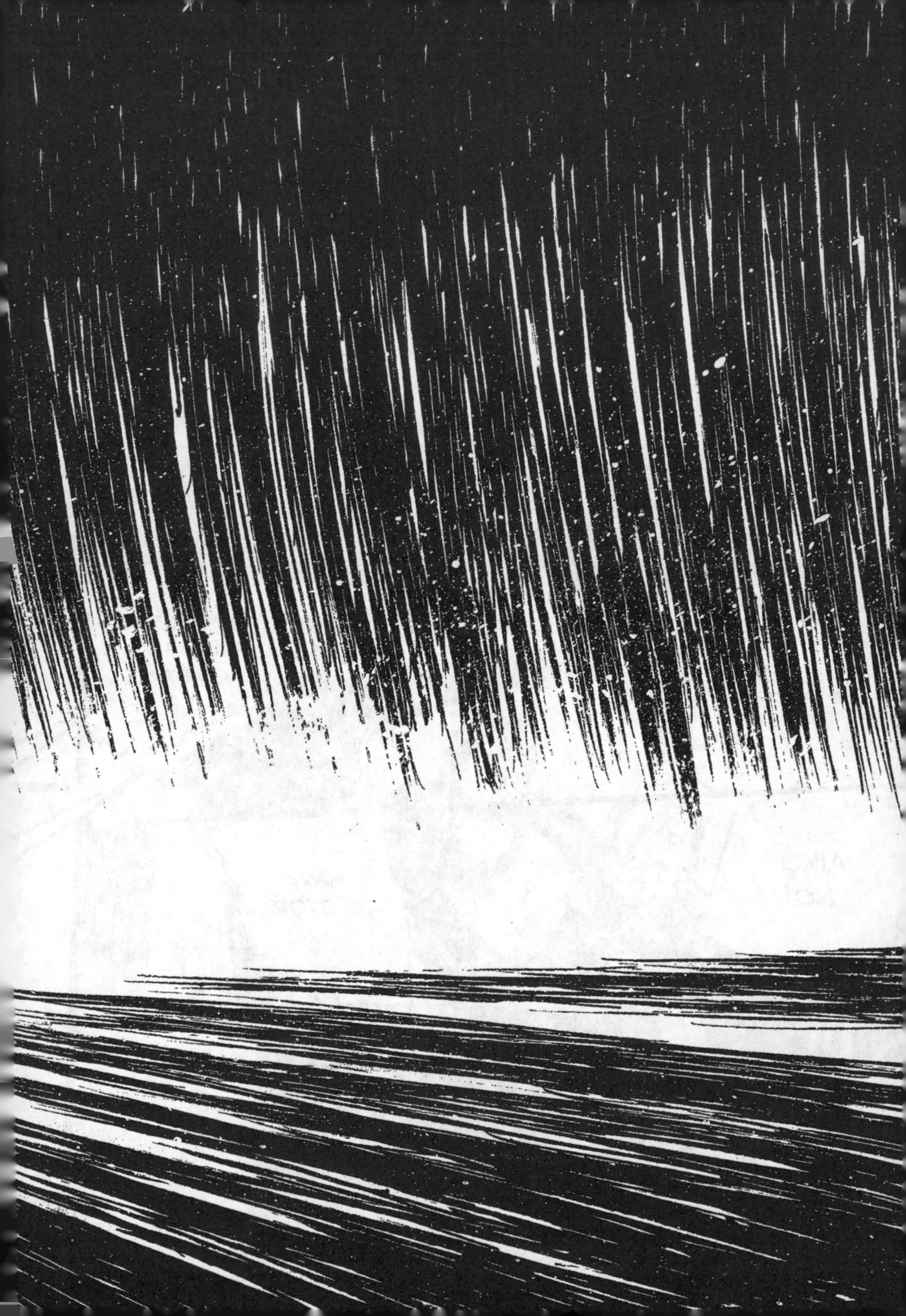

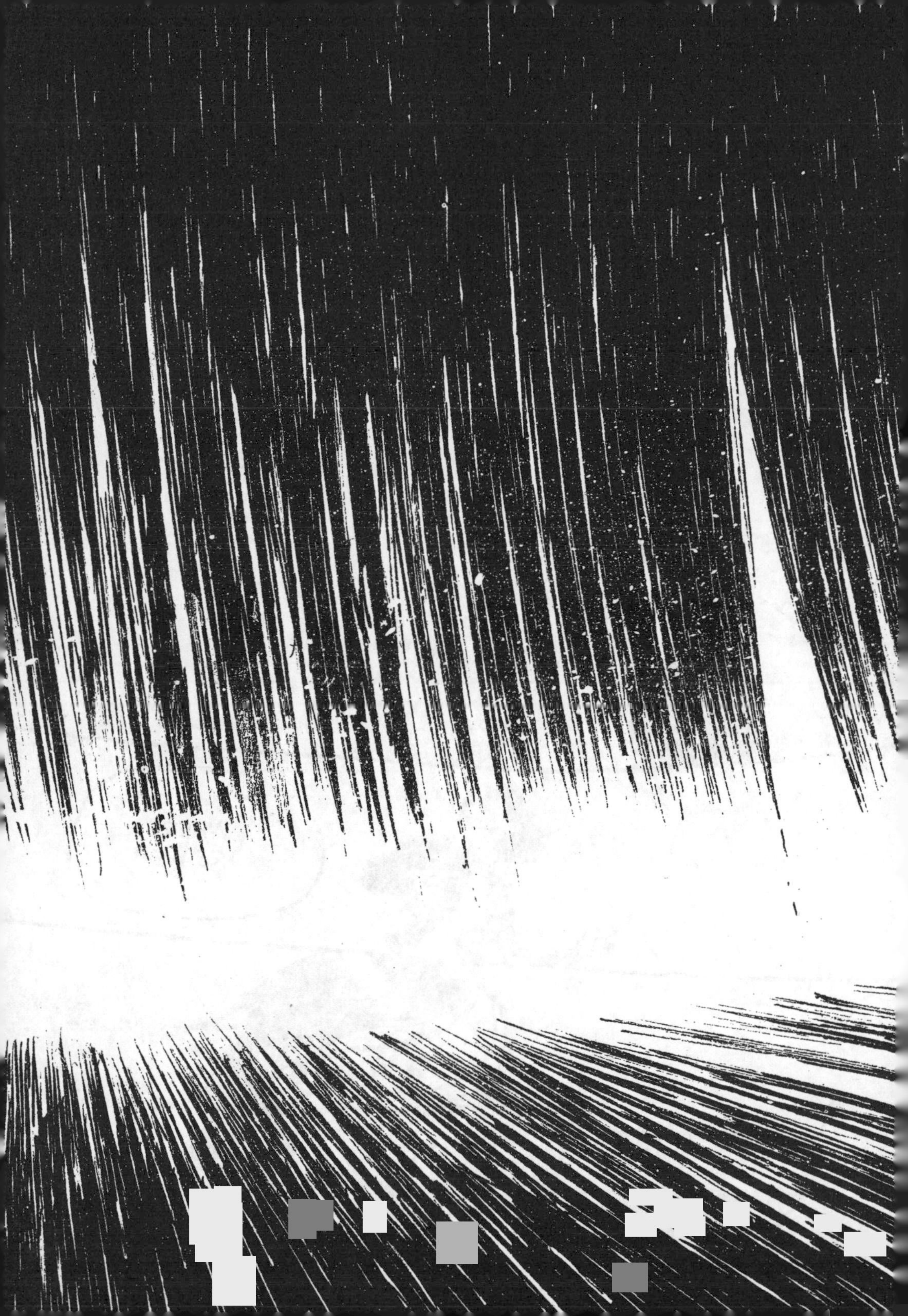

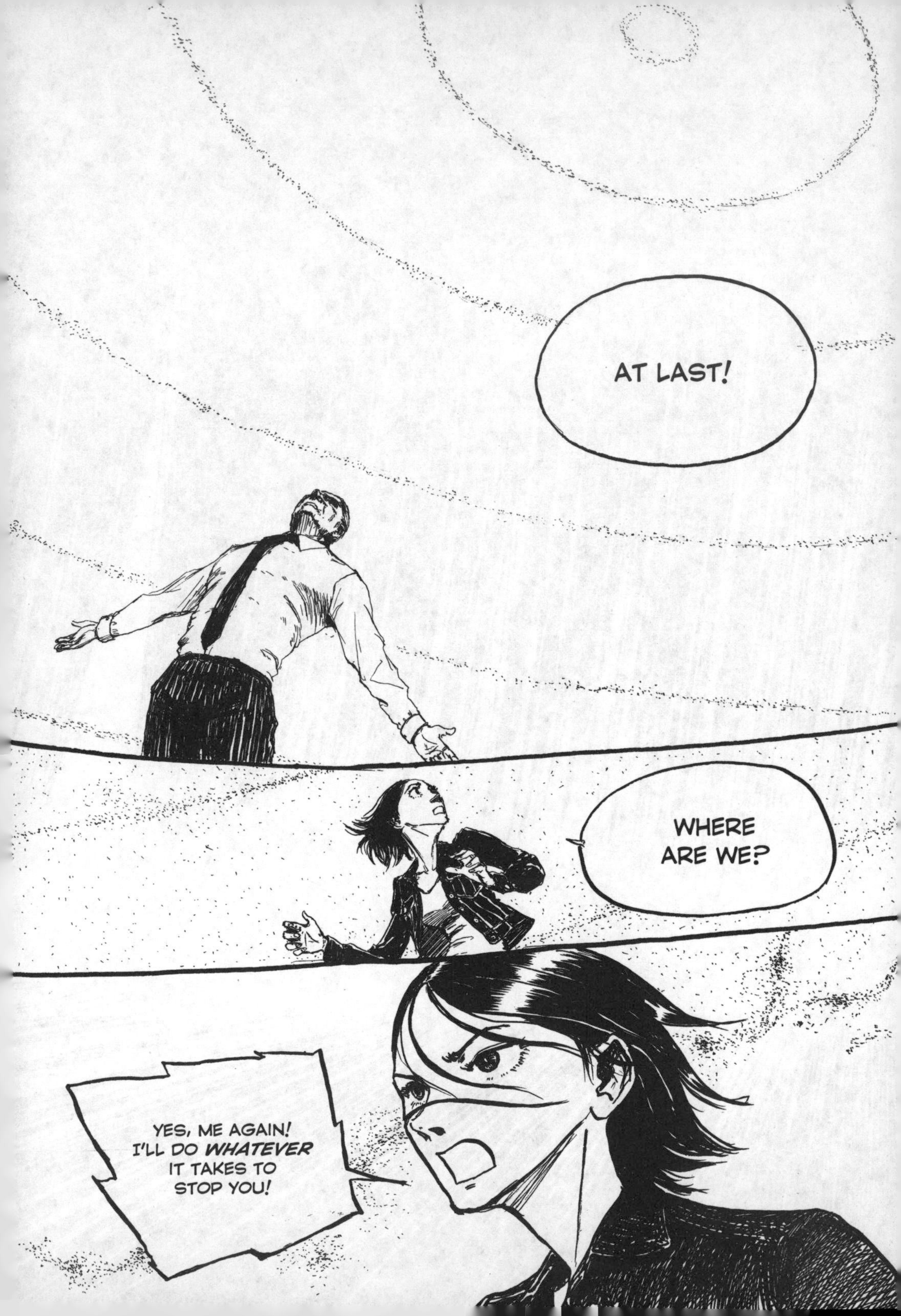
AT LAST!
WHERE ARE WE?
YES, ME AGAIN! I'LL DO *WHATEVER* IT TAKES TO STOP YOU!

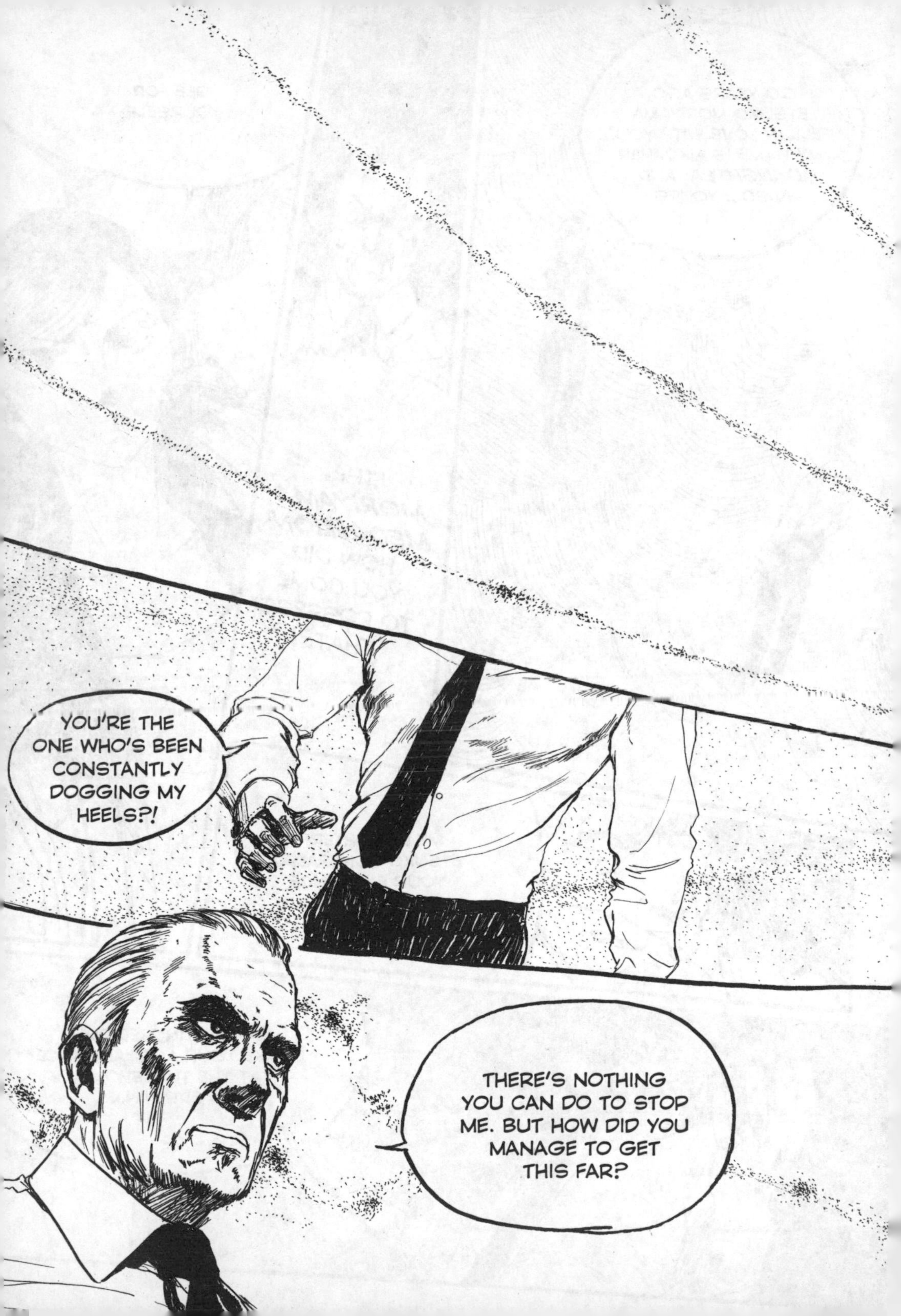
YOU'RE THE ONE WHO'S BEEN CONSTANTLY DOGGING MY HEELS?!
THERE'S NOTHING YOU CAN DO TO STOP ME. BUT HOW DID YOU MANAGE TO GET THIS FAR?

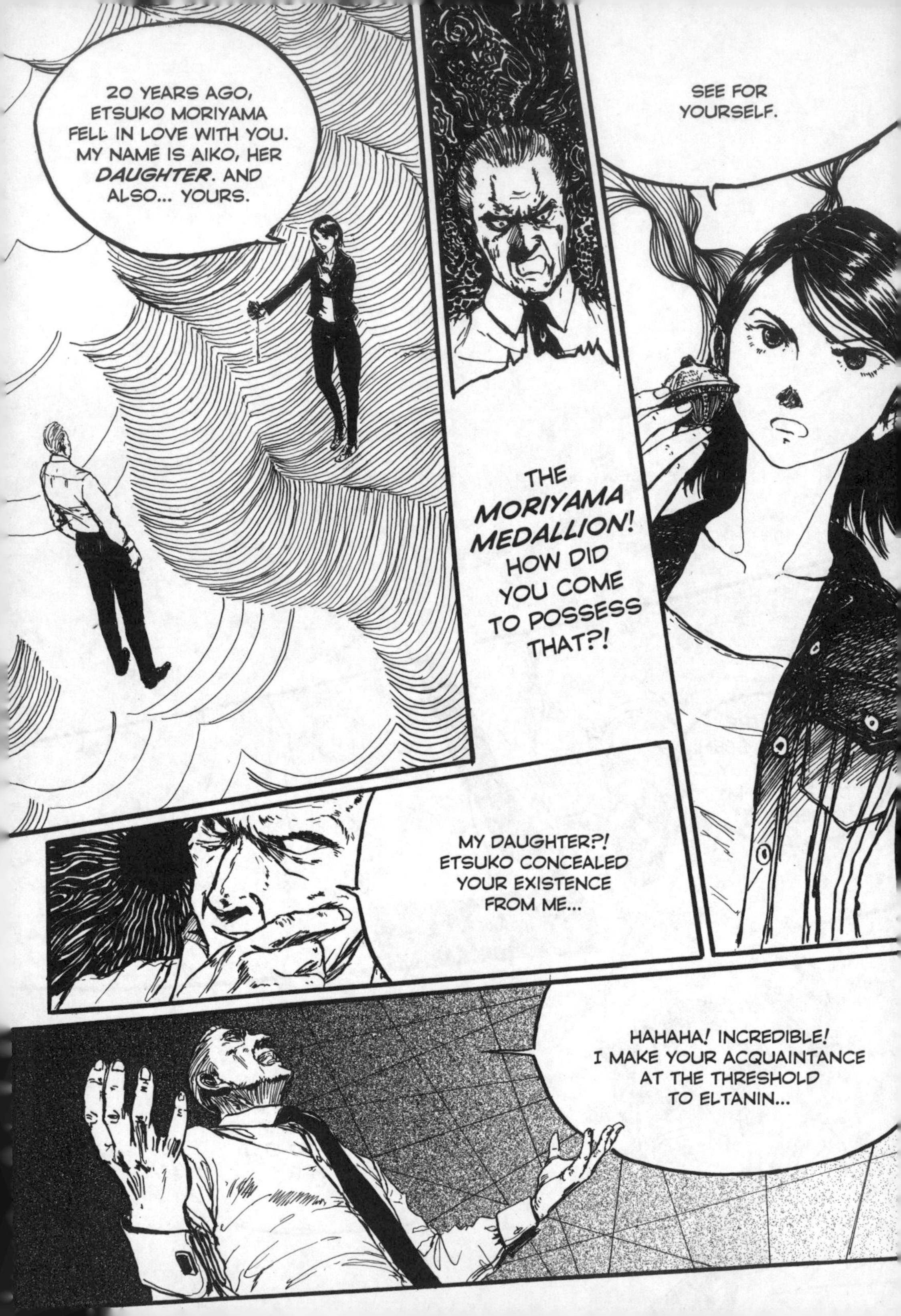
SEE FOR YOURSELF.
THE *MORIYAMA MEDALLION*! HOW DID YOU COME TO POSSESS THAT?!
20 YEARS AGO, ETSUKO MORIYAMA FELL IN LOVE WITH YOU. MY NAME IS AIKO, HER *DAUGHTER*. AND ALSO... YOURS.
MY DAUGHTER?! ETSUKO CONCEALED YOUR EXISTENCE FROM ME...
HAHAHA! INCREDIBLE! I MAKE YOUR ACQUAINTANCE AT THE THRESHOLD TO ELTANIN...

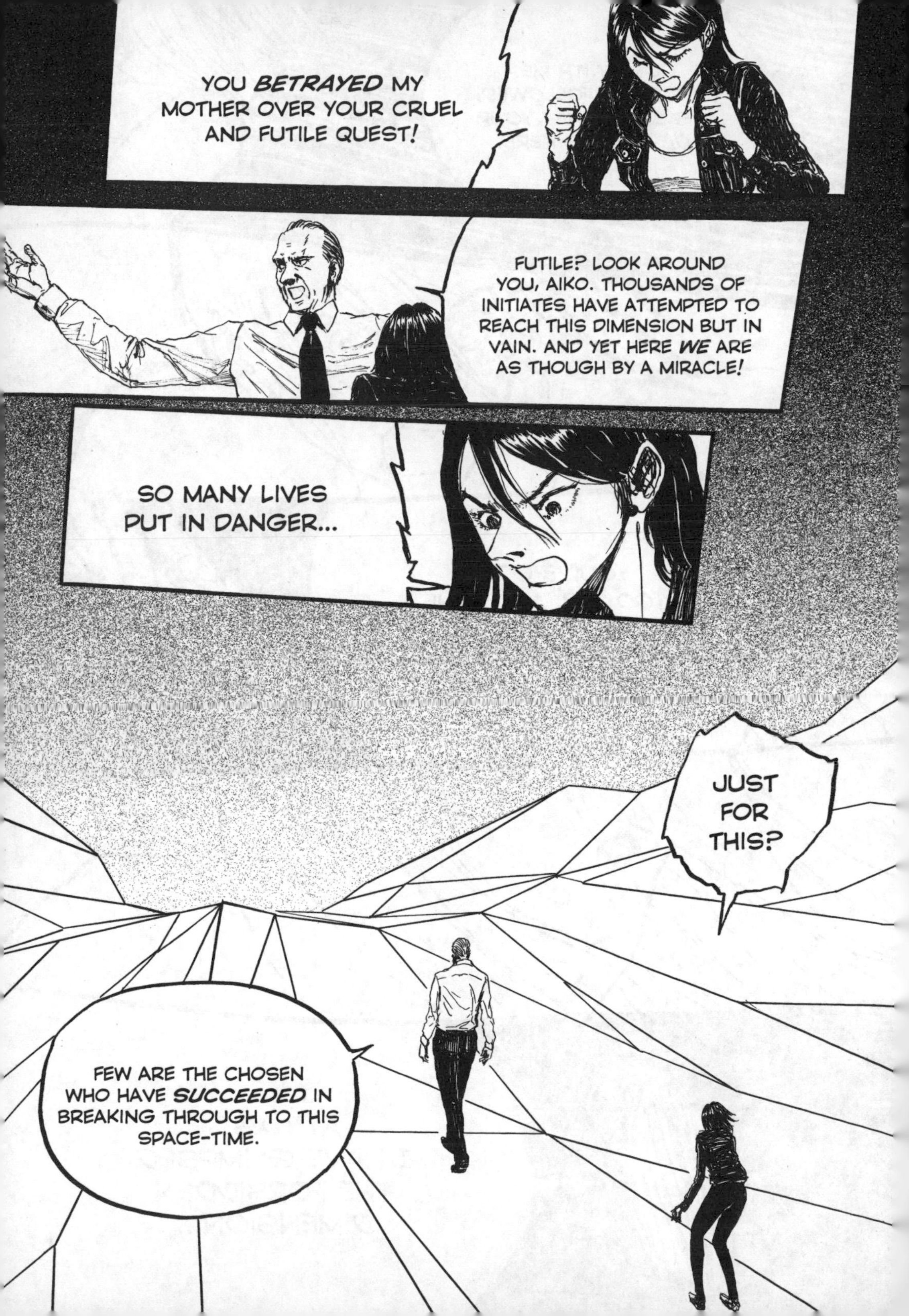
YOU *BETRAYED* MY MOTHER OVER YOUR CRUEL AND FUTILE QUEST!
FUTILE? LOOK AROUND YOU, AIKO. THOUSANDS OF INITIATES HAVE ATTEMPTED TO REACH THIS DIMENSION BUT IN VAIN. AND YET HERE *WE* ARE AS THOUGH BY A MIRACLE!
SO MANY LIVES PUT IN DANGER...
JUST FOR THIS?
FEW ARE THE CHOSEN WHO HAVE *SUCCEEDED* IN BREAKING THROUGH TO THIS SPACE-TIME.

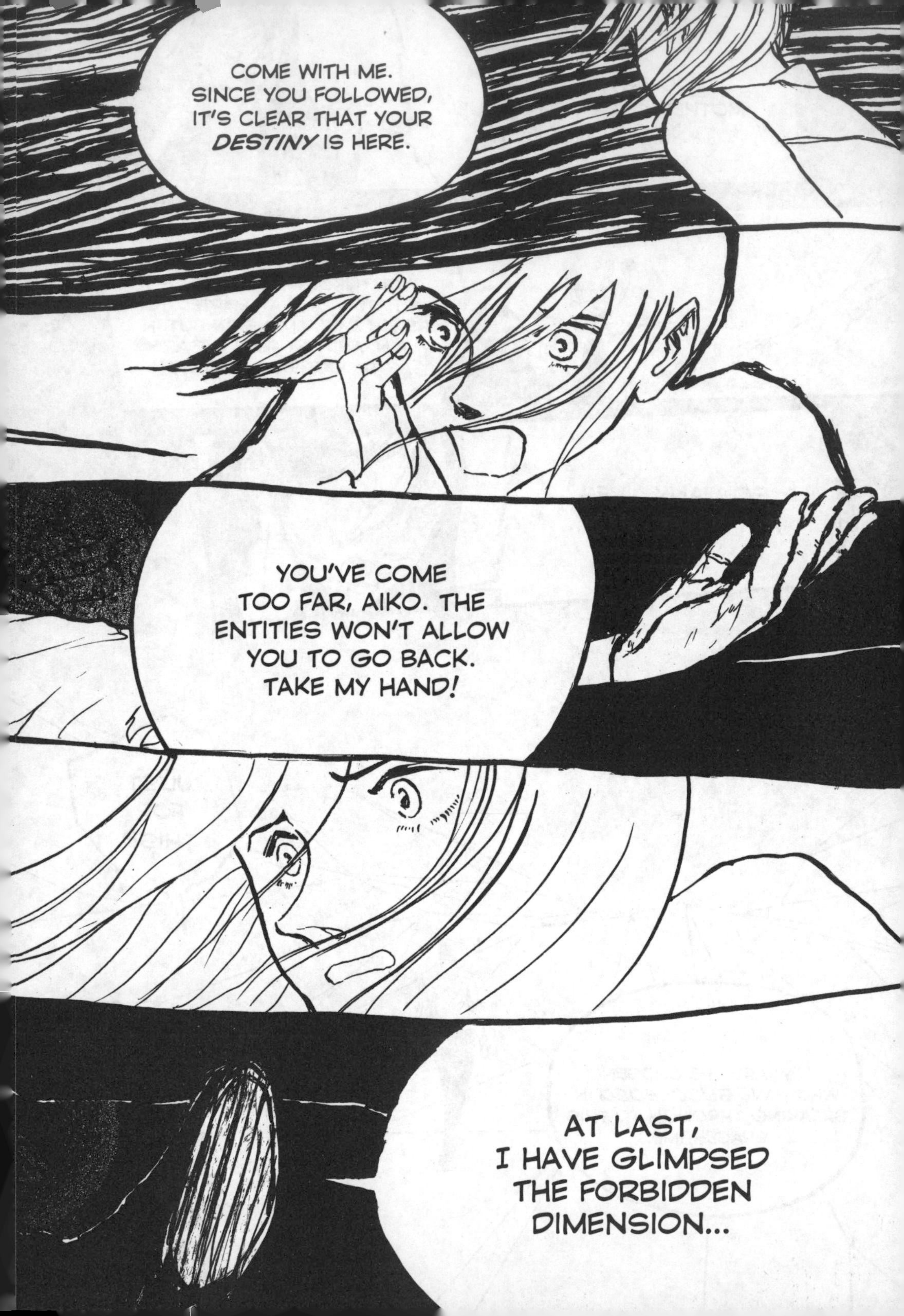
COME WITH ME. SINCE YOU FOLLOWED, IT'S CLEAR THAT YOUR *DESTINY* IS HERE.
YOU'VE COME TOO FAR, AIKO. THE ENTITIES WON'T ALLOW YOU TO GO BACK. TAKE MY HAND!
AT LAST, I HAVE GLIMPSED THE FORBIDDEN DIMENSION...

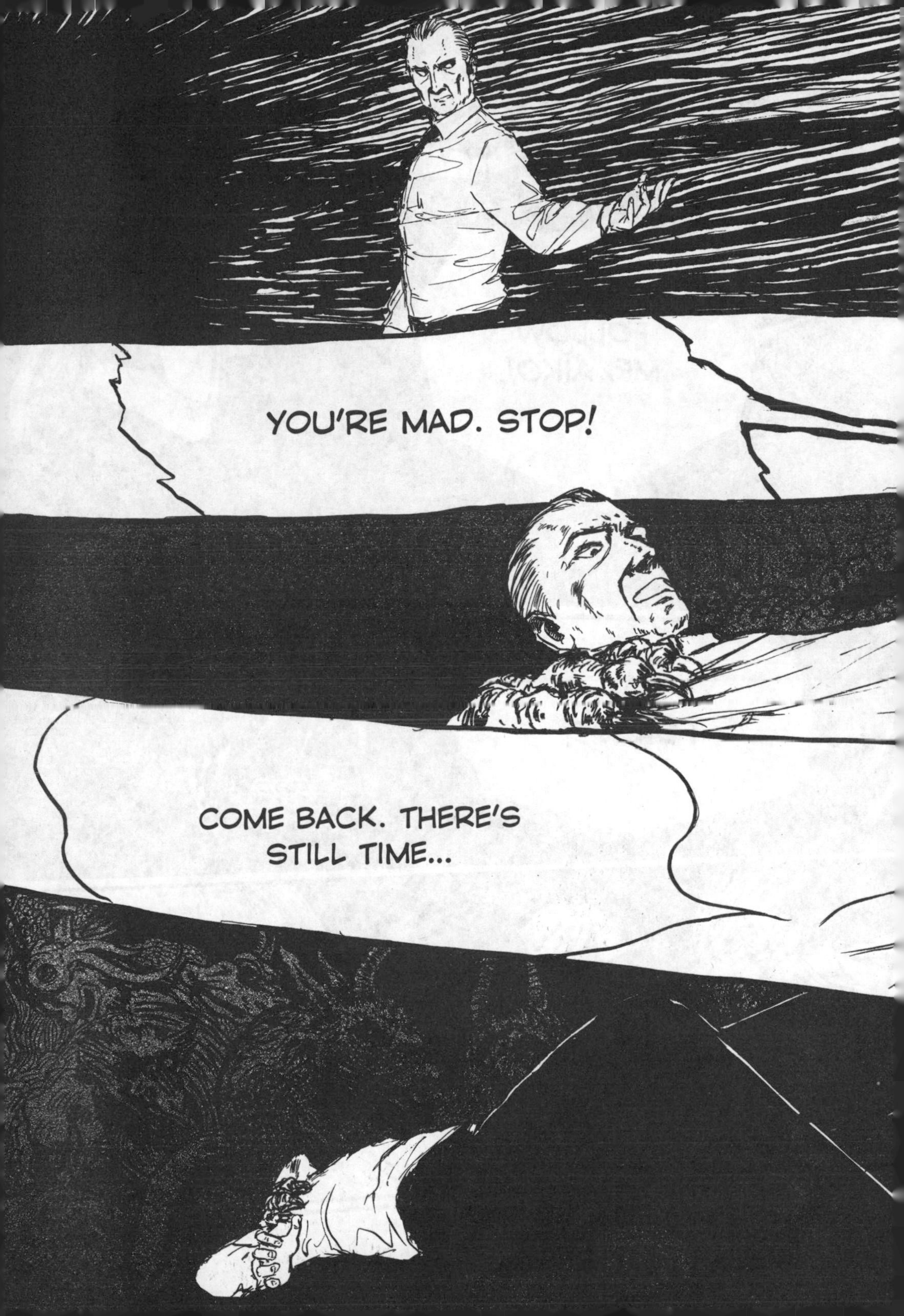
YOU'RE MAD. STOP!
COME BACK. THERE'S STILL TIME...

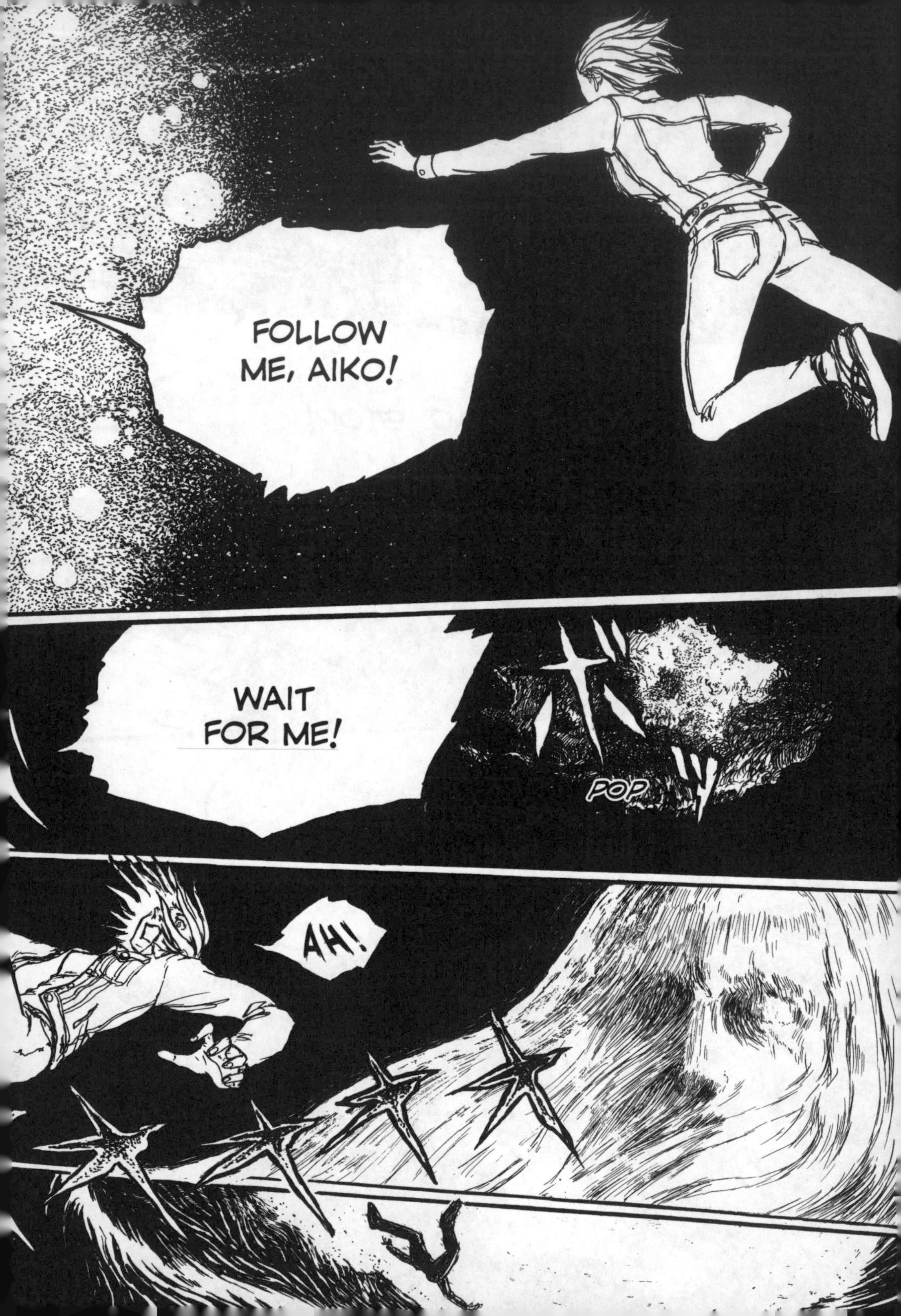
FOLLOW ME, AIKO!
POP
WAIT FOR ME!
AH!

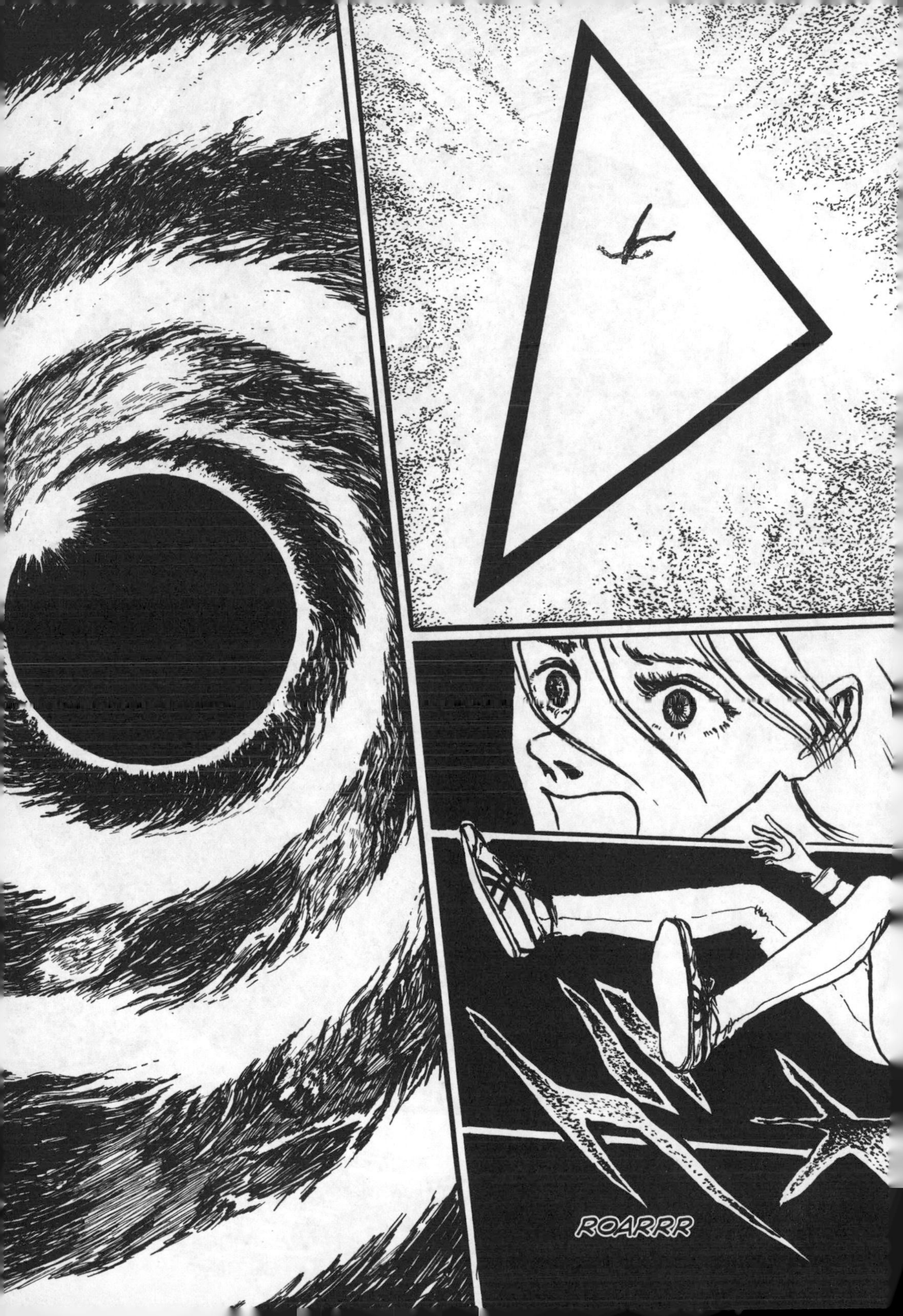
ROARRR

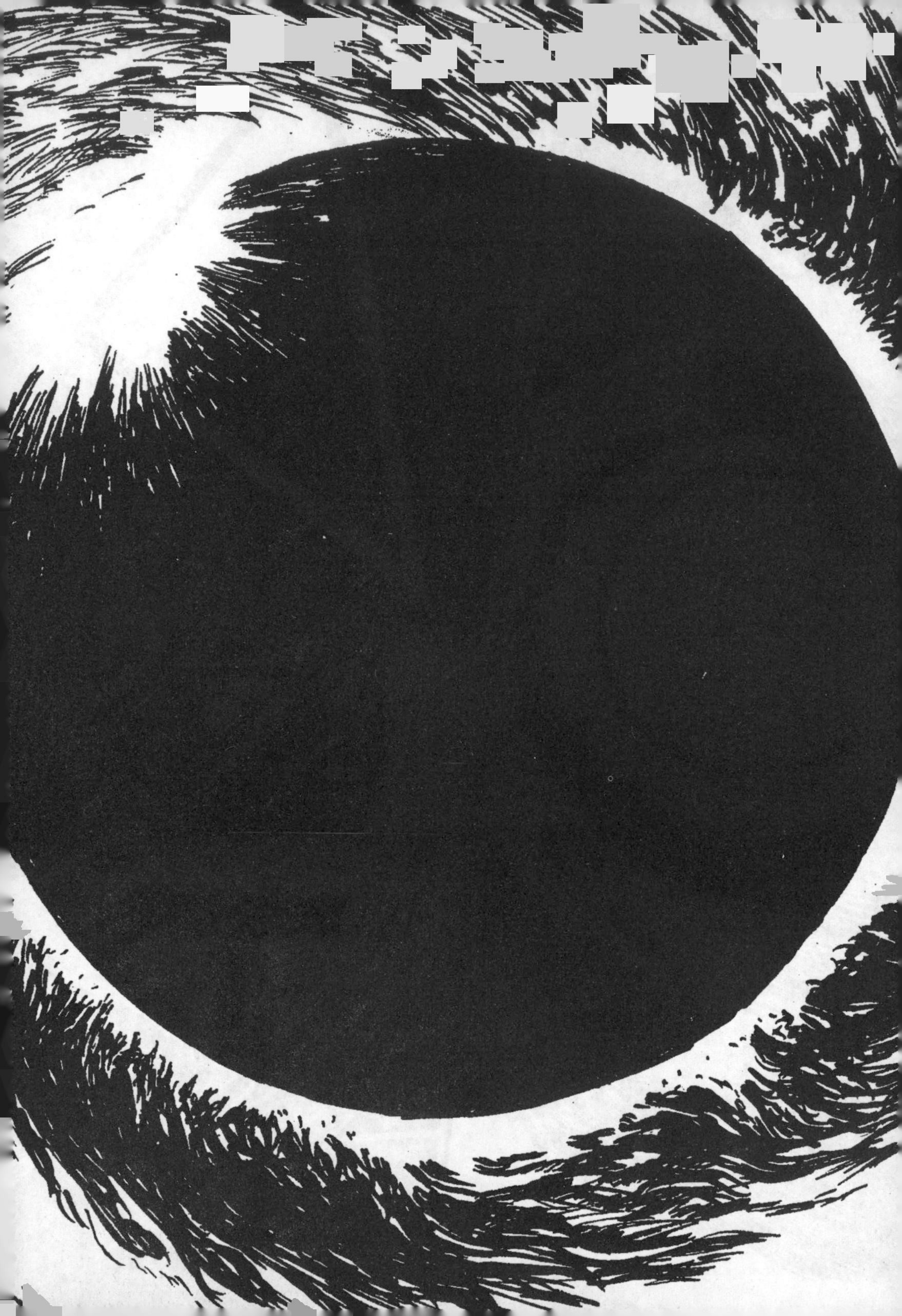

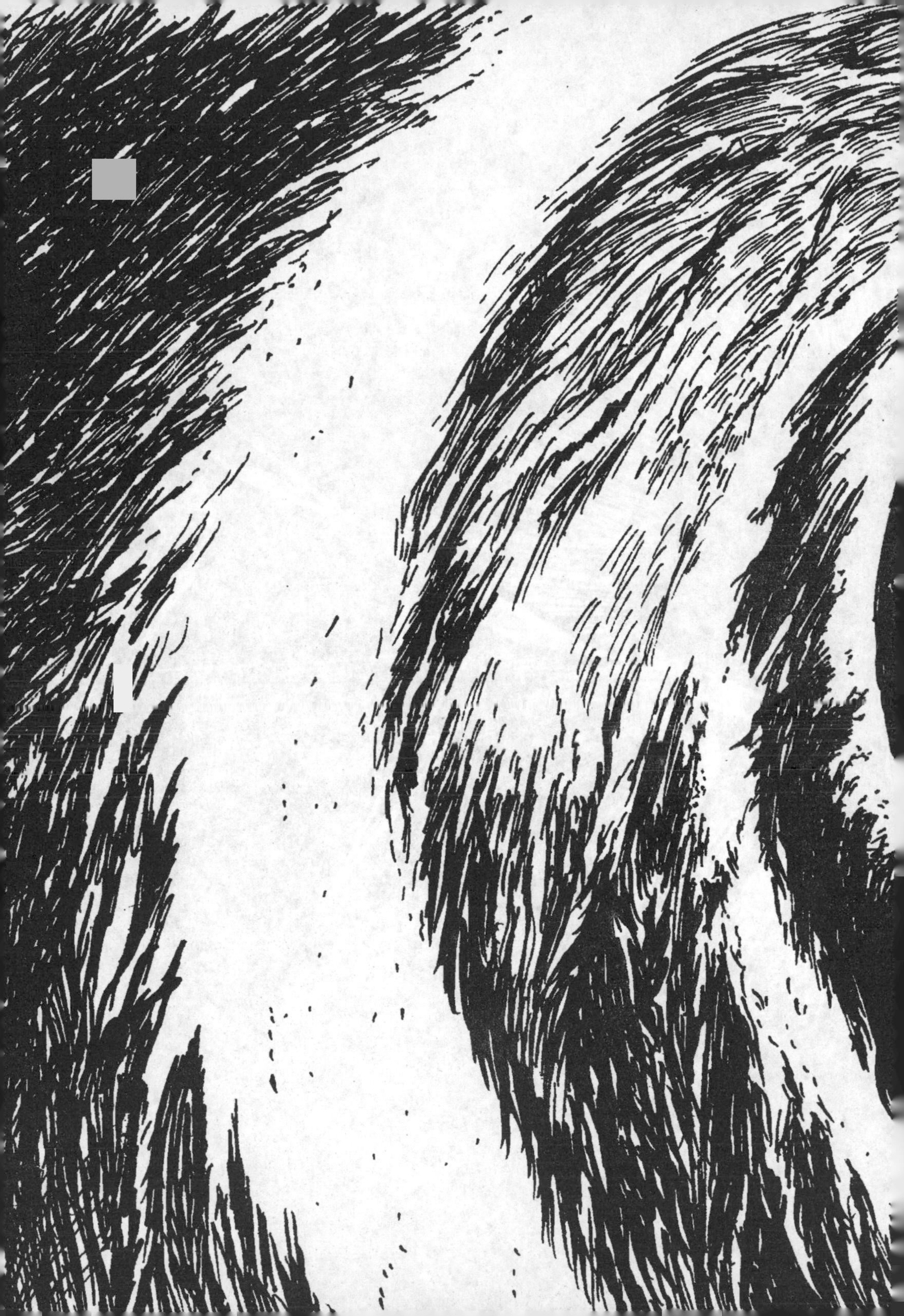

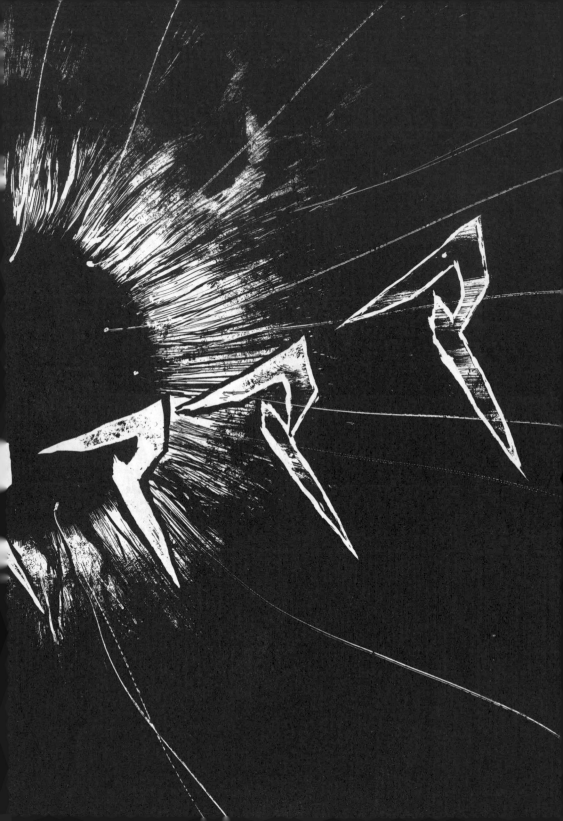

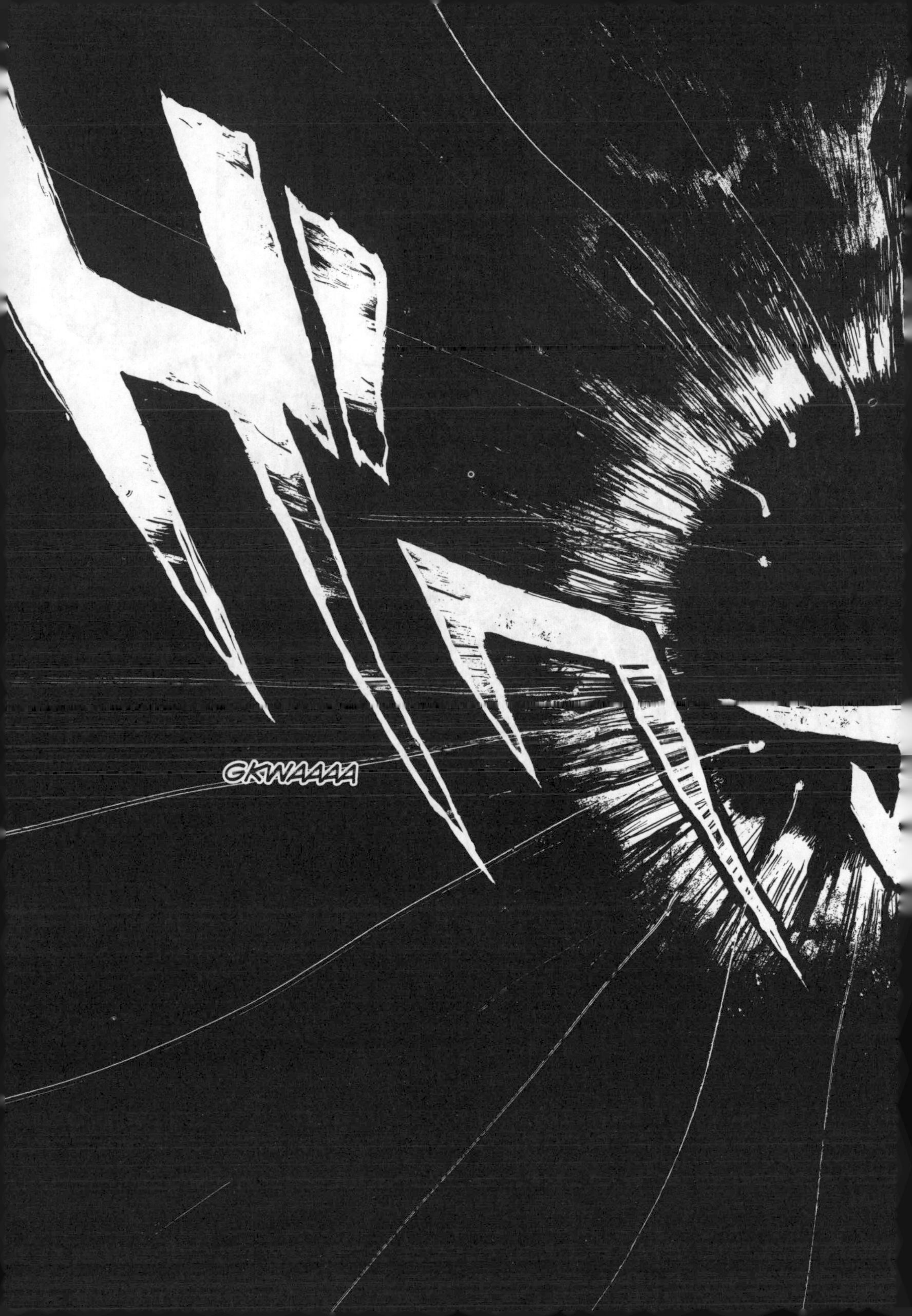
GKWAAAA

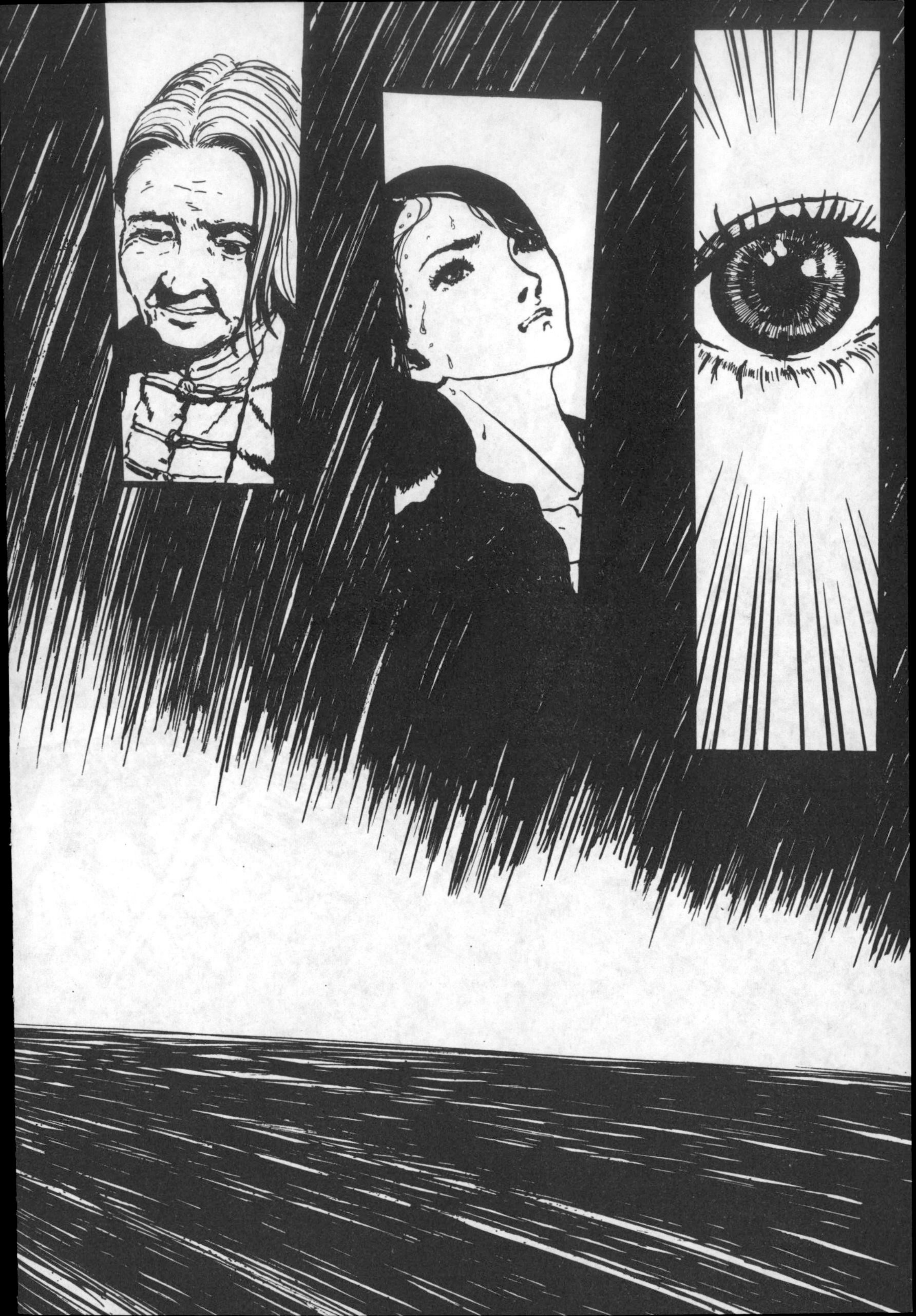

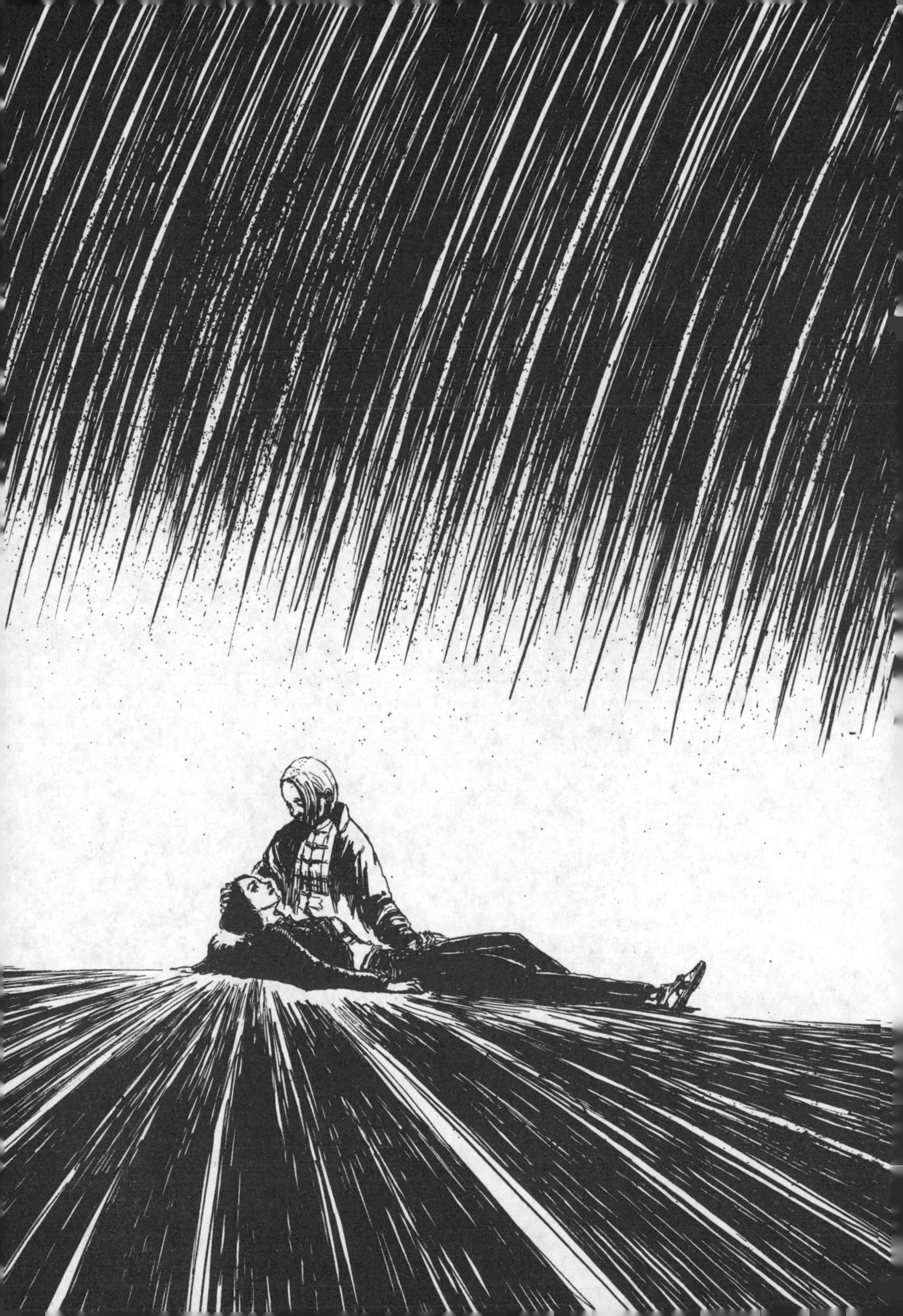

EPILOGUE

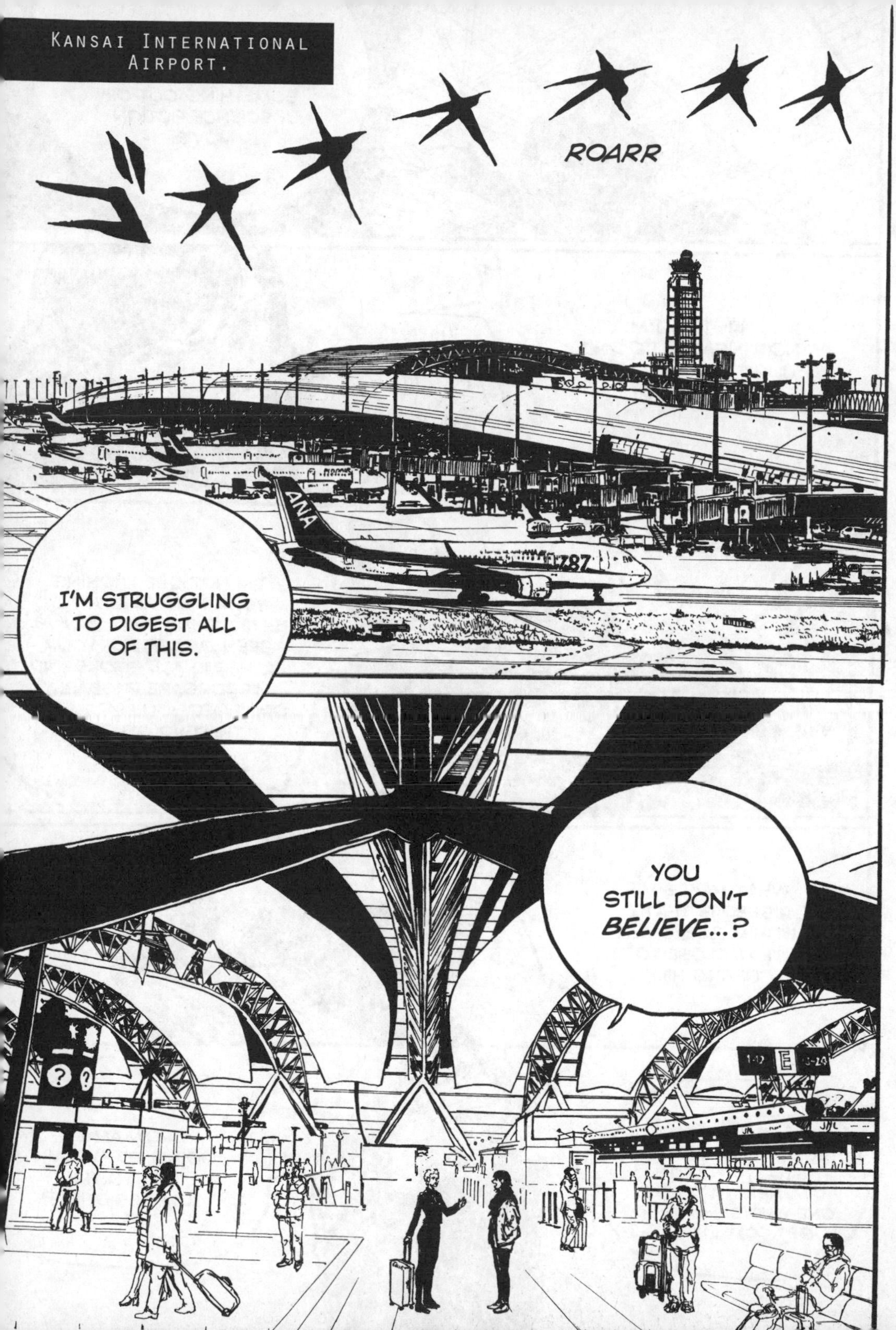
KANSAI INTERNATIONAL AIRPORT.
ROARR
I'M STRUGGLING TO DIGEST ALL OF THIS.
YOU STILL DON'T *BELIEVE*...?

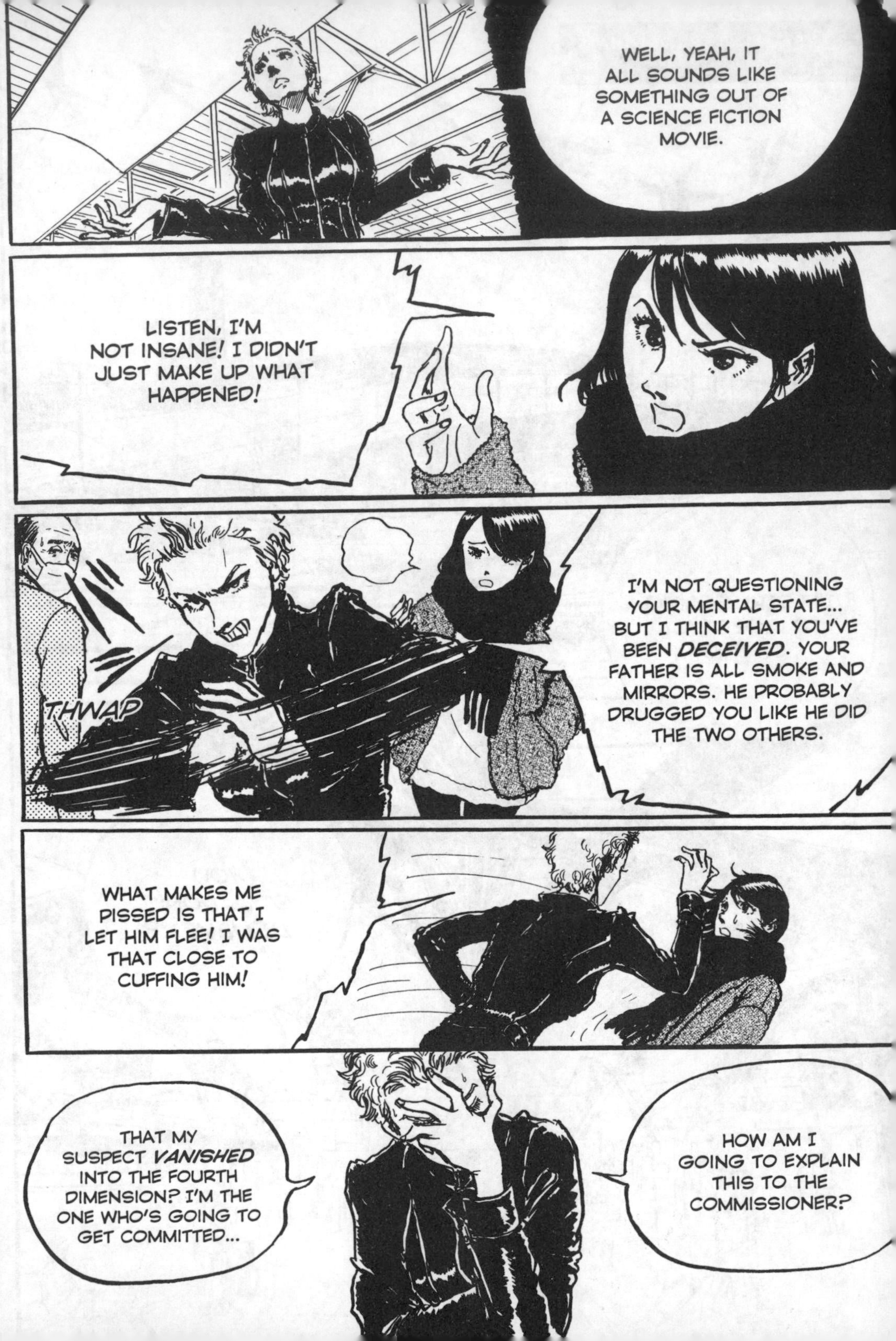
WELL, YEAH, IT ALL SOUNDS LIKE SOMETHING OUT OF A SCIENCE FICTION MOVIE.
LISTEN, I'M NOT INSANE! I DIDN'T JUST MAKE UP WHAT HAPPENED!
I'M NOT QUESTIONING YOUR MENTAL STATE... BUT I THINK THAT YOU'VE BEEN *DECEIVED*. YOUR FATHER IS ALL SMOKE AND MIRRORS. HE PROBABLY DRUGGED YOU LIKE HE DID THE TWO OTHERS.
THWAP
WHAT MAKES ME PISSED IS THAT I LET HIM FLEE! I WAS THAT CLOSE TO CUFFING HIM!
HOW AM I GOING TO EXPLAIN THIS TO THE COMMISSIONER?
THAT MY SUSPECT *VANISHED* INTO THE FOURTH DIMENSION? I'M THE ONE WHO'S GOING TO GET COMMITTED...

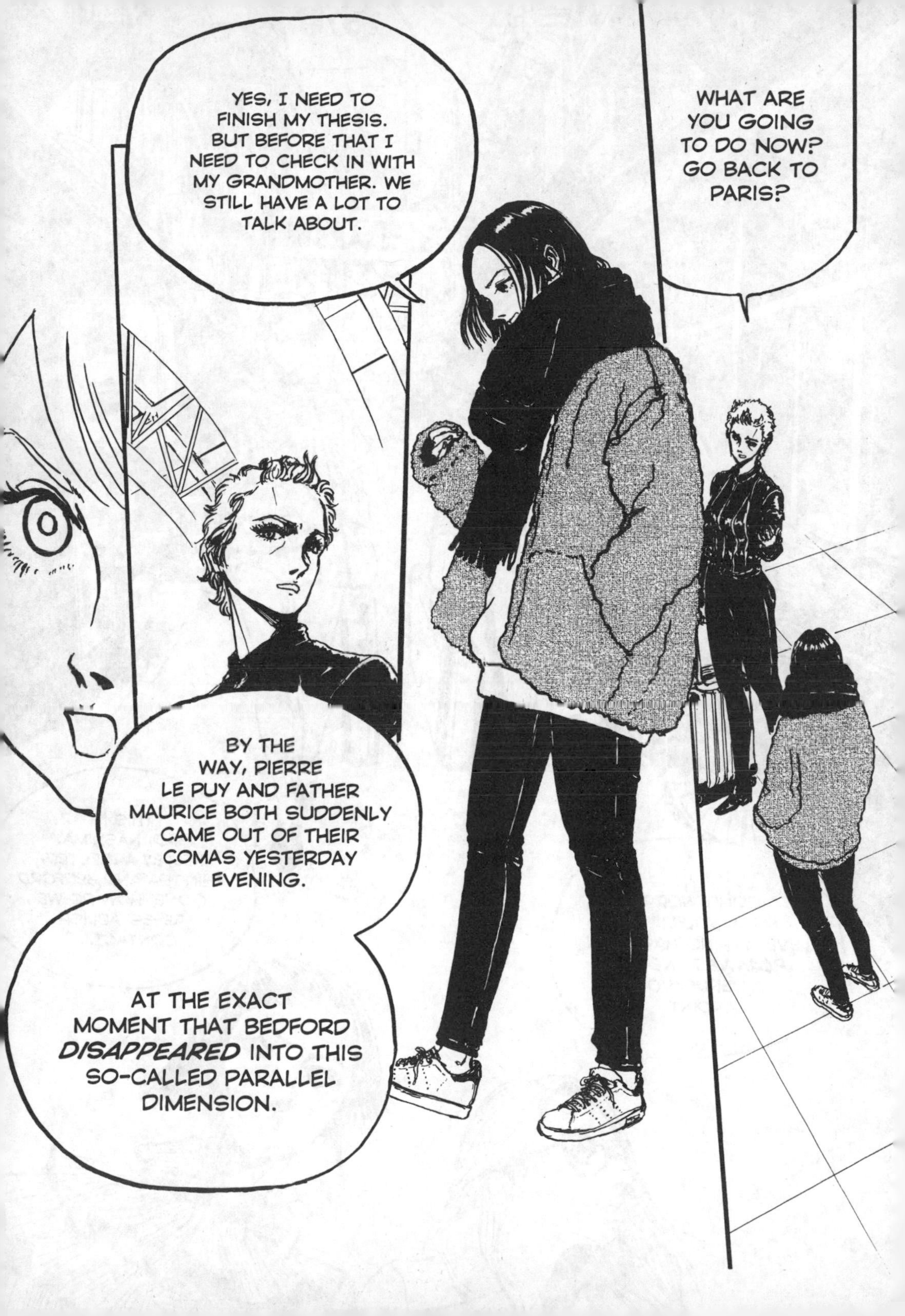
WHAT ARE YOU GOING TO DO NOW? GO BACK TO PARIS?
YES, I NEED TO FINISH MY THESIS. BUT BEFORE THAT I NEED TO CHECK IN WITH MY GRANDMOTHER. WE STILL HAVE A LOT TO TALK ABOUT.
BY THE WAY, PIERRE LE PUY AND FATHER MAURICE BOTH SUDDENLY CAME OUT OF THEIR COMAS YESTERDAY EVENING.
AT THE EXACT MOMENT THAT BEDFORD *DISAPPEARED* INTO THIS SO-CALLED PARALLEL DIMENSION.

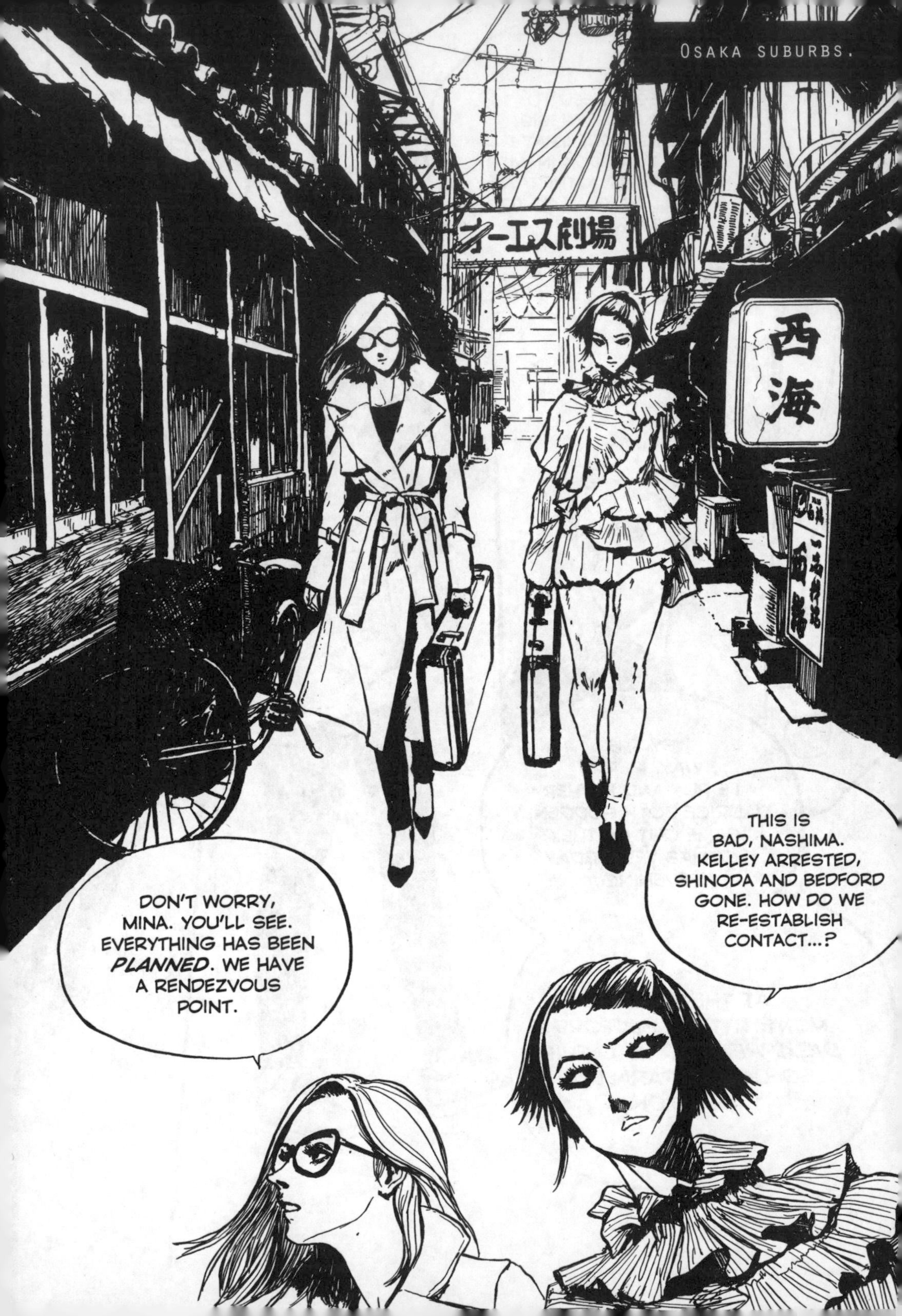
OSAKA SUBURBS.
オーエス劇場
西海
THIS IS BAD, NASHIMA. KELLEY ARRESTED, SHINODA AND BEDFORD GONE. HOW DO WE RE-ESTABLISH CONTACT...?
DON'T WORRY, MINA. YOU'LL SEE. EVERYTHING HAS BEEN *PLANNED*. WE HAVE A RENDEZVOUS POINT.

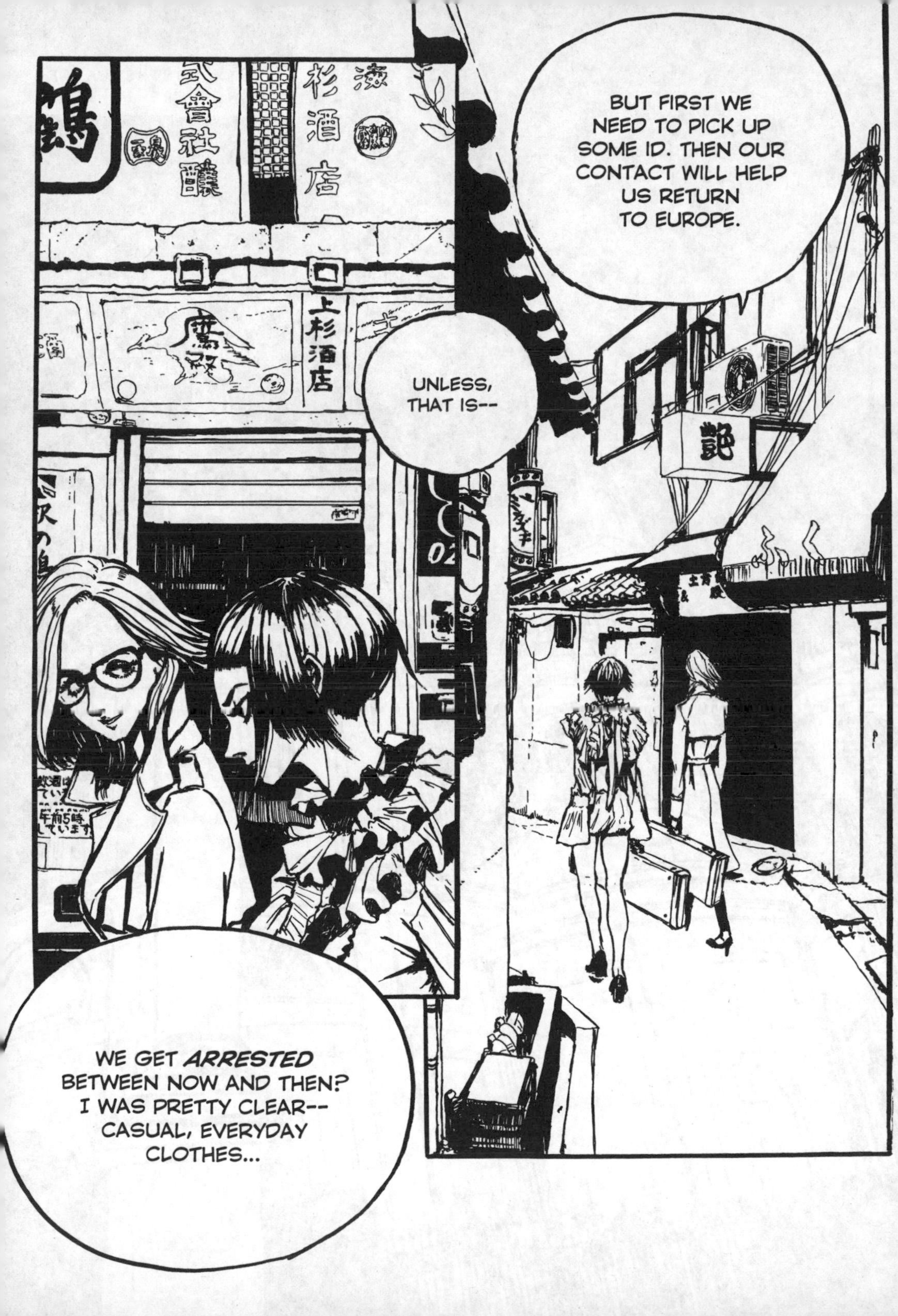
BUT FIRST WE NEED TO PICK UP SOME ID. THEN OUR CONTACT WILL HELP US RETURN TO EUROPE.
UNLESS, THAT IS--
上杉酒店
WE GET *ARRESTED* BETWEEN NOW AND THEN? I WAS PRETTY CLEAR-- CASUAL, EVERYDAY CLOTHES...

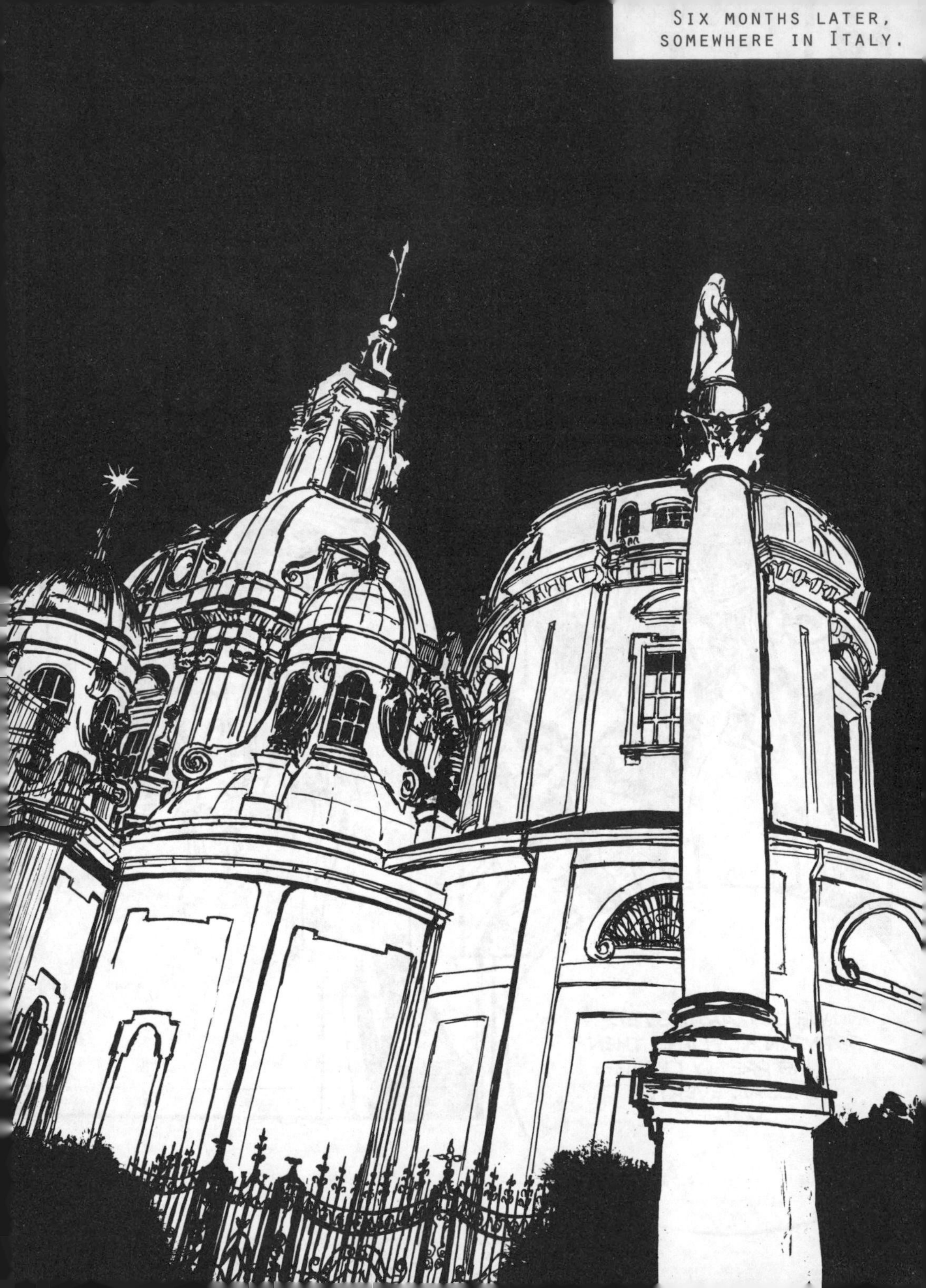
SIX MONTHS LATER,
SOMEWHERE IN ITALY.

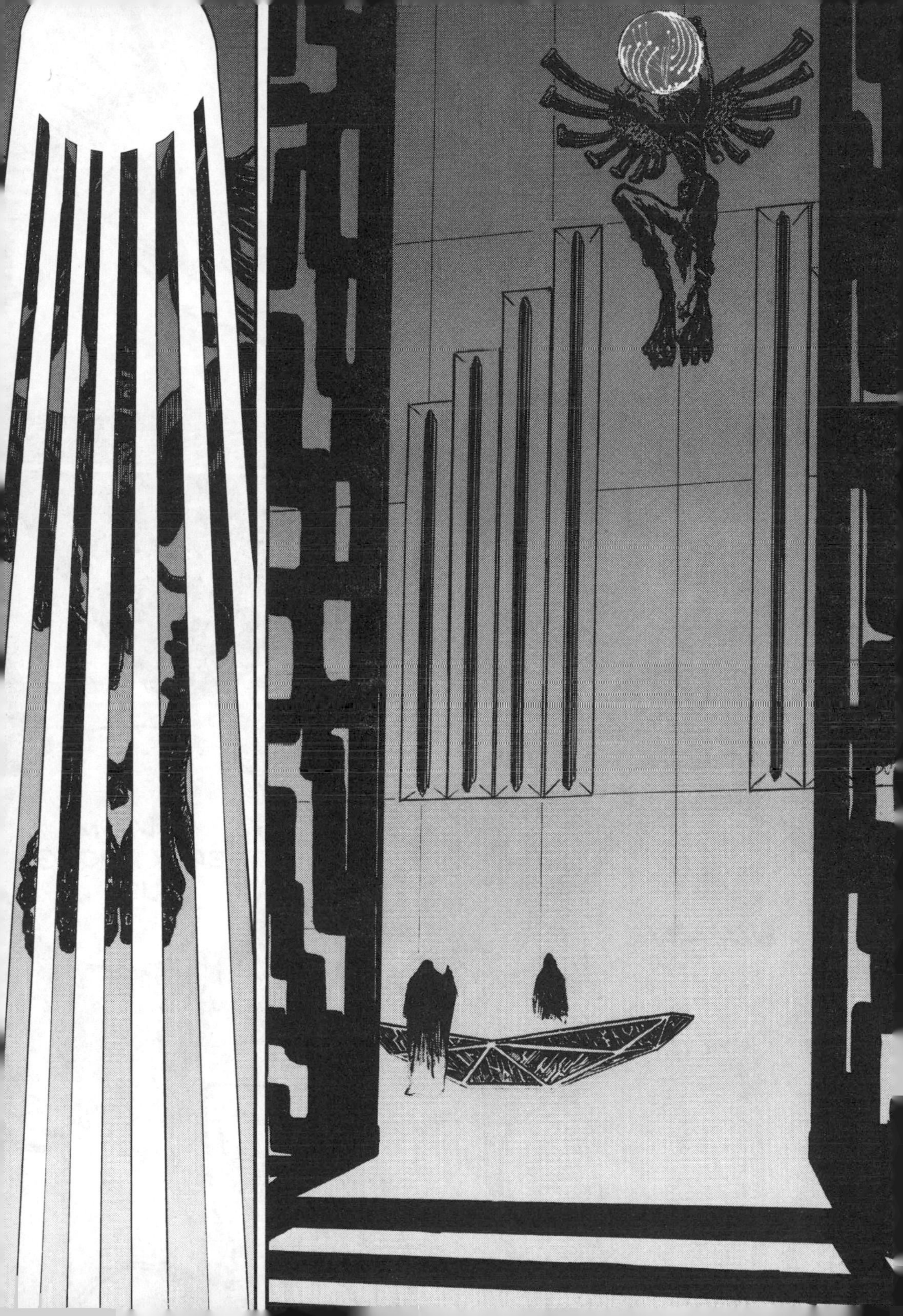

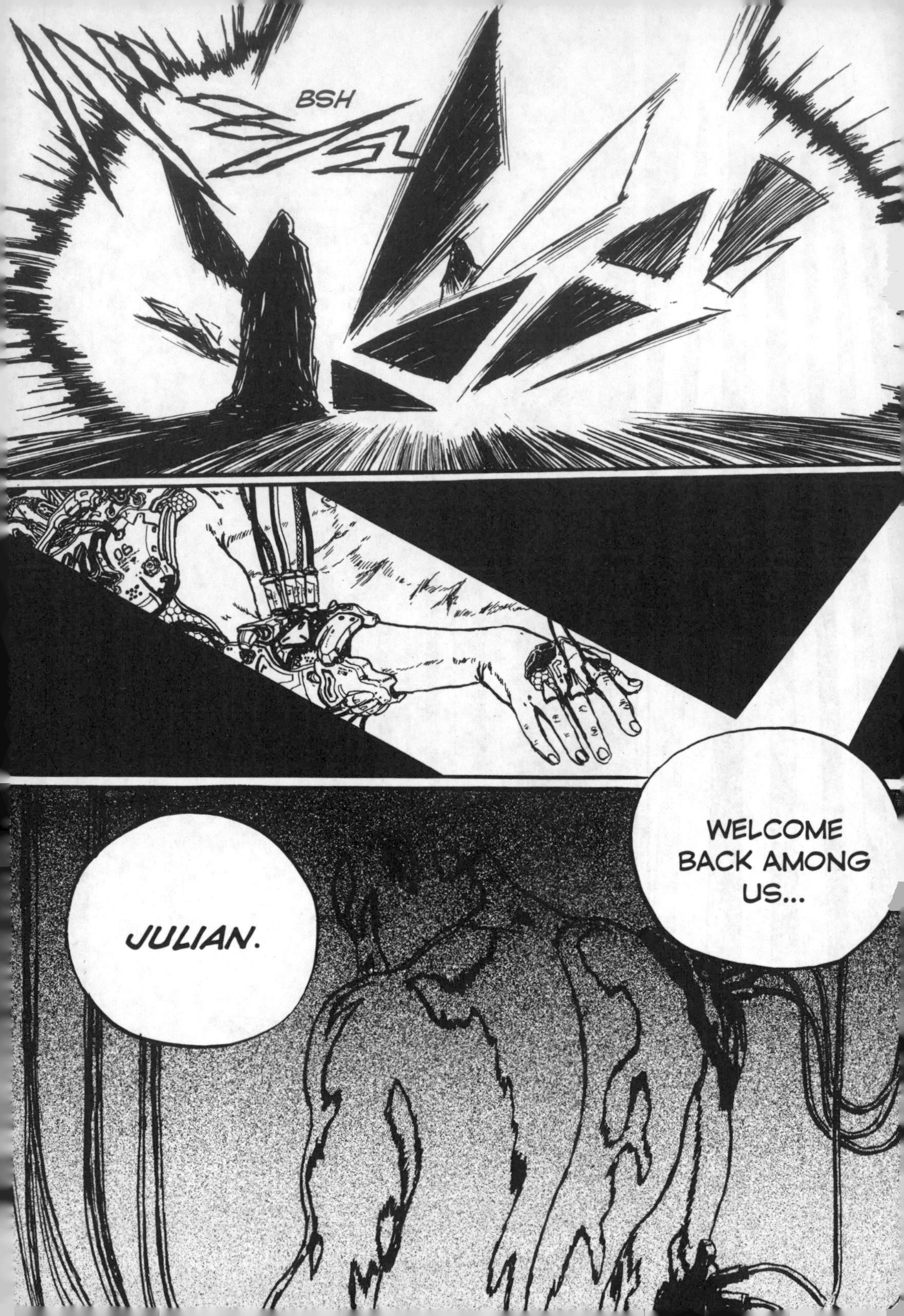
BSH
WELCOME BACK AMONG US...
JULIAN.

BIOGRAPHIES

BENOIST SIMMAT

Benoist Simmat is a journalist who contributes to *Le Journal du Dimanche*, as well as an essayist and scriptwriter.

A wine specialist, he is a long-time contributor to *La Revue du Vin de France*. In 2008, he co-authored a book, *In Vino Satanas*, with the editor of *La Revue*, Denis Saverot. It details the French government's subverting of the French wine industry in favor of pharmaceutical companies.

Simmat is not only the author of thirty books, but has penned the comic book *Robert Parker: Les Sept Pêchés Capiteaux*, with artist Philippe Bercovici – a satire of wine critic Robert M. Parker, Jr.

ELDO YOSHIMIZU

Born in Tokyo, Eldo Yoshimizu is an artist, sculptor, musician, and photographer.

As a sculptor, Yoshimizu creates vast, jewel-like shapes and sinuous, vivid outlines which are among Japan's most significant pieces of public art. His work has been exhibited in galleries all over the world, and he has held positions as an artist in residence in Italy, France and New York.

Yoshimizu's character of Ryuko has appeared in art galleries around Japan and Europe, and she made her jump to manga in 2019.

embezzlement, and the financing of terrorism, by investigating specifically the finance industry (investment funds and businesses in the private sector).

Louis Charbonneau-Lassay
Historical and religious writer of the early 20th century (1871-1946), originally of Loudun (Poitou), and well-versed in numerous traditional disciplines: symbolism, heraldry (the study of coats of arms), engraving, sigillography (the study of seals), numismatics, etc. He is famous for his monumental study of Christian iconography *The Bestiary of Christ* (1940).

Pelican
This bird has been worshiped since time immemorial. Christians made use of its symbolism to represent the sacrifice of Christ as redemption for sinners. For Alchemists, the pelican piercing its own flanks embodies the alembic; its seven children, the seven stages in the transmutation of metal.

Abbey Saint-Martin de Ligugé
Benedictine monastery in the centre of Poitou (Ligugé, south of Poitiers), known for being founded by Saint Martin in 361, which makes it the oldest Christian abbey still active in the west (even if those activities have been interrupted a few times throughout the ages). Its famous library (350,000 works) is entirely closed to the public.

Joris-Karl Huysmans
Parisian novelist and art critic of the late 19th century (1848-1907). This complex character was by turns a traditionalist poet, a naturalist writer, a militant of impressionism and, towards the end of his life, a Christian author in the defense of religion. He remains in the collective memory a 'decadent' novelist, with his penetrating works *À Rebours* and *Là-bas*.

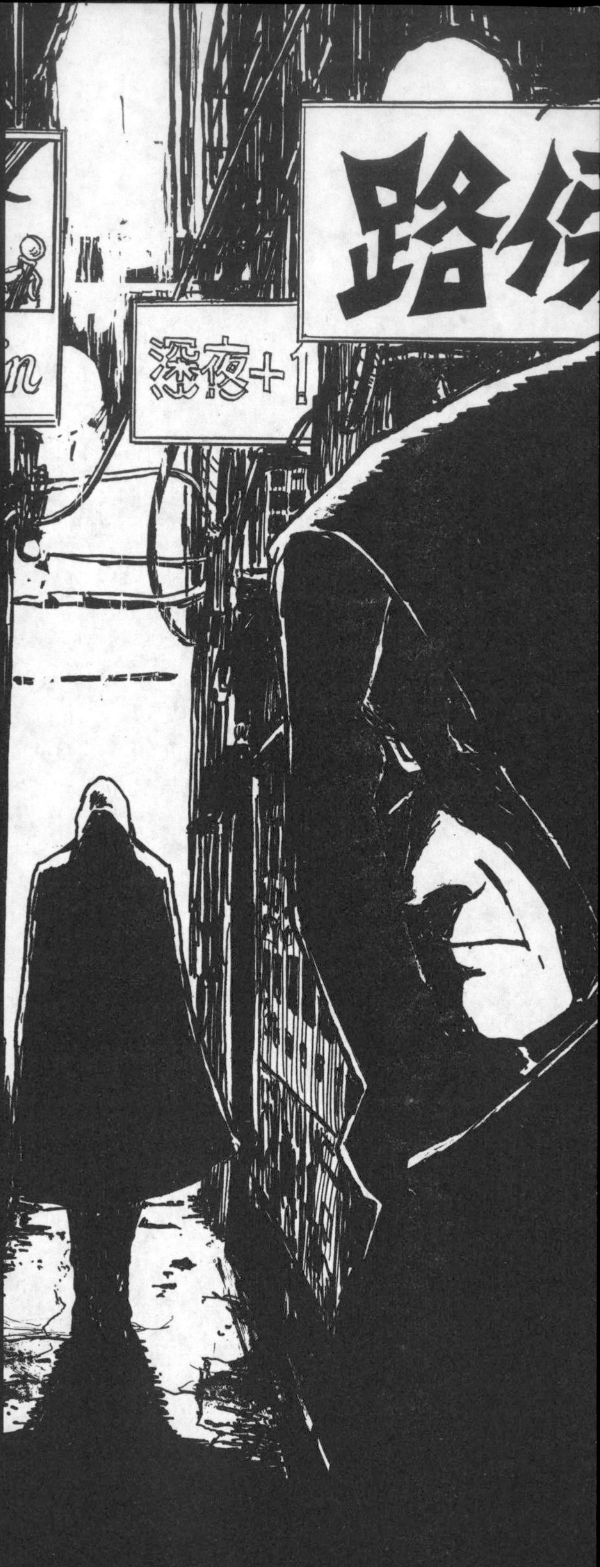

NOTES ON THE TEXT

JAPANESE CATHOLICISM
Christianity was introduced to Japan in the sixteenth century by Jesuit missionaries, notably Saint Francois Xavier, who landed at Kyushu (a large island in the south of the country) in August 1549. The Catholic confession now counts around half a million faithful in Japan (who frequent a thousand churches), particularly numerous in the dioceses of Nakasaki and Osaka.

36 QUAI DES ORFÈVRES
36 Quai des Orfèvres (or '36'), on L'île de la Cité, in Paris, is the historic building which sheltered every service of the Parisian judicial police until 2017. They have since been transferred to the XVII arrondissement, a new '36', this one on the rue du Bastion. Certain services (like the ex-antigang B.R.I) remain in the historical 36.

THE EMERALD TABLET
The Tabula Smaragdina is an alchemical text a dozen allegorical verses in length, referenced passionately since the Middle Ages – from which we derive the famous 'As below, so above, and as above, so below'. According to tradition, they are said to be the posthumous teachings of the mythical Hermes Trimegiste (Corpus Hermeticum). The Emerald Tablet is also the name of a famous esoteric bookshop on the rue de la Huchette, in the area of Saint-Michel.

GAMMA DRACONIS / ELTANIN
The dragon constellation, known since antiquity (as described by Ptolemy), is, by size, the 8th largest of the 98 visible constellations in the night sky. Gamma Draconis, the giant orange star, is its brightest. In 2016, the international astronomical union gave it back its traditional name: Eltanin.

UTSURO-BUNE
An unknown vessel resembling a flying saucer ('empty boat' in Japanese) which was said to have come ashore at the beginning of the 19th century as an ovoid shape transporting a pretty young woman, herself the guardian of a treasure she held in her hands. It is a very well-known story in Japan.

TOGO MURANO
This Japanese architect is a master·of 20th century modernism (1891-1984), and is the creator of many public buildings, hotels, and large shops associated with the Sukiya-Zukuri style (using traditional materials). He conceived the Catholic church in Takarazuka, 'as having the shape of a whale', and the Cistercian monastery in Nishinomiya.

JOHN DEE
English scientist and astrologer of the 16th century (1527-1608), renowned in particular for his knowledge of mathematics, astronomy, and navigation as well as his research into magic and alchemy. Thanks to contact with 'angelic' entities who had bestowed upon him their occult language, the Enochian alphabet, Dee claimed (in his *Monas Hieroglyphica*) to have touched upon the Universal Knowledge.

BLACK MIRROR
An artifact of black obsidian (of Aztec origin apparently) that once belonged to John Dee and supposedly allowed him, as well as Edward Kelley, his medium, to converse with 'angels' (supernatural entities dwelling in another dimension). This object, sacred amongst those in hermetic circles, is kept today in the British Museum and regularly exhibited, along with other relics that once belonged to Dee, in the King's Library.

FINANCIAL INTELLIGENCE UNITS
Units created in every country of the European Union. Their role is to jointly battle against fraud,

STOP!

This manga is presented in its original right-to-left reading format. This is the back of the book!

Pages, panels, and speech balloons read from top right to bottom left, as shown above. SFX translations are placed adjacent to their original Japanese counterparts.